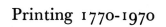

Printing 1770-1970

Michael Twyman

Printing 1770-1970
an illustrated history of its development and uses in England

Printed and published by
Eyre & Spottiswoode, London
Her Majesty's Printers
on the occasion of their bicentenary 1970

SBN 413 264203 2
© 1970 Michael Twyman
First published 1970
Printed in Great Britain
for Eyre & Spottiswoode (Publishers) Ltd
11 New Fetter Lane, London, EC4
by Eyre & Spottiswoode Ltd, printers at
Thanet Press Margate and Grosvenor Press Portsmouth

Contents

Author's acknowledgements

Any student interested in non-book printing owes a considerable debt to John Johnson, Printer to the University of Oxford from 1925 to 1946, who had the foresight to build up a collection of printed material of all kinds which he called the Constance Meade Collection. Much of the material must have been considered of little value at the time, but the collection, which passed to the Bodleian Library in 1968 and is now known as the John Johnson Collection, is a mine of information for the social and economic historian as well as for the historian of printing. I am particularly grateful to the present Printer, Vivian Ridler, for allowing me to use the collection while it was in his care, and to Harry Carter, the Archivist of the University Press, and his assistant, Lil Thrussell, for their most generous help over a number of years. My thanks are also due to Michael Turner, curator of the collection since its move to the Bodleian Library, for his help during the later stages of the work. It would be difficult to mention all the other librarians, archivists, and curators who have helped to make my task easier, but I should like to thank in particular the Librarians and staff of the St Bride Printing Library and Reading University Library, and the Keeper and staff of the Museum of English Rural Life, Reading University. For their help in obtaining either photographs or material to be photographed I should also like to thank the following: E.F.Andrews, R.E.Bailey, Christopher Bradshaw, Marilynne Burbage, J.D.G.Foster, C.N.Hadlow, Elizabeth Harris, A.D.B.Jones, Richard Kauffman, Caspar Mitchell, David Prout, K.H.Rogers, Herbert Spencer, M.Stocks, Walter Tracy, J.C.Wittich, and Berthold Wolpe.

Credits for the illustrations are included in the captions, but in addition formal thanks are due to the Arts Council of Great Britain for 844, 845; Associated Newspapers Ltd for 412, 838; Automobile Association for 632, 635, 636; Barclays Bank Ltd for 212; British Campaign for Peace in Vietnam for 664; British & Foreign Bible Society for 343; British Railways Board for 527, 528, 529, 530, 531, 547; Bryant & May Ltd for 335, 336; Campaign for Nuclear Disarmament for 663; Estate of Marcel Duchamp and the Arts Council of Great Britain for 863; East Kent Road Car Co. Ltd for 598; A.C.Frost & Co. for 307; Galérie Anderson Mayer, Martha Jackson Gallery, Mrs Lilian Somerville, Sir Basil Spence, and the Calouste Gulbenkian Foundation for 880; Maurice Goldring for 342; Calouste Gulbenkian Foundation for 879; Hampton & Sons for 306; Harris-Intertype Ltd for 147; Harrison & Sons Ltd for 134; IBM United Kingdom Ltd for 152; Institute of Printing for 341; Leicester Galleries for 854, 855, 856; Linotype & Machinery Ltd for 142; London Group for 859, 874; London Transport Executive (formerly London Transport Board) for 277, 316, 597, 603, 605, 606, 607, 608, 610; Lund Humphries Publishers Ltd for 328, 329, 330, 860, 861; Marlborough Fine Art Ltd for 876, 877, 878; Martin & Pole for 305; Monotype Corporation Ltd for 144, 145, 146, 202; Penguin Books Ltd for 108; Sir Isaac Pitman & Sons Ltd for 211; Rank Xerox Ltd for 81; Estate of Eric Ravilious and the British Broadcasting Corporation for 187; Reading *Evening Post* for 153; Roland, Browse & Delbanco Art Gallery for 862; Ross & Co. for 309; Rotaprint Ltd for 59; Royal Academy of Arts for

869, 870, 871, 872; Shell-Mex and B.P. Ltd for 189; Lord Strachie and the Arts Council of Great Britain for 875; Madame Tussaud's Ltd, London, for 766-80; Times Newspapers Ltd for 672; Ministry of Transport for 617-29; A. Zwemmer Ltd for 858. 676, 677, 693, 695-704, 708, 716, 717, 735-43 are Crown copyright, reproduced by permission of the Controller, Her Majesty's Stationery Office; 79, 80, 117, 124, 135, 141, 148, 149, 150, 151 are Crown copyright, Science Museum, London; and 317 rights reserved A.D.A.G.P. If inadvertently there has been any oversight in this matter, apologies are hereby offered to those concerned.

Readers familiar with John Lewis's *Printed ephemera* will at once recognise its influence on the second half of my book, and this is a debt I readily acknowledge. Less obvious, though no less genuine, is my debt to James Mosley, Librarian of the St Bride Printing Library; my own understanding of printing history has been greatly enriched through years of personal friendship and professional cooperation with him, and I am well aware that more parts of this book than I am able to acknowledge reflect his influence.

Elizabeth Harris, Gillian Riley, Christopher Bradshaw, Ernest Hoch, and James Mosley have read the text at some stage in its preparation. I am grateful to all of them for their corrections and helpful comments, though I must take full responsibility for both the accuracy of the material and for the ideas expressed. For help on specific points of information I should also like to thank W.A.Cook, T.A.B.Corley, Maurice Goldring, A.D.B.Jones, James Moran, E.A.Smith, and Berthold Wolpe.

Though I have called on the services of many photographers, the bulk of the work fell on the shoulders of I.MacLean and the staff of the Photographic Department of Reading University Library. Over the years they have helped to build up a photographic archive of printing and letterforms in connection with the teaching of typography in the University, and this book would have been a much more difficult venture but for their skill, patience, and willing help.

Finally, I must thank my typist, Brenda Tucker, for her interpretative skills in making sense of my rough draft and all those in the publishing and printing offices who have helped in the production of this book.

November 1970   Michael Twyman

Part I Text

Introduction

This book is concerned with the birth of modern printing and its development over the last two hundred years. The period it covers begins towards
the end of the eighteenth century, when the Industrial Revolution was
gathering momentum and shortly before the old order began to be shaken
by events in France and the radical ideas associated with them. The main
causes of the rapid growth and spread of printing in this country from the
end of the eighteenth century onwards – the increase in population,
expansion of trade, improved means of communication, advances in technology, and pressure for the propagation of ideas – were in fact much the same
as those which brought about a change in society generally. Printing has
always had a rather special relationship with the community it serves and has
been closely involved with the events, ideas, products, and tastes of its time. In
this short history I have approached the subject of English printing in the
period 1770–1970 from two different directions in an attempt to show it in
this light. In a series of introductory essays I have discussed a number of
aspects of printing history, and in the section of plates I have tried to show
how examples of printing can throw light on some general themes from the
history of this period.

Like most writers of history, whether they choose to admit it or not, my
approach has been moulded by my own attitudes and interests; and, though
I have probably touched on most aspects of printing in England in the last
two centuries, I have concentrated on those which seem to me to have
special relevance today. I have tried to correct the imbalance, which seems
to exist in histories of printing, between the treatment given to books and
other kinds of printing; and for this reason I have avoided the field of book
production almost entirely. Most historians of printing have tended to
concentrate on this aspect, partly because of its close link with the development of scholarship and ideas, but mainly, I suspect, for the simple practical
reason that books have been conveniently preserved in quantities in libraries
all over the world, while many other kinds of printing have not. Furthermore, books have a useful characteristic for the historian in that they are
usually dated and bear the name of the printer. Yet while as many as forty-
eight copies of Gutenberg's 42-line Bible have been traced, we know of only
unique examples of certain fifteenth-century playing cards and devotional
prints, and many others have presumably not survived at all. The position
in the nineteenth and twentieth centuries is not so very different. Most books
published in this period survive in at least a few copies, yet there must have
been millions of items of printing which have disappeared without trace – for
even if many have survived there is the problem of locating them. Moreover,
books were designed from the outset to be repositories of knowledge, to be
kept and, in many cases, treasured. By tradition they have been embellished,
and often marked with the monogram or device of the owner, and may even
have been bound to suit the shelves or cases of a particular library. Most other
items of printing survive only by chance: items of stationery find their way
into business files; printers preserve their work to show clients; collectors
with all kinds of interests paste examples of printing into guard books; and,

more fortuitously, items of printing have survived in the bindings of books, as shelving or lining paper, as book marks, and, in the case of packaging, as receptacles for storing buttons, letters, and knick-knacks.

It is hardly surprising therefore that, with one or two notable exceptions, historians have avoided the subject of jobbing and other non-book printing. What has been traced is clearly only the tip of the iceberg of even surviving material; and since such little work has been done in this field any printing history of this kind is bound to be a rather personal interpretation of the past. Even so, it seems very clear that the most important innovations in printing after about 1800 were not made by the book printers, but by numerous craftsmen, engineers, artists, and designers, many of whom may not warrant individual mention, and some of whom will probably never be identified. It is true that a number of exceptional and influential books were published in the nineteenth century, and most short-lists of such works would include William Daniell's *A voyage round Great Britain* (1814–25), Owen Jones's *Alhambra* (1836–46), and William Morris's *Chaucer* (1896), but these were far removed from the typical productions of the period and the general level of nineteenth-century book design was certainly not high. Furthermore, there were few significant changes in the design of books in this period, and most of these affected the cases or covers rather than the text pages. The few printers who did make a real contribution to book design, such as Charles Whittingham and William Morris, found inspiration in the work of the past and, however admirable their books may be, they did little to come to terms with the kinds of problems that affected most printers. In many ways the most original aspects of printing since 1800, both from the design and technical standpoints, are seen in jobbing and periodical printing. Unlike the book printer of the period, who continued with conventions established some three hundred or more years before, jobbing and periodical printers were faced with new problems to solve, new processes and materials to use, new clients to serve, new kinds of information to translate into print. What emerged was a new approach to design which distinguishes the nineteenth-century printer from his eighteenth-century counterpart and leads to the new profession of graphic design in the twentieth century.

This book is primarily intended for the layman interested in printing and social history and for the student of typography and graphic design who might want to have an introduction to the history of the field in which he intends to practise. I have tried to write concisely so that the narrative, which covers the printing of both pictures and words, as well as the growth of techniques, technology, and design, can be taken as a whole; and, wherever possible, I have avoided using technical terms which may not be generally understood. Besides dealing with some familiar aspects of printing history I have touched on a few topics which may not be so well known. Anyone working in this field can hardly fail to be aware of the dangers he runs in committing his ideas to print, and my experience of studying a few aspects of nineteenth-century printing in some depth has made me realise only too clearly that I must be writing from a position of relative ignorance about many others. Vast areas of the subject are virtually uncharted and much work still needs to be done on specialised aspects before an adequate history of printing in this period can be written. This book should therefore be regarded merely as a starting point: it will have served its purpose only if the bibliography is well used and, in the course of time, some of its gaps filled.

In the section of plates I have chosen to approach the subject from a different direction. Rather than provide a miscellaneous selection of illustrations, I have selected five themes which will, I hope, not only convey something of the variety of printing produced during the last two hundred years, but also provide a vivid documentation of some aspects of the history of the period. A few of the illustrations are well known, but many of the items have not survived in quantity and are almost certainly reproduced for the first time. The main subject headings – Ceremony, Rural Life, Transport, Wars, and Exhibitions – have been chosen to provide a range of work from prestige printing in colour and gold by leading metropolitan printers to the humble work of provincial craftsmen, and to show visually exciting images as well as routine documentary and information printing. I have tried to select items which show some of the new kinds of problems the printer or designer had to cope with, such as the designing of timetables, forms, catalogues, pictorial posters, and have included some modern parallels of earlier items; and wherever possible I have given preference to pieces of printing which seem to me to have some intrinsic historical interest.

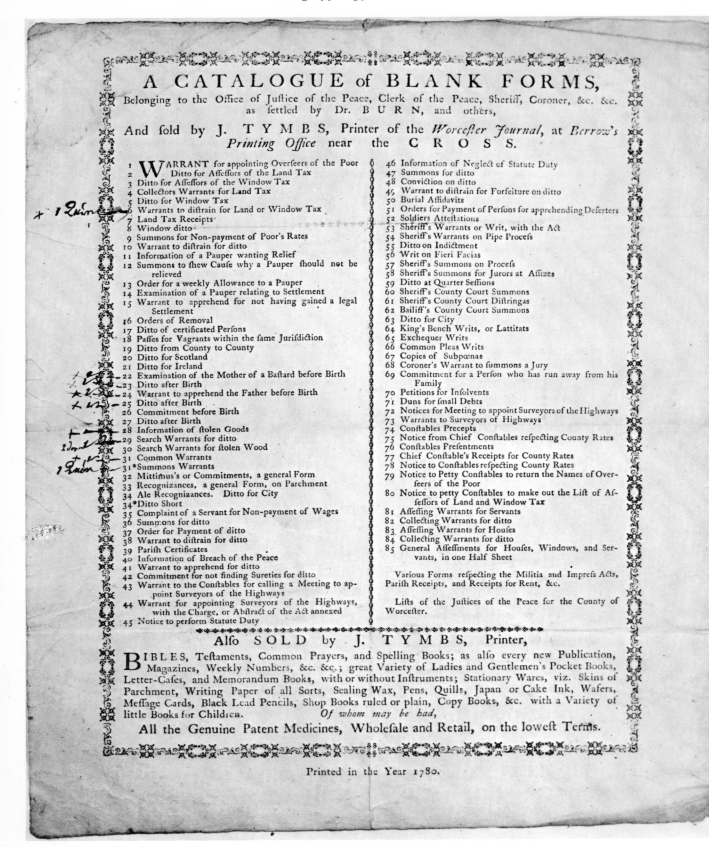

A CATALOGUE of BLANK FORMS,

Belonging to the Office of Justice of the Peace, Clerk of the Peace, Sheriff, Coroner, &c. &c. as settled by Dr. BURN, and others,

And sold by J. TYMBS, Printer of the *Worcester Journal*, at *Berrow's Printing Office* near the CROSS.

1 WARRANT for appointing Overseers of the Poor
2 Ditto for Assessors of the Land Tax
3 Ditto for Assessors of the Window Tax
4 Collectors Warrants for Land Tax
5 Ditto for Window Tax
6 Warrants to distrain for Land or Window Tax
7 Land Tax Receipts
8 Window ditto
9 Summons for Non-payment of Poor's Rates
10 Warrant to distrain for ditto
11 Information of a Pauper wanting Relief
12 Summons to shew Cause why a Pauper should not be relieved
13 Order for a weekly Allowance to a Pauper
14 Examination of a Pauper relating to Settlement
15 Warrant to apprehend for not having gained a legal Settlement
16 Orders of Removal
17 Ditto of certificated Persons
18 Passes for Vagrants within the same Jurisdiction
19 Ditto from County to County
20 Ditto for Scotland
21 Ditto for Ireland
22 Examination of the Mother of a Bastard before Birth
23 Ditto after Birth
24 Warrant to apprehend the Father before Birth
25 Ditto after Birth
26 Commitment before Birth
27 Ditto after Birth
28 Information of stolen Goods
29 Search Warrants for ditto
30 Search Warrants for stolen Wood
31 Common Warrants
31*Summons Warrants
32 Mittimus's or Commitments, a general Form
33 Recognizances, a general Form, on Parchment
34 Ale Recognizances. Ditto for City
34*Ditto Short
35 Complaint of a Servant for Non-payment of Wages
36 Summons for ditto
37 Order for Payment of ditto
38 Warrant to distrain for ditto
39 Parish Certificates
40 Information of Breach of the Peace
41 Warrant to apprehend for ditto
42 Commitment for not finding Sureties for ditto
43 Warrant to the Constables for calling a Meeting to appoint Surveyors of the Highways
44 Warrant for appointing Surveyors of the Highways, with the Charge, or Abstract of the Act annexed
45 Notice to perform Statute Duty

46 Information of Neglect of Statute Duty
47 Summons for ditto
48 Conviction on ditto
49 Warrant to distrain for Forfeiture on ditto
50 Burial Affidavits
51 Orders for Payment of Persons for apprehending Deserters
52 Soldiers Attestations
53 Sheriff's Warrants or Writ, with the Act
54 Sheriff's Warrants on Pipe Process
55 Ditto on Indictment
56 Writ on Fieri Facias
57 Sheriff's Summons on Process
58 Sheriff's Summons for Jurors at Assizes
59 Ditto at Quarter Sessions
60 Sheriff's County Court Summons
61 Sheriff's County Court Distringas
62 Bailiff's County Court Summons
63 Ditto for City
64 King's Bench Writs, or Lattitats
65 Exchequer Writs
66 Common Pleas Writs
67 Copies of Subpœnas
68 Coroner's Warrant to summons a Jury
69 Commitment for a Person who has run away from his Family
70 Petitions for Insolvents
71 Duns for small Debts
72 Notices for Meeting to appoint Surveyors of the Highways
73 Warrants to Surveyors of Highways
74 Constables Precepts
75 Notice from Chief Constables respecting County Rates
76 Constables Presentments
77 Chief Constable's Receipts for County Rates
78 Notice to Constables respecting County Rates
79 Notice to Petty Constables to return the Names of Overseers of the Poor
80 Notice to petty Constables to make out the List of Assessors of Land and Window Tax
81 Assessing Warrants for Servants
82 Collecting Warrants for ditto
83 Assessing Warrants for Houses
84 Collecting Warrants for ditto
85 General Assessments for Houses, Windows, and Servants, in one Half Sheet

Various Forms respecting the Militia and Impress Acts, Parish Receipts, and Receipts for Rent, &c.

Lists of the Justices of the Peace for the County of Worcester.

Also SOLD by J. TYMBS, Printer,

BIBLES, Testaments, Common Prayers, and Spelling Books; as also every new Publication, Magazines, Weekly Numbers, &c. &c.; great Variety of Ladies and Gentlemen's Pocket Books, Letter-Cases, and Memorandum Books, with or without Instruments; Stationary Wares, viz. Skins of Parchment, Writing Paper of all Sorts, Sealing Wax, Pens, Quills, Japan or Cake Ink, Wafers, Message Cards, Black Lead Pencils, Shop Books ruled or plain, Copy Books, &c. with a Variety of little Books for Children. *Of whom may be had,*

All the Genuine Patent Medicines, Wholesale and Retail, on the lowest Terms.

Printed in the Year 1780.

1 A catalogue of blank forms sold by
J. Tymbs, printer, Worcester, 1780.
Letterpress. 412 × 331 mm. *John Johnson Collection.*

Chapter 1
The information explosion

Undoubtedly the most important single point to emerge from a study of the history of printing during the last two hundred years is the steadily increasing part it has played in the everyday life of the community. In the eighteenth century and earlier the educated well-to-do man may have had his own private library, but books were expensive and even among those who were able to read few would have been in a position to buy them. Invitation cards, tickets, bank-notes, trade cards, bills of fare, letterheads, theatre bills, notices, and legal documents [1] were common enough in the late eighteenth century, and there was also a flourishing trade in pictorial prints of all kinds; but it seems likely that the printer of such items catered for much the same area of the public as the book printer. Only proclamations and similar public notices, the popular broadsheets and ballads which were sold on the streets for a penny plain or twopence coloured, and of course the Bible, can really have made much of an impression on the ordinary person of the late eighteenth and early nineteenth centuries. The impact of jobbing printing on the community is certainly difficult to gauge, but since the majority of printers worked in London and there were only comparatively few in the provinces before the late eighteenth century, it is fairly safe to assume that it had little influence on the country as a whole. Before the effective development of the postal and transport systems the jobbing printer really needed to work within the community he served; if he was any considerable distance from potential clients there was no real possibility of his being used for printing work of a very topical nature.

Towards the end of the eighteenth century, however, the position began to change and printing moved into the country towns of the regions. The little research on provincial printers that has been done by local historians has yet to be gathered together, but the valuable work of Professor Peter Isaac and his team in their study of the book trade in the north-east of England confirms the impression that it was only in the last three decades of the eighteenth century that printing really began to spread from London and the large towns into the country as a whole. And it was in the rural areas and small country towns where most people lived in the eighteenth century. More information is available about London printers, and it is clear that the number working in the capital increased steadily between 1785 and the middle of the nineteenth century. 124 letterpress printers were recorded by Pendred in 1785,[1] 216 by Stower in 1808,[2] and 316 by Johnson in 1824,[3] and by the middle of the century the directories reveal that the number had risen to around 500. The new trade of lithographic printing developed just as rapidly. In 1818 the number of lithographic printers in London could be counted on the fingers of one hand, but twenty years later there were at least forty and thereafter the trade probably grew even more rapidly. In the middle of the century London was still the centre of printing in this country and accounted for well over a third of the total labour force and over half the total output of the British letterpress printing industry,[4] but with the increasing cost of land, premises, and labour in the capital some

[1] J.Pendred, *The London and country printers, booksellers and stationers vade mecum* (London, 1785), edited with an introduction by Graham Pollard (London, Bibliographical Society, 1955), pp.1–4

[2] C.Stower, *The compositor's and pressman's guide to the art of printing* (London, 1808), pp.127–32

[3] J.Johnson, *Typographia, or the printers' instructor* (London, 1824), vol. ii, pp.649–51

[4] B.W.E. Alford, 'Business enterprise and the growth of the commercial letterpress printing industry, 1850–1914', *Business History*, vol. vii, no. 1, January 1965, p.1

of the largest and oldest-established firms set up factories in the provinces. Clowes purchased the Caxton Press at Beccles, Suffolk, in 1872, and Wyman, Waterlow, and Harrison all opened branches within reasonable striking distance of London in the first decade of the twentieth century. Since then the drift from the capital has continued steadily and London printers have accounted for a decreasing proportion of the nation's printing.

The majority of printers working in the eighteenth century were letterpress printers. Some concentrated on book printing, but many were prepared to take on anything that came their way, from the local newspaper to a window bill or visiting card. Much the same equipment would have been used in this period, regardless of the job in hand. Copper-plate printing was usually practised by separate firms, though many letterpress printers, especially those in the country towns, were prepared to take on copper-plate printing as a sideline. The trade of lithographic printing, which began to emerge quite quickly after 1820, was also practised separately, though there were some printers who undertook the whole range of letterpress, copper-plate, and lithographic printing [2]. In the course of the nineteenth century it became increasingly necessary for a printer to specialise, not only in terms of the processes used, but also in terms of the kinds of jobs undertaken. The newspapers had forced the issue early in the nineteenth century because of the organisational problems involved in meeting pressing deadlines and the special machinery which had to be built to cater for the large numbers of copies needed, but other printers began to specialise in labels and packaging, books, stationery, posters, legal work, security printing, and similar categories as the century wore on.

2 Trade card of Nathaniel Pearce, London, mid-nineteenth century. Engraved. 75 × 115 mm. *John Johnson Collection.*

One characteristic feature of the printing industry has always been the very small size of the majority of printing works. In all probability many jobbing printers of the late eighteenth century consisted of only the master printer and his assistant, and both would have had to be competent in most branches of the trade. One person could hardly have managed on his own as it was usual for the actual operation of taking a pull from the press to be carried out by two people working together, one inking the forme of type, the other laying the paper on, operating the press, and removing the printed sheets. In any case, one person would have had to see clients from time to time – and not all of them would have come for printing. Many provincial and country printers sold stationery, books, and newspapers, and even items like patent medicines, perfumes, and fancy goods [3]; in addition, they often acted as local agents for the coaches, theatres, and lotteries. The book printer was usually rather larger, and the University presses in particular had been sizable houses for centuries, but the general pattern of the printing industry in the late eighteenth century was of numerous small units. During the first half of the following century, however, some newly founded printing houses grew to be quite large, and by 1850 four London firms – Clowes, Eyre & Spottiswoode, Hansard, and Spottiswoode & Co. – each employed over two hundred men. The largest of these were Clowes and Eyre & Spottiswoode, both of whom employed about four hundred men in this period. Even so, 80 per cent of the five hundred or so printing firms in London in the mid-nineteenth century employed three men or fewer.[5]

The structure of the printing industry has not changed significantly since then. The larger firms have increased in size, but they still form a very small proportion of the total number of firms. It is estimated that large firms employing 200–1,000 workers formed rather less than one per cent of the total number of printing firms in Great Britain in 1914,[6] and an analysis of the British printing industry made by the British Federation of Master Printers in 1964 revealed that only 37·8 per cent of member firms employed twenty-

[5] B.W.E. Alford, 'Government expenditure and the growth of the printing industry in the nineteenth century', *Economic History Review*, 2nd series, vol. xvii, no. 1, August 1964, p.107

[6] Alford (1965), *op. cit.*, pp.10–11

JOHN SOULBY,
PRINTER, BOOK-BINDER, BOOK-SELLER AND STATIONER,
ULVERSTON;

BEGS leave to return his most grateful thanks to his FRIENDS and the PUBLIC for all favors; and assures them he is determined to exert his utmost abilities, to promote and secure that confidence and support hitherto so liberally bestowed upon him, which he will ever acknowledge with gratitude, and hopes from his steady attention to Business, to merit their future encouragement.

HE SELLS THE FOLLOWING ARTICLES (ON THE LOWEST TERMS,) VIZ.

WRITING PAPERS

Pott
Fool's-cap
Pott, faint lines
Fool's-cap; ditto
Thick Post
Ditto wove
Ditto faint lines
Thin Post
Thin Post wove
Extra Post
Thick gilt Post
Thin ditto
Mourning Post
Draft Paper
Tissue Paper

WHATMAN'S DRAWING PAPERS

Antiquarian
Double Elephant
Imperial
Super royal
Royal
Medium
Demy
Fool's-cap

PATENT RULED PAPERS

For MERCHANTS' ACCT. BOOKS of all sizes, from Super-royal to Fool's-cap, with faint lines, ruled to any pattern, and bound in Russia Bands or Plain Bindings.

WRAPPING PAPERS

Of various sorts

Cartridge and Log-book Paper
Bills of Lading
Ship Articles

ATKINSON'S TIDE TABLE,
Calculated for
LIVERPOOL and *ULVERSTON,*
And the time of Crossing
ULVERSTON and LANCASTER
SANDS

MOORE'S Navigation. Last Edition
Common Prayer Books, in a variety of elegant and plain Bindings
Dictionaries of all kinds
Bibles and Testaments
School Books of all sorts, in strong Bindings
A great variety of entertaining Books
Ditto of Songs and Jests
German Flutes tipt with Ivory and Silver Keys, or plain
English Flutes and Fifes of all sorts
Instruction Books for the Violin, German Flute, Fife, &c.
Violin Strings and Bows, best kind
A variety of Songs set to Music

Music Paper
Marble Paper of all sorts
Pink, green, yellow, and many other coloured Papers
Blossom and blue Demy for hanging Rooms
Blossom blotting Demy
Bonnet and Shaloon Papers
Quills and Pens,——common and clarified
Ink,——very choice common black, red, Patent Cake, Japan and Indian
Cammel's hair Pencils
Drop Paints
Black lead Pencils of the best manufactory
Metal Pencil Tops and Caps
Silver Pencil Cases
Gold and Silver Tooth Picks, with Silver Cases
Indian Rubbers, for cleaning Paper, Drawings, Satin, Gloves, &c.
Writing Parchment
Sealing Wax,——superfine Dutch and English, black and red
Wafers,——Irish and various sorts
Sand and Sand Boxes
Pounce
Black leather, brass and paper Ink-stands
Message Cards with ornamental borders
Ditto plain
Pocket Books,—— morocco and black leather, with straps, locks or clasps, made to any pattern
Morocco Etwee Cases, with instruments
Morocco Purses and Wallets
Asses Skin Books in morocco and black leather cases
Black and red leather Paper-cases
Port Folios for paintings and drawings
Round Rulers
Gunter's two feet Scales
Compasses with double steel joints
Counting Slates, and Slate Pencils
Letter Files

Court, or Ladies Sticking Plaister
Large two sheet Maps of England, Europe, &c.
Large and small Copper-plate Prints
Copper-plate slip Copies for schools
Copy Books
Letters for marking Linen
Frames for ditto
Black and red Ink for ditto
Memorandum Books of all sorts
Children's Books, by NEWBERRY, MARSHALL, &c.——a large assortment
Pocket Ledgers with pockets and flap
Cheap Repository, for religious and moral tracts, at ½d. 1d. and 1½d. each
Tin Pens for ruling
Blacking Balls for shoes, &c.
Puzzling Cards
Waste Cards for directions
Printed Bill Books

With many other articles in the BOOK-SELLING and STATIONARY Businesses

PATENT MEDICINES, SOLD BY AUTHORITY

Daffy's Elixir
Anderson's Scotch Pills
Bateman's Drops
Hooper's Female Pills
British Oil
Godfrey's Cordial
Molineux's Smelling Medicine
Cephalic Snuff
Steer's Opodeldoc
Essence of Pepper-mint
Rooke's Matchless Balsam
Turlington's Balsam of Life

Subscribers regularly supplied with REVIEWS, MAGAZINES, and every monthly, or other periodical publications, with great care and punctuality

A large CIRCULATING LIBRARY; to which will be added every new publication of merit

. Copper Plates taken off in the neatest manner

3 Trade list of John Soulby (senior), Ulverston, *c.* 1807. Letterpress. 287 × 173 mm. *Barrow Public Library.*

five or more persons and only 0·2 per cent one thousand or over.[7] Nevertheless, large firms have been responsible for a considerable proportion of the total production of the printing industry: the four largest printers in London accounted for over a third of the total output of London printers in the 1850s,[8] and just over a century later firms with one thousand employees or over, though representing only 1·4 per cent of the total number of firms in the country, accounted for 22 per cent of net output.[9] Apart from a few specialist printers, such as newspaper and periodical houses, most large firms of the nineteenth century installed greater quantities of exactly the same kind of equipment as the small printer; and this situation has not changed significantly this century. The small printer has, of course, always been slower in taking up new ideas for want of sufficient capital, but, allowing for this time lag, the methods he has used for composing type and printing have been much the same as those employed by the larger firms. The small printer has survived because so many jobs in printing are related to the scale of human needs and the relatively stable size of social groups; and while the increased capacity of a large printing works allows more ambitious jobs to be undertaken more efficiently, the small printer can often undertake small jobs just as well and, because his overheads are less, very much more economically.

Until the second half of the nineteenth century hardly any printers worked in premises specially built for the purpose. Before then the most typical printing works was the private house, with its floors shored up to take the extra weight of tons of metal and equipment. Expansion was normally effected by buying up neighbouring property and adding wings and outhouses, so that the plan of the original building was usually adapted beyond recognition. Judging from contemporary descriptions, the conditions in such houses were chaotic and appallingly squalid, and men were crammed together in badly lit rooms with little ventilation in summer and no source of warmth in winter. Stocked with reams of paper and quantities of oil and turpentine, and with the naked candle the usual form of illumination, such printing houses were a great fire risk, and many ended up in flames. Charles Manby Smith, who worked for a time in one of the largest of the London firms (probably Hansard's), described the premises as little better than a ruin in the 1830s, and claimed that though money had been spent on repairs not even the oldest workman could remember a single sixpence being spent for the purpose of cleanliness or sanitary precaution:

'The ceilings were black as printers' ink with the candle-smoke of two or three generations, and the walls, save where they were polished to a greasy brown by the friction of the shoulder, were of the same colour. The wind and the rain were patched out from the clattering casements and the rotting window-frames by inch-thick layers of brown paper and paste. Type of all descriptions, old as the building itself, or shining new from the foundry, was abundant as gravel in a gravel-pit, and seemed about as much cared for. Pots, pans, dishes, and cooking-utensils ground the face of it as it lay upon the men's bulks, and the heels of the busy crowd, as they tracked their sinuous path through the piles of forms stacked together in every available space, razed the corners of the pages nearest the ground.'[10]

Such conditions may not have been absolutely typical, but they were not exceptional, and the unsanitary nature of the printing trade in general is supported by the incidence of pulmonary disease amongst printers. A Royal Commission, quoted by the London Society of Compositors in 1866, recorded that the death rate of printers was 47 per cent higher than that of the community at large, and that 70 per cent of the deaths could be ascribed to some form of chest disease.[11]

[7] British Federation of Master Printers, *Economic study of the printing industry* (1965), p.25

[8] Alford (1964), *op. cit.*, p.107

[9] Census of Production, 1958. Quoted British Federation of Master Printers, *Economic study of the printing industry* (1965), p.25

[10] C.M.Smith, *The working man's way in the world*, 3rd issue (London, 1857), with preface and notes by Ellic Howe (London, Printing Historical Society, 1967), pp.242–3

[11] E.Howe, *The London compositor; documents relating to wages, working conditions, and customs of the London printing trade 1785–1900* (London, Bibliographical Society, 1947), p.270

4 The principal composing room of the Temple Printing Office, built for James Moyes in 1825. Wood-engraving by Samuel Williams from *Specimens of the types commonly used in the Temple Printing Office*, 1826.

5 A printer's workshop of the 1820s or 1830s. Wood-engraving by Thomas Kelly. *St Bride Printing Library.*

One of the first large premises known to have been constructed in the nineteenth century specially for printing was the Temple Printing Office, built in Bouverie Street for James Moyes in 1825 after his previous premises had been destroyed by fire. The illustration of the principal composing room [4] certainly presents a very different picture from that painted by Charles Manby Smith, but it should be pointed out that Moyes's building was designed as a model establishment. Probably more typical is the printing works used by Thomas Kelly as the basis for his wood-engraving of the 1820s or 1830s [5], which shows both composing and printing being practised in the same room. Though the room is well lit and comparatively spacious, there are indications of real activity and of the chaos described by Smith; and this

illustration certainly has a ring of truth about it that others lack. Towards the end of the nineteenth century factories began to be specially built as printing works as London firms moved into the provinces, and since then the industry as a whole has changed drastically; but the small printer, working in conditions not so very different from those described by Smith, survived for many years [6] and is not unknown even today.

The printer's lot in the nineteenth century may not have been any worse than that of the average industrial worker, and was a good deal easier than that of some, but this should not disguise the fact that the printer worked long hours under conditions of considerable strain. During the first half of the century a twelve-hour day was not exceptional; what is more, a printer could be called upon to work from six in the morning until ten at night, and in some houses had to be prepared to work for as long as two whole days without a break for sleep in order to meet a deadline for some Parliamentary printing or other urgent work. Regular employment was not easy to find in the printing trade in this period, and labour was only taken on when it was needed. Apprenticeship lasted seven years, after which the successful boy became a journeyman printer and earned full rates of pay. There was no limit, as there is today, to the number of apprentices a master printer could employ, so that many preferred to exploit cheap boy labour. Consequently, as soon as an apprentice became a journeyman he found it more difficult to find work, and some printers even travelled to the continent to earn a living at their chosen trade.

6 A composing room in the Great Hall of 'Colston's House', Small Street, Bristol. Photographed before 1868. *Reproduced by courtesy of Reece Winstone Esq.*

Nevertheless, there were compensations in the work of the printer. The compositor in particular would have had every chance to meet authors and clients, some of them of great distinction, and may even have been able to discuss problems and requirements around the printing frame. Because of the nature of the work, the printing trade attracted some of the most intelligent boys and provided as good a means of self-education as any occupation for those who wished to take advantage of the opportunities it offered. In addition, the trade had evolved over the centuries its own mysterious customs which helped to create a strong corporate unity amongst printers. Each printing house had its own organisation, known as the Chapel, to which all journeymen printers belonged. The chapels functioned in a disciplinary capacity to ensure that work ran smoothly on the shop floor, for printing is a trade in which departure from a stringent code of conduct can lead to chaos; but they were also benevolent and social bodies, and their complex and imaginative rules gave plenty of opportunity to break the tedium of work by making some procedure or punishment an excuse for quenching the thirst with a pot of beer. The chapels also gave corporate voice to grievances, and it was largely through their initiative that the printing trade became one of the first to secure wage agreements. In the course of the nineteenth century some of the functions of the chapels were taken over by the unions, the first of which was founded in 1801, shortly after the Combination Acts had legislated against trade societies. Numerous unions associated with the printing and allied trades were formed after the repeal of the Combination Acts in 1824/5, and towards the end of the nineteenth century they moved towards a nation-wide federation which was eventually founded in 1902 and called the Printing and Kindred Trades Federation. Well before this, however, the unions had successfully negotiated for better rates of pay and working conditions. As a result of their efforts the weekly hours of the printer were gradually reduced until the eight-hour day became the norm by the end of the nineteenth century.

The proliferation of printing houses and the growth of existing ones continued throughout the nineteenth century and brought about a steady increase in the quantity of work produced. The Census of Production for 1907 reveals that in terms of net output the printing and bookbinding trades stood in tenth position among all industries of the United Kingdom. It is difficult to give any reliable statistical record of the growth of the printing trade itself during the last two hundred years, as output for the early period is not known, but the general pattern is probably revealed by the growth of the dependent trades of book publishing and paper-making. The number of books published annually in the United Kingdom rose from an average of fewer than six hundred in the first quarter of the nineteenth century[12] to 32,393 in 1969. Paper production in the United Kingdom shows a similar rate of growth: 11,000 tons were produced in 1800, 100,000 tons in 1860, and 652,000 tons in 1900.[13] These figures provide some general indication of the growth of the printing industry and its impact on the community in the period as a whole. A more specific assessment of its growth in a particular period has been made by B. W. E. Alford, who estimates that the gross output of the letterpress printing industry of Great Britain doubled in the twenty years from 1831 to 1851, when it grew from £750,000 to £1,500,000.[14]

Something of the influence of printing on the environment in the nineteenth century can be gleaned from studying contemporary prints, paintings, and photographs of London, many of which show posters displayed on every available piece of wall [8 – 10]. Billposting was one of the new trades of the nineteenth century, and illustrations of the billposter in sets of London characters or books of trades usually show him respectably setting about his work [7]. In fact, the billposter's job was really rather a disreputable one, and he often worked surreptitiously at night so as to be able to disfigure a private wall or paste over a competitor's advertisement. Sampson describes the billposter as 'a nuisance of the most intolerable kind',[15] and records that his peak period of activity was early on Sunday mornings, when he would aim to be early enough to avoid detection, but not so early as to run the risk of having his work disfigured by rival billposters.

7 A billposter of the early nineteenth century. From an etching by John Miller in Griffin & Co.'s *Book of trades*.

[12] C.H.Timperley, *A dictionary of printers and printing* (London, 1839), p.901

[13] S.H.Steinberg, *Five hundred years of printing* (Harmondsworth, 1955), p.191

[14] Alford (1964), *op. cit.*, pp.96–7

[15] H.Sampson, *A history of advertising from the earliest times* (London, 1874), p.25

8 John Parry, London street scene, 1835. Water-colour painting. 760 × 1065 mm. *Alfred Dunhill Ltd, St James's.*

9 Alfred Concanen, 'A railway station in 1874'. Lithograph in five colours, printed by Stannard & Son. From H. Sampson, *A history of advertising from the earliest times*, 1874. Image 158 × 309 mm.

10 Poster-covered wall of the Alhambra Theatre, Leicester Square, 1899. Photograph. *Reproduced by kind permission of Aero Films and Aero Pictorial Ltd.*

Sandwichmen have been another familiar part of the London scene since before the middle of the nineteenth century. They first made their mark when two hundred of them paraded the streets of London to announce the first number of the *Illustrated London News* which appeared in May 1842 [11].

11 Sandwichmen advertising the first number of the *Illustrated London News*, 1842. Wood-engraving from the *Illustrated London News*, 14 May 1842. 75 × 225 mm.

Another standard method of advertising was to employ men to thrust bills into the hands of passers-by at street corners, railway stations, and other vantage points. William Smith, the enterprising manager of the New Adelphi Theatre, records in a little book on advertising a walk he made through London during the week of the Cattle Show in 1861 when he accepted everything he was offered and collected 250 bills, books, and pamphlets.[16] Smith was a precursor of the market researchers of our own day, and he estimated that if only half the people following the same route had taken half of what they were offered the number of items distributed during nine hours on that day would have amounted to 2,300,000. In the following year, during two hours spent at the Smithfield Cattle Show, he was given 104 items of printing; and as he was just one of 50,000 visitors that day, he estimated, on the same basis of half the number taking half bills, that some 1,300,000 items must have been distributed in the course of the one day.[17]

The proliferation of printed matter in the last two hundred years has been self-generating. On one level, the publishing of information created a demand for still more information, on another, printing which had persuasion as its prime motive needed to be larger and more widely circulated in order to be able to outdo its competitors. This tendency towards larger and bolder printed advertising is seen very clearly in the work of three different generations of printers in Ulverston, a small market town in the Furness area of Lancashire: John Soulby (senior), who was printing from about 1795 to 1817; his son, John Soulby (junior), who worked from about 1820 to 1827; and William Kitchin, who was working during the last quarter of the nineteenth century. The set of illustrations printed opposite [12 – 14] shows the largest surviving poster of each of these printers. They are reproduced to scale, and the comparison is a valid one since the work of all three of these printers has survived in quantity and the largest item in each case is not exceptional. The growth in the size of posters in the nineteenth century was commented upon by William Smith, who compared the six-sheet posters (probably 90 × 40 in.) he was ordering for the New Adelphi Theatre in the early 1860s with a little theatre bill of half a century earlier which measured only 8 × 3 in.

In addition to the greater impact of printing gained by sheer size, there also emerged in the course of the opening decades of the nineteenth century a method of display and copy-writing which was consistent with the need for emphasis. The use of larger, bolder, and more eye-catching typefaces for

[16]W. Smith, *Advertise. How? When? Where?* (London, 1863), pp.86–7
[17]*Ibid.*, pp.87–8

12 Religious tract in the form of a theatre bill, *c.* 1810. Letterpress, printed by John Soulby (senior), Ulverston. 432 × 257 mm. *Barrow Public Library.*

13 Circus poster, 1823. Letterpress, printed by John Soulby (junior), Ulverston. 545 × 450 mm. *Museum of English Rural Life, Reading University.*

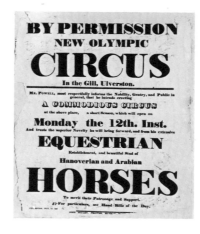

14 Concert poster, *c.* 1890. Letterpress, printed in green on three sheets of paper by William Kitchin, Ulverston. 1875 × 1015 mm. *Museum of English Rural Life, Reading University.*

15 Reward notice, 1810. Letterpress, printed by John Soulby (senior), Ulverston. 270 × 197 mm. *Barrow Public Library.*

16 Reward notice, 1823. Letterpress, printed by John Soulby (junior), Ulverston. 176 × 225 mm. *Museum of English Rural Life, Reading University.*

17 A view of the packaging department of Huntley & Palmers, Reading, showing the application of paper labels to tin boxes. Water-colour drawing, probably produced in connection with the international exhibition of 1862. *Huntley & Palmers.*

important words or lines will be discussed in a later chapter. The linguistic equivalent of this, copy written in such a way that individual words could be emphasised and a message put over in almost telegraphic form, anticipates the work of experimental psychologists, copywriters, and typographers in this century. The essence of this approach can be seen by making a further comparison of similar work produced by two of the Ulverston printers mentioned above. John Soulby (senior) continued to work in the late eighteenth-century conventions [15], while his son began to organise his material differently and adopted an approach which prevailed throughout the nineteenth century [16].

The reason for this change in the method of writing and organising copy obviously relates to the need to achieve impact by making the most important words as large as possible so that they could be picked out at a glance by a passer-by; but it may also have some connection with the emergence of a new semi-literate public who could take in the essential meaning of a poster by reading one or two words, but may have been unable to read the whole text.

It is not difficult to find reasons for the sudden growth of printing in this country during the last two hundred years, and they are all closely related to one another. In the fifteenth century printing had been nurtured on theology and Renaissance humanism and, although commercially based, had been directed to meet the needs of scholarship. The growth of printing in England in the late eighteenth and nineteenth centuries was much more closely related to the expansion of industry and trade. Though slow to become industrialised itself, the printing trade was quick to reap the rewards of industrial society and changed its course accordingly. The reorganisation of English manufacturing from cottage-based industry to centralised factories in urban areas brought with it a society much more dependent on organised commerce, and created a demand for new kinds of printing. Large firms needed printing in order to identify, describe, and advertise their products [17], and labels, trade catalogues, and circulars were printed in lengths of run previously required only for newspaper and periodical work. The organisation of trade involved correspondence and accounting, and this created the need for letter-heads, invoices, receipts, statements, bills of lading, and other business printing which had in the past often been written by hand. In its turn the expansion of business and trade conducted on a national and international

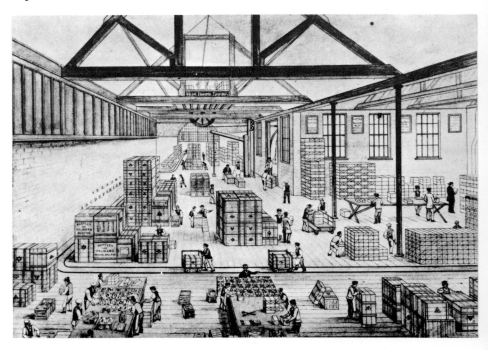

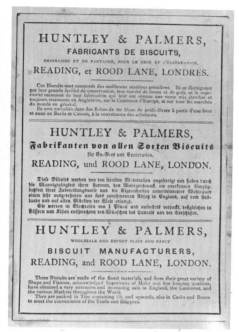

18 Bank-note of the Cornish Bank, 1825. Engraved on copper by J. Bateman. 99 × 177 mm. *John Johnson Collection.*

19 Multilingual advertisement of Huntley & Palmers, produced for the Paris exhibition of 1867. Letterpress, printed in red and blue. 143 × 98 mm. *Huntley & Palmers.*

20 Penny post notice, 1840. Letterpress, printed by C. E. Brown, Cambridge. 340 × 212 mm. *Cambridge Folk Museum.* (The notice is mounted on wallpaper, which has stained the paper.)

21 Notice of a festival and diversions at Chippenham to celebrate the passing of the Reform Bill, 1832. Letterpress, printed in blue by Alexander, Chippenham. 375 × 250 mm. *Wiltshire County Record Office.*

level necessitated the printing of postage stamps, cheques, and a reliable paper currency [18].

Allied to the growth of trade was the breaking down of the isolation of parts of Britain by improvements in communication. On a physical level the canals, roads, and bridges of engineers such as Telford and Macadam, the network of railways which spread across the country in the middle of the nineteenth century and, later, the invention of the internal combustion engine, made possible the efficient movement of goods and people. In terms of ideas and information the growth of a cheap national press, the development of the postal system, and the invention of the electric telegraph helped to promote an interest in affairs outside a particular locality. This new mobility and ease of communication had the effect of taking selling and the exchange of information and ideas out of the market place on to a national and international level [19]. The printing industry was one of the principal beneficiaries of this movement and it expanded rapidly as the demands of advertising, business, and information printing increased. A crucial factor in this change was the introduction of the penny post in 1840 [20] as a result of the tireless efforts of Rowland Hill. This established a cheap postal service based on a pre-paid standard fee of one penny per half ounce, whatever the distance a letter was to be sent, and it played a significant part in the growth of the printing industry because of its influence on commerce and literacy. A natural consequence of the improvement in transport and communication was that it was no longer so necessary for the printer to serve merely local needs; and, particularly this century, there has been a tendency for larger printing firms to rely less, if at all, on local custom.

While the structure of British industry was changing rapidly during the last quarter of the eighteenth century, the political and intellectual climate underwent an even more significant upheaval, and this too had its effect on the printing industry. The example of the French Revolution left its mark on British society, and radical thinkers inspired by Tom Paine's book *The rights of man* (1791–2) did much to shake the complacent attitudes of eighteenth-century England. Parliament gradually emerged as a more democratic body and, with the rise of the trade unions and the gradual extension of the franchise, the ordinary person began to become involved in the major issues of his time [21] and felt that he had a right to a say in the machinery of government. Despite the ruthless suppression of the press during Pitt's

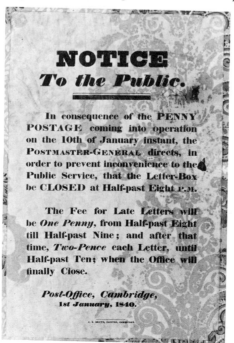

c

ministry at the close of the eighteenth century, and occasionally thereafter, printing eventually provided an effective means for the propagation of radical ideas and became a powerful platform in the reform movement. *Cobbett's Weekly Political Register* [22], which sold at only twopence a copy, was so successful that it achieved a circulation of 40,000, a figure not approached by any daily newspaper of the period.

An effective nation-wide commercial structure and the active involvement of the people in government both depend on there being an efficient means of communication. In the nineteenth century this really meant printing; and printing implies a literate public. The development of education and the growth of literacy were therefore closely linked with the expansion of society generally. Statistics relating to literacy in Britain are numerous and usually misleading because the term is so difficult to define; but even taken on the basis of a simple skill, such as an ability to sign the marriage register, the first nation-wide report of 1840 showed that only 67 per cent of males and 51 per cent of females were literate. But returns such as these, which indicate over the century a steady increase in the percentage of literates, reveal absolutely nothing about the essential factor in reading, the ability to understand what has been written.

At the close of the eighteenth century there was no national pattern of education in England. The old-established grammar schools still survived, and on another level there were the charity schools, Sunday schools, and dame schools. It was not until the beginning of the nineteenth century that two religious foundations, the British and Foreign School Society (1810) and the National Society (1811), established the basis of an educational system. After voluntary effort had shown the need, the state stepped in hesitantly and established the first state Committee for Education in 1839. Thereafter, successive Education Acts, particularly those of 1870, 1902, 1918, and 1944, extended the period of education, widened its scope, and improved its quality. The beginning of the nineteenth century also witnessed the growth of adult education for skilled workers in the form of the Mechanics' Institutes. The original idea for these came to Dr Birkbeck while he was teaching at Glasgow University, and when he moved to London he was the guiding spirit behind the foundation of the London Mechanics' Institute in 1823. Thereafter, Mechanics' Institutes and similar bodies for the education of the working classes were founded in most large industrial towns and many small ones as well and

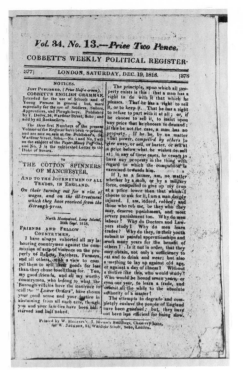

22 *Cobbett's Weekly Political Register*, 19 December 1818. Letterpress, printed by W. Molineux, London. Page size 225 × 138 mm.

23 Northampton Clickers' Early Closing Association, notice of a lecture at the Mechanics' Institute, 1857. Letterpress with manuscript alterations, printed by Lea, Northampton. 275 × 193 mm. *John Johnson Collection.*

24 Notice of Stansted Literary Association lecture, 1851. Letterpress, printed by Mullinger, Bishop's Stortford. 250 × 316 mm. *Essex County Record Office.*

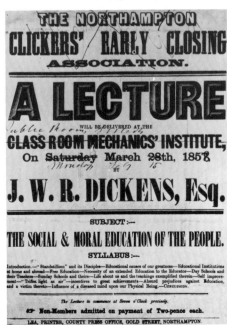

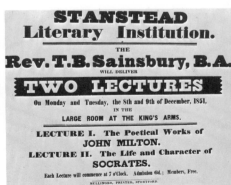

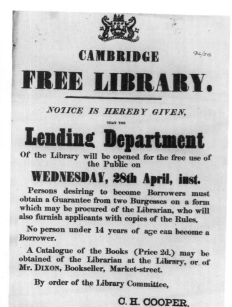

played a major part in the growth of education [23]. In the same period higher education took a leap forward with the foundation of University College (1826) and King's College (1828), which were later combined to form the University of London.

Education took many other forms, and the need men felt to educate themselves was reflected in the activities of bodies like the Literary and Philosophical Societies [24] and particularly in the pressure for the means of self-education. Reading for pleasure and education increased enormously and the private circulating libraries [25], which catered virtually alone for borrowers' needs prior to the middle of the nineteenth century, soon proved to be inadequate. Edward Edwards, a member of the staff of the British Museum, who was called as a witness by the Select Committee appointed in 1849 to look into the question of the public libraries, reported that 'most of our great towns have no libraries at all that can in any proper sense be termed public . . .'.[18] The Public Libraries Act of 1850 gave councils of towns with over 10,000 population the authority to levy a rate not exceeding one halfpenny in the pound for the provision of public libraries and museums; in 1855 the levy was raised to one penny and the population limit lowered to 5,000. A number of towns soon took advantage of the new legislation: Winchester in 1851, Bolton, Ipswich, Manchester, and Oxford in 1852, Blackburn, Sheffield, and Cambridge in 1853 [26]. By the close of the century there were over three hundred public libraries in the country, most of them with facilities for lending books, and it is estimated that in the year 1895–6 over 26 million books were issued by the lending libraries of the United Kingdom.[19]

The development of a system of free education for all, however unsatisfactory it may have been in reality, at least gave children the opportunity of a few years at school; the libraries of the Mechanics' Institutes and the public libraries gave them a chance to continue their education on leaving. Moreover, the pioneering spirit of the times, the growth of trade and science, and improvements in transport and communication gave people an incentive to do so. Society was becoming increasingly dependent on the printed word in everyday affairs, and by the middle of the nineteenth century most people would have been brought face to face with new kinds of printing – forms to fill in, timetables to read, instructions to follow, puzzles to solve, advertisements to understand. All this meant a growing market for the printers' wares.

25 Notice of Troughton's circulating library, *c.* 1800. Letterpress, 262 × 171 mm. *Barrow Public Library.*

26 Notice of the opening of the lending department of Cambridge Free Library, 1858. Letterpress on blue paper, printed by Naylor and Co., 'Chronicle' Office, Cambridge. 310 × 205 mm. *Cambridge Folk Museum.*

[18] W.A.Munford, *Penny rate: aspects of British public library history 1850–1950* (London, 1951), p.12

[19] M.G.Kendall (ed.), *The sources and nature of the statistics of the United Kingdom*, 2 vols (London, 1952–7), M. Deane, 'Publishing', vol. i, p.349

Chapter 2
New processes

In the middle of the eighteenth century there were very few printing processes and, for one reason or another, they were all rather limited in their application. There were two basic kinds of printing, relief and intaglio, and both of them stemmed from the fifteenth century or before.

Printing from movable types and woodcuts, which had been the basic techniques of the book and jobbing printer for centuries, fall into the category of relief printing. Solid text was usually composed from thousands of small units bearing letterforms in reverse which received the ink and transferred it to paper under pressure. Most ephemeral printing in which text played an important part, such as window bills, proclamations, notices, and ballads, was also printed in this way. Popular pictorial images were mostly printed from wood because of the simplicity of the technique and the cheapness and availability of the material [27]. Woodcuts were frequently used for the decoration and illustration of books as they were easily printed along with type, and they were also used for the printing of wallpaper and textiles. But, though such artists as Dürer and Holbein brought great distinction to woodcutting in the late fifteenth and early sixteenth centuries, it remained for the most part a rather crude process.

Work of a more refined nature, where quantity and cost were not so crucial, was normally engraved on copper and printed intaglio. There are various kinds of intaglio printing, but in all of them the printing image lies below the surface of the plate. Printing is effected by rubbing ink into the hollows of the plate, wiping its surface clean, and then forcing the ink out on to the paper under great pressure. In copper-engraving, the oldest form of intaglio printing, the marks are physically engraved in the metal with a lozenge-shaped tool called a burin [28]. Copper-engraving was first practised by artists in the fifteenth century as an autographic process, but it soon became a popular means of reproducing drawings and developed its own very complex syntax of marks. It was also widely used for the illustration of books and was for centuries the most common process for both map and music printing. A few isolated books have been engraved throughout on metal but, as far as text is concerned, metal engraving was usually limited to rather more elaborate work, such as trade and invitation cards, music covers, billheads, and book plates [29], where the lettering was combined with some kind of decoration.

The other old-established branch of intaglio printing is etching. An etched plate is printed in exactly the same way as an engraved one, but the image is made by removing part of an acid resistant ground with a steel point and then etching the lines into the metal by immersing the plate in a bath of acid. Since its first use by artists at the beginning of the sixteenth century, etching has remained the province of the original draughtsman, largely because it accommodates personal handling; but from the seventeenth century onwards it also began to be used commercially in conjunction with engraving as a convenient means of doing preliminary work on copper before adding finishing touches with the burin.

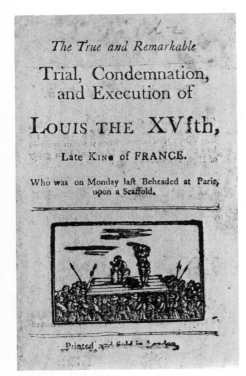

27 Cover of popular pamphlet, c. 1793. Letterpress with woodcut, printed in London. 179 × 113 mm. *Reading University Library.*

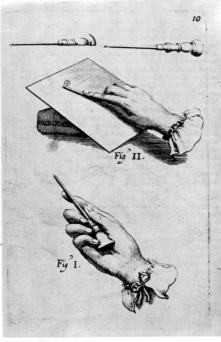

28 The copper-engraver's burin. From Abraham Bosse, *Traicté des manières de graver en taille douce*, 1645.

18

Other kinds of intaglio printing which were popular before 1770 are mezzotint, crayon-engraving, and stipple-engraving. They were principally used to reproduce the work of fashionable artists and tended to have very specific applications. In mezzotint [30, 31] the whole of a copper plate is worked over in numerous directions with a toothed tool, called a rocker, until it presents a roughened surface all over. In this state the entire plate would hold printing ink, and would therefore print black, but the actual process of engraving in mezzotint consists of reducing the grain of the plate with a scraper in proportion to the degree of light required. The richest blacks are left untouched, while the lightest areas are produced by removing the grain entirely with a tool called a burnisher. Mezzotint is capable of a wide range of subtly gradated tones, and in the eighteenth century was primarily used for the reproduction of oil paintings, particularly fashionable portraits. Crayon-engraving and stipple-engraving are closely related to one another, and were primarily used to capture the effects of drawings made with crayon or pastel. In stipple, which is much the older of the two, tonal effects are produced by making a conglomeration of dots or short strokes with an etching needle or with the point of a stipple engraver. In crayon-engraving, tools, known as roulettes, are used which have toothed wheels with different kinds of grains to match the various textures of the actual lines of a chalk drawing. Crayon and stipple work were combined to such an extent in the eighteenth century that it is misleading to consider them separately. In both processes preliminary work was usually done through an etching ground and subsequently etched, and further work was then added with the burin directly on to the plate as in engraving.

29 Copper-engraved book plate, eighteenth century. 134 × 86 mm.

30 John Raphael Smith, mezzotint after a painting by W. Peters, 1778. 414 × 323 mm.

31 Detail of Plate 30. 120 × 95 mm.

The differences between the two major branches of printing, relief and intaglio, go far beyond technical differences of production. Relief printing, whether of images or words, has traditionally been the province of the common printer who was mainly concerned with the printing of solid text; intaglio printing stemmed from the work of the craftsman in metals and has ever since been linked with the artist and pictorial imagery. The letterpress printer sometimes commissioned illustrations and occasionally may even have made his own wood-block images, the copperplate engraver and printer often moved into the field of lettering and jobbing printing; but there remained a fundamental difference of outlook between the two.

These traditional processes all continued to be used well into the nineteenth century, though the importance of some of them diminished considerably as new processes were developed. All have been revived from time to time and have been used by artists for making pictorial prints. This application

32 Theatre bill, mid-nineteenth century. Woodcut, printed in black on green stained paper. 755 × 500 mm. *John Johnson Collection.*

apart, copper-engraving survived the longest and continued to be used for prestige printing, such as the reproduction of works of art, well into the second half of the nineteenth century. More refined relief processes soon ousted the woodcut, and by the middle of the nineteenth century it was virtually limited to posters and popular broadsheets where the scale was sufficiently large to stand the coarseness of cutting [32].

The last quarter of the eighteenth century saw the beginnings of a great period of experimentation in printing processes and initiated a movement which bore fruit commercially in the following century. The experiments took many directions, but there seem to have been two main areas of interest. First of all, there were attempts to extend the range of existing pictorial processes so that they were more in keeping with artists' needs, either in terms of the end result or the convenience of working. Secondly, there were attempts to find cheaper methods of working which would allow text and images to be combined and would also stand up to very long runs.

Before the nineteenth century was very old, improvements had been made to some of the old-established graphic processes. The first such improvement was aquatint [33, 34], a tonal extension of etching. The origins of the process are somewhat obscure, but it was introduced to England from the continent around 1770 and used successfully by the water-colour painter Paul Sandby from 1775 onwards. Aquatint gave as close an imitation of a water-colour painting as could be hoped for, and was used almost exclusively for this kind of work. The relation between the growth of water-colour painting and aquatint was very close, and many of the leading landscape and topographical painters produced originals which skilled engravers translated into aquatint. The usual stages in the production of a contemporary water-colour painting, in which a linear drawing was first given a monochrome tonal base and then local colour, were matched exactly in the production of an aquatint print: the plate was etched in line, given a tonal structure by means of the aquatint process, and the print itself was then often coloured by hand afterwards. Scores of superb volumes with hand-coloured aquatint plates were produced in the early nineteenth century, and Rudolph Ackermann and other publishers specialised in this kind of work. The heyday of aquatint was quite short, and after about 1840 the process was rarely used for any kind of commercially-produced work.

33 'Pembroke College', hand-coloured aquatint, engraved by J. C. Stadler after a water-colour by A. Pugin. From *A history of the University of Cambridge*, 1815. 276 × 207 mm. *Reading University Library.*

34 Detail of aquatint tone from the top of Plate 33. 46 × 40 mm.

Another branch of etching which was developed during the late eighteenth century was soft-ground etching. The process is similar to the usual method of etching, except that the drawing is done with a pencil on thin paper stretched over the surface of a grounded plate. The lines take on something of the quality of the texture of the paper and, consequently, soft-ground etchings look very much like drawings made with a soft pencil. The process had little commercial application as its role was soon taken over by lithography, but its limited use did at least demonstrate the draughtsman's need for a more direct method of multiplying his drawings.

The improvements made to the process of taking prints from wood, though rather more significant commercially than developments in intaglio printing, are less easy to define. They are embodied in the process we usually call wood-engraving [35, 36]. A simple distinction between woodcutting and wood-engraving can be made by stating that woodcuts are made with a knife on the long grain of a plank of wood, while wood-engravings are made with tools similar to the engraver's burin on a piece of close-grained wood, such as box, cut across the grain; or by stating that woodcuts appear as black images on a light ground, while wood-engravings appear as a series of white lines against a dark ground. But though both statements are broadly true, neither is strictly accurate. The distinction cannot really be made on the basis of either technique or style alone. Some fifteenth- and sixteenth-century woodcuts are conceived in white lines and it is easy enough to produce the effect of a black-line woodcut on a wood-engraving block. All that can usefully be said is that a method of working on boxwood with tools like the engraver's burin became popular in England during the last quarter of the eighteenth century and that it allowed for a full tonal rendering of a small-scale image which could be printed along with type.

35 Thomas Bewick, wood-engraved vignette from his *A history of British birds*, 1809 edition. 58 × 81 mm.

36 Detail of Plate 35. 24 × 30 mm.

37 Thomas Bewick, *A history of British birds*, 1809 edition. Letterpress with wood-engravings, printed by Edward Walker. Page size 200 × 120 mm.

This proved to be a most significant development, and can be attributed to Thomas Bewick (1753–1828), who lived and carried on his business for most of his life in and around Newcastle-upon-Tyne. Bewick's name soon became well known in the various fields of ornithology, book production, and popular art through the publication of his *General history of quadrupeds* (1790) and *History of British birds* (1797–1804) [37] and has been handed down to posterity in literature by Charlotte Brontë, who used the vignettes of the second of these publications to stir the imagination of the young Jane Eyre in the opening pages of the novel which appeared nearly fifty years later. Our concern here is that Bewick raised the craft of making printed images from wood to a new level and paved the way for a revolution in communication in the nineteenth century. For the first time there existed a refined but cheap process which could be used in conjunction with type for the printing of large editions. Bewick's method of working depended on technical improvements in the manufacture of paper which allowed fine lines and small areas of rich black to be printed properly. One such development was wove paper, which differs from the older form of laid paper in that it does not have the parallel lines of rather thinner paper which result from the use of thick chain wires to strengthen the wire mesh on which the paper is made. Wove paper was introduced around the middle of the eighteenth century and, together with improvements in presswork, had much to do with the success of Bewick's technical methods.

Despite Bewick's isolation in the north of England, his reputation and methods spread quickly by means of his publications and the school of assistants who left his employment to find work in London. His pupils were responsible for training the next generation of wood-engravers whose images fill the pages of the journals and books of the nineteenth century; but while Bewick often worked from his own delightful wash drawings, his pupils and later wood-engravers usually worked from originals supplied to them by other draughtsmen [38]. This led to the gradual movement away from the style of work done in Newcastle, which derived from the simplest kinds of marks which could be engraved on wood, to virtuoso performances in copying the complex hatchings of pen drawings and translating washes of ink or paint [39, 40]. Though the appearance of wood-engraving changed to suit the requirements of different artists' styles, the basic technique remained much the same. Craftsmanship became more skilful and certain refinements were introduced to make the process better suited to machine printing, and by the middle of the century wood-engraving had developed into a veritable industry [42].

38 Birket Foster, illustration from William Cowper, *The task*, 1855, engraved on wood by Edmund Evans. 100 × 87 mm.

39 J. E. Millais, 'The finding of Moses by Pharaoh's daughter'. Wood-engraving from *Lays of the Holy Land*, 1858, engraved by the firm of Dalziel. 138 × 101 mm.

40 J. E. Millais, 'The finding of Moses by Pharaoh's daughter'. Water-colour drawing for *Lays of the Holy Land*, 1858. 152 × 114 mm. *Victoria & Albert Museum.*

The progress of wood-engraving was given a considerable boost in the 1820s with the perfection and widespread use of the plaster of Paris method of stereotyping. Stereotype plates were used to provide duplicates of printing formes, which meant that the original could be preserved from damage in printing and that more than one forme could be printed at a time when large editions were needed quickly. Providing nothing unforeseen happened, wood-engravings could stand up to the wear of very long runs. Bewick estimated that as many as a million prints had been taken from one of his engravings, Spielmann reports that after 70,000 to 80,000 prints had been taken for the foreign edition of *Punch* the wood-engravings were still in good enough condition for electrotyping,[20] and Mason Jackson claimed that the blocks for the Christmas number of the *Illustrated London News* of 1882 had 425,000 impressions taken from them.[21] A crucial technical innovation in wood-engraving was the invention by Charles Wells about 1860 of a method of assembling large blocks in parts, so that they could be separated after the drawing had been made on them and bolted together again for printing [41]. This had important implications for illustrated journalism as it meant that the laborious work of engraving could be divided among a whole team of craftsmen when deadlines were tight.

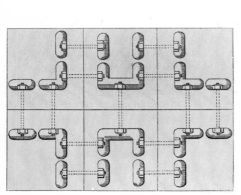

41 Drawing of the back of a half-page block for the *Illustrated London News* showing how the parts are bolted together. From Mason Jackson, *The pictorial press: its origin and progress*, 1885.

A far reaching improvement in intaglio printing was the substitution of steel plates for copper ones. Steel-engraving had its origins in the movement towards greater security in bank-note printing, and its invention is usually credited to the American Jacob Perkins (1766–1849) who developed, during

[20] M. H. Spielmann, *The history of 'Punch'* (London, 1895), p.251

[21] M. Jackson, *The pictorial press: its origin and progress* (London, 1885), p.326

42 Ed. Badoureau, view of the interior of the workshop of the firm of Ed. Badoureau showing the manufacture of boxwood blocks. Wood-engraving, printed in black and a tint for the firm's calendar, 1886. 307 × 178 mm. *John Johnson Collection.*

the first decade of the nineteenth century, a new method of hardening steel as part of his process of siderography. This was a process by which an engraving made on soft steel was hardened by a special method of heating and sudden cooling and then impressed repeatedly on different parts of a soft steel cylinder. This cylinder was subsequently hardened by the same method and used to impress the image on to a sheet of soft steel. In its turn this sheet was hardened and used for printing. In 1810 an English patent was taken out on Perkins's behalf by Joseph Dyer for improvements in intaglio printing which depended on the process of siderography, but some years passed before steel-engraving was taken up commercially. However, Perkins's process was the means by which the new material and method of hardening it were introduced to English engravers. As steel plates were tougher than copper ones even very fine lines could withstand the wear of printing, and

43 Steel-engraving by W. Miller after an original by J. M. W. Turner from an edition of Samuel Rogers, *Poems*, 1838. 83 × 92 mm.

44 Detail of Plate 43. 26 × 28 mm.

45 Specimen bank-note, engraved on steel by Perkins, Bacon & Petch. From Granville Sharp, *The Gilbart prize essay on the adaptation of recent discoveries and inventions to the purposes of practical banking*, 1854. 110 × 190 mm.

46 Detail of Plate 45. 8 × 27 mm.

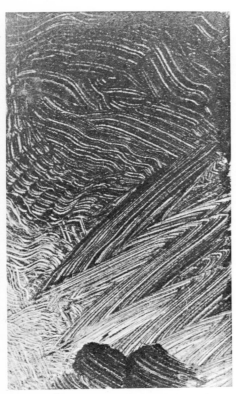

47 Specimen of Palmer's electrotint, printed intaglio, 30 × 18 mm. From Thomas Sampson, *Electrotint or the art of making paintings in such a manner that copper plates and 'blocks' can be taken from them by means of voltaic electricity*, 1842.

the commercial life of intaglio plates was lengthened considerably. Steel-engraving first made its mark in the fashionable drawing-room annuals of the 1820s. It was widely used after this for work, such as landscape illustrations in guide books and other popular publications, which combined the need for great delicacy and long runs [43, 44]. Perkins came over to England and took out a patent for his improvements in 1819. In the same year he established a successful business with the style Perkins, Fairman & Heath (later Perkins & Bacon, and Perkins, Bacon & Petch), which exploited his siderography for the production of bank-notes [45, 46]. One of the firm's most significant achievements was the printing of the Penny Black postage stamp. Later in the century the problem of wear and tear on copper plates was solved by giving them a thin coating of steel by means of electrolysis.

The close of the eighteenth century and the first half of the nineteenth century were periods of great experimentation in the graphic processes. The most important discoveries were undoubtedly lithography and photography, but many other processes were developed which have since fallen into obscurity. An important source for these is W. J. Stannard's *The art exemplar*, which is a kind of encyclopaedia of descriptions and actual examples of printing processes which the author compiled and issued about 1859 in an edition of only ten copies. Stannard lists the names of 156 processes that he had heard of, though some of the techniques he describes appear under more than one name. Some of the new methods were extremely novel and, taken together, they tend to invalidate any tidy definition of the word 'printing'. In one of these processes, Gardiner's wire-plate engraving (1836), thousands of fine wires were packed together to form a plate. The image was 'engraved' by drawing on one side of the plate so that the wires were forced out on the other; when the drawing was finished the wires were held fast with resin or wax so that a relief print could be taken from either side of the plate. In another process, Felix Abate's thermography (1854), a wood-engraving was damped with dilute hydrochloric or sulphuric acid and pressed on to paper; when the paper was heated strongly for a short time the image appeared on it as a scorched pattern.

These two processes were of the kind that had little, if any, practical application and, along with many others, are now forgotten; but some of the more experimental processes were practised for a short time. Many of them were quite complicated and cannot be described very meaningfully in this context, but there seem to have been three profitable lines of experiment. One, which included William Blake's method of relief etching on metal (1789), some of Schmidt's and Senefelder's first experiments in working on stone (1790s), Lizar's *alto relievo* (1819), Schoenberg's acrography (*c.* 1835), Woone's gypsography (1837), and Branston's relief metal process (1838), was concerned with finding cheaper and more flexible methods of relief printing; another, which included Palmer's processes of electrotint (1841) [47] and glyphography (1842), utilised the newly invented electric battery; the third, which included the experiments of Niepce, Daguerre, Fox Talbot, and others in photography, Auer and Bradbury's nature printing (1852) [48, 49], and new methods of working with existing processes, such as Bate's anaglyptography or medal engraving (1832), was concerned with verisimilitude. Apart from photography, the practical importance of

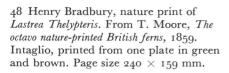

48 Henry Bradbury, nature print of *Lastrea Thelypteris*. From T. Moore, *The octavo nature-printed British ferns*, 1859. Intaglio, printed from one plate in green and brown. Page size 240 × 159 mm.

49 Detail of Plate 48. 27 × 21 mm.

most of these processes from a commercial point of view was not very great; but collectively they are an obvious symptom of the experimental approach which shattered the simple structure of eighteenth-century printing.

One experimental process of this period which did eventually have wide commercial application was a chemical method of printing from stone or metal plates called lithography. The process was invented by Senefelder in Munich around 1798 after he had spent nearly two years trying out ways of etching the stone for relief and intaglio printing. The essence of lithography rests on two simple physical phenomena: that grease and water do not mix with one another and that both are absorbed by a porous substance. Greasy marks drawn on stone will therefore repel water, while the porous stone absorbs it. A subsequent application of greasy printing ink will adhere to the drawn marks, but not to the damped surface. Both the printing and non-printing areas can therefore be on the same level, and for this reason lithography is often referred to as the first of a new category of printing called planographic.

50 Benjamin West, 'Angel of the Resurrection', 1801. Pen and ink lithograph published in *Specimens of polyautography*, 1803. 327 × 225 mm. *Victoria & Albert Museum.*

Alois Senefelder (1771–1834) came to England in 1800 in the hope of applying his invention to the printing of textiles. He stayed about six months, just time enough for him to take out a patent for his invention, but when he returned to Germany the process was still only imperfectly understood in England. Apart from an impressive collection of original prints by artists and amateurs, called *Specimens of polyautography* (1803 and 1806) [50], and two collections of pen lithographs by Thomas Barker of Bath, very few of the surviving examples of lithography produced in England during the first two decades of the century are noteworthy. Lithography was mainly taken up by amateur artists who were fascinated by what seemed to them to be the almost magical properties of a process which did not depend on physical differences of relief. J. T. Smith, who later became Keeper of Prints in the British Museum, described in his book *The antiquities of Westminster*

51 J. T. Smith, *The antiquities of Westminster*, 1807. Pen and ink lithograph of 'Internal view of painted chamber', drawn by Smith and printed by Philipp André. 187 × 159 mm.

52 Imitation of wood-engraving in lithography. Printed by Rudolph Ackermann for A. Senefelder, *A complete course of lithography*, London, 1819. 112 × 91 mm.

53 Francis Nicholson, 'Hardraw Force, in Wensleydale', 1822. Chalk lithograph, printed by Rowney & Forster. 335 × 285 mm.

54 Experimental lithotint, 1841, drawn by J. D. Harding and printed by C. J. Hullmandel. From a collection of proof impressions and experiments made by Hullmandel. 152 × 133 mm. *St Bride Printing Library*.

(1807) how one of the plates was made by means of lithography [51], and affirms that '. . . there could be no deception. At one time four persons, among whom was the author, were present, and saw the whole; two of them, medical men of distinguished abilities, and very skilful chymists, and the other two fully acquainted with every branch of copper-plate printing.'[22]

One of the main problems was that even those few people who were successful in setting up in England as lithographic printers did not really understand how the process worked, and during the Napoleonic Wars it was not easy to go over to Germany to find out. It was not until Rudolph Ackermann and Charles Joseph Hullmandel set up their presses in London after visits to Munich that the process really made any headway in England. Hullmandel, in particular, was largely responsible for the success of lithography in this country. He set sufficiently high standards in printing to attract competent draughtsmen to draw on stone, and in the 1820s and 1830s was responsible for making many important improvements to the process.

One of the main virtues of lithography and, paradoxically, one of its drawbacks, was its versatility. Senefelder had shown in his treatise on lithography, which was originally published in Germany in 1818, that practically any kind of mark could be made on stone, and that the stone itself could be used as a printing surface in a number of different ways. As a result, imitation etchings, engravings, aquatints, mezzotints, and wood-engravings [52], in addition to straightforward drawings in chalk and ink, were all produced on stone. Some of these methods actually involved using the stone as a substitute for the wood block or copper plate and printing from it in a semimechanical manner. It was also possible to transfer a print made by one of the traditional processes on to the stone and then to print it off lithographically. All this meant that it took some time for lithography to find its own identity, and it was not until after about 1820 that it settled down in England as a graphic process in its own right. Thereafter, two quite distinct lines were developed, though for the most part they were practised alongside one another by the same printers.

One important characteristic of lithography was its simplicity as a process for artists. It was much the most direct of the graphic processes and could be used for both chalk and ink drawing with comparative ease. Lithography was soon taken up by landscape draughtsmen [53], partly because of the popularity of this kind of work in England, but also because a ready market for topographical prints had already been established through the use of

[22]J.T.Smith, *The antiquities of Westminster* (London, 1807), p.49

aquatint. Lithography became so popular in this field that it soon ousted aquatint from its own stronghold. Portraiture, satirical prints, and the production of drawing books were other important areas for the lithographic draughtsman; but the influence of landscape on the techniques of drawn lithography was paramount, and a whole range of methods of working on stone were developed by Hullmandel and others to cater for the needs of the landscape draughtsman [55]. It is no exaggeration to say that the approach to lithographic drawing was determined, as in aquatint, by the demands of the water-colour painter; the main difference was that the methods of water-colour painting had begun to change in the intervening

55 C. J. Hullmandel, *The art of drawing on stone*, 1824. Specimen plate showing stages in the building up of tones with lithographic chalk. 139 × 218 mm.

56 Announcement of sale of Stagenhoe Park, Hertfordshire, 1836. Lithograph, printed by Day & Haghe. 368 × 492 mm. *John Johnson Collection.*

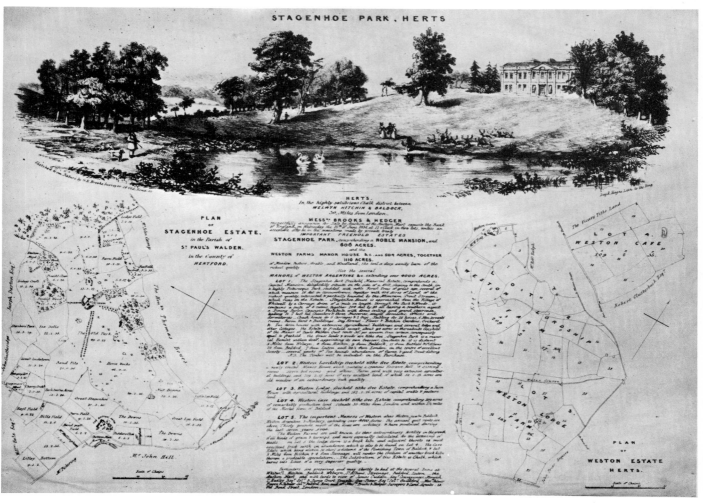

years. In the period 1818–40 a number of the most popular methods of drawing on stone, including a complicated system of laying in tones with crayon, the dabbing style, and tinted lithography, were made with the water-colour painter in mind. The search for a fully tonal method of working in lithography culminated in Hullmandel's process of lithotint (1840) by which prints could be taken from drawings made on stone with diluted washes of ink [54].

Lithography was also used for jobbing work where it had, in theory at least, two main advantages. The first of these was the comparative ease of writing on stone or of transferring to it text which had been written or printed on transfer paper; the second was its suitability for the printing of work which combined text with images [56]. Lithography was quicker and cheaper than copper-engraving, both in the production of the image and in the printing, and it also gave longer runs; but compared with letterpress printing it was very slow indeed. For the most part, therefore, lithographic jobbing printing in the first half of the nineteenth century was limited to fairly short runs, or to jobs where text and drawn work needed to be combined.

One very interesting prefigurement of recent trends in lithographic printing was the development of what is today usually called in-plant work, where a firm undertakes its own business printing. In 1809 the War Office became the first body in England to set up its own lithographic press. After a hesitant start the press began to flourish and in the year 1826 alone it is credited with having produced nearly 170,000 copies of maps, plans, and circulars [57]. Other institutions followed suit in the course of the first half of the nineteenth century; special presses were manufactured for this kind of work, and the introduction of metal plates as a substitute for the cumbersome slabs of limestone gave the movement considerable encouragement. The firm of Waterlow, which developed its own 'autographic presses' for use in businesses and institutions [58], claimed in 1859 that it had sold nearly two thousand models. This evidence alone is sufficient to indicate that jobbing printing was quite a flourishing branch of lithography by the middle of the nineteenth century, though such was the nature of the work produced that little has survived. Circulars, stationery, accounts, estate plans, maps, and diagrams are the main kinds of work that were produced by lithographic jobbing printers.

Towards the middle of the nineteenth century, lithography began to replace copper-engraving as the principal process for music printing. In the second half of the century, when colour printing became cheap enough to be popular, lithography had a virtual monopoly in the production of valentines, Christmas and other greeting cards, post cards, Sunday school texts, and the scraps which were sold for the decoration of albums and boxes. It also became the standard process for posters and other large-scale work, and was widely used for the reproduction of all kinds of paintings, from the cheapest popular images to expensive reproductions of the old masters.

While letterpress remained the only really important process for text printing well into the twentieth century, lithography was fast catching it up technically. One by one the factors which had held lithography back from its full flowering as a commercial printing process were mastered. The gradual introduction of powered lithographic machines after 1851, some forty years after letterpress printing began to be mechanised, helped to narrow the gap between the two processes; and the subsequent development of offset printing on paper early this century and, more recently, the introduction of web-fed machines have put lithography more on a par with letterpress. By the end of the nineteenth century metal plates were well on the way to replacing lithographic stones, which were expensive, difficult to obtain in the right quality,

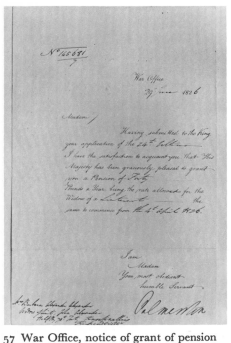

57 War Office, notice of grant of pension to the widow of a soldier, signed by Palmerston, 1826. Lithograph, probably printed at the War Office. 328 × 205 mm. *John Johnson Collection.*

58 Waterlow's autographic press for office printing, patented in 1850. From an advertisement of 1854. *John Johnson Collection.*

and awkward to store. But the persistent long-term problem which prevented lithography from competing effectively on all fronts with letterpress concerned the setting of text. The original method was to set type by hand, proof it on special transfer paper, and then transfer the image to stone; later, type was set on a composing machine, proofed, and then photographed down on to a plate. But in both methods there was an initial stage when the text could just as well have been printed in an edition by letterpress. With the development of photosetting this century, there existed for the first time a method of text composition which put lithography on level, if not more favourable, terms with other methods of printing. It was only after the Second World War, and in England in the late 1950s, that photosetting really became a commercial reality; but in the short period since then it has already contributed considerably to the rise of lithography.

Another important feature in the growth of lithography has been the development of small offset printing for stationery and similar work [59]. This was a trend which spread from Germany soon after the Second World War. Its success, too, was linked with an improved method of text composition – the electric typewriter, with characters of variable width and new kinds of ribbons, which could be used to type either directly on to a plate or on to paper or film to be photographed down. This method of text composition is used for offset lithography by professional printers, but it has also attracted a new body of specially trained printers working in small units within firms and public bodies, and there are now many more such units in this country than there are trade printing houses. This development echoes the pattern in the first half of the nineteenth century when similar business printing was done by amateur lithographers who wrote out their text on specially-prepared transfer paper, transferred it to stone or plate, and printed on small presses manufactured specially for the purpose. Furthermore, much the same criticism of the amateur's ability to cope with such a situation is heard today as was voiced in the mid-nineteenth century.

Though technical aids, such as ruling machines, pantographs, and mechanical tints, were frequently used [60], until the last decade of the nineteenth century most pictorial images continued to be printed from blocks or plates that had been made by hand. The invention of photography had an enormous influence on draughtsmen, but it took at least half a century before it was effectively harnessed to the printing processes themselves. In one sense, of course, photography was itself a printing process. The branch of photography invented by Fox Talbot in 1835 involved the use of paper negatives from which repeatable images could be produced, and this aspect of photography was developed further with the use of glass and celluloid negatives. Actual photographs were sometimes used as illustrations in books and, on occasions, even when the original was itself an engraving.

Draughtsmen soon began to use photography as an aid to their image making, and around 1860 Thomas Bolton discovered a method of sensitising the surface of a piece of boxwood so that a photographic image could be exposed on it [61]. This meant that the artist's original drawing, which had hitherto usually been made directly on the block, could now be preserved, and that the wood-engraver could make a direct translation of the complex tones of an actual photograph [62] in addition to being able to copy exactly the positive lines of a drawing originally made on paper.

A more fundamental change came about when it became possible for the printing surface itself to be produced by means of photography. The actual dates of discoveries are of only limited significance when charting the progress towards the effective commercial production of photo-engraved printing plates and, in any case, there were probably as many experimental photographic printing techniques in the second half of the nineteenth century as

59 Rotaprint small offset lithographic machine (R10/75QC).

60 Specimen wood-engraving produced with the Royle-Richards ruling machine. From *Penrose's Pictorial Annual*, vol. 12, 1906-7. 111 × 111 mm.

61 Thomas Bolton, specimen wood-engraving made from a photograph on wood of a relief sculpture by Flaxman. From J. Jackson, *A treatise on wood engraving*, 2nd ed., 1861. 124 × 90 mm.

62 Wood-engraving after a photograph of 'Penguins and Mollymawks, Bounty Islands', published in the *Graphic*, 16 March 1889. 177 × 225 mm.

PENGUINS AND MOLLYMAWKS, BOUNTY ISLANDS

INSTANTANEOUS PHOTOGRAPHY IN THE SOUTHERN SEAS

there were autographic ones in the first. Broadly speaking, these processes can be considered in two main categories: those which reproduced an artist's line drawing, and those which reproduced a photograph or a tonal drawing.

The first photographic processes to be developed for wide commercial use were those in which a line image was reproduced for relief printing. A number of different methods were tried. The first of them was the Pretsch process, which was developed by Paul Pretsch of Vienna in 1853 and practised commercially in England from about 1872 by the firm of Alfred Dawson. It was similar to the process we now call collotype and, like it, involved the use of a plate of metal or glass coated with light-sensitised gelatine. Parts of the gelatine hardened when it was exposed to light through a photographic negative, and those parts which had not been hardened swelled when the plate was later immersed in a bath of water. As a result the image appeared in relief, the positive parts of the original appearing as sunken areas. An electrotype cast was then taken from the swollen gelatine matrix so that the image could be printed as a relief block [63]. This process gave excellent results, but it was expensive compared with other methods and consequently had only a limited application.

More popular were the albumen and bitumen processes, which involved the direct etching of zinc. They were similar to one another, except that in the first a zinc plate was coated with a light-sensitive preparation consisting of

63 Pen and pencil drawing reproduced by the swelled gelatine process. From C. G. Harper, *A practical handbook of drawing for modern methods of reproduction*, 2nd ed., 1901. 64 × 92 mm.

64 Pen and pencil drawing reproduced by the bitumen process. From C. G. Harper, *A practical handbook of drawing for modern methods of reproduction*, 2nd ed., 1901. 64 × 92 mm.

white of egg and bichromate of ammonia in water, while in the second the coating was of bitumen. In the albumen process a reversed photographic negative of a drawing was placed in contact with a suitably prepared plate. When the image was sufficiently exposed to light, the surface of the plate was rolled over with printing ink thinned down with turpentine, and then washed carefully in cold water. The action of light on the prepared ground had the effect of making it insoluble, so that only the lines of the image remained. After a few precautions had been taken the plate was in a state to receive a series of etchings in a bath of dilute nitric acid, which ate away the bare metal to leave standing in relief only those parts covered with ink. In the other process, bitumen was used as the light-sensitive medium, and was dissolved in the unexposed parts by means of turpentine [64].

Both processes gave good results very cheaply and began to be widely used from the mid-1880s onwards, though the albumen process survived the longer. One firm was reported in 1894 as having an annual production of 63,000 blocks made by the albumen process,[23] and by the end of the century there were over a hundred process engravers in London alone [65]. Process engraving attracted many of the artists who had previously worked for the wood-engravers, and at the outset their style of drawing hardly changed at all. Some of the wood-engravers who found their livelihoods threatened also turned to process engraving, and it was standard practice to work up a process block with the burin to reduce some of the darker tones and lines. By the end of the century process engraving had established some of its own methods of drawing, including the use of a range of specially-prepared drawing papers and cards with different surfaces or with patterns

65 Etching room for process work, drawn by F. G. Kitton in 1894. From J. Southward, *Progress in printing and the graphic arts during the Victorian era*, 1897.

66 Line block of a pencil drawing made on a board with a perpendicular grain. From C. G. Harper, *A practical handbook of drawing for modern methods of reproduction*, 2nd ed., 1901. 49 × 69 mm.

67 Line block of a pencil drawing made on canvas-grain clay-board with the lights scraped away. From C. G. Harper, *A practical handbook of drawing for modern methods of reproduction*, 2nd ed., 1901. 48 × 69 mm.

68 Examples of Ben Day's shading mediums. From C. G. Harper, *A practical handbook of drawing for modern methods of reproduction*, 2nd ed., 1901. Each example about 47 × 25 mm.

printed on them [66, 67], and shading mediums made of thin sheets of gelatine with lines or stippled patterns engraved on them so that they could be rolled up with printing ink and applied to the block before etching [68]. As far as half-tone images are concerned, photography was first applied successfully to those branches of printing where it could have least impact – lithographic and intaglio printing. Relief printing, which alone satisfied the enormous public demand for inexpensive pictorial journalism in the nineteenth century, was the last to benefit commercially from the use of photographic half-tones.

From the middle of the nineteenth century numerous experiments were made, both in England and abroad, to find a suitable method of printing from plates bearing half-tone photographic images. Some of the early results obtained abroad in the early 1850s by Lemercier, Pretsch, and Poitevin are extremely competent, but the commercial development of their ideas had to wait until the perfection of the half-tone screen. This was a device used to break down the tonal image of a photograph into a series of small dots. The sizes of the dots depended on the amount of light passing through a mesh of lines engraved on glass and on the coarseness of the mesh itself. The essence of the technique was devised by Fox Talbot (1852) who suggested using what he called 'photographic screens or veils' in connection with his discovery of

[23] C.G.Harper, *A practical handbook of drawing for modern methods of reproduction*, 2nd ed. (London, 1901), p.28

69 'Edward L. Wilson', an early Ives process half-tone from the *Philadelphia Photographer*, June 1881. 113 × 88 mm. *Smithsonian Institution, Washington.*

70 *Strand Magazine*, vol. i, 1891, with half-tone blocks engraved by Meisenbach & Co. Page size 235 × 163 mm.

71 Half-tone process engraving of an oil sketch in Payne's grey of 'Hadleigh Castle: spring sunset'. From C. G. Harper, *A practical handbook of drawing for modern methods of reproduction*, 2nd ed., 1901. 95 × 136 mm.

72 Wood-engraving after an oil sketch in Payne's grey of 'Hadleigh Castle: spring sunset'. From C. G. Harper, *A practical handbook of drawing for modern methods of reproduction*, 2nd ed., 1901. 97 × 138 mm.

73 Detail of Plate 71. 36 × 45 mm.

74 Detail of Plate 72. 36 × 45 mm.

[24] C.G.Harper, *A practical handbook of drawing for modern methods of reproduction*, 2nd ed. (London, 1901), pp.12, 74–7

a photographic intaglio process. Many different kinds of screens were proposed by A. J. Berchtold (1855 and 1857), Frederick von Egloffstein (1865), Joseph Swan (1866), William Leggo (1871) and others, but most of them were used in conjunction with lithographic and intaglio printing. The first really successful commercial method for creating letterpress half-tones was patented in 1881 by Frederick Ives of Philadelphia, but though he found a method of breaking up the photographic image into dots of varying size he did not make use of a screen of any sort [69]. A year later George Meisenbach of Germany patented a half-tone process in England based on ideas previously put forward by Berchtold and Swan. He used single-lined screens that were turned during exposure to produce cross-lined effects, and was the first to achieve any real commercial success with relief half-tones. Frederick Ives and the brothers Louis and Max Levy took the process a stage further in America shortly afterwards with the invention and commercial production of good cross-lined screens.

The need for a relief half-tone process was proved by its almost immediate success. Meisenbach founded a company in London as early as 1884, and soon after 1890 half-tone blocks were appearing regularly in the popular journals [70] and were beginning to oust wood-engravings from some of them. Artistic recognition followed soon afterwards with the inclusion of half-tone process engravings in the literary and art journals of the 1890s. In 1901 two of the leading wood-engravers of the nineteenth century, George and Edward Dalziel, admitted openly in their book, *A record of fifty years' work*, that the standard of ordinary commercial process engraving was so high that the days of the professional wood-engraver were really over.

One reason for the rapid success of process engraving was its cheapness compared with wood-engraving. The writer of a contemporary handbook on drawing for reproduction records in 1901 that a process engraving cost approximately a fifth as much as a similar wood-engraving. At that time the cost of an average quality wood-engraving worked out at from 3s to 5s a square inch, while letterpress half-tones cost between 8d and 1s 6d, line blocks made by the swelled-gelatine process between 1s and 1s 3d, and those produced by the albumen and bitumen processes between 2½d and 6d (with hand touching extra).[24]

75 *Graphic*, 27 July 1895, showing an illustration by Frank Brangwyn engraved in half-tone. Page size 394 × 290 mm.

76 Detail of Plate 75 showing the use of the burin in the highlights. 55 × 50 mm.

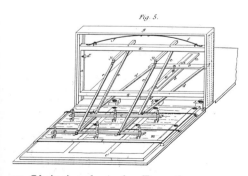

77 Obrion's polygraphe. From the French patent specification, 1821.

Yet for all this, many of the early half-tone blocks were not as satisfactory as wood-engravings for reproducing some kinds of images. Very fine-screen process engravings did not print as well as wood-engravings on poor quality paper, and much of the precision of an image tended to be lost in reproduction when coarse screens were used. For this reason wood-engravings continued to be used well into the twentieth century, particularly in technical catalogues. In any case, early half-tone process engravings relied a great deal on hand touching with the burin [75, 76], especially for increasing contrast in the highlights and softening the edges of vignetted blocks, and many wood-engravers found an outlet for their skills in such work.

By 1900 photolithography, photogravure, and collotype had all reached a very high technical standard, especially when they were used for quality printing such as the reproduction of works of art. The twentieth century has since seen the widespread commercial development of photography in all three major branches of printing. Each has its own particular value: photolithography has developed as a most useful all-purpose process, giving great definition on a wide range of papers; photogravure is mainly used for magazine work, packaging, and quality reproduction of paintings; half-tone letterpress is still widely used for newspapers, and for most books and small-scale jobbing printing. The process of collotype, which was one of the first successful photographic printing methods, is now practised by only one firm in the country and has been superseded by very fine-screen lithography.

The two most important new graphic processes that have been developed commercially in this century are silkscreen printing and xerography. Silkscreen is really no more than a refined form of stencilling, in which non-printing areas are masked out on a sheet of silk or organdie stretched on a frame. Ink is forced through the image areas by means of a rubber blade known as a squeegee. The origins of silkscreen printing are still obscure, but the process was being used for the mass production of signs in both America and England just before the First World War. After the war it was developed for a wide range of commercial purposes, including the printing of fabrics and a variety of advertising work. In recent years silkscreen has been given a new lease of life as a result of the application of photography to it and the introduction of fine-mesh nylon and stainless-steel screens. Very precise work can now be printed by silkscreen on machines capable of thousands of impressions an hour, and the process is used for a wide range of commercial printing, particularly on surfaces other than paper.

Xerography is usually regarded as a reprographic process rather than a branch of printing because it is limited to the multiplication of an already existing image. It rests on the familiar natural phenomenon of static electricity and was invented in America by Chester Carlson, who produced his first experimental xerographic print in 1938. Since then other methods of xerography have been developed, but the original version invented by Carlson is a dry copying process in which very fine powder is transferred from an electrically charged surface to a sheet of paper, and then fixed by heating. Shortly after the Second World War xerography was developed commercially, and since then it has been taken up with remarkable speed all over the world as the most convenient method of reproducing copies of a line document. This had been a desideratum for years, and many people from the late eighteenth century onwards experimented with methods of obtaining a limited number of copies of a document. One novel solution to the problem was proposed by Obrion, a French mathematician, who took out a patent in 1821 for an instrument he called a polygraphe [77], which allowed several pen heads to move in unison. A more practical method, which was used widely in the nineteenth century, was transfer lithography; manuscripts written on special paper in greasy ink could

LETTER COPYING MACHINES,

SOLD BY

NISSEN AND PARKER,

Nos. 42 & 43, MARK LANE, 68 & 69, GREAT TOWER STREET,

LONDON.

The hitherto exceedingly high prices of LETTER COPYING MACHINES have been the principal, if not the sole, objection to their more general adoption. On the Continent every person, of whatever rank, engaged in Commerce, is provided with a Machine for taking Copies of Correspondence, Contracts, Debits, &c., &c., whilst thousands of the Commercial Community of Great Britain have, perhaps, neither seen or heard of such an instrument; by these Machines Letters are Copied after writing, either upon loose sheets, or at once into a bound volume, and from ten to twenty letters may be thus copied in a few minutes—the Copy possesses all the durability and blackness of Ink, the letter itself suffers no deterioration whatever, whilst the freedom from any possibility of error is rendered a certainty. These Machines are now made in various sizes, and at a very considerable reduction in price; formerly the purchase of a Copying Machine was a subject of deliberation, the cheapest having been seven or eight guineas, ranging upwards to £15 or £20. The liberal postal arrangements of the Government, added to the great increase in all branches of trade and manufactures of this country, have induced NISSEN & PARKER to make arrangements for supplying Copying Machines, at the lowest remunerating profit upon the actual manufacturing prices, which they respectfully submit in the following Scale.

No. 1. Lever Copying Machine.

QUARTO—11 by 8½ in.	£	s.	d.	FOOLSCAP—13 by 9in.	£	s.	d.	FOLIO—18 by 11 in.	£	s.	d.
Machine with Polished Mahogany Stand and Damping Box	3	3	0	Machine with Polished Mahogany Stand and Damping Box	3	18	0	Machine with Polished Mahogany Stand and Damping Box	5	0	0
Machine only.........	2	2	0	Machine only.........	2	10	0	Machine only.........	3	3	0
Fittings, viz.—				Fittings, viz.—				Fittings, viz.—			
Pads 4 0				Pads 4 0				Pads 5 0			
Brush.......... 2 3				Brush.......... 2 3				Brush.......... 2 3			
Damping & Drying Book .. 2 9	0	10	6	Damping & Drying Book .. 2 9	0	10	6	Damping & Drying Book .. 2 9	0	12	6
Oil'd Sheets 1 6				Oil'd Sheets 1 6				Oil'd Sheets 2 6			

These Presses are made of the best materials; the working parts are steel well hardened, so as to secure the greatest durability; and the pressure surfaces, being correctly ENGINE-PLANED, are warranted to give a clear, distinct and equal copy.

No. 2. Screw Copying Machine.

	QUARTO. 12 by 9¾ in.			FOOLSCAP. 13 by 9 in.			FOLIO. 18 by 12 in.		
	£	s.	d.	£	s.	d.	£	s.	d.
Machine only	3	3	0	5	10	0	6	6	0
Damping Box...............	0	12	6	0	15	0	0	17	6
Fittings	0	10	6	0	10	6	0	12	6
Machine, Mahogany Stand, with One Drawer, Damping Box and Fittings complete	5	5	0	7	7	0	9	9	0
Machine, Polished Mahogany Stand, Two Drawers, Flaps, Damping Box and Fittings complete...............	7	17	6	9	9	0	11	11	0

These Presses are made with that mathematical nicety that only one-fourth of the Pressure is required to obtain a perfect Copy, consequently, no breakage can take place.

COPYING INK (more certain in its effects than any yet introduced), Pints 18s, Quarts 36s ⅌ dozen.

COPYING PAPER (finest French) ⅌ ream, 10s 6d—half ream, 5s 6d—quarter ream, 3s.

COPYING LETTER BOOKS for taking Copies direct from the Machine, neatly and strongly half-bound, with index, and every book paged in type, 6s 6d, 9s 6d, 12s 6d, and 15s each.

GUARD BOOKS for preserving loose Copies, half bound, with index (every book paged), 6s, 9s, 12s, 14s, and 20s each.

78 Advertisement for Nissen & Parker's letter-copying machines. From one of their copy books, *c.* 1850. Sheet size 267 × 224 mm.

79 Watt's portable copying press, 1794. *Science Museum, South Kensington, London.*

80 Apparatus for Gestetner's 'Cyclo-style' stencil duplicating process, probably of the 1880s. *Science Museum, South Kensington, London.*

81 A Rank Xerox 3600 copier/duplicator in use at Massey-Ferguson Ltd, Coventry.

easily be transferred to stone, and in 1839 two French lithographic printers, Paul and Auguste Dupont, took out a patent for an improved transfer process by which lithographic copies could be made even from leaves of old books. Yet another method was proposed by Benjamin Franklin in the late eighteenth century for multiplying French 'assignats', and taken up again by Gassicourt in 1821. It allowed copies of recently written documents to be made by putting the writing slightly in relief with an application of dust or powder and then taking a cast of it in soft metal for intaglio printing.

The problem of duplicating documents in limited numbers was partly solved with the invention of carbon paper and wet copying processes. Ralph Wedgwood patented 'carbonated paper' for use in duplicating writing as early as 1806, but it is not clear how soon it was generally used. Wet copying processes were considered even earlier, and in 1780 James Watt took out a patent for a method of copying letters by writing with a special ink which could be partially transferred to a sheet of moist paper under pressure [79]. Similar processes were used throughout the nineteenth century, and many kinds of portable presses were developed for them [78]. In the 1880s Gestetner took out a series of patents for his stencil duplicating process [80] which, along with a variety of spirit duplicating processes, has been widely used this century for the printing of short runs of circulars. In addition, various photocopying methods have been developed for the copying of existing documents. But xerography has proved to be both quicker and more conven-ient than all previous methods; individual Xerox copies can be produced in a matter of seconds, and the most recent machines are capable of taking thousands of copies an hour [81]. More and more reading is being done from originals that have been reproduced by xerography and, with the increasing use of computers for information retrieval, it may well be that a process of this kind, used on demand for one-off jobs, will become as important as the printing processes themselves.

While new processes have been developed and some older ones neglected, one consistent trend can be traced through the nineteenth and twentieth centuries. At the beginning of the nineteenth century artist, craftsman, and printer often worked side by side in the same workshops, and sometimes one person undertook all aspects of a job. But during the second half of the century, with the mechanisation of printing and the development of photo-engraving, this gradually ceased to be practicable; and by the end of the century there had emerged a very clear distinction between the autographic techniques, which the artist could still understand and practise, and the industrial techniques which, though sometimes carrying the same name, were really quite different. This polarity has been accentuated in the present century, and the resulting separation of conception from production has helped to create the need for the new profession of graphic design.

Chapter 3
Printing in colour

As far as the man in the street was concerned, the discovery of cheap methods of making colour prints must have been one of the most exciting developments in nineteenth-century printing. He would probably not have been able to distinguish between a wood-engraving and a copper-engraving, nor between a pen lithograph and an etching, but he could hardly have escaped noticing the advent of cheap colour-printed images just before the middle of the nineteenth century. For the first time in history cheap pictorial images printed in full colour were readily available and, however crude they may appear to our eyes, their impact on the public at the time must have been considerable.

Coloured prints had, of course, existed before the nineteenth century, but such images were normally printed in monochrome and coloured by hand. The widespread use of line reproductions of woodcuts has tended to obscure the fact that fifteenth-century woodcuts were often hand-coloured. The popular print of the fifteenth century was as much a substitute for a painting as the colour print of the nineteenth century. It was only from Dürer onwards that the monochrome print began to be accepted as a work of art in its own right. The early tradition of hand-colouring prints continued in some of the new processes, and most landscape aquatints and lithographs would not have been considered complete unless coloured by hand. The practice of adding colour to prints in this way continued right through the nineteenth century, either where it was more economical than colour printing or where the work was considered important enough to warrant this special attention.

Printing with coloured inks was not new either and from 1457, when Fust and Schoeffer produced their Psalter in Mainz with a series of superb colour-printed initial letters, it has presented a challenge to printers in all processes. Isolated examples of colour printing occur throughout history, and the use of a red printing for lines of type or initial letters in imitation of manuscript rubrication became part and parcel of the letterpress printer's repertoire. Great strides were made in colour printing in the early years of the eighteenth century in England by Jacob Christoph Le Blon, who developed a process of intaglio colour printing which relied on successive workings in yellow, red, and blue to produce fully colour-printed images. His successor, J.-G. d'Agoty, took the process a stage further in France by adding a black printing to give greater richness of tone. Another kind of colour print which was popular in the eighteenth century, particularly in France, involved inking up a single intaglio plate in a variety of different colours. A third method, in which colours were printed from several wood blocks, was used by John Baptist Jackson and others for the printing of wallpapers and reproductions of paintings. All these processes were slow and expensive, and tended to be restricted in their application to work that appealed to only a limited market, such as the reproduction of works of art and scientific illustration, in both of which reliability of colour was important. For the most part, however, it was still cheaper to colour prints by hand in the eighteenth and early nineteenth centuries than it was to print them in colours.

As the nineteenth century wore on, it became increasingly necessary to find more efficient methods of making coloured images to keep pace with the growing public demand for printing and the greater output of the new printing machines. Hand colouring may have been economical when runs were short, but large edition sizes virtually necessitated a colour-printing process, and particularly one which could be geared to machine production.

The need for such a process was accentuated by other factors in the first half of the nineteenth century. The publication in France in 1839 of M.-E. Chevreul's treatise on the harmony and contrast of colours, which had a great influence on some of the painters of the period, stimulated a new interest in the use of colour in many other fields as well. Chevreul discussed the value of his principles in relation to architecture, clothing, and tapestries, and also devoted sections to the printing of fabrics, paper hangings, the colouring of maps and engravings, and the use of coloured papers in letterpress printing. An English translation of Chevreul's work was published in 1854 with the title, *The principles of harmony and contrast of colours, and their applications to the arts*, and its success in this country can be judged by the fact that it soon ran into three editions.

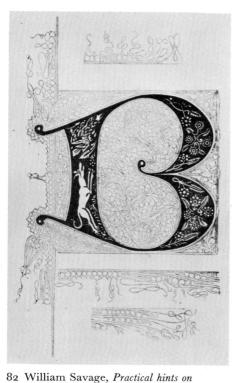

82 William Savage, *Practical hints on decorative printing*, 1822. Wood-engraving by J. Byfield after a drawing by R. Thomson of an initial B in Fust and Schoeffer's Psalter of 1457, printed in red and blue. 188 × 111 mm.

The rise of colour printing was also connected with the widespread interest in medieval art, and particularly illuminated books. The Gothic Revival had begun to create an interest in the decoration of medieval manuscripts in the eighteenth century, and by the beginning of the next century scholars and antiquarians were becoming familiar with books which were illuminated by hand in a wide range of rich colours. This helped to establish a taste for decorated borders and initial letters which, in turn, led to the need for a means of printing them in colour. An interesting indication of the contemporary printer's eagerness to fulfil this need (and at the same time match the skills of one of the earliest printers) was the choice of one of Fust and Schoeffer's colour-printed initial letters from the Psalter of 1457 as an example through which Senefelder, Savage, and Hansard all chose to display in their manuals their own achievements in colour printing [82]. Improvements in colour printing continued to be made as interest in medieval manuscripts grew, and numerous colour facsimiles of manuscripts were brought out by Henry Shaw, Owen Jones, Noel Humphreys and others. These publications drew attention to the fact that it was only since the invention of printing that the book had become predominantly monochrome. They also helped to promote an interest in a style of decoration and lettering which soon attracted Victorian artists, who turned it to their own ends with the confidence and enthusiasm typical of the period. And one of the ingredients of this style was the use of strong colour.

A further incentive for developing colour printing was the real need for a reliable method of producing a number of identical, or as nearly identical as possible, copies of a scientific diagram or illustration. It was the need for exactly repeatable copies of texts and illustrations that helped to promote printing in the fifteenth century and, although the printer could not ensure that texts and illustrations were accurate, he could at least make almost certain that they were equally accurate or inaccurate as the case may be. Much the same could be said of colour printing in the nineteenth century. The careless hand-colourist rapidly applying washes to hundreds of copies of a map, for instance, could so easily make an error of cardinal importance. In a colour-printed version, however much inks may have discoloured with the passage of time, the location of colours will at least either be precise or out of register in such a way as to be obvious. The scientific value of colour printing as a means of ensuring more or less reliable copies of a coloured image tends to be overlooked because of the understandable enthusiasm for its visual and technical qualities.

The commercial use of colour-printed images in the nineteenth century depended on a number of technical factors. The first and most crucial of these concerned the manufacture of coloured inks. Though independent ink manufacturers are known to have existed from the early sixteenth century, most printers probably continued to make their own inks until the middle of the nineteenth century. Coloured inks were much more troublesome to make than black inks, and the pigments themselves, which had to be bought from the ink manufacturers, were mostly much more expensive than black. These reasons alone could well have been sufficient to prevent the widespread use of colour in jobbing printing. It is not clear what made the ink manufacturers start making a variety of coloured inks – unless it was just sound business judgement – but as soon as coloured inks became readily available from the ink manufacturers around the middle of the nineteenth century, colour printing developed very rapidly.

The other technical problem was the accurate registration of the colours so that successive blocks or plates could be printed in exactly the right place on the paper. This was a much greater problem in the past than it is today because nearly all printing was done on damp paper until the last quarter of the nineteenth century. Paper stretches when it is damped, and in order to get perfect registration successive printings had to be taken while the paper was equally damp. A number of different methods and devices were developed to help with the actual problem of registration, and they played an important part in the commercial development of colour printing.

Three main techniques were commonly used in the nineteenth century for the printing of coloured images: relief printing from wood or metal, chromolithography, and a mixed process depending on both intaglio and relief printing. These categories are singled out for the sake of clarity, but in each case it was possible to work in such a variety of ways that, for instance, a chromolithograph could be made to look more like a coloured wood-engraving than like other chromolithographs. There were many other approaches to colour printing in the nineteenth century, but these three were the ones to have the widest commercial application.

Interest in the practicability of printing in colour was first aroused in this period by William Savage (1770–1843), a letterpress printer who published a book in 1822 called *Practical hints on decorative printing* [83]. This contains numerous specimen plates showing his method of colour printing from relief wood blocks, including plates showing the progressive stages in the production of a simple colour print [84]. The book is a virtuoso performance

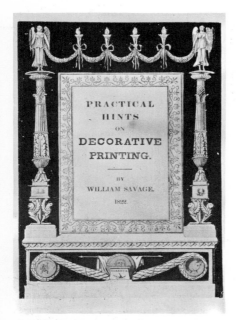

83 William Savage, *Practical hints on decorative printing*, 1822. Decorative title-page, designed by T. Willement and engraved by Robert Branston, printed in gold and seven colours. Image size 200 × 142 mm.

84 William Savage, *Practical hints on decorative printing*, 1822. Progressive proofs of a simple colour print, drawn by W. M. Craig and engraved by Robert Branston. Finished image 200 × 120 mm.

in colour printing. One of the plates, 'Ode to Mercy' [85, 86], was printed from as many as twenty-nine different blocks and is a masterpiece of technical skill, if not in conception. Savage's major contribution was to refine and extend the basic technique used by John Baptist Jackson in the eighteenth century by introducing rich colours and a great many more workings. To

85

86

85 William Savage, *Practical hints on decorative printing*, 1822. 'Ode to Mercy', engraved on wood by G. W. Bonner after a painting by W. H. Brooke, printed from twenty-nine separate wood blocks. 211 × 145 mm.

86 Detail of Plate 85. 113 × 82 mm.

87 Charles Knight, *Old England*, 1844-5. 'Entrance to the Chapel of Edward the Confessor', engraved by S. Sly after an original by J. Scandrett and printed in nine colours from relief blocks by William Clowes (the red and green added by hand). 248 × 175 mm.

88 Detail of Plate 87. 95 × 63 mm.

ENTRANCE TO THE CHAPEL OF EDWARD THE CONFESSOR.

87

88

89

90

91

92

89 George Baxter, 'The hop garden',
1856. Aquatint base with twelve relief
blocks. 152 × 105 mm. *John Johnson
Collection.*

90 Detail of Plate 89. 20 × 28 mm.

91 Le Blond & Co., 'The hop garden',
1868, printed from Baxter's blocks but
with the signature trimmed from the foot.
147 × 105 mm. *Museum of English Rural
Life, Reading University.*

92 Detail of Plate 91. 20 × 28 mm.

93

94

95

96

97

93 Kate Greenaway, illustration from
Mother Goose, 1881. Colour wood-engraving
by Edmund Evans, printed in nine colours.
115 × 70 mm.

94 Detail of Plate 93. 39 × 27 mm.

95 Trade card of David Leighton,
Sheffield, 1848. Lithograph, printed in
seven colours. 285 × 206 mm. *John
Johnson Collection.*

96 *Illustrated London News*, Diamond
Jubilee number, *Her Majesty's Glorious
Jubilee 1897*, 1897. Chromolithography,
printed in about ten colours by Orford
Smith & Co., St Albans. Page size 401 ×
302 mm.

97 Detail of Plate 96. 48 × 70 mm.

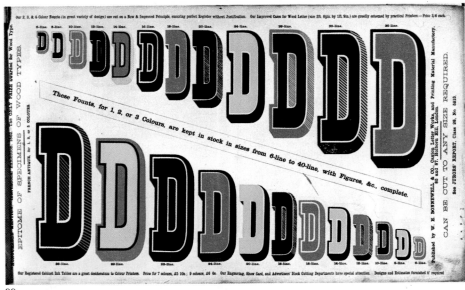

99

100

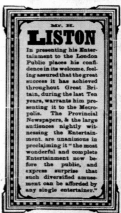

98 Sunday School texts, *c.* 1880. Chromolithography in six colours, the actual texts overprinted letterpress. 115 × 45 mm.

99 W. H. Bonnewell & Co., *Specimens of wood type*, *c.* 1870. Two- and three-colour letters. Page size 310 × 505 mm. *St Bride Printing Library.*

100 Ream label. Letterpress, rainbow printed. 178 × 110 mm. *John Johnson Collection.*

101 James Upton, Birmingham, notice of entertainment, *c.* 1870. Letterpress, printed in four colours. 752 × 499 mm. *John Johnson Collection.*

prevent the unsightly spread of oil, which mars so many earlier examples of colour printing, Savage used a base of copaiba balsam for his inks. Time has proved the success of his method, for the colours have retained their brilliance remarkably well in many copies.

Savage had no immediate followers and, as far as is known, his method had no application outside his *Practical hints on decorative printing*. But Charles Knight (1791–1873), one of the most enterprising publishers of the century, patented a relief colour process in 1838 called 'Illuminated printing' which certainly owed something to Savage. Knight used a wood-engraved key block and then added a series of colours in simple shapes from relief-printed metal blocks. Like almost all nineteenth-century colour printers since, Knight reverted to the traditional oil as a base for his inks. There was nothing particularly new in Knight's actual process, but he managed to bring colour-printed images to a far wider public than Savage by reducing the number of colours and speeding up the operation of printing. He developed a special press, which allowed each block to be brought over the paper in succession, and printed one colour on top of the other while the ink was still wet. Knight used his process commercially in popular publications, such as *Old England* (1844–5) [87, 88], and it was taken up by Leighton Brothers who reprinted from some of Knight's blocks.

Knight had developed a practical method of producing colour-printed images, but his prints cannot be compared in quality with those of Savage. He was limited by practical considerations in the number of colours he could use, and most of his prints look more like tinted drawings than fully-coloured images. But he proved the commercial limitations of Savage's method by showing that a technique depending on a wide range of simple areas of colour matching those of the original was incompatible with mass-production. The approach to relief colour printing which caught on commercially depended much more on the engraving of complex tones on the wood blocks themselves and the subtle optical fusion of juxtaposed tints.

This approach was pioneered by George Baxter (1804–67) in connection with his method of printing in colour from wood-engravings on to a mono-chrome base [89, 90]. Baxter patented his method of colour printing in 1835 and used it successfully for twenty years, a few of his prints being produced in editions of hundreds of thousands. His method was to engrave the original in either aquatint or mezzotint, or occasionally draw it in litho-graphy, and to print this plate or stone as a monochrome base. He then added as many colours as were necessary to give an accurate facsimile of the original, which usually meant between eight and twelve workings, and occasionally many more. Though Baxter did produce some very big prints, most of his work is on a small scale, and many of his prints are no larger than a postcard. In his best work he managed to capture a remarkable range of colours and tones, and to achieve most skilful feats of registration. From 1849 Baxter began to grant licenses to use his process, and Le Blond & Co., Bradshaw & Blacklock, Kronheim, Dickes, Mansell, and Myers & Co. all bought the right to do so. In general, they failed to match the quality of the inventor's printing, and this is particularly noticeable when Le Blond reprinted from some of Baxter's own blocks [91, 92].

Baxter had shown the possibilities of wood-engraving as part of his colour-printing process; others soon saw the practical advantages of abandoning the intaglio key plate and relying on relief printing alone. Because wood-engravings were comparatively easy to print in large editions, this soon became one of the two major colour-printing techniques of the second half of the nineteenth century. The principal exponents of colour wood-engraving were Leighton Brothers, who produced some fine facsimiles of water-colour paintings, Benjamin Fawcett, who specialised in natural history illustration, and Edmund Evans, who is best known for his engravings of illustrations for children's books drawn by Randolph Caldecott, Walter Crane, and Kate Greenaway [93, 94]. All three printers relied on far fewer colours than Baxter, and in some cases used only six workings to produce fully-coloured illustrations. Because of its relative simplicity this method of colour printing was widely used, though it tended to be limited to the illustration of books.

The third of the major colour-printing processes was chromolithography. Isolated attempts had been made right from the beginning of the century to produce colour-printed lithographs, though nothing was printed of any consequence. Experiments with other processes forced the issue in the 1830s and in 1837 Godefroy Engelmann patented a process in Paris which he called *chromolithographie*. There was nothing substantially new in the idea. The image was merely drawn on a number of different stones in much the same way as in Baxter's process, except that the nature of lithography allowed for a range of marks with both soft and hard edges. In England the crucial figure in chromolithography was Hullmandel. He printed the superb plates for T. S. Boys's folio volume of *Picturesque architecture in Paris, Ghent, Antwerp, Rouen* (1839) which proved convincingly the technical possibilities of colour lithography. In the 1840s chromolithography was still finding its feet, but after the middle of the century scores of lithographic printers turned to the process. While relief printing in colour was limited to rather more respectable images, chromolithography supplied the mass market of the second half of the century with a welter of cheap colour printing in the form of scraps, greeting cards, valentines, postcards, Sunday school texts, and popular reproductions of all kinds.

At the outset, most work in chromolithography was conceived in rather simple areas of solid colour [95], with perhaps a suggestion of half-tones drawn in chalk. With the introduction of fast-running powered lithographic machines in the second half of the century it ceased to be practicable to work in chalk, as the stones for use on such machines had to be given a polished surface. In order to build up tones on polished stones the chromolithographer revived an older lithographic technique of stippling with the pen [96, 97]. As a result, the standard technique of chromolithography, which lasted well into the twentieth century, was born. It involved breaking up the image into a number of colours, varying usually from four to about a dozen, and interpreting the colour values in terms of dots and solid areas. Where many printings were needed the colours were chosen to suit the image to be copied, but in some of the cheaper examples of printing a standard range of yellow, red, and blue (with perhaps a pink and grey as well) catered for most situations [98]. While this technique relates to the processes of Le Blon and others in the eighteenth century, it also anticipates the photographic colour-printing processes and the techniques of neo-impressionist painters later in the nineteenth century. Chromolithographs were often varnished and given a surface texture in an attempt to make them look more like original paintings.

One interesting method of colour printing which was occasionally adopted in the nineteenth century in both letterpress printing and lithography was known as rainbow printing. This was a technique of producing a multi-coloured print from a single printing surface by using a roller charged with a range of variegated colours. This very simple and ingenious method was an effective means of producing fascinating results quite cheaply. Rainbow printing could be practised both with the hand roller and on a machine, and the technique was used for many kinds of printing, from the large posters of Chéret and others to smaller items such as music covers and labels [100]. Sometimes rainbow printing was used in combination with other methods in order to reduce the number of workings, and in such cases it was often quite cleverly disguised.

102 Compound-plate print in red and black. From J. H. Ibbetson, *A practical view of an invention for better protecting bank-notes against forgery*, 2nd ed., 1821. 65 × 65 mm.

103 Ream label of Wilmot, Sundridge Mill, Sevenoaks, 1827. Compound-plate print. 150 × 132 mm. *John Johnson Collection.*

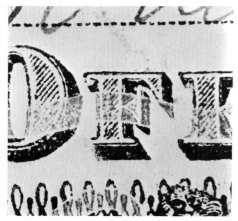

104 Detail of Plate 103. Height of 'O' 10 mm.

105 Lottery bill of T. Bish, 1815. Letter-press, printed in three colours by Gye & Balne, London. 206 × 165 mm. *John Johnson Collection.*

25 T.C.Hansard, *A treatise on printing* (Edinburgh, 1841), p.144

Another interesting method of colour printing in which a number of colours could be printed at one pull of the press was compound-plate printing. It was developed at much the same time by both J. H. Ibbetson and Sir William Congreve as a solution to the problem of bank-note forgery. Ibbetson's method of dividing up a relief block into a number of parts, inking them separately in different colours, and fitting them together again for printing, was described in his *A practical view of an invention for better protecting bank-notes against forgery* (1819) [102], though he had previously submitted his idea to the Royal Commission which had been set up to investigate an improved method of making bank-notes. Sir William Congreve (1772–1828) was one of the Commissioners, and Ibbetson hinted in his pamphlet that the methods of compound-plate printing which Congreve developed might have stemmed from his idea. In both methods the printing block was composed of interlocking parts which could be inked separately in different colours and brought together for printing at a single impression; but the process Congreve protected by patents in 1819 and 1820 allowed for more complex treatment, and he also devised a special machine to facilitate the inking and printing of his plates. Congreve's plates were made in the following way. First of all a simple design was cut or stamped through a piece of sheet metal so that it appeared rather like a stencil. This stencil plate was then placed on a flat metal surface and a more fusible metal was melted and poured over it, filling the holes and covering its back, so that the two parts held together but could be separated easily. The face of this compound plate was therefore all on one plane, though it consisted of two parts made of different metals. The whole plate was then engraved with a design for relief printing in such a way that the lines crossed the boundaries between the two parts. After engraving, the two parts of the plate were separated, charged with different coloured inks, and brought together again to produce a perfectly registered print at a single impression.

One of the first major applications of Congreve's process was the printing by Branston & Whiting of the tickets for the coronation of George IV in 1821 [397, 398]. Thereafter, it was frequently used for printing borders for official documents, labels for sealing reams of paper [103, 104], and other printing which needed to suggest authenticity. After about 1824 Congreve yielded his patent rights to Branston & Whiting, who continued to use the process. The firm of Whiting continued in business well into the second half of the nineteenth century, and the process of compound-plate printing was still being used at Somerset House for the printing of government medicine seals as late as 1920.

The use of colours for the printing of type on work such as posters became popular at much the same time as colour-printed images, and this seems to support the view that it was the lack of suitable inks that delayed the wide-spread commercial development of colour printing. Some of the attractive lottery bills produced in the decade before the abolition of the state lotteries in 1826 by printers such as Branston & Whiting and Gye & Balne were printed in two or three colours [105], but the impression gained from surviving work generally is that the majority of letterpress jobbing printing was in monochrome until the 1840s. This view is confirmed by Hansard who pointed out with some regret in his *Treatise on printing* (1841) that while colour printing was frequently used for pictorial work connected with the fine arts it had been entirely neglected in run-of-the-mill printing.[25] In the early 1840s circus and theatre bills and posters advertising balloon ascents and other festive occasions began to appear in two or three colours. J. W. Peel of Lambeth was one printer (though there were probably many others) who seems to have specialised in this kind of work, and he produced numerous posters for such occasions printed in two colours, usually red with either blue, green, or black [106]. Pictorial woodcuts and decorative designs in three or

106 J. W. Peel, theatre bill, London, 1843. Letterpress, printed in green and red. 754 × 239 mm. *John Johnson Collection.*

four colours began to find their way on to posters, and by the early 1860s wood-letter cutters, such as Bonnewell & Co., had begun to supply special letters, each consisting of two or more units, for printing in different colours [99, 107]. Commercially available letters and ornaments of this kind were, of course, an enormous stimulus to the development of colour printing.

Though jobbing printing in colour had become quite widespread by this time, some printers appear to have specialised in this kind of work. The imprint of James Upton of Birmingham, for instance, figures on a number of surviving posters which incorporate multi-coloured pictorial images and letterforms [101]. Small-scale jobbing work in colour received great encouragement in the 1860s from the introduction of the jobbing platen press, which gave accurate registration and helped to make colour printing quicker and cheaper.

Printing in gold and silver was also developed in the nineteenth century for both letterpress and lithographic work, though the usual practice was to print with a tacky ink or varnish and to dust the paper with bronze or silver powder afterwards. Ready-mixed metallic inks do not seem to have been available until well into the second half of the century.

The Great Exhibition of 1851 marked a turning point in the progress of colour printing as it did in so many other fields. The most interesting and visually appealing category of printing to be exhibited at the Crystal Palace was certainly colour printing, and many of the leading letterpress and lithographic printers brought along their latest masterpieces for inspection. The market for printing offered by the exhibition itself in the form of commemorative views, souvenirs, handbooks, and catalogues also provided the colour printer with a fine opportunity to display his skills [794–802].

Hand-drawn colour printing processes depended not only on the skill of the draughtsman or engraver who actually made the marks, but more particularly on the visualiser who decided how many printings were needed to achieve an accurate facsimile of the original and what colours they should be. Some of the more ambitious chromolithographs, such as the facsimiles published by the British Museum towards the end of the nineteenth century, sometimes involved as many as twenty-four workings, and even second-rate posters were usually printed in a dozen or more colours. This method of producing chromolithographs flourished right up to the Second World War for certain kinds of work, and is still practised in the lithographic studios of Mourlot *frères* in Paris for the production of posters for exhibitions and the reproduction of paintings. Thomas Griffits, who began his apprenticeship as a lithographic artist in the nineteenth century, claimed that the eight colour lithographs he made for the King Penguin edition of *The Bayeux Tapestry* (1943) [108] were the last examples of hand-drawn reproductive lithography to be produced in this country, though in fact the technique lingered on in the world of commercial printing for a good many more years.

Once printers had come to terms with monochrome photography it was natural that they should turn their attention to the reproduction of coloured photographs. The path was prepared for them by Clerk Maxwell, who demonstrated in 1860 how separate colour filters could be used to record photographically the blue-violet, green, and red constituents of a subject, and how these could be combined to produce a fully-coloured image. The first printing process to be used in connection with this idea was collotype, and Josef Albert of Munich, and many others on the continent, began printing colour collotypes as early as 1870. The process was much slower to take root in this country, but from the early 1890s onwards a number of firms were using it. Particularly fine examples were the series of Medici Society

107 W. H. Bonnewell & Co., *Specimens of wood type*, c. 1870. The components of a two-colour letter printed separately and together. Height of letters 85 mm. *St Bride Printing Library.*

108 Thomas Griffits, detail of hand-drawn lithograph. From E. Maclagan, *The Bayeux tapestry*, 1943. Printed in seven colours by the Baynard Press. 71 × 56 mm.

reproductions of famous paintings which began to appear in 1908. Though excellent work was produced in colour collotype, the process was very slow and expensive and there was great wastage. It was certainly not the solution to the problem of inexpensive colour printing.

As in monochrome half-tone printing, economical colour half-tones depended on the use of screens. Frederick Ives of Philadelphia, who developed the cross-lined screen in the mid-1880s, soon adapted it for colour work. In England, the Photochromatic Printing Co. was the first firm to practise three-colour process relief printing on a commercial scale, and by the turn of the century many others in this country had followed suit.

Numerous experiments in the printing of coloured photographic images were made in the last quarter of the nineteenth century, and many of them, as in the hand-drawn processes, involved the colouring of a monochrome base or the inking up of a single plate in different colours. The development of three- and four-colour intaglio and lithographic process printing was really delayed by the limitations of the printing processes themselves. Around 1908, just over ten years after the Rembrandt Intaglio Printing Co. developed the half-tone screen in connection with monochrome rotogravure, it began producing colour prints; similarly, the application of offset lithography to printing on paper in the early years of this century prepared the way for the experiments made by George Mann & Co. in photographic colour lithography in 1909–10. By the beginning of this century, therefore, the path was prepared for the wide commercial application of photography to colour printing in all the three major processes. Since then the most significant advances have been the development of electronic photo-engraving machines, such as the Klischograph, for making separate colour plates for three- and four-colour printing, and the printing of newspapers in full colour by web-offset lithography.

Even in the second half of the nineteenth century the techniques used for making commercial colour prints were becoming so complicated that the artist could no longer effectively involve himself in their production, and in the twentieth century the separation has become almost absolute. It is true that painters like Chéret and Lautrec worked in lithographic studios to produce their posters and that, inspired by this precedent, undertakings this century such as 'School Prints', 'Lyons' Lithographs', and the London Transport poster campaign have provided some kind of link between the artist and the process of manufacture. But these are exceptions, and for the most part the complexities of industrial methods, quite apart from the social problems of the printing industry, have tended to separate the two. The artist's involvement in the making of autographic colour prints dates from the last decades of the nineteenth century, which is precisely the period when the hand-drawn processes were beginning to be superseded commercially by photographic ones.

Chapter 4
From craft to technology

In 1800 the methods used in the printing and allied industries had hardly changed from those of 350 years before. Paper continued to be made by hand and the methods of making punches, striking matrices, casting types, setting text, and inking and printing from the forme remained much the same as in the fifteenth century. But the demands of a new reading public, coupled with the growth of trade, created a climate which encouraged experiment in all branches of printing in the early nineteenth century. Furthermore, inventiveness and engineering skills existed in plenty and had already been applied to other manufacturing industries.

A new era began in printing with the opening of the nineteenth century, and at its close nearly all the processes were fully mechanised. Comparison of production speeds can be very misleading, but such figures do nevertheless give some general indication of the extent of the revolution which swept through the printing and allied industries. The hand compositor, even when working most efficiently from simple prose, could only be expected to set something in the order of 2,000 ens (or about 350 words) an hour: the keyboard operator working on one of the composing machines of the late nineteenth century would have set text at least three or four times as quickly and for short periods might have attained speeds of 10,000 ens an hour. A pressman working with his assistant on a wooden hand press [109] could produce perhaps as many as 200–250 sheets in an hour, though it is doubtful whether he could sustain that speed for long and very much lower average speeds were reported: the rotary machines used for newspaper printing at the end of the nineteenth century could print 24,000 copies of a complete twelve-page newspaper in the same space of time. The vatman of the early nineteenth century [110] would have counted his sheets of paper by the ream, but by the middle of the nineteenth century the daily output of giant machines was being measured in miles, and at the end of the century one British mill was producing nearly 600 tons of paper a week. During the nineteenth century many other activities relating to printing, such as ink making, folding and trimming of paper, wire stitching, sewing, the making of envelopes, and the casing of books, were also mechanised to keep pace with the growing output of paper and printing machines.

Dates of the introduction of particular machines are rarely an accurate guide to their impact on the trade but, as other information is hard to come by, this is often all that can be given. It should be borne in mind, however, that wooden presses were still in use some fifty years after the development of iron presses, that the powered letterpress machine was not widely used until some thirty or forty years after its invention, and that even the composing machines developed in the late nineteenth century took two or three decades to find their way into the works of provincial book and jobbing printers. The master printer of the nineteenth century was steeped in the traditions of the trade and did not always take readily to new ideas; the journeyman, seeing his livelihood threatened by the machine, viewed it with some suspicion; others resisted the machine because they thought it produced work which fell short of the very highest standards of the hand craftsman. In general,

109 A wooden hand press or common press. From a wood-engraving in J. Johnson, *Typographia*, 1824.

110 Making paper by hand. From a wood-engraving in *Arts and manufacture: paper*, 1842.

however, the time lag between the introduction of a new machine or system and its widespread commercial exploitation seems to have diminished with the passing of time. With the appearance of the first printing trade journals in this country in the second half of the nineteenth century and the growth of national and international printing exhibitions there has been an increasing acceptance of the need to keep up to date with the latest technical developments.

There was little possibility of significant growth in the printing industry without a corresponding increase in the production of paper. The paper-making machine was virtually a prerequisite for the exploitation of the printing machine and, as it happened, it was developed first. In the early years of the nineteenth century a number of attempts were made to develop paper-making machines in England, but the first successful machine was conceived in France by N.-L. Robert, a clerk in the paper mills of Léger Didot at Essonnes near Paris, who took out a French patent for his invention in 1799. With the encouragement of Didot, Robert's idea was pioneered in England by John Gamble (Didot's brother-in-law) who took out an English patent in 1801 and, with the stationers Henry and Sealy Fourdrinier and the engineer Bryan Donkin, began to produce a machine in 1802. It is almost impossible to sort out the contributions of these six men, all of whom were concerned in some way with the enterprise, but the outcome of their combined activities was the first successful paper-making machine which was in use in Hertfordshire by about 1804.

111 A Fourdrinier paper-making machine. From a wood-engraving in *Arts and manufacture: paper*, 1842.

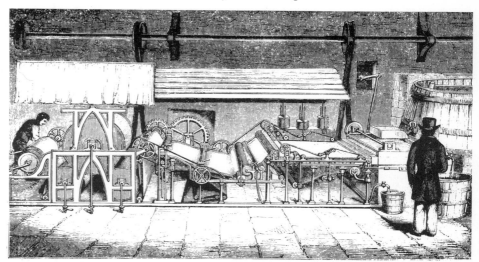

The actual process of paper-making remained much the same as it had for centuries, it was merely mechanised by feeding paper pulp on to a continuous, agitating web of wire mesh [111]. The first machines were powered by water and produced individual sheets of paper about twenty-four inches wide. Fourdrinier claimed that by 1822 forty-two of his machines had been installed in this country, but all the same the mechanisation of the paper industry probably did not really get under way until after 1830. By 1835 it was being claimed that machines were producing as much paper in as many minutes as it had previously taken weeks to make by hand. The effect of the introduction of machines to the paper industry was to produce very much larger industrial units and, as a result, the number of paper manufacturers actually decreased between 1800 and 1860. The old centres of paper-making in Kent, Hertfordshire, and Buckinghamshire, which mainly supplied the London printers, remained; but many of the more remote mills declined and there was a rapid growth in industrial areas of the north where transport facilities were good and where there was a ready supply of coal to provide power to drive the machines. Between 1800 and 1860 the output of paper in the United Kingdom increased ninefold, and by the end of that period only

4 per cent of the total production was made by hand. Despite the high cost of raw materials, the reduction of labour costs brought a steady decline in the average cost of paper which fell 60 per cent in the period 1800 to 1860.

Even before the advent of paper-making machines the problem of supplying rags from which paper was made was becoming acute, and by the end of the eighteenth century their cost had risen sharply. The situation was made worse by the cutting off of continental supplies of rags during the Napoleonic Wars [112]. The reliance of the paper industry on such an unpredictable material as rags had caused a number of men to look for substitutes in the eighteenth century and even before; but the search was intensified in the nineteenth century and John Evans of the firm of John Dickinson & Co. reported to a Select Committee in 1861 that there had been 'upwards of 100 patents taken out for different materials for the manufacture of paper'.[26] In fact, of the 120 patents relating to the materials used in paper manufacture in the period 1800 to 1859, just over three-quarters were taken out from 1850 onwards. In the early years of the nineteenth century Matthias Koops actually set up a large mill based on his experiments in re-pulping paper and the use of hay, straw, and thistles; but though some paper was made at the mill his company soon faced bankruptcy. It soon became quite common for low grade papers to be made partly from old ropes, mill-sweepings, and straw, but all sorts of other materials were proposed, such as coconuts, nettles, and rhubarb, which had little if any application. In 1854 *The Times* offered a prize of £1,000 for a suitable substitute for rags, but it was never awarded, and in 1861 rags still accounted for half the cost of paper.

The need for new materials for making paper had been made more acute by the great demand for European rags to supply the rapidly growing American paper-making industry, and also by the repeal of the newspaper stamp duty in 1855 which led to an increase in the circulations of many newspapers and journals. Soon after the middle of the century esparto grass and wood, the two materials which were later extensively used in the paper industry, began to be the subject of experiment. Both had been considered earlier in the century as possible alternatives for making paper, but for one reason or another had not been developed commercially. The use of esparto grass was pioneered by Thomas Routledge, who began to manufacture paper from it at his mills at Eynsham, near Oxford, in 1857. Wood pulp was used in Germany as an ingredient of paper in the 1840s, and experiments began to be made with it in this country too from the 1850s onwards. In the first place, a purely mechanical method was used to break the wood down into small fibres, but in the 1870s the first successful chemical process was introduced into this country from abroad. Between them esparto grass and wood pulp provided a solution to the problem of supplying vast quantities of cheap material to feed the paper machines and satisfy the voracious demands of the public for cheap literature. By 1860 both materials were being commercially developed, and well before the end of the century they had replaced rags as the major constituent of paper. The figures recording the import of raw materials into Britain at the beginning of this century are sufficient to give a general indication of the change which had taken place in paper manufacture: in the one year 194,000 tons of esparto grass and 448,000 tons of wood pulp were imported, but only 16,000 tons of rags.[27] The majority of paper used today is made primarily from wood pulp (both mechanically and chemically produced) and esparto grass, with the addition of various agents, such as china clay and size, depending on the characteristics required. For the most part rags are now used only for the very best quality papers.

The first significant improvements made to printing equipment concerned the design of the press. About the year 1800 Earl Stanhope proposed an

Many a little makes a Mickle.

AT a Time like the present when every Article requisite in Housekeeping is so dear that Labourers and Mechanics, who have large Families to support, can scarcely make both Ends meet,

A Penny saved is a Penny got

is a Proverb that well deserves their Attention, and indeed that of Housekeepers in general.

When an Opportunity like the present occurs, Mistresses of Families need never be in Want of *Pinmoney*, *fine Gunpowder Tea*, and *Snuff*, by saving their old WHITE LINEN RAGS, which are too frequently thrown into the Fire or out of Doors, and for which they may receive *Three-pence a Pound*, at J. SOULBY's Shop, King-street, Ulverston.

J. S. also gives the best Price for GOOSE FEATHERS

August, 1810.

J. Soulby, Printer, Ulverston.

112 Advertisement for white linen rags, possibly for use in the local paper industry. Printed by John Soulby (senior), Ulverston, 1810. 197 × 156 mm. *Barrow Public Library.*

[26] D.C.Coleman, *The British paper industry 1495-1860* (Oxford, 1958), p.339

[27] *Ibid.*, p.344

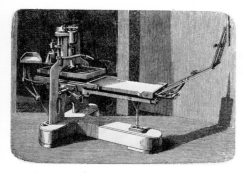

113 A Stanhope hand press. From a wood-engraving in C. Stower, *The printer's grammar*, 1808.

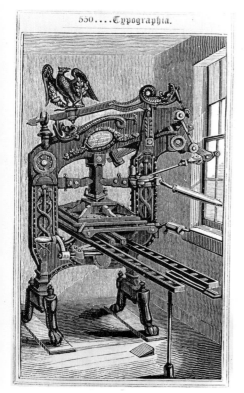

114 A Columbian press. From a wood-engraving in J. Johnson, *Typographia*, 1824.

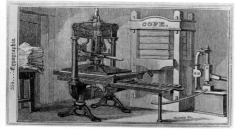

115 An Albion press, manufactured by R. W. Cope. From a wood-engraving by Mosses in J. Johnson, *Typographia*, 1824.

alternative to the traditional wooden or common press and constructed a press made entirely of iron [113]. Stanhope's press incorporated a system of compound levers, which made it capable of greater pressure than the common press, and it had a platen which covered the whole forme, whereas the common press had a platen only about half this size and needed two pulls of the press to print a full-size forme. These improvements led to a saving of human energy and, when large formes were to be printed, a saving of time, and Stanhope presses were soon used by book and newspaper printers, among them the proprietors of *The Times*. Many other kinds of iron presses followed; the most popular versions were the Columbian [114], which was introduced from America in 1817, and the Albion [115], which was invented and originally manufactured by R. W. Cope in or before 1822. Such presses soon became the standard equipment of book and jobbing printers, and continued to be widely used commercially for printing posters and proofing well into the twentieth century. Indeed, Albion presses continued to be manufactured right up to the outbreak of the Second World War.

These new iron presses were certainly easier and quicker to work than the old common presses and, once printers had got used to them, probably gave better results; but the increase in speed of working was of no great consequence to the book or jobbing printer, and altogether insufficient to satisfy the requirements of the successful newspaper publisher. Newspapers were needed in large editions and, just as important, the whole edition had to be printed as quickly as possible so that the latest news could be included without delaying despatch. In the days of the hand press it was often the custom to put the latest news on the inside pages, which were set up twice and printed simultaneously on two presses to save time. One French periodical is even recorded as having been printed from four identical formes so as to satisfy the necessary deadlines for a large edition. It was the readers of newspapers and periodicals, therefore, who really created the need for powered printing machines, and throughout the nineteenth century it was the newspaper industry that pioneered the major developments in their design.

To the forefront in this movement was *The Times*, the only daily newspaper in the country during the first half of the nineteenth century to have an edition size large enough to justify the use of printing machines. During the first three-quarters of the century most of the important improvements in printing machinery were sponsored by *The Times* in an effort to keep pace with its rapidly increasing circulation, which rose from an average daily figure of around 1,500 in the eighteenth century to 11,000 in 1830, 38,000 in 1850, and 70,000 in 1870. Before this last date it had been overtaken by the *Daily Telegraph* which had a circulation of over 100,000 in the 1860s and twice that number in the 1870s. The circulations of both these newspapers were made to appear insignificant with the founding in 1896 of Lord Northcliffe's *Daily Mail* which soon achieved a record circulation of one million copies. Nevertheless, most of the major developments in fast-speed letterpress printing had been anticipated by 1870 and, thereafter, other papers began to exploit them.

The powered printing machine was the invention of Frederick Koenig (1774–1833), a German engineer who was temporarily living in this country. His first experiments were directed at applying steam power to a press constructed along traditional lines in which pressure was applied by the vertical movement of a flat platen, and on this machine he printed an edition of 3,000 of one sheet of the *New Annual Register* for 1810. In the course of the next two years Koenig turned his attention to adapting and mechanising the pressure system used in the rolling presses of the copper-plate printer and patented and manufactured a power-driven cylinder press with automatic

51

E

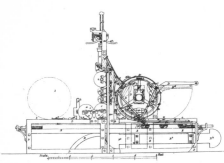

116 Diagram of Koenig's cylinder printing machine. From K. Faulmann, *Illustrirte Geschichte der Buchdruckerkunst*, 1882.

117 Model of Applegath and Cowper's perfecting cylinder machine, 1818. *Science Museum, South Kensington, London.*

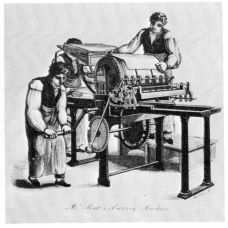

118 Rutt's cylinder machine. Wood-engraving by James Lee from T. C. Handsard, *Typographia*, 1825.

inking [116]. His machine had a moving bed on which the forme travelled successively under inking rollers and an impression cylinder, and it is this principle which has formed the basis for a wide variety of cylinder presses manufactured to this day. From Koenig's time onwards the story is one of successive improvements.

One of Koenig's cylinder machines was put on display in the office of the printer Thomas Bensley who, along with other printers, had entered into partnership with him to develop the invention. The proprietor of *The Times*, John Walter II, was persuaded to take an interest in it and ordered two machines with duplicate feeding stations and impression cylinders on the understanding that each machine was capable of printing 1,100 sheets an hour. The first machine was secretly installed in Printing House Square and on 29 November 1814 the first issue of *The Times* to be printed on a steam-driven machine was produced. Koenig was under contract to make improvements to his invention and in 1816 developed a perfector, which printed almost as many sheets on both sides of the paper at one pass through the press as had previously been printed on one side only. On Koenig's return to Germany in 1818 Edward Cowper and Augustus Applegath were engaged by *The Times* as engineers. They made many improvements to Koenig's basic design, including a number of modifications to the inking apparatus, and it continued to be used by *The Times* until 1827 [117].

Though originally sponsored by book printers, Koenig's machines were not quickly taken up by the trade in general. In reply to a request from Koenig in Germany, Brockhaus wrote in 1820 to the effect that there were still only eight powered machines in London, including the two operating at the offices of *The Times*; and the printer R. Taylor, who owned one of these machines, is reported by Johnson in his *Typographia* of 1824 as preferring to do all his book printing on hand presses. For the most part, in any case, book printers must have found it difficult to justify the capital cost of such equipment. In the 1830s some of the major book-printing houses began to introduce powered cylinder machines into their works, and Eyre & Spottiswoode and William Clowes are known to have had batteries of them in this period. Clowes is reported as having had almost a score of steam-driven printing machines in the 1830s, and in 1851 fifteen such machines were used to print 290,000 copies of the small *Official Catalogue* of the Great Exhibition [784, 785] in just forty-two days. Much more common in this period were small hand-operated cylinder presses, such as Rutt's machine, which were driven by turning a handle [118]. In fact, powered machines remained novelties to most printers, and certainly to the small printer, for years to come and long after 1850 many firms still proudly boasted in their imprints that they were 'steam printers'.

The pressure for improved performances in the speed of printing machines had little to do with the general and book printers; it came from the newspaper and periodical press, and initially almost exclusively from the proprietors of *The Times*. The success of this paper was such that its circulation in 1850 was nearly eight times that of its nearest rival daily paper, the *Morning Advertiser*. Considerable impetus had been given to the demands of the periodical press by the abolition of the so-called 'taxes on knowledge' which had been a persistent factor in pushing up the prices of periodical literature. The advertisement duty imposed in 1815 at 3s 6d was reduced to 1s 6d in 1833 and finally abolished in 1853; the newspaper stamp duty, first imposed in 1712, was reduced from 4d to 1d in 1836 and repealed in 1855; and in 1861 the 1½d per pound duty on paper was also removed. The outcome of all these changes was reflected in an increase in both the sizes and circulations of newspapers.

119 Applegath's vertical rotary printing machine at *The Times*. From Lardner, *The Great Exhibition and London in 1851*, 1852.

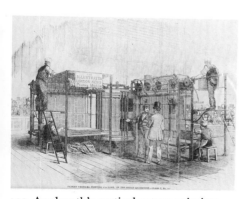

120 Applegath's vertical rotary printing machine belonging to the *Illustrated London News* in operation at the Great Exhibition of 1851. From the *Illustrated London News*, Exhibition Supplement, 31 May 1851.

The main factor limiting the speed of printing was not so much the machine itself as the feeding of the sheets by hand; and in the case of newspaper printing the paper was so large that the most one man could feed in an hour was about 1,500 sheets. The first solution to this problem was to increase the number of feeding stations on presses, and in 1827 Applegath and Cowper built a four-feeder which printed four sheets during one movement of the forme and produced well over 4,000 sheets an hour printed on one side of the paper only. Machines of this kind were used by *The Times* for over twenty years and by other London and provincial newspaper printers as well. But by the 1840s even the four-feeder was not sufficient to keep pace with the growing circulation of *The Times*, and this caused Applegath to consider replacing the clumsy and mechanically inefficient reciprocating movement of a flat bed and forme with the rotating movement of a wide cylindrical forme. The result of his experiments was a rotary press [119] in which the type was mounted on to a vertical cylinder or, more accurately, a polygon consisting of a series of flat facets corresponding to the columns of a newspaper. The cylinder revolved continuously while paper was fed from eight stations to pass between eight impression cylinders and the printing drum. Mammoth vertical rotary machines of this kind were used to print the inner forme of *The Times* from 1848 and attained speeds of up to 12,000 impressions an hour. Two of them managed to cope with the extra large edition of 70,000 copies which were needed for the Wellington funeral issue of 14 November 1852. A similar press was later used by the *Standard*, and the *Illustrated London News* was printed on a vertical four-feeder which was one of the sights of the Great Exhibition [120].

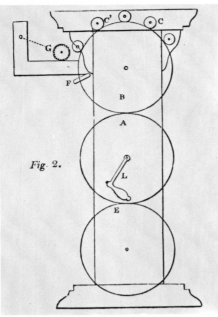

121 Diagram of William Nicholson's proposed rotary printing machine. From W. Savage, *A dictionary of the art of printing,* 1841.

122 The Hoe ten-feeder horizontal rotary printing machine. From a catalogue of the firm R. Hoe & Co., 1867. *Smithsonian Institution, Washington.*

Applegath's vertical rotary machines were no real answer to the problem of rotary printing, which engineers had toyed with persistently since the late eighteenth century. The principle of rotary printing was adopted for calico printing in the eighteenth century, and in 1790 William Nicholson took out a patent for a machine in which paper passed between a cylindrical printing surface and an impression cylinder [121]. Thereafter numerous attempts were made to construct both letterpress and lithographic machines on this principle, but all were thwarted because of the difficulty of producing satisfactory curved printing surfaces. In 1816 Edward Cowper took out a patent for a method of printing from stereotype plates which had been cast from flat plaster of Paris moulds of formes and heated and curved afterwards, but the first real step towards solving the problem of producing curved letterpress printing surfaces was taken by Jean-Baptiste Genoux in France in 1829 with the invention of a method of making stereotype casts of formes by means of moulds or 'flongs' made of papier mâché. Such moulds could be bent and used for making curved surfaces from flat ones, and in 1845 Worms and Philippe in France returned to the idea of making curved stereotype casts which could be fitted to the cylinders of presses. Papier mâché stereotyping was covered in England by the patents of Moses Poole (1839) and J. M. Kronheim (1844), but it only began to be used in this country after the middle of the century. It was successfully practised by James Dellagana, who made the first whole-page stereotype casts of *The Times* in 1857 and began experimenting with curved stereotype plates soon afterwards. The difficulties encountered were considerable, and it was not until about 1860 that the process which continued as the basic method of producing printing surfaces for newspaper production for over a century was introduced commercially by *The Times* for use on its new Hoe rotary machines.

At much the same time as Applegath and Cowper were developing their vertical rotary machines, American engineers were experimenting with horizontal rotaries. A press of this kind manufactured by Hoe was installed in this country in 1857 to print *Lloyd's Weekly Newspaper,* which ran to an average weekly circulation of half a million copies in the early 1860s, and later in the same year *The Times* ordered two of Hoe's giant ten-feeders [122]. These machines were capable of printing nearly 20,000 impressions an hour,

and when put into operation by *The Times* in 1858 the old vertical rotaries of Applegath were soon made obsolete. In the 1860s Hoe rotary machines with four, six, eight, or ten feeding stations were more widely used than any other machines for printing national and provincial newspapers: in 1866 the *Standard* installed five Hoe machines and in 1867 the *Daily Telegraph* had at least four ten-feeders at work.

Up to this point in time all machines used in the newspaper industry had been sheet-fed by hand, and most had printed on only one side of the paper at a time; but it was already fairly obvious to printing engineers that the most efficient machines would be those which could print on both sides of a moving web of paper at one pass through the press. In America William Bullock of Philadelphia manufactured such a press in 1865; in this country the initiative was once again taken by *The Times*. As early as 1862 John Walter III embarked upon a project to design a reel-fed rotary machine; a prototype was built in 1866 and, after a period of secret trial running, four 'Walter' machines were working in Printing House Square in 1869. These presses [123] were much more compact than their predecessors, they needed fewer men to operate them, and produced about 10,000 perfected sheets of an eight-page paper in an hour. This represented such an improvement that *The Times* could be printed in less than half the time previously needed. The 'Walter' press marked a turning point in the evolution of fast-running letterpress machines, and also pointed the way for the later development of lithographic and gravure printing. In the 1870s reel-fed rotary presses were installed by many of the large-circulation newspapers,

123 'Walter' rotary presses. From J. Southward, *Progress in printing and the graphic arts in the Victorian era*, 1897.

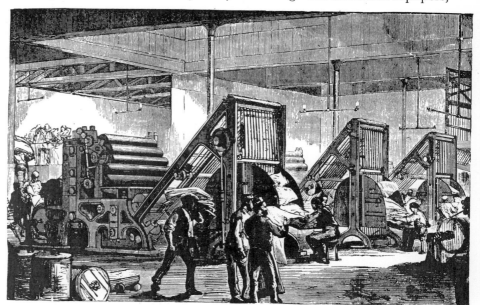

such as the *Daily Telegraph*, the *Standard*, and the *Daily News*, and by 1880 in provincial newspaper offices as well. Folding apparatus was incorporated in the 'Victory' rotary machine, which was introduced in 1870, and was added to 'Walter' presses about 1885. The 'Walter' presses used by *The Times* were finally ousted in 1895 by Hoe machines which were capable of printing, cutting, and folding 24,000 copies of a complete newspaper in an hour.

Such has been the increase in the volume of printing produced in this century that some of the principles applied in the nineteenth century to newspaper presses have since been applied to presses designed for other sorts of printing where long runs are required, such as paperback books, catalogues, directories, and year books. The use of both reel- and sheet-fed rotary machines for this kind of work has been greatly advanced in recent years by the development of plastic and other composition plates which can be made relatively easily for use on rotary machines by even the medium-size printer.

124 A stop-cylinder printing machine manufactured by Henry Ingle about 1875. *Science Museum, South Kensington, London.*

The evolution of large-scale machinery for very fast printing does not tell the whole story of the mechanisation of letterpress printing. The book and jobbing printers may not have been so interested in speed of printing as the newspaper proprietors, but by the middle of the nineteenth century they too found that the hand press no longer satisfied their needs, and numerous power-driven presses were designed specially for them.

Most of the presses built for the book printer derived from one or other of Koenig's cylinder machines. It is not possible to give even a brief outline of the development of the numerous kinds of cylinder presses manufactured since then; but two versions which had remarkable success over a long period were the Wharfedale, a stop-cylinder machine developed by David Payne in 1858, and the Miehle two-revolution machine which was invented by Robert Miehle in Chicago in the 1880s. These presses, and others like them [124], were built in a range of sizes which related to book and paper sizes in common use, and improved versions of both kinds of machines are still in production.

New platen presses were also designed to cater specifically for the needs of the jobbing printer. The first step was the development of small self-inking treadle presses, and experiments were made along these lines by two American printers, Stephen Ruggles and George Phineas Gordon. In 1839 Ruggles produced and marketed a press in which the type forme was held upside down above the platen, but in 1851 he adopted the now conventional practice of placing the bed in a vertical position [125]. This second idea was taken up by Gordon, who developed a press in which a hinged platen moved from a nearly horizontal position to meet the printing forme [126]. Gordon showed his press at the International Exhibition in London in 1862 and it soon became very popular in this country where it was manufactured by the firm of Cropper [127]. Other versions were soon built for particular purposes, and later in the century presses designed on this principle were power driven. Platen presses of this kind are still very popular machines for small-scale jobbing work.

The gradual adoption of electricity from the close of the nineteenth century as a source of power to drive printing machinery, and the development after the First World War of really satisfactory machines with automatic feed and delivery, were important improvements which affected all kinds of machines.

125 A Ruggles press of about 1851, lacking treadle attachment, feed board, and rollers. *Smithsonian Institution, Washington.*

126 A Gordon treadle platen press of about 1856-8. *Smithsonian Institution, Washington.*

127 The Cropper-Charlton 'Acme' treadle platen machine. From a catalogue of Cropper, Charlton & Co. Ltd, Nottingham, *c.* 1906. *St Bride Printing Library.*

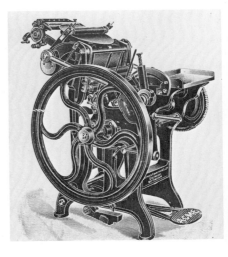

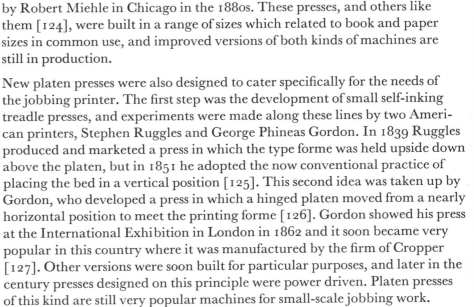

128 Wooden lithographic hand press, *c.* 1820, imported from Germany and used by William Millington of Trowbridge. *From an old photograph in the St Bride Printing Library.*

129 A Sigl lithographic machine. From the *Journal für Buchdruckerkunst,* 1852.

130 Ira Rubel's rotary offset press, said to have been built in about 1904 and put into operation in San Francisco in 1906. Standing by the press is Albert Madsen, who was associated with Rubel from 1907. *Smithsonian Institution, Washington.*

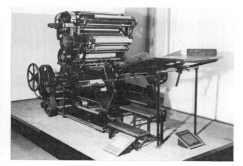

131 Harris's rotary offset press, 1906. *Smithsonian Institution, Washington.*

[28] A. Senefelder, *A complete course of lithography* (London, 1819), p.180

The mechanisation of the other two major branches of printing was delayed very much longer. The new process of lithography was on the point of challenging the monopoly of letterpress in certain branches of printing just as Koenig's powered cylinder machines were beginning to be used; and Senefelder even predicted in his treatise on lithography that his invention would not be perfected 'till the impression can be produced wholly by good machinery'.[28] As it was, however, no successful powered lithographic printing machine was developed, either in this country or abroad, during the first half of the nineteenth century. Throughout this period the maximum speed of printing even the smallest and simplest lithographic image on a hand press [128] was in the region of 100 to 120 impressions an hour, which compared most unfavourably even with the production of the letterpress printer working on a common press. Numerous proposals were made in an attempt to speed up lithographic printing, including printing from cylinders made of lithographic stone and using apparatus for damping and inking the stone mechanically, but no machines were developed beyond the experimental stage until the middle of the century.

In 1851 an Austrian engineer, Georg Sigl, took out patents in Austria and France for a powered machine which printed from flat lithographic stone and incorporated rollers which damped and inked it automatically [129]. By 1854 the Imperial Printing Office in Vienna was using a Sigl machine which printed at the rate of 800 to 1,000 sheets an hour and Maclure, Macdonald & Macgregor, who pioneered the use of lithographic machines in England, claimed to be able to print in one hour on a machine the equivalent of four days' work on a hand press [132]. The effect of the use of powered machines in lithography was quite as momentous as that of Koenig's powered machine in letterpress printing some forty years earlier; furthermore, lithography was able to profit from the experience gained by engineers who had made letterpress machines and soon began to close the gap.

A major obstacle was the lithographic stone, which could not be adapted very easily to rotary printing; but lithography was given a tremendous boost by the development of offset printing and the commercial production of metal plates to replace slabs of limestone. Offset printing was first practised in 1875 by Robert Barclay, of the firm of Barclay & Fry in London, for printing on tin plate. Barclay printed from a flat lithographic stone on to the surface of a cylinder covered with specially prepared cardboard, from which the image was transferred to sheets of metal. A few years later Barclay replaced the cardboard offset blanket with one made of rubber-coated canvas. The tin-box firm of Huntley, Boorne & Stevens of Reading began to print on tin by offset lithography under licence from about 1880, and when Barclay's patent lapsed in 1889 many other metal-box decorators began to exploit the new process.

The real significance of the offset principle was only felt when it was adapted for printing on paper from a metal plate sleeved on to a cylinder. This was first proposed in America in the latter part of 1903 by Ira W. Rubel, who stumbled upon the idea of offset printing quite independently as a result of accidentally offsetting a print from a rubber impression cylinder. In the following year Rubel went into partnership with Kellogg of New York and Sherwood, a Chicago lithographer, and built three prototype offset lithographic machines [130]. Soon afterwards the partnership split up and each developed the idea independently. Rubel came over to England and collaborated with manufacturers here in building offset presses, and similar machines were manufactured in America by the Potter Printing Press Co. and by Harris [131]. The first British-designed offset presses were built in this country by George Mann, who took out a patent for his own version in 1906. Offset presses consist of three main cylinders

132 Maclure, Macdonald & Macgregor, specimen of lithographing by steam power, *c.* 1852. 258 × 170 mm. *John Johnson Collection.*

which work in unison with one another; one carries the printing plate (which is damped and inked by a further set of rollers), the second is clothed in rubber and receives the image from the first cylinder and then transfers it to paper which is fed between it and a third impression cylinder.

Rotary machines which printed direct from metal plates were also developed for lithographic printing, and by the outbreak of the First World War many kinds of direct and offset rotary machines, some of which were capable of as many as 5,000 impressions an hour, were being built by George Mann, Furnival, Hoe, Harris, and other manufacturers. The first rotary lithographic machines were sheet fed. Web-fed lithographic machines were developed for direct rotary printing just before the First World War, but it was not until web-fed offset machines began to be widely used in this country in the 1960s that lithography became fully competitive with letterpress for newspapers and other work which was needed in long runs.

In the last decade, too, the offset principle has been applied to printing from relief plates. The process goes under a variety of names – offset letterpress, dry offset, letterset, and indirect letterpress – and is still in rather an experimental stage; but in recent years most of the leading manufacturers of printing machines have brought out either dual-purpose presses designed for both offset lithography and offset letterpress, or presses for offset lithography which can easily be modified to take wraparound relief plates. Though it is too early yet to predict a certain future for offset letterpress in general-purpose printing, it has already made firm inroads into branches of the industry concerned with the printing of packaging, business forms, labels, and other work required in very long runs.

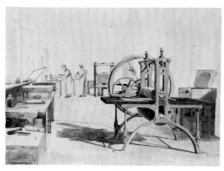

133 Interior of part of the new premises built for the copper-plate printer W. B. McQueen in 1832. Wash drawing. 432 × 711 mm.

Intaglio printing was even later than lithography in becoming mechanised. It was much the slowest of the three major printing processes in the era of the hand press [133], and for this reason presented no serious challenge to either letterpress or lithographic printing in the nineteenth century. Special powered presses for intaglio printing were developed to help produce the enormous quantity of postage stamps needed in the second half of the nineteenth century, but not until the 1890s, when the half-tone screen began to be used for making photographic intaglio plates, did the process make any general commercial headway. Though it was possible to print from screen-made photogravure images on flat plates, the process was developed for rotary printing right from the beginning and, in practice, the terms photogravure and rotogravure have come to mean much the same thing. Photogravure was brought to a state of commercial application in Vienna by Karl Klíč who came to England and began to print on rotary presses at his Rembrandt Intaglio Printing Co. in Lancaster about 1895. A few years before the First World War fast-speed rotary photogravure presses began to be used for newspaper and magazine printing. First in the field was the German newspaper *Freiburger Zeitung*, the illustrations of which were printed by photogravure in 1910. The weekly *Southend Standard* was printed by photogravure in 1912, and the *Illustrated London News* began experimenting with a single section in the same year, turning to the process for the whole production shortly after the First World War. By this time reel-fed rotogravure machines were capable of printing 3,000 impressions an hour on both sides of the paper. Thereafter, reel-fed rotary gravure began to be accepted as perhaps the most suitable process for printing illustrated magazines with very large circulations and other pictorial work required in vast numbers, including the nation's postage stamps [134].

134 A reel-fed rotary photogravure machine printing postage stamps at the High Wycombe works of Harrison & Sons Ltd.

The other major operations connected with printing to be mechanised in the course of the nineteenth century were the casting and setting of type. For most of the first half of the century these activities were continued in the time-honoured ways and as separate crafts; type was cast manually by the typefounder and set by hand by the compositor. But by the end of the nineteenth century these operations were fully mechanised and machines were in use which cast and composed types in one operation.

Traditionally, type was cast by means of a hand-held mould and a ladle of molten metal [135]. The output for one man was something in the region of 400–500 pieces of book-size type an hour, and even then the type had to receive further treatment before it was ready for the compositor. During the first half of the nineteenth century a number of attempts were made to speed up this laborious process, but typefounders were suspicious of anything that might threaten their livelihood and did everything in their power to prevent the introduction of mechanical aids. The first effective type-casting machine was invented in 1838 by David Bruce of New York and was capable of producing 6,000 pieces of type an hour [136, 137]; but though quickly taken up in America and Germany this pivotal caster was not introduced into

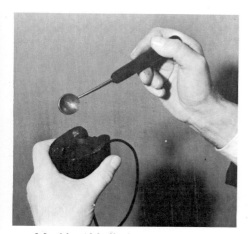

135 Mould and ladle for casting type by hand. *Science Museum, South Kensington, London.*

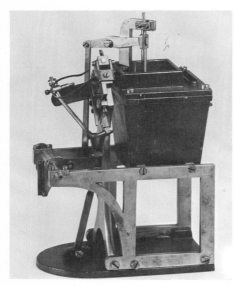

136 David Bruce's typecasting machine, patent model, 1843. *Smithsonian Institution, Washington.*

137 Pivotal typecasting machine, developed by David Bruce between 1838 and 1845. *Smithsonian Institution, Washington.*

138 Young and Delcambre's typesetting machine, invented in 1840.

Britain until around the middle of the century. The Edinburgh typefounders Miller & Richard were using it in 1849, despite the opposition of English founders, and the printing firm of Clowes produced on a mechanical caster the fifty tons of type needed to set the catalogues of the Great Exhibition of 1851. Pressure for the supply of vast quantities of type came primarily from the rapidly expanding newspaper industry, and various improvements were made to the design of casting machines. The most successful model was the rotary caster invented by Frederick Wicks and patented by him in 1881. It had one hundred moulds and was reputed to be capable of producing as many as 60,000 finished types an hour. Wicks machines were used to cast the large quantities of type needed to set *The Times* before the first hot-metal composing machines were introduced there in 1909, and typecasting machines continued to be used by founders for the casting of moderate quantities of type for hand setting.

The problem of composing text quickly proved to be much more troublesome than mechanising type-casting and occupied the minds of hundreds of inventors during the nineteenth century. One proposal for speeding up the compositor's work was made by Henry Johnson who took out a patent in 1778 for a method which involved casting up to five letters on one body of combinations of letters which occurred regularly, such as short words, prefixes, suffixes, and common syllables. The rights of this patent were acquired in 1784 by John Walter who founded what he called the 'Logographic Press' and, in the following year, began to produce a whole stream of rather inaccurately printed books and pamphlets using logotypes. In 1785, too, he founded the *Daily Universal Register* (or *The Times* as it became from 1788) which was printed logographically until the beginning of 1792. Another approach to speeding up the setting of type was an organisational one, known as the 'clicker' system, whereby a small group of compositors working on piece rates under the direction of a 'clicker' collaborated on a job in order to meet a press deadline and worked at frantic pace on small sections of text. The system was practised throughout most of the nineteenth century and was vividly described by Charles Manby Smith in *The working man's way in the world* (1851–2), but, not surprisingly, it left little opportunity for the consideration of typographical niceties.

Both these approaches were stop-gap measures and did little to solve the long-term problems created by the growing demand for printing. More fundamental experiments took the form of attempts to mechanise the traditional operation of composing types of predominantly individual letters into lines, and numerous ingenious machines were devised to this end. The first of these was patented in England in 1822 by an American, William Church, though there is no evidence that a machine of the kind he proposed was ever built. It incorporated a keyboard which governed the release of individual types, and in this respect it is important as it pointed the way to the development of successful machines later in the century. A workable typesetting and distributing machine produced by a Hungarian, Joseph Kiegl, was put on exhibition in Bratislava in 1839, but the first composing machine known to have been installed in a printing office was invented by Young and Delcambre of Lille, who took out a joint English patent for it in 1840. This machine, known as the 'Pianotyp' [138], was similar to the one proposed by Church in that the types were released on the depression of a keyboard and slid down channels to be assembled into lines for justification by hand later. It was used for setting Edward Binns, *The anatomy of sleep* (1842) and the weekly *Family Herald* (founded 1842) but, because of mechanical deficiencies and the vociferous opposition of compositors who feared losing their livelihood, the few machines that were constructed ceased to be used within a year or two.

The 'Pianotyp' was followed by a host of other machines designed to facilitate the organisation of type into lines, and speeds varying from 6,000 to 10,000 characters an hour were claimed for them. The most successful of those installed in this country were the Hattersley, Kastenbein, and Thorne, all of which were used almost exclusively for newspaper composition. The Hattersley was the earliest, and the first machines of this kind were installed in 1866 at the offices of the *Eastern Morning News* in Hull. Thereafter, the Hattersley was used by a number of provincial papers, including the *Manchester Guardian*, and even lingered on in the offices of the *South Wales Daily News* until as late as 1915. The Kastenbein [139] was much less widely used, and in this country was virtually limited to the offices of *The Times*. It was installed at Printing House Square in 1872 and, after a few years of experimentation, began to be used regularly until 1909 in conjunction with type produced on the Wicks rotary caster. Both the Hattersley and the Kastenbein required an additional mechanism to distribute the type after use, but the Thorne combined the two operations of composing and distributing in the one machine. It was introduced from America and was chiefly used in this country by the *Bradford Observer*, which had ten such machines in the 1890s.

All these machines were handicapped by the lack of a mechanical system for justifying the lines of type once they had been set, and this was the problem which still concerned most designers of composing machines in the 1890s, and especially American ones. The most sophisticated of all composing machines using pre-cast type was perfected in this period. It was developed over a couple of decades by J. W. Paige of Rochester, New York, and set, justified, and distributed the type; but it was soon abandoned because it had already been superseded by the new hot-metal Linotype machines by the time it was commercially installed in the offices of the *Chicago Herald* in 1894.

In retrospect it can be seen that the mistake of the designers of early composing machines was to concentrate on the organisation of existing type.

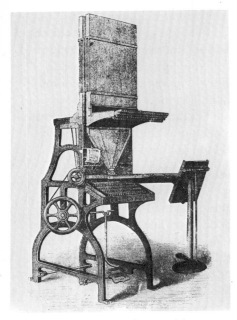

139 Kastenbein typesetting machine. From K. Faulmann, *Illustrirte Geschichte der Buchdruckerkunst*, 1882.

140 An early version of Mergenthaler's Linotype composing machine, 1885. *Smithsonian Institution, Washington.*

141 A Linotype composing machine of the design introduced about 1890. *Science Museum, South Kensington, London.*

142 A Linotype slug.

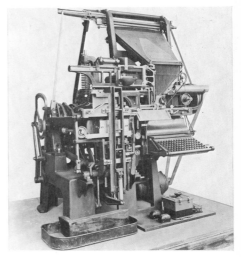

During the last decades of the nineteenth century new approaches were explored and machines were built which controlled the position of individual letter matrices so that type could be cast and set simultaneously. The idea had been toyed with by Charles Westcott of New Jersey, who invented a machine in 1872 which cast single pieces of type on the operation of a keyboard, but the first practical machine was the Linotype [140]. An early model of the Linotype machine was installed in the offices of the New York *Tribune* in 1886, but only after a few more years of patient experiment was it developed commercially [141].

The Linotype composing machine was designed by a young German mechanic, Ottmar Mergenthaler (1854–99), who had recently emigrated to America, and it worked by assembling and spacing rows of individual matrices and taking casts of complete lines or 'slugs' from them [142]. The matrices were stored in magazines not unlike those previously used in composing machines using pre-cast type, but Mergenthaler introduced an ingenious method of returning them to the magazines after use. The certainty that some characters would be used many times in the composition of an average length line meant that many matrices had to be held for each letter. This put a heavy demand on the punch-cutter and matrix maker, and the practical development of the Linotype (and other machines of this kind) would have been out of the question but for the invention in 1884 of a satisfactory punch-cutting machine, based on the pantographic principle, by Linn Boyd Benton of Milwaukee. Though it lacked some of the refinements of hand setting, the Linotype composing machine was an almost immediate success; the first models in England were installed at the offices of the *Newcastle Chronicle* (1889) and *Leeds Mercury* (1890), and within four years over 250 models are known to have been at work in the provinces alone. Along with other slug-composing machines of this kind, the Typograph (1890) and the Intertype (1913), Linotype machines are still widely used, especially for newspaper work.

The other kind of hot-metal composing machine used throughout the world in this century is the 'Monotype' machine [143], which was developed by Tolbert Lanston (1844–1913) of Washington between 1885 and 1897. It consists of two separate units, a keyboard [144] which produces perforated paper tape, and a caster [145] which is controlled by this tape to produce individual pieces of type in lines. The matrices in the caster are not selected

143 The heading of the *Monotype Recorder*, no. 1, January 1902, showing early models of the 'Monotype' keyboard and caster. *St Bride Printing Library.*

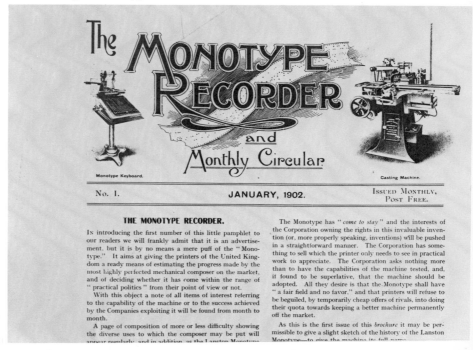

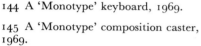

144 A 'Monotype' keyboard, 1969.

145 A 'Monotype' composition caster, 1969.

146 'Monotype' matrices and matrix case.

from a bank to form words, as in line-composing machines, but one matrix only of each character is arranged on a grid system in a steel case [146]. On receiving instructions from the perforated tape the case moves so that the appropriate matrix is above a mould and jet of hot metal. The spacing between words is determined before casting, and the types are produced in lines, one character at a time. The idea of controlling typesetting by perforated tapes was not new, and had been successfully applied by Alexander Mackie in 1867. Other machines invented since then have adopted similar systems, but only the 'Monotype' machine has been developed commercially. The first limited fount 'Monotype' machines were sent to this country in 1897, and in the same year a British company was founded. The first sale of a 'Monotype' machine was made to Cassell's of London three years later. Whereas Linotype and Intertype machines were used in England mainly for setting newspapers and periodicals, 'Monotype' machines gradually began to replace the hand compositor for the setting of books and jobbing work. Initially, there was a certain amount of resistance to their introduction from the purists, but even such a stickler for perfection as Bruce Rogers admitted in his *Report on the typography of the Cambridge University Press* (1917) that 'recent developments in the machines themselves now permit the possibility of doing quite as good work as by the older and slower method'.

The latest major development in type-composing machines to record is the invention of typesetting by photography. The idea of entirely replacing metal for text composition was given impetus by the practical application of photography to the making of printing plates; and from 1896, when E. Porzholt patented a keyboard-controlled machine that projected single characters by reflected light on to a sensitised plate, there have been numerous attempts to develop a satisfactory system of setting type photographically. Between the two world wars several machines were constructed and the problem attracted considerable attention. First in the field was the Uhertype, invented by Edmund Uher in Augsburg in 1925, which was controlled by perforated tape and produced strips of film from negatives of letters on a glass cylinder. It was not until after the Second World War, however, that photosetting became a commercial reality, and since 1945 technical developments have been rapid. The first British photosetting machine was George Westover's Rotofoto system, which was manufactured in 1948 and put into limited use in the following year. Meanwhile, photosetting machines were being developed by all the manufacturers of hot-metal composers. The first to make an impact commercially was the Harris-Intertype Fotosetter [147],

147 The Harris-Intertype Fotosetter.

148 Burt's 'Typographer', 1829 (replica). *Science Museum, South Kensington, London.*

[29] F.Balzer, 'Survey of filmsetting installations in Europe', *Print in Britain*, September 1967, pp.22–7

[30] L.W.Wallis, 'Filmsetting in focus', *Monotype Recorder*, vol. 43, no. 2, Summer 1965, p.75

which was installed in the Government Printing Office in Washington as early as 1946, but since then the Photon-Lumitype range, 'Monophoto' filmsetter, Linofilm systems, and a variety of other machines have been put on the market.

Photosetting can now be said to have developed beyond the experimental stage, and though the number of installations is still not very large – only four hundred and ten were recorded in the whole of Europe in a survey made in 1967[29] – it accounts for a growing proportion of our printed material. The commercial growth of photosetting has not been particularly rapid, partly because of the large proportion of his capital the small printer has locked up in hot-metal machines, and partly because it is still not usually competitive for short runs which make up the majority of printed work. The economic advantages of photosetting do not lie in the setting itself, which is quite as expensive as conventional hot-metal methods, but in the practical advantages ensuing from its use. First among these is the link with lithography and photogravure; plates for these processes can be made more directly from film than by using conventional methods of setting – all of which involve taking reproduction proofs from type and photographing them before a similar stage can be arrived at. The second major advantage lies in the ease of storing and transporting film. It has been calculated, for instance, that the whole of the text of an edition of *War and peace* occupied less than one-fifth of a cubic foot on film, compared with approximately twenty-two cubic feet which would have been needed to store the equivalent material in metal.[30]

A new kind of photosetting system has been specially developed over the last few years for use in conjunction with computers for very high speed setting. The Linotron 505 is such a machine, and it produces its letterforms by scanning a cathode-ray tube through letter matrices and then photographing them. The models which were installed recently at the Hilsea plant of the Portsmouth *Evening News* are capable of setting one hundred and twenty newspaper lines a minute and are being adapted for even faster working. Such speeds are very much faster than those obtainable from photosetting systems involving the use of film matrices, but are still very slow when compared with the capabilities of the latest computers.

One other machine designed for the setting of text should be mentioned – the typewriter – though it has only recently been considered in relation to printing. The idea of the typewriter goes back to at least 1714 when Henry Mill took out a patent for 'an artificial machine or method for the impressing or transcribing of letters singly or progressively one after another, as in writing ... so neat and exact as not to be distinguished from print ...' – though there is no evidence that such a machine was actually produced at this time. Many kinds of writing machines were invented in both Europe and America in the nineteenth century, but W. A. Burt of Detroit (1829) and X. Progin of Marseilles (1833) developed the two earliest models that are known to have worked [148–150]. An American printer, Christopher Latham Sholes, is usually considered the father of the modern typewriter (1867–76), and it was he who introduced the 'Universal' arrangement of the keyboard now commonly used on typewriters and also on 'Monotype' composing machines. His associate, James Densmore, submitted a model to E. Remington & Sons who put the first reliable typewriter on the market in America in 1874 [151]. By the end of the century scores of different typewriters were available both in America and in this country. Since then many improvements have been made in the design of typewriters and, with the development between the wars of electrically-driven machines and, later, of models with one-time ribbons and letterforms of varying width, such as the IBM 'Executive' (1941), they began to be used for making originals which could be photographed

149 The underside of the swinging sector of Burt's 'Typographer' showing the types (replica). *Science Museum, South Kensington, London.*

150 Facsimile of a letter to his wife written on the 'Typographer' by W. A. Burt, 1830. *Science Museum, South Kensington, London.*

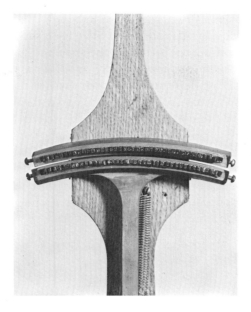

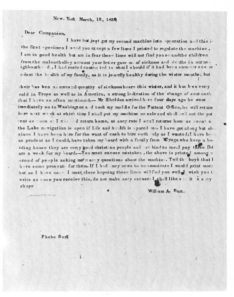

151 The Sholes and Glidden typewriter as built by E. Remington & Sons, 1874-6. *Science Museum, South Kensington, London.*

152 An IBM 72 Selectric Composer.

153 A keyboard operator at work on an electronic keyboard in the composing room of the *Evening Post*, Reading.

and printed by offset lithography. This has had significant repercussions on the structure of the printing industry in this country and has encouraged the growth of small lithographic printing units within firms and other organisations. In recent years this new branch of printing has been given a considerable boost by the development of sophisticated composers, based on the principle of the typewriter, which can imitate tolerably well the letterforms used by the printer and can be made to produce text which is set with a straight right-hand edge. Composers of this kind, such as the VariTyper and IBM 72 Selectric Composer [152], which were first marketed in this country in 1958 and 1966 respectively, are already beginning to find their way into the works of traditional printers and even newspaper offices.

During the last decade considerable attention has been given by engineers and computer programmers to the problem of speeding up the setting of text by controlling part of the operation by means of computers. The pressure to develop satisfactory methods of automated setting has been enormous and, though the first system was only put into operation at the Imprimerie Nationale in Paris in 1960, computer-aided typesetting is already widely used in America and has found a firm foothold in this country too. The position at present is that copy and information about its design can be fed into a computer, which is able to determine certain functions, such as the breaking of lines, the make-up into pages, and the placing of running headlines and folios, and to control the working of a photosetting machine or hot-metal composer. The major drawback at present is that the copy has to be fed into the computer by means of a manually operated keyboard [153]. This operation is faster than keyboard work on conventional composing machines because the text is tapped out without decisions being made about line breaks, but there is some evidence to suggest that the theoretical gain in speed is partly offset as a result of boredom arising from the lack of decisions that have to be made by the operator. Keyboarding remains the bottleneck in the system, though machines are being developed for the optical scanning of types, and even some forms of handwriting, which may eventually replace it.

The real advantages of computer-aided setting are felt at present only when it is combined with some kind of processing of the copy, such as the updating of directories, gazetteers, and bibliographies and the classification and costing of advertisements. In America computers are already being used for the setting of most telephone directories and many newspapers; in England progress has been slower, but the first computer-set newspaper, Reading's

Evening Post, was issued in September 1965. Since then a number of complex large-scale works have been produced in this country with the help of computers, including the sixteenth volume of the Aslib *Index to theses accepted for higher degrees* (1968), *Treasures of Britain* (1968), produced by Drive Publications Ltd for the Automobile Association, and an edition of the Bible (1968) published for the British & Foreign Bible Society by William Collins. Many such projects have been carried out in the nature of experiments, and it is too early yet to assess the economic advantages of the use of computers in printing. Though few can doubt that the computer will play a significant role in the development of printing in the future, there is good reason to believe that most of the methods of text composition described will continue to have a place in the production of smaller jobs for many years to come.

Chapter 5
Types and other letterforms

Whilst newspapers and periodicals were largely responsible for the technical advances made in the printing industry in the nineteenth century, the most significant changes in type design in this period were made on behalf of the humble jobbing printer for use on handbills, window bills, and similar kinds of advertising. Throughout most of the eighteenth century no special types existed for this sort of work, and the letterpress printer merely used the largest available sizes from the ranges of book types supplied by the founders. In the course of the second half of the eighteenth century, however, types specially designed for display purposes began to be produced. The initiative was taken in France by P.-S. Fournier, who designed a range of floriated letters in the 1760s to match the lively curves of the prevailing rococo style. In England it was not until the 1780s that the leading typefounders of the day, William Caslon III and Fry, issued specimens which included decorated letters. These were less flamboyant than Fournier's, and the most popular designs took the form of simple inline types with a white line engraved down the thick strokes of each letter [154]. Though widely used at the turn of the eighteenth and nineteenth centuries in jobbing work, they were still conceived as book types; they preserved the familiar proportions of book types and, more important, were only produced in sizes up to five-line Pica (slightly more than two centimetres high).

Meanwhile, some English typefounders had begun to produce larger letters for use on posters. This innovation is usually credited to Thomas Cottrell, who showed a twelve-line Pica letter (about five centimetres high) in a specimen of about 1765 [155], but other typefounders followed suit and letters of this

154 Ornamented two-line, or inline, letters. From E. Fry & Co., *A specimen of printing types*, 1788. *St Bride Printing Library.*

155 Twelve-line Pica letters. From T. Cottrell, *A specimen of printing types*, c. 1765. *St Bride Printing Library.*

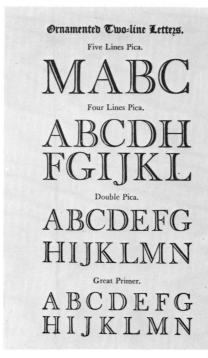

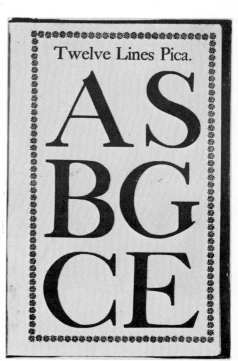

156 Billhead of John Knowlton, 1820. Engraved by W. Alexander, London. 107 × 188 mm. *John Johnson Collection.*

157 Announcement of sale, 1826. Letterpress, printed by John Soulby (junior), Ulverston. 202 × 244 mm. *Museum of English Rural Life, Reading University.*

158 Lottery bill of the firm of Swift & Co., 1810. Letterpress, with wood-engraved lettering. 225 × 136 mm. *John Johnson Collection.*

kind can be found on some of the largest posters of the late eighteenth century that have survived. In copper-plate printing, which catered almost exclusively for rather more refined small-scale jobbing work, the choice of lettering was only really limited by the skill and imagination of the engraver. It was copper-engraving that was used to reproduce the writing books of the period, and the scrolls and flourishes which the great writing masters indulged in are echoed in the decorative letters which grace the printed invitations, billheads, documents, and music titles of the late eighteenth and early nineteenth centuries [156].

In the course of the first two decades of the nineteenth century the whole pattern of jobbing printing changed with the introduction of large, bold, eye-catching types which were designed specially for the purposes of advertising [157]. It was one of those very sudden developments which take place from time to time and for which no really satisfactory reasons can be given. Conditions generally were certainly ripe for such a development: the growth of trade on a wide front had brought with it the need to advertise more competitively, and a new generation was becoming at least partially literate. In the printing and allied industries recent technical developments had prepared the way for the effective use of large display types: the new paper-making machines offered greater supplies of cheaper paper than had existed hitherto, and the new iron presses enabled the printer to produce large areas of dense type much more easily. But the actual origins of the type designs the founders produced to satisfy such needs are still obscure. The most likely explanation is that many of them were based on the letterforms of those craftsmen who had previously been responsible for street advertising – the signwriters. The typefounders may also have learned something from the wood-engravers who produced, from at least as early as 1808 onwards, some very inventive decorative letters in the form of logotypes for lottery bills [158] and the headings of popular broadsheets. Many of the new type designs introduced by the founders were not absolutely original, and precursors of most of the letterforms they produced can be found from many periods, and particularly in work such as mosaic, embroidery, and watermarks, where technical factors were paramount in determining the shapes of letters.

It is difficult to sort out the contributions of the various typefounders who produced display types in the first decades of the nineteenth century, and even more difficult to give very accurate dates for the introduction of particular designs. We rely almost entirely on the type specimens issued by the founders and, since they were only intended as ephemeral catalogues and were replaced by later issues as soon as they were out of date, they have now become very scarce. But the most important founders in the period 1800–32, when most of the basic designs made their first appearance, were Robert Thorne, William Thorowgood, William Caslon IV, Caslon & Catherwood, Bower & Bacon, and Vincent Figgins. By 1810 founders had begun to show specimens which included large, bold display letters, but the earliest specimen book to show a good range of these new designs was the *Specimen of printing types* which was issued from 1815 by Vincent Figgins (1766–1844). Figgins's specimen continued to be updated with new designs as they were produced, though the date on the original title-page was retained until 1821.

The first of the types to be designed specifically for the printer of posters and handbills was the fat face [159, 160]. It derives from the modern-face types of the latter part of the eighteenth century which had markedly contrasting thick and thin strokes and a pronounced vertical bias in the position of thick strokes in curved letters. But in the early nineteenth century the contrast in the proportion of the thick and thin strokes was increased to such an extent that the thick strokes sometimes grew to be more than a third of

Eleven Lines Pica. Cast in Mould & Matrixes.

MINE mane

V. FIGGINS.

159 Fat-face types. From Vincent Figgins, *Specimen of printing types*, 1815. Dr Berthold Wolpe.

2 LINE GREAT PRIMER ROMAN, No. 4.

The Fann Street Letter Foundry will be carried on with the same spirit and liberality as before, by W. THOROWGOOD. £1234567890.

160 Fat-face types. From *Thorowgood's new specimen of printing types*, 1821. St Bride Printing Library.

Five Lines Pica.

And be it further hereby enacted, ¶ ABCDEFGH

Figgins.

161 Fat-faced black letters. From Vincent Figgins, *Specimen of printing types*, 1815. Dr Berthold Wolpe.

FIVE LINES PICA, SHADED.

ABCDEFGH IJKLMNOP RSTUVWX.

V. FIGGINS.

162 Shaded types. From *Specimen of printing types*, 1815. Dr Berthold Wolpe.

FIVE LINES PICA ANTIQUE.

MANKIND

163 Egyptian types. From Vincent Figgins, *Specimen of printing types*, 1817. Oxford University Press.

164 The first sanserif type. Two lines English Egyptian of William Caslon IV. From Blake, Garnett & Co., *Specimen of printing types*, c. 1819. St Bride Printing Library.

31 J. Mosley 'The nymph and the grot: the revival of the sanserif letter', *Typographica*, no. 12, 1965, pp. 2–19

the height of the letters themselves. The development from the modern face was gradual, so that it is impossible to state when the fat face really came into being, but contemporary printers such as William Savage and T. C. Hansard regarded the typefounder Robert Thorne as the originator of the new fashion. No specimens produced by Thorne showing these designs have survived, but by 1810 William Caslon IV and Bower, Bacon & Bower had each issued a specimen book showing a range of fat faces, and by 1820 most of the other leading typefounders had followed suit. A variant of the fat face was the fattened version of the medieval black letter, which was a vigorous and dynamic transformation of the rather stilted Gothic lettering of the late eighteenth century. The first appearance of the fat-faced black letter in a type specimen book was in Vincent Figgins's specimen of 1815 [161].

At much the same time the typefounders brought out the first shaded letters, most of which were based on the forms and proportions of the fat face. These types were really imitation three-dimensional letters, and were drawn in outline with heavy black shadows to the right and on the undersides of the letters to make them appear to be standing in relief [162]. Figgins (1815) was again the first founder to produce a specimen showing these letters, but during the 1820s most founders produced their own versions to replace the elegant inline types of the previous decades.

Along with the fat face and its variants, the most popular of the early display letters was the Egyptian, or Antique as it was originally called. The main characteristics of the Egyptian were an almost uniform thickness of line throughout and thick slab serifs. Of all the letterforms of the period it was capable of giving the densest concentration of black ink while still remaining legible, and in its boldest and most extreme forms it is best imagined as a rectangular area of black from which small areas of white have been removed. The design appeared first as an upper-case roman fount in a version of Figgins's specimen which was probably issued in 1817 [163]. Four years later Figgins showed an italic version of it, and during the 1820s most of the leading typefounders included a range of Egyptians in their specimen books.

The other display types introduced in the period before 1832, the sanserif (which was originally called Egyptian or Antique by the typefounders), Tuscan, and Italian, were rather less widely used at the time. Since then, however, one of these designs, the sanserif, has emerged as the most influential innovation in nineteenth-century type design. As James Mosley has recently shown,[31] the sanserif was revived as a deliberate attempt to capture the spirit of the first Roman letterforms which, like their precursors in Attic Greece, had no serifs and were basically monoline. The use of the sanserif by sculptors and others as a neo-classical letterform dates from the close of the eighteenth century, and this is one instance where we can be virtually certain that type design was following a pattern already made popular in other fields. Though we tend to regard the sanserif as a modern letter, the product of the machine age, this was not the spirit which prevailed when it was originally cast in type. The first sanserif types made an assured, though modest, one-line appearance in William Caslon's specimen book of 1816, where they are rather confusingly given the name Egyptian.

W CASLON JUNR   LETTERFOUNDER

They appear again in the same form in the specimen book of Caslon's successor, Blake, Garnett, of about 1819 [164] but, as far as is known, no further types without serifs were issued until the early 1830s when Vincent Figgins and William Thorowgood issued specimens showing new versions under the two terms now used to describe such letters – sanserif (Figgins) and grotesque (Thorowgood).

165 Tuscan types. From Vincent Figgins, *Specimen of printing types*, 1817. *Oxford University Press.*

166 Italian types. From Caslon & Livermore, *Specimen of printing types*, 1825. *St Bride Printing Library.*

167 Slate gravestone from Wadebridge Parish Church, Cornwall, showing the influence of type designs. Though the stone records the dates of deaths in 1816 and 1820, it may have been carved later.

The Tuscan types of the nineteenth century relate to another Roman letterform, one which was brought to perfection in the fourth century and is still to be found in some of the catacombs and earliest churches in Rome. Its principal characteristics are curled and elongated serifs which grow vigorously from the letters and often begin to divide their stems in half. In nineteenth-century versions the faces of the letters were often decorated in a manner not unlike the contemporary style of working light against dark called Etruscan. It may well be the style of this decoration, therefore, which has given these types the name Tuscan, for the region of central Italy now known as Tuscany coincides approximately with ancient Etruria or Tuscia. The first Tuscan types appeared in the 1817 issue of Figgins's crucial specimen where they are called, perhaps significantly, 'ornamented' [165].

The last major kind of display type to be introduced in this early period was the Italian [166]. In a way its very introduction can be seen as evidence of the success of the new fashions and proof of the confidence of the typefounders to master all aspects of type design, for it is a mannerist letter in which the established conventions of lettering are deliberately overthrown. The roles of the thick and thin strokes are reversed so that the emphasis is on the horizontal rather than the vertical, and the triangular serifs are perversely joined to the stem at one of their points rather than along one side. The Italian was one of the few new display types which may not have originated in this country, and was probably used in France before its first recorded appearance in Caslon & Catherwood's specimen of 1821.

The new types brought out by the typefounders were not appreciated by all printers of the period, and Savage complained that the thicks of fat faces had been carried to an unnecessary extent and that 'some founts have been cut, totally unfit for Book printing, which have nevertheless been used for that purpose'.[32] All the same, they caught on with remarkable speed, even in the provinces, and are found in the work of printers from all parts of the country in the 1820s. In cases where printers could not afford to buy complete founts from founders they often cut their own versions of current designs for odd words or lines on posters. Something of the part played by the provincial printer in popularising the new letterforms can still be seen in places as far afield as Wales and Cornwall [167], where the sculptors of the first half of the nineteenth century began to adapt type designs for use on slate gravestones within a few years of their first recorded appearance in the typefounders' specimen books.

168 Thirteen-line Pica decorative letters, engraved on wood in the first half of the nineteenth century as patterns for display types. *Oxford University Press.*

Smaller sizes of display types were usually cast in metal from copper matrices in the traditional manner. Larger sizes were probably cast from sand moulds or stencil matrices, or were cut on wood. Wood letter-cutting emerged as a trade at much the same time as the new display letters began to appear, and thereafter grew steadily; but as each character had to be engraved individually by hand the output was very slow [168]. It is very likely, therefore, that some of the decorative types issued by the founders in the nineteenth century were cast from matrices made either by plunging wood-engravings into solidifying type metal or by striking them into soft metal in a cold state. The widespread use of large-scale wooden letters later in the

[32] W. Savage, *Practical hints on decorative printing* (London, 1822), p.74

70

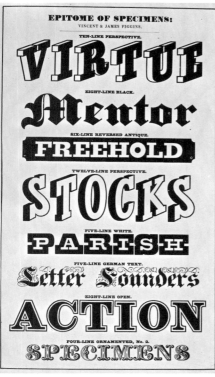

169 Specimen of fourteen-line wood letters showing the influence of the routing machine. From W. H. Bonnewell & Co., *Specimens of wood type, c.* 1870. *St Bride Printing Library.*

EPITOME OF SPECIMENS:
VINCENT & JAMES FIGGINS.

TEN-LINE PERSPECTIVE.
VIRTUE

EIGHT-LINE BLACK.
Mentor

SIX-LINE REVERSED ANTIQUE.
FREEHOLD

TWELVE-LINE PERSPECTIVE.
STOCKS

FIVE-LINE WHITE.
PARISH

FIVE-LINE GERMAN TEXT.
Letter Founders

EIGHT-LINE OPEN.
ACTION

FOUR-LINE ORNAMENTED, No. 2.
SPECIMENS

170 Display types of the 1840s. From V. & J. Figgins, *Epitome of specimens, c.* 1850. *St Bride Printing Library.*

171 A range of sizes of one of the sanserif type designs in V. & J. Figgins, *Epitome of specimens, c.* 1850. *St Bride Printing Library.*

172 A range of sizes of one of the sanserif type designs in W. Thorowgood & Co., *A general specimen of printing types,* 1848. *St Bride Printing Library.*

century was made possible by the invention in America in 1827 of the mechanical router. This machine facilitated the manufacture of large quantities of wooden type and, as the router tended to make certain curved shapes more easily than others, also had some influence on the actual forms of the letters [169].

Typefounders continued to introduce new kinds of letter designs throughout the nineteenth century, and the styles and moods of the types they evolved in response to the changing tastes of the time have been discussed critically by Nicolete Gray in her now classic book, *19th century ornamented types and title pages* (1938). In the 1830s a number of new varieties of types began to appear in the specimen books of the founders, including outline and three-dimensional letters, white letters on dark grounds, and some very powerful sets of ornamental letters with fruit, flowers, and pictures of farmyard implements and animals engraved on their faces [478, 479]. It was in the following decade, however, that the typefounders produced some of their most striking designs [170] and introduced elongated and rustic types as well as many elaborately decorated versions of earlier forms.

The sanserif, which had figured sporadically in the specimen books of the 1830s, really came of age in the late 1840s when both Figgins [171] and Thorowgood [172] issued a good range of sizes of two different designs. Other founders were encouraged to follow suit, and by 1860 the sanserif had become a standard feature in the specimen books and was beginning to be widely used by printers. The black letter also received a new lease of life in the 1840s and, having been virtually neglected since fat-faced versions were introduced in 1815, became the subject of renewed interest. In the following decades the traditional Gothic letters were transformed and enlivened according to the whims of Victorian designers, and a host of types appeared with fascinating and perverse forms under names with a variety of medieval connotations. These new gothicised letters had a significant influence on the design of roman letterforms, and on occasions it is extremely difficult to make any real distinction between the two categories. One other

FIVE-LINE PICA SANS-SERIF, No. 2.
BEDMINSTER

FOUR-LINE PICA SANS-SERIF, No. 2.
ROMAN EMPIRE

TWO-LINE GREAT PRIMER SANS-SERIF, No. 2.
BRITISH AND FRENCH CORRESPONDENT.

TWO-LINE PICA SANS-SERIF, No. 2.
BRITISH HOUSE OF COMMONS OPENED BY COMMISSION.

TWO-LINE BREVIER SANS-SERIF, No. 2.
HISTORY OF THE ROMAN EMPIRE IN NUMBERS CHINESE CUSTOMS AND CEREMONIES.

TWO-LINE NONPAREIL SANS-SERIF, No. 2.
JUST PUBLISHED THE THIRD EDITION PRICE NINEPENCE, MEMORIALS OF THE REFORMATION IN EUROPE.

TWO-LINE PEARL SANS-SERIF, No. 2.
CHARNOCK'S HARMONY OF HISTORY WITH PROPHECY IN SIX NUMBERS, BROUGHAM ON THE INSTINCT AND PLEASURES OF SCIENCE.

BREVIER SANS-SERIF, No. 2.
THIRD EDITION OF CARPENTER'S INTRODUCTION TO THE STUDY OF THE SCRIPTURES, SUGGESTIVE HINTS TOWARDS IMPROVED SECULAR INSTRUCTION BY DAWES.

N-SPARIL SANS-SERIF, No. 1
WISEMAN ON THE CONNEXION OF SCIENCE AND RELIGION, HANDSOMELY BOUND IN FOURTEEN VOLUMES.
ROBERTSON'S HISTORY OF THE TRANSMISSION OF ANCIENT BOOKS TO MODERN TIMES.

The whole of these Founts are complete with Figures.

FOURTEEN LINES GROTESQUE
MINERS

SEVEN LINES GROTESQUE
BRIDGENORTH communion

FIVE LINES GROTESQUE
NORTHUMBERLAND £2134507.

THOROWGOOD & Co. LONDON.

DOUBLE PICA CLARENDON.

Quousque tandem abutere Catilina, patientia nostra? quamdiu nos etiam furor iste tuus eludet? quem ad finem sese effrenata jactabit audacia? nihilne te nocturnum præsidium palatii, nihile urbis vigiliæ, nihil timor populi, nihil consnesus bonorum omnium, nihil hic munitissimus habendi senatus locus, nihil horum ora vultusque moverunt? patere tua consilia non sentis? constricta jam omnium horum conscientia teneri conjurati-

SALES BY PUBLIC AUCTION.

ABCDEFGHIJKLMNOPQRSTUVWXYZÆŒ

£1234567890

173 Clarendon types. From W. Thorowgood & Co., *A general specimen of printing types*, 1848. *St Bride Printing Library.*

174 Nineteenth-century copies of medieval and other inscriptions. From an album of alphabets and illuminations arranged in 1872 by Frederick Hendriks from his own collection and those of Dawson Turner and Thomas Willement. Manuscript. Page size 365 × 260 mm.

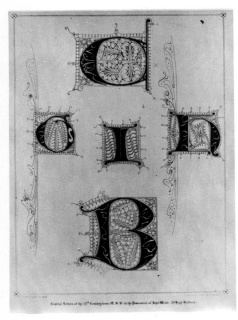

175 John Weale, capital letters of the 14th century, from his *Monograms, old architectural ornament, sacred illustrations, borders and alphabets; collected on the continent and in England.* Lithograph in three colours, drawn by F. Bedford and printed by Standidge & Co. 260 × 187 mm.

important kind of letter was introduced in the 1840s. This was the Ionic or Clarendon [173], which was registered in 1845 by Besley, successor to Thorne and Thorowgood at the Fann Street Foundry in London. The Clarendon is similar to the Egyptian letter, but differs from it by having clearly defined thick and thin strokes and slab serifs which are bracketed, that is, joined to the stem of the letter by curves.

The wealth of invention displayed by the designers and craftsmen who produced these types in the nineteenth century derived partly from the antiquarian, archaeological, and palaeographical activities of the period. Interest in lettering and inscriptions from the past was aroused in England in the second half of the eighteenth century in two main ways – by the excavation of classical sites at Herculaneum and Rome, and by the growing fashion for things Gothic. Later on, the growth of travel generally and the discoveries made by explorers and archaeologists in many parts of the world drew attention to unfamiliar and 'exotic' languages. This interest was greatly stimulated by the discovery of the Rosetta Stone in the Nile Delta in 1799 and by the subsequent deciphering of its early Egyptian inscription by Champollion. Attention at first centred on the textual aspects of inscriptions, but in order to publish even the texts of hitherto unknown or rarely-recorded languages the letters had first to be engraved or lithographed. Facsimiles of such texts began to be published in the early nineteenth century and interest was gradually awakened in the actual appearance of the letters and other symbols used. Antiquarians made copies of manuscripts and drawings and rubbings of inscriptions they had found [174] and began writing

to the journals about them; and in the 1840s Owen Jones, Henry Shaw, John Weale, and Noel Humphries in England, and others abroad, published selections of alphabets, ornamental letters, and manuscript pages [175]. The exact connection between this antiquarian interest in lettering and the actual letterforms which were designed in the same period has yet to be established; but the use of the names Antique and Egyptian, which were given to both the early sanserif and slab serif types, suggests a positive link with archaeological studies. The practice of engraving decorative initial letters on wood, which was revived in book design in the 1820s and lasted throughout the century, may likewise be seen as a revival of an earlier idiom.

The enormous variety of new display letters introduced by the typefounders, and the technical ingenuity with which they disguised the fact that their

176 The Lord's Prayer, designed by Harttwieg. Printed lithographically and published at Friedel's Establishment, London, 1837.
345 × 251 mm. *John Johnson Collection.*

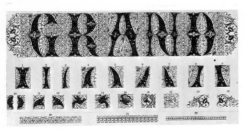

177 Type units for making ornamented letters. From V. & J. Figgins, *Epitome of specimens*, c. 1850. Height of large letters 26 mm. *St Bride Printing Library.*

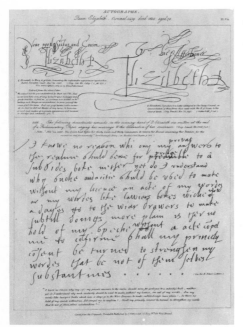

178 Joseph Netherclift, *Autograph letters from the correspondence of illustrious and distinguished women of Great Britain*, 1838. Lithographed plate showing autographs of Queen Elizabeth I, copied from originals and printed by Netherclift. 300 × 210 mm.

179 Detail of lithographed lettering on the title-page of Samuel Prout, *Illustrations of the Rhine*, 1822-6. 70 × 87 mm. *Victoria & Albert Museum.*

180 Music cover of the 1860s. Lithograph, printed in red, green, and black. 347 × 255 mm.

181 Music cover, c. 1895. Lithograph, printed in black and two shades of stone. 330 × 245 mm.

types were manufactured as individual units [177], were partly the result of competition with the lithographic writer and printer [176]. There were few technical restrictions on the kinds of letters which could be drawn on the lithographic stone: there was no need to conform to straight parallel lines; positive and negative marks could be made equally easily; letters could be expanded, condensed, or distorted to suit the needs of the occasion; and, perhaps most important, different letterforms could be created for every job.

England lagged behind the continent in the commercial exploitation of lithography in the first half of the nineteenth century, but by 1820 specialists were emerging in lithographic writing even in this country. One of the most successful of these was Joseph Netherclift who was in his time an acknowledged expert in the reproduction of written texts by lithography. He specialised in the copying of historical documents and autographs, and in the second quarter of the nineteenth century published many facsimiles of this kind with the help of a transparent transfer paper which he had invented [178]. Professional letterers were originally employed in lithography to letter the titles and imprints on pictorial lithographs and to produce title-page and wrapper designs for collections of plates, but they soon began to be used for a range of jobbing printing as well, including maps, plans, circulars, and stationery. By about 1830 most of the larger lithographic printers can be assumed to have employed specialists to do this kind of work. The earliest lithographic letterers merely copied the current styles of the copper-plate engraver [179], but they soon began to invent letters which exploited the possibilities of their own process, and some of the designs they evolved were later copied by the typefounders. Most of the major publications which brought medieval manuscripts to the notice of the public were produced by lithography because it was the most convenient process both for copying documents and for colour reproduction. The historical and technical influences on the design of mid-nineteenth century letterforms are thus curiously linked.

By 1840 lithographers had evolved their own approach to lettering. In letter-press printing type and image were usually conceived and manufactured separately, but in lithography they were produced together and were often inextricably linked. Examples of this can be seen on the title-pages of illustrated books and on numerous covers to popular pieces of music, where freely-drawn letters are often combined with pictures and decorations [180, 181]. By the middle of the century full-colour lithography was a commercial proposition, and this made it even more suitable for jobs needing striking

letterforms. This was the first real challenge that letterpress printing had faced and, in answer to purpose-drawn lithographic letters, the typefounders were obliged to produce a wide and ever-changing range of letterforms which could match the variety, freedom, and invention of the lithographic draughtsman. In response to the challenge of colour the manufacturers of wooden letters brought out designs in which the individual letters were made in two, three, or even four parts to be inked and printed separately in different colours [99, 107].

The Victorian conception of lettering was a very elastic one, and letterforms were often elaborated and distorted with abandon either for decorative purposes or in order to create an overall mood. Legibility, if it was considered at all, was usually of minor importance, and in some examples of the period lettering is so effectively integrated with the total design that it is hardly even noticed. The same concern for overall effect links the very ornate high Victorian style with the more organic and sinuous letters of Art Nouveau. This later style began with a flourish in printing in 1883 with the remarkable title-page of A. H. Mackmurdo's *Wren's city churches*; but thereafter, though the style left its mark on the decorative designs of Walter Crane and others, and on the lettering of Lewis F. Day [182], its influence on type design was hardly felt at all in this country.

Towards the end of the nineteenth century this fertility of imagination in lettering began to fade, and in the first decade of the twentieth century there developed a strong puritanical reaction to the excesses of the letter designs of the previous age. Two related influences were brought to bear which had a profound effect on the subsequent development of lettering in this country. The first of these to make itself felt was a revival of interest in classical Roman inscriptions, and particularly the now well-known inscription on the base of Trajan's column in Rome. A cast of this inscription had existed in the Victoria and Albert Museum since 1864 [183], but it seems to have attracted no great attention until the calligrapher and letter designer Edward Johnston (1872–1944) reproduced photographs from it in his *Writing & illuminating & lettering* (1906). The craft of letter-cutting was also revived in this period, and Johnston's pupil, Eric Gill, who was greatly influenced by the Trajan model, provided a stone-cut inscription which Johnston reproduced in his book. Thereafter, the influence of the Trajan model was paramount and, largely because of the availability of the cast in the Victoria and Albert Museum, reproductions and reconstructions of it have since been published in numerous handbooks on lettering. From the wide range of letterforms produced by the ancient Romans one version only was selected, and its admittedly fine proportions and forms were soon established as inviolable canons. These still exert a profound influence on lettering of all kinds, regardless of purpose or means of production, and have acted as a powerful brake on the development of new letterforms.

The other important influence on the design of letters in England this century has been the sanserif, and it was Johnston again who was responsible for its popularity. In 1913 Frank Pick, the enterprising commercial manager of the London Underground Railway, commissioned Johnston and Gill to design an alphabet for use on signs and publicity. The instructions were to produce a design which would have 'the bold simplicity of the authentic lettering of the finest periods and yet belong unmistakably to the XX century'.[33] In fact, Gill took no part in the enterprise, but Johnston began work late in 1915 and by the middle of 1916 the first signs began to appear in the new letterforms. Johnston's main concern was to design simple, legible letters, and he did so by drawing them with the help of compass and rule and by stripping them of all inessentials. He fulfilled his brief to the letter: in proportion and many other features both the upper- and lower-

182 Lewis F. Day, *Alphabets old & new*, 1898. Plate showing playful treatment of 'Modern capitals derived from Gothic'. Each panel 136 × 88 mm.

183 Part of a plaster cast of the inscription on Trajan's column, Rome, AD 114. *Victoria & Albert Museum.*

[33] Quoted P. Johnston, *Edward Johnston* (London, 1959), p.199

case alphabets relate to traditional forms, but the geometry of the letters, the constant thickness of line, and the lack of serifs all help to convey something of the spirit of the machine age [184, 185]. Johnston's letters were not only modern in conception, and therefore popular, but they were also easily copied. For these reasons, and because of their unmistakable quality, they have had an enormous influence on the design of both drawn lettering and printing types. Johnston's letters were not originally designed as types, though they were produced as such in 1916, but his pupil Gill, who owed much to his influence, produced a range of sanserif types which swept the country in the 1930s.

184,185 Edward Johnston, original drawings for the sanserif alphabets designed for the London Underground, 1916. *Victoria & Albert Museum.*

The Trajan inscription and Johnston's sanserif letters for the Underground, though admirable in themselves, have nevertheless had an inhibiting effect on the development of lettering in this country, and very little has been produced so far this century in the field of display lettering to compare with the fertile designs of the nineteenth century. The specimens of the wood-letter manufacturers show a depressing range of emasculated nineteenth-century designs and an abundance of condensed sanserifs, and the type-founders have fared little better in the display types they have produced. A number of designers who worked mainly in the inter-war years, amongst them Edward Bawden, Barnett Freedman [186], Ashley Havinden, McKnight Kauffer, W. G. Raffé, and Eric Ravilious [187], produced drawn lettering for their own posters and jacket designs; but, with the exception of Gill, who designed a range of display types in the 1930s based on his original sanserif design, and Berthold Wolpe, whose Albertus type (1935–40) [188] has been popular over a long period, the letter-cutters and calligraphers of this century have not been much involved with the design of display types.

186 Barnett Freedman, twelve of a set of initial letters called Baynard Claudia designed for the Baynard Press. From *Signature*, no. 1, November 1935.

187 Eric Ravilious, cover of a BBC talks pamphlet, *British art*, 1934. Letterpress, printed by the Kynoch Press, Birmingham. 247 × 184 mm.

ALBERTUS

188 Albertus, designed for the Monotype Corporation by Berthold Wolpe, 1935–40.

189 Advertisement for the series of Shell Guides. From *Typography*, no. 6, 1938. Letterpress. 279 × 228 mm.

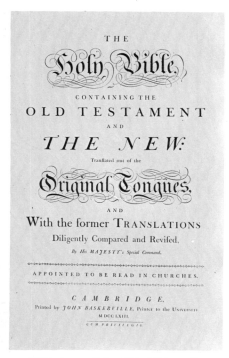

190 Title-page of the *Holy Bible*, 1763, printed by John Baskerville from types designed by himself. 492 × 315 mm. *Reading University Library*.

Two Lines Great Primer, No. 1. NEW.

Quousque tandem abutere, Catilina, patientia nostra? quamdiu nos etiam furor iste tuus eludet? quem ad finem sese effrenata jactabit audacia? nihilne te nocturnum præ ABCDEFGHIJKLMNOPQRST UVWXYZÆŒABCDEFGHIJKLM NOPQRSTUVWXYZÆŒ£1234567890

191 Robert Thorne's modern face. From his specimen book of 1803 in the *St Bride Printing Library*.

The paucity of early twentieth-century display types was implicitly acknowledged in the 1930s by a revival of interest in the type designs of the nineteenth century. This was sparked off by Frederick Horn in an article in *Penrose's Annual* of 1934, and soon afterwards found expression in a number of ways – in the Shell Guides of John Betjeman, in the journal *Typography* (1936–9) edited by Robert Harling [189], in Nicolete Gray's book, *19th century ornamented types and title pages* (1938), and in a number of pale reflections of nineteenth-century designs which were issued by the founders. After the Second World War the fashion was taken up again in connection with the Festival of Britain in 1951. Since then, rather more full-blooded revivals of nineteenth-century types have appeared, and the fashion is by no means exhausted yet. Alphabet books providing liberal selections from old specimens are still widely used in advertising agencies and television studios; but there are signs that a movement that began by encouraging mere pastiche is now leading to the design of modern equivalents of the display letters of the past.

A study of the development of types in composition sizes for use in books and for text setting generally reveals a contrary pattern, and in this field the nineteenth century was a particularly lean period as far as quality is concerned. In the last quarter of the previous century the general standard of book types in Britain was remarkably high, largely because of the influence of William Caslon and John Baskerville who worked earlier in the century. The types which Caslon began designing in the 1720s stemmed directly from contemporary Dutch models, which in turn could trace their ancestry back through France in the sixteenth century to the types produced by Jenson and Aldus in Venice in the fifteenth century. Baskerville, on the other hand, who was trained as a writing master, approached the design of types from a rather different standpoint. He based his types more on the style of writing which prevailed in the eighteenth century and introduced designs which show more regular proportions and details and a greater tendency for the stress of the thick strokes to be upright [190]. Baskerville's types were first shown in 1754 and in his lifetime were used only by his press, but their influence spread rapidly and at the time of his death in 1775 were already being copied. Before the end of the century a number of such types, strongly influenced by Baskerville's designs, were available from the foundries of Robert Martin, William Martin, Alexander Wilson, Fry, Figgins, and William Caslon III.

The next stage in the development of book types was the accentuation of these new features and the evolution of what is now called the modern face, which is characterised by vertical stress, abrupt and exaggerated modelling of the thick strokes, and sharply defined serifs. The modern face was the direct result of an attempt to translate into type the style of lettering popularised by the writing masters, and it was made feasible by improvements in the manufacture of paper and refinements in the construction of the printing press. The first fully-formed modern-face types are found in France, but by 1788 Richard Austin had cut for John Bell of the British Letter Foundry a type which exhibited some of the features of the modern face. The first fully-developed modern-face types in this country are usually credited to Robert Thorne who produced a specimen which included some examples in 1803 [191]. Thereafter, the fashion caught on quickly, and what was to be the prevailing style of type design throughout the nineteenth century was soon firmly established. The older transitional types, though still preferred by the printer Hansard and other purists, were melted down in the interests of fashion and replaced by the new modern-face types.

One innovation which gained ground as type designs were changing at the turn of the eighteenth and nineteenth centuries was the dropping of the

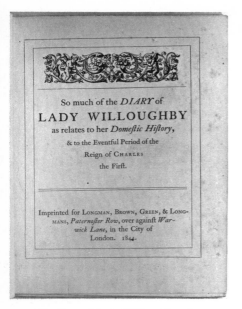

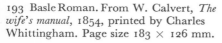

192 *The diary of Lady Willoughby*, 1844.
Set throughout in Caslon and printed by
Charles Whittingham. Page size 210 × 165
mm.

long ʃ – the only lasting change to be made during the past 200 years in
the actual range of letters used. The enterprising publisher John Bell first
dispensed with it as a regular practice in his edition of *Shakespere* published
in 1785, and over the next two years his own newspapers the *English Chronicle*
and the *World* also made the change to the short s. In 1803 *The Times*
followed suit, and in 1808 the long ʃ began to be dropped from the pages
of even the conservative *Gentleman's Magazine*.

The fashion for modern-face types, which gave a rather mean look to the
page, continued unchecked until 1840. In that year Charles Whittingham
the younger (1795–1876) began to introduce Caslon capitals on the title-
pages of some of the books he printed at the Chiswick Press for the publisher
Pickering, and by 1844 he had produced an edition of *The diary of Lady
Willoughby* which was printed throughout in Caslon [192]. Other printers
followed suit in the 1840s and 1850s, though the use of Caslon tended to be
limited to the printing of jobs with a rather special flavour, such as devotional books, and probably did not affect routine commercial work at all.
The transitional types of the late eighteenth century were also revived in the
1850s by the Figgins foundry and by the Camden Press, which the Dalziel
brothers founded for printing the rather special books they illustrated with
their own wood-engravings. In 1857 the Caslon foundry revived the Caslon
types which had been removed from its specimens in 1805. These were the
first conscious revivals of older types in the history of printing and they
parallel the revival of interest in medieval lettering which occurred at much
the same time. In the early 1850s Whittingham went a stage further and used
a type known as Basle Roman, which was cut specially for him, complete
with a long ʃ, in imitation of early types [193]. The actual sources for these
designs were the types of the early sixteenth-century Basle printer, Johann
Froben, though in fact they show many characteristics of fifteenth-century
types.

Such revivals and imitations of earlier designs, though limited to a very small
and special class of work, are sufficient to indicate the beginnings of a shift
away from modern-face types. In order to meet the new demand for old-face
types the Edinburgh foundry of Miller & Richard brought out a compro-
mise design called Old Style, which it showed in a range of eight sizes in a

193 Basle Roman. From W. Calvert, *The
wife's manual*, 1854, printed by Charles
Whittingham. Page size 183 × 126 mm.

194 Miller & Richard's, Great Primer
Old Style types. From their *Specimens of
Old Style type*, Edinburgh, 1860. *St Bride
Printing Library*.

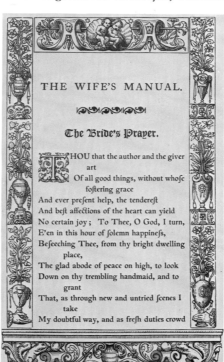

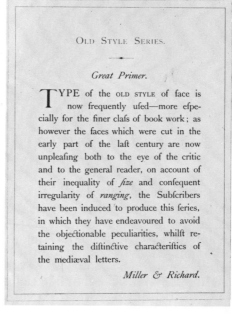

specimen of 1860 [194]. Old Style was a modernised and regularised adaptation of old-face types; the bracketed serifs and gradual transition from thick to thin strokes belonged to the old-face tradition, though the vertical direction of thick strokes found in modern-face types was retained. Despite its hybrid nature, Old Style was a commercial success and began to be imitated by other founders. By 1870 it was being widely used, even for the setting of newspapers. Between them, modern-face and old-style designs accounted for most of the text setting in book and jobbing printing in the last quarter of the nineteenth century, and they were the first two designs to be produced in England for use on 'Monotype' machines in 1900.

A more scholarly and devoted return to early type designs was made at the beginning of the last decade of the nineteenth century by William Morris (1834–96). In an attempt to revive the spirit and standard of craftsmanship of the past Morris studied historical examples, and when he came to design his own types he turned to the great masters of fifteenth-century printing. Morris's most important type design, the Golden Type [195], made its first appearance in 1891, and was produced as a result of studying the roman types of Renaissance printers and making modifications to them by working on top of photographic enlargements [196]. Morris was followed by others who worked in the same spirit, and in the first decade of the twentieth century in particular many designs were cut for the private presses, nearly all of which were inspired by the great figures of Italian printing. Like Morris's, however, such types were designed and cut for printing by hand on hand-made paper, and their influence on the printing trade generally was negligible.

An ideal opportunity to reconsider the types used for text setting came with the introduction of hot-metal composing machines. In the first instance the designs of founders' types in common use were merely adapted for use on the new machines, but with the general acceptance of mechanical composition in the early twentieth century numerous specially designed faces began to be issued. The method of casting complete lines of type on Linotype and Intertype machines imposes considerable limitations on type design, especially in italic founts, and the contributions made by these companies to type design in this country have in the main been limited to newspaper types [197]. The 'Monotype' machine, which casts individual types, is rather more flexible, and in this century the Monotype Corporation has taken over from the type founders the role of principal patron and promoter of new type designs.

The first notable types to be produced for 'Monotype' machines were Imprint (1912), an old-face design specially produced to the specification of J. H. Mason and Gerard Meynell for their journal *The Imprint* (1913),

195 William Morris's Golden Type. From his edition of Caxton's *The golden legend*, 1892.

196 Detail of a photograph, probably from Aretino's *Historia Fiorentina*, 1476, used by William Morris in connection with the designing of his Golden Type. From a collection of enlarged photographs of early types collected by William Morris [1891]. *St Bride Printing Library.*

197 Linotype news founts. From *Linotype news and book type founts*, c. 1895. *St Bride Printing Library.*

Imprint 101 ABCDefghijkl

Plantin 110 ABCDefghijklm

198

Garamond 156 ABCDefghijkl

Baskerville 169 ABCDefghijkl

Blado 119 ABCDefghijklm

Poliphilus 170 ABCDefghijklm

Fournier 185 ABCDefghijklm

Bembo 270 ABCDefghijklmn

Bell 341 ABCDefghijklm

Walbaum 574 ABCDefghijkl

Ehrhardt 453 ABCDefghijklm

199 A selection of types issued by the Monotype Corporation between 1922 and 1937.

Perpetua 239

abcdefghijklmnopqrstuvwxyz

ABCDEFGHIJKLMNOPQRST

ABCDEFGHIJKLMNOPQRSTUV

abcdefghijklmnopqrstuvwxyz

200

TimesNewRoman327

abcdefghijklmnopqrstuvwxyz

ABCDEFGHIJKLMNOPQ

ABCDEFGHIJKLMNOPQR

abcdefghijklmnopqrstuvwxyz

201

and Plantin (1913), a most successful reinterpretation of a sixteenth-century type [198]. But the company's real contribution to type design dates from 1922 when it appointed the distinguished scholar and typographer Stanley Morison as typographical adviser and initiated an ambitious scheme of revivals of the most famous types of the past. Garamond (1922), Baskerville (1923), Blado (1923), Poliphilus (1923), Fournier (1925), Bembo (1929), Bell (1932), Walbaum (1933), and Ehrhardt (1937), which the Monotype Corporation issued between the wars, were the fruits of Morison's enthusiasm for printing history [199]. They are based on some of the finest types chosen from a number of periods and countries but, unlike some of the types revived by the private presses, were carefully adapted to the requirements of modern printing machinery.

The scholarly interest which Stanley Morison, Oliver Simon, Francis Meynell, and others took in printing history in this period found an outlet in the typographic journals *The Fleuron* (1923–30) and *Signature* (1935–40), and had a profound effect on printing and type design in the inter-war years.

In addition to its programme of reviving historic types, the Monotype Corporation was also responsible for commissioning new types from eminent letter designers. Eric Gill (1882–1940), the best-known English letter-cutter of this century, designed a number of book types for founders and printers between the wars, most of which kept something of the quality of his stone-cut letters. The most popular of Gill's seriffed type designs was his Perpetua [200], which was commissioned by the Monotype Corporation in 1927 and first issued in 1930. Every effort was made to retain the chiselled quality of Gill's inscriptional lettering, and the types depart considerably from the traditional calligraphic forms in some of their details. Perpetua was very widely used for some twenty years and still finds a place in certain 'prestige' printing, though it now tends to look somewhat precious and idiosyncratic.

A less personal and therefore more timeless type design is Times New Roman [201]. This was produced under the supervision of Stanley Morison for use by *The Times*, and is perhaps the most significant seriffed type to be designed this century. The requirements were absolutely clear: a good looking type which gave maximum legibility with the minimum waste of space, and which would print well under rigorous newspaper conditions. The designs of the types were prepared only after elaborate technical and optical researches, and were completed in 1930. The experimental founts were made by the Monotype Corporation and the final forms were produced for use on Linotype machines, and *The Times* went to print in the new face for the first time on 3 October 1932. The main features of Times New Roman are short ascenders and descenders, unusually narrow letters, and rather strong modelling; but like so many of the best types it owes its quality to subtle characteristics which cannot easily be described in words. For a year the type remained the exclusive property of *The Times*, but in October 1933 it was released to the trade. The first quality book to appear in Times New Roman was printed by the Nonesuch Press in 1934, and three years later it was adopted by Penguin Books for the printing of paperback books. It gained ground during the war, when the regulations governing the use of paper emphasised its value as a space-saver, and since then it has become one of the most valuable all-purpose types in the printer's arsenal.

In Britain, as in Europe and America, one of the most significant trends in type design this century has been the increasing popularity of the sanserif. As we have seen, the sanserif was originally developed in the early nineteenth century as an upper-case display type, and only later in the century did it become available with a lower-case alphabet and in small sizes for text composition. By 1900, however, the value of sanserif types had been firmly established, and this was fully realised by the Monotype Corporation which brought out a number of sanserif founts for its new composing machines in the first decade of the twentieth century. But in style and spirit these types still belonged to the nineteenth-century tradition and, after the First World War, they must have begun to look rather old-fashioned compared with the new letterforms of Edward Johnston which were beginning to be used for new signs and printing by the London Underground. Johnston's alphabets were extremely influential; they mark the real birth of the new sanserif movement in this country and were not without influence on a parallel movement in Germany. Though originally intended for use on signs, Johnston's sanserif was very soon produced as type and was in use in this form by 1916. It had begun to create a taste for a new kind of lettering among a few discerning people but, since the London Underground had exclusive rights to its use, it could not be produced to satisfy any general demand.

Stanley Morison's choice of Eric Gill to design a sanserif type for the Monotype Corporation ten years later seems in retrospect to have been inevitable. Gill was the foremost letter-cutter of his age and was already engaged in designing Perpetua for the Monotype Corporation; he had joined with Johnston in the initial discussions about the London Underground lettering, and had himself worked on a number of signposting schemes which used sanserif letters unmistakably related to the Johnston pattern. Morison was prompted to commission a sanserif type from Gill after seeing an example

202 A display of 'Monotype' Gill Sans. From the *Monotype Recorder*, vol. 34, no. 4, Winter 1935-6. Page size 282 × 215 mm.

of sanserif lettering which he had painted on a facia board in 1926 for Douglas Cleverdon's bookshop in Bristol. Gill began work on the drawings for the type in the summer of 1927. There was no restrictive brief, but what emerged was a type face closely related to Johnston's in weight, proportion, and spirit [202]. Gill's sanserif was even more rationally conceived than Johnston's, and he dispensed with some of the traces of traditional calligraphy that remained in Johnston's design, such as the curling terminal of the lower-case l.

Monotype Gill Sans made its first appearance in 1928, and very soon afterwards its commercial success was ensured when it was chosen by the newly appointed publicity manager of the London and North Eastern Railway as the basis for establishing a corporate identity in timetables, notices, brochures, and other printed matter, and on station signs as well. It was also taken up by the small *avant-garde* movement in English typography and was used for the setting of the very modern-looking catalogue which was produced for Greenly's second exhibition of modern advertising in 1930 [331–334], and for the brochure published in connection with an exhibition of the typographical work of Jan Tschichold in 1935 [328, 329]. What began as an experimental venture soon became the stock-in-trade of the printer, and during the following ten years Gill adapted his basic design to satisfy the demands of printers and designers for related types in a variety of weights and in condensed, expanded, and shaded forms. New designs continued to appear even after Gill's death in 1940. In Gill's own day his sanserif was very popular for display work in advertising and also in jobbing printing, where the very clear numerals made it particularly valuable for tabular work. The use of any sanserif for the setting of text in journals and books would not have been seriously countenanced at the time, and Gill Sans was no exception, but it has weathered the trough of disfavour which usually follows a period of great success to emerge in recent years as one of the best sanserif types for the setting of text and tabular work in small sizes.

Gill Sans was not without competition from other sanserif types in the 1930s, and some of the modern German types, Erbar (1922–30), Kabel (1927–9) [203], and Futura (1927–30), began to be used by some of the more enterprising typographers and advertising agencies. The Monotype Corporation's own Grotesque series 215 and 216 (1926) and series 126 (1927) [204] were also brought out shortly before Gill Sans. Broadly speaking, however, the name Gill Sans was synonymous with sanserif in the mind of the ordinary British printer for something like a quarter of a century. Only after the Second World War did it begin to be ousted by Grotesque series 215 and 216 and, more recently, by types of continental origin such as Venus, Standard, Folio, Helvetica, and Univers.

One innovation in type design this century, and one which has particularly affected sanserif types, has been the introduction of a range of weights and styles within a single family of types designed for text composition. In the nineteenth century it was common practice for founders to produce composition types in a limited number of different styles or weights. This practice was taken a stage further in the early years of this century with the rather miserable Cheltenham family of types [205] which included different weights of the same basic design and a range of expanded, compressed, inline, outline, and shaded versions. Gill Sans can claim to have sired the largest family of this kind and has appeared in a range of over twenty related designs. Between 1931 and 1937 the Dutch type designer Jan van Krimpen created a rather more cosmopolitan kind of type family which included related weights of both seriffed and sanserif founts as well as a condensed version, a script, and a Greek fount. Most sanserif types of this century now appear in families and many traditional seriffed types have been supplied with bold versions.

203 Kabel, designed by Rudolf Koch. From the cover of a specimen book of Kabel light issued by the Klingspor Foundry, Offenbach, 1927. *Ralph Beyer Esq.*

Grotesque 215 ABCDefghijk

Grotesque 216 ABCDefghi

Grotesque 126 ABCDefghijkl

204

Cheltenham Oldstyle
Cheltenham Wide
Cheltenham Italic
Cheltenham Oldstyle Condensed
Cheltenham Medium
Cheltenham Medium Italic
Chelt. Medium Expanded
Cheltenham Medium Condensed
Cheltenham Bold
Cheltenham Bold Italic
Chelt. Bold Extended
Cheltenham Extrabold
Cheltenham Bold Condensed
Cheltenham Bold Condensed Italic
Cheltenham Bold Extra Condensed
CHELTENHAM BOLD EXTRA COND. TITLE
Chelt. Inline Extended
Cheltenham Inline
Chelt. Inline Extra Cond.
Cheltenham Bold Outline
Cheltenham Bold Shaded
Chelt. Bold Italic Shaded
Chelt. Extrabold Shaded

205 The Cheltenham type family of twenty-three varieties.

Univers light 685 ABCDefghijklm

Univers medium 689 ABCDefghij

Univers bold 693 ABCDefghij

Univers extra bold 696 ABCde

Univers medium 689 ABCDefghij

Medium Expanded 688

Medium Condensed 690 ABCDefghijklm

Medium Extra Condensed 691 ABCDefghijklm

206 'Monotype' Univers shown in a range of weights and widths.

IBM Univers light ABCDEfghijklmn

IBM Univers medium ABCDEfghijk

IBM Univers bold ABCDEfghijklmn

207 IBM Univers, designed for the 72 Selectric Composer.

What appears at present to be the ultimate in this search for a comprehensive type family is Univers, designed by Adrian Frutiger of Paris. From the outset Univers was conceived as a complete family of twenty-one variants; each size of type was to exist in a range of weights, and each weight in a series of different widths [206]. Univers was commissioned by the French founders Deberny & Peignot for use on the Lumitype photosetting machine, and work began on the designs in 1952. Univers has since been adapted for use on both 'Monotype' and 'Monophoto' machines and is also available as cast type from Deberny & Peignot and American Typefounders. In addition, Frutiger has made substantial adaptations to bring Univers in line with the more limited range of character widths of the typewriter and a version of it is available for use on the IBM 72 Selectric composing machine [207]. Since its introduction to this country in 1961 the success of Univers has been rapid. Despite the initial reluctance of the printing trade to commit itself to the considerable capital cost, and the justifiable criticism of certain features of its design, it has already become as much the bread-and-butter sanserif type as Gill Sans was in earlier decades.

In the course of this century research into problems relating to the legibility of letterforms and types has had a growing influence on their design. Interest in problems of this kind seems first to have been aroused on a broad front in the 1880s and has grown steadily since the American psychologist Miles Tinker began publishing the results of his researches into reading in the late 1920s. In recent years the attention of letter designers and typographers has been drawn to the importance of experimental work, and the new signs on roads and at railway stations and air terminals are the fruits of such optical research. In type design Stanley Morison led the way by inviting Sir William Lister to act as ophthalmic adviser in the designing of Times New Roman. Since then some of the findings of perception psychologists have been borne in mind by typographers, and the greater use of the lower-case alphabet in recent decades must partly be seen as a response to such research.

In the 1920s in Germany strong arguments were advanced for the use of a single alphabet, on the grounds that it was unnecessary to have both upper- and lower-case forms when one alone would suffice. Special alphabets were designed on the continent between the wars, some of them basically lower-case [208], others combining features of both upper- and lower-case letters [209], but even where no special single-alphabet form was used typographers often dispensed with upper-case letters. This practice found some favour in England in the late 1920s and early 1930s, when *avant-garde* typographers began to stop using capitals for the beginnings of proper nouns. Though this proved to be only a passing fashion, based essentially on style, it has had the long-term effect of reducing the excessive and unthinking use of capital letters for the beginnings of words and of undermining the view that setting words in capitals gives them importance. The concept of a single alphabet has come to the fore again in recent years in

208 Herbert Bayer, study for his universal alphabet, 1927. 445 × 645 mm.

209 A. M. Cassandre, Peignot, issued by Deberny & Peignot in 1937. From a review in *Printing Review*, no. 27, Summer 1938.

abcdefghi jklmnopqr stuvwxyz a dd

P E I G N O T

The engraved letters of the inscription cutter form the basis of this radical essay in letter-formation

It will be noted that a certain lower-case quality appears to persist in the Peignot fount, i. e. the presence of ascenders and descenders. They are preserved in the Peignot type because, in the act of reading, the eye does not regard separate letters but the silhouette of the complete word or even group of words. Hence, ascenders and descenders are of great use as sighting points to the eye. The extension of the perpendicular in such letters as b,

83

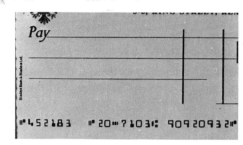

210 Phonetic printing types. From *A general specimen of printing types issued by Isaac Pitman*, Bath, 1850. *Reading University Library*.

211 The initial teaching alphabet, devised by Sir James Pitman and first introduced into British schools in 1961. Specimen setting from J. Downing, *The initial teaching alphabet explained and illustrated* 2nd ed., 1964.

212 E13B, developed for the American Bankers Association in 1958. Detail of a Barclays Bank cheque, with the numbers printed in magnetic ink.

213 OCR-B, designed by Adrian Frutiger for the European Computer Manufacturers Association for both optical and machine reading.

connection with computers, which at present are usually made to 'communicate' with man by means of a single alphabet comprising capital letters and other symbols.

New kinds of symbols have also been developed in order to find a closer parallel between the written and spoken forms of English than is possible using the traditional Roman alphabet. Sir Isaac Pitman took the initiative in the mid-nineteenth century [210], but the movement has gained strength this century. The phonetic alphabet promoted by Bernard Shaw and designed by Kingsley Read, the special symbols used in the study of linguistics and language teaching which record the phonemes of language, and Pitman's Initial Teaching Alphabet [211], are all attempts to solve this problem. But, on the whole, the Roman alphabet and the forms of its letters have been remarkably resistant to change. The printed letters of the fifteenth century in Italy, which were themselves translations into metal of contemporary calligraphic forms, have been adapted to meet the requirements of hot-metal composition, photosetting, the typewriter, and computer-controlled cathode-ray tube display without any significant alterations being made to their forms.

The most powerful challenge to the traditional shapes of letters came in the late 1950s when alpha-numeric characters were designed to satisfy as a first consideration the requirements of electronic reading equipment and, only secondarily, those of the human reader. Some of the first characters of this kind that were designed departed considerably from the traditional shapes; they found their way on to our cheques [212] and have been exploited by designers for their association with the computer age. But, even in this field, technical advances and design ingenuity have since led to the appearance of alpha-numeric characters which relate closely to traditional forms and can be read freely by both man and machine [213]. Having survived this major challenge, it does seem unlikely that the letterforms in present use will be substantially altered as a result of technical considerations in the foreseeable future.

Chapter 6
Pictures into print

This chapter covers an enormous range of work – from anonymous images of the humblest kind which were reproduced by the thousand for popular consumption, to the work of well-known painters who occasionally turned to the graphic arts and made illustrations for rather special books or limited editions of original prints. It is misleading, however, to equate the satisfaction of commercial or other purposes with mediocrity and freedom from such restrictions with quality. The fallacy of such a simple distinction is seen particularly clearly in the visual arts of nineteenth-century England; for while it must be admitted that the general standard of painting and sculpture in this period was not very high, work of considerable quality was produced in fields such as satire, topography, scientific and technical drawing, and the illustration of books and journals.

For most of the nineteenth century English artists were working in a backwater, either unaware of or deliberately blind to developments in France which formed the mainstream of European painting at the time. Throughout most of the century English painting was literary in character and was concerned with telling a story as completely and unambiguously as possible. Such characteristics, which proved to be a stumbling block as far as the painter was concerned, were valuable assets in illustration, and in this field artists were able to exploit their narrative talents and utilise their undoubted skills as draughtsmen. Furthermore, most printed illustration was in black and white by necessity, so that the worst excesses of Victorian colouring were avoided. Hundreds of skilful draughtsmen, some of them hardly known today, helped to make the second half of the nineteenth century one of the finest periods in English illustration. The quality of their drawing was admired by contemporary painters in France, and Van Gogh even made a collection of illustrations from English journals to help him with his own drawing. From this host of professional illustrators, who worked day in day out on commissions and often had rigorous deadlines to meet, some have emerged to be considered among the finest draughtsmen of their time.

One consistent thread which runs through the history of picture printing in the nineteenth century is the gradual tendency for the draughtsman to become separated from the actual process of making the printing surface. In the late eighteenth century the landscape painter Paul Sandby etched and aquatinted plates after his own water-colour drawings [214]; Thomas Bewick made engravings on wood from his own keenly observed originals [215, 216];

214 Paul Sandby, 'Harlech Castle', from his *Twelve views in North Wales*, 1776. Aquatint. 241 × 316 mm. *Victoria & Albert Museum.*

215 Thomas Bewick, wash drawing. *Hancock Museum, Newcastle.* 46 × 90 mm.

216 Thomas Bewick, *A history of British birds*, 1809 edition. Wood-engraved vignette based on the drawing reproduced in Plate 215. 39 × 80 mm.

217 J. D. Harding, 'Folkestone', from *Britannia delineata*, 1822-3. Lithograph, printed by Hullmandel. 238 × 324 mm. *John Johnson Collection.*

218 J. D. Harding after a sketch by Robert O'Callaghan Newenham, from the latter's *Picturesque views of the antiquities of Ireland*, 1830. Lithograph, printed by Hullmandel. 159 × 220 mm.

219 William Morris, proof pages of the *Works of Geoffrey Chaucer*, 1896. The illustrations were designed by Burne-Jones, the borders by Morris, and both were cut on wood by William Hooper. Page size 424 × 290 mm. *John Johnson Collection.*

and William Blake's imagery actually grew out of his own method of working, whether it was with the conventional processes of line- and wood-engraving or with his own invention of printing from relief-etched metal plates. There were many artists, it is true, who had their paintings reproduced for them in aquatint and mezzotint by professional craftsmen, but there was still a strong tradition in the late eighteenth and early nineteenth centuries for the artist to be involved, at least partially or on occasions, with the printing processes. Indeed, many artists served their apprenticeships with engravers or worked as colourists of prints.

The connection between water-colour painting and printmaking was particularly strong in this country; most of the leading water-colour painters worked for the engravers and lithographers and many of them practised as both original artist and professional craftsman on different occasions. A particularly good example of this versatility is provided by William Westall (1781–1850) who worked as a water-colour painter and as a painter in oils, supplied drawings for numerous plates in topographical volumes which were engraved or aquatinted by others, made drawings on stone from both his own and others artists' drawings, and also worked as a professional engraver and aquatinter. Louis Haghe (1806–85) and James Duffield Harding (1797–1863) worked in much the same way in lithography. They produced collections of plates made from their own drawings [217], but were quite prepared to translate another artist's drawing into lithography or even to touch up an amateur's sketch and copy it on to stone for publication [218]. A similar tradition existed in wood-engraving. In Bewick's own workshop there was such an interplay of roles between draughtsmen and engravers that it is impossible to establish exactly who did what, and throughout the nineteenth century commercial wood-engravers were expected to be competent draughtsmen. The two leading houses for wood-engraving in the second half of the nineteenth century, those of Joseph Swain and the Dalziel brothers, both required their engravers to attend classes in drawing; some wood-engravers acted as illustrators in their own right and many of the best illustrators of the period served their apprenticeships as wood-engravers.

As graphic processes became more complex with the commercial application of colour printing, and as the pressure of news reporting made it essential for images to be produced more quickly to meet publication deadlines, there came about a more distinct separation of the functions of draughtsman and professional craftsman. Finally, with the introduction of photo-mechanical engraving in the last quarter of the nineteenth century, the draughtsman became separated entirely from the process of manufacturing the printing surface. As far as the industrial aspects of printing are concerned this situation has continued throughout the present century.

But just as the artist's connection with the printing processes was being severed in the industrial field, there was a revival of printmaking as a craft and of the production of hand-made illustrations in books. In wood-engraving the initiative came from William Morris who employed William Hooper, a professional engraver, to work closely under his guidance at the Kelmscott Press in the 1890s [219]. Morris's use of wood-engraving stemmed from his belief in the integrity of craftsmanship and the unity of the book, and his ideas were taken a stage further at the beginning of this century by a host of other private presses which commissioned artists to design and cut their own illustrations on wood.

There was also a revival of interest in the making of original artists' prints, which stemmed from the *peintre-graveur* movement in France. James McNeill Whistler (1834–1903) was the first important figure in the revival of printmaking in England. When he settled here in 1859 he began practising the art of etching which he had learned in Paris and, nearly twenty years later, started making lithographs under the guidance of Thomas Way, a professional lithographic printer [220]. Many lesser artists soon followed suit and by the close of the century etching and lithography had begun to be regarded once again as natural extensions of the art of drawing. In this century the artist has continued to participate in the making of original prints of all kinds, with particular processes coming in and going out of fashion as styles of painting have changed. Such works are, of course, often as much articles of commerce as the prints of the early nineteenth century. They provide an opportunity for people to buy original works of art of a size they can hang on their walls and at a price they can afford and, equally important, the artist welcomes the opportunity of finding a respectable commercial outlet for his work.

The illustration of books is excluded from this story, but it is impossible to neglect entirely because its development in the nineteenth century was inseparable from that of picture printing generally. The distinction is in any case often very difficult to make: prints were usually published in parts, each consisting of a few plates with or without explanatory letterpress, and at the close of publication were often available bound in volume form; in the field of illustration the same artists contributed to books and journals, and serialised illustrated novels were sometimes published in book form afterwards. It is perhaps sufficient to emphasise that in the nineteenth century the illustrated book ceased to be the exception, and that in certain fields, such as natural history and travel, it became the norm.

In the eighteenth century all illustrations of any precision or refinement had to be engraved on copper, and this was expensive, not only because the printing of copper plates was very slow, but because they had to be printed separately from the text. Illustrations in this period usually took the form of full-page plates [221] and decorative head- and tail-pieces to chapters. With the perfection of the technique of engraving on wood in the closing decades of the eighteenth century there existed for the first time a satisfactory pictorial process which could be fully integrated with letterpress text. Wood-engraving soon became the main process for the illustration of the ordinary book, and it remained so throughout the nineteenth century. At the outset its typical form was a small vignette, deriving in style and technique from Bewick, which served the dual purpose of illustrating the text and decorating the page [222]. The age of the vignetted wood-engraving lasted well into the nineteenth century but, as well-known painters turned to illustrating books, engravings began to be squared up and treated as pictures which had a significance independent of their typographical surroundings [223]. The great period for wood-engraved illustration in England was the 1860s when Millais, Rossetti, Hunt, Sandys, Hughes, Pinwell, and many others made illustrations which were engraved for both books and periodicals by firms such as Swain and the Dalziels.

From the 1820s onwards lithography and steel-engraving began to be used for the illustration of books. Though the use of these processes involved a

220 James McNeill Whistler, *The toilet*, 1878. Lithotint, printed by Thomas Way. 257 × 165 mm.

221 John Milton, *Paradise lost*, 8th ed., 1775, showing an engraving by C. Grignion after an original by F. Hayman. Page size 288 × 227 mm.

222 Northcote's *Fables*, 2nd ed., 1829, with wood-engravings by John Jackson after drawings by William Harvey. Page size 197 × 117 mm.

223 Illustration by J. E. Millais, engraved on wood by the firm of Dalziel for *Dalziel's illustrated nights' entertainment*, 1865. Page size 260 × 185 mm.

separate printing, they had certain advantages over wood-engraving – lithography in cases where the artist wanted to produce the printing plate himself, and steel-engraving where greater precision was needed. By the middle of the nineteenth century even colour-printed images had begun to find their way into quite ordinary books. In the prevailing concern for mass education hardly any kind of book escaped this enthusiasm for visual stimulus and instruction, and novels, poetry books, travel books and guides, natural history books, religious tracts, bibles, textbooks, and technical manuals were all regularly produced with illustrations throughout most of the nineteenth century.

One important kind of picture-making in England which was particularly popular from the beginning of our period until the middle of the nineteenth century was the production of topographical and landscape prints. It was closely associated with the flourishing native school of water-colour painting, and most prints of this kind were intended as facsimiles of water colours. The interest in landscape views at home was partly inspired by William Gilpin (1724–1804) who began publishing in 1783 a series of descriptions of picturesque tours he had made in various parts of Britain. His books were illustrated with sepia hand-coloured aquatints made from his own drawings and had an extraordinary influence on English taste in landscape, besides helping to popularise the new process of aquatint. The first important collection of aquatint views to be published in this country was Paul Sandby's series of *Views in Wales* (1775–7), and from this time until about 1830 aquatint was the most popular process for reproducing water-colour drawings of landscape and architectural subjects. The most ambitious publication of this kind was *A voyage round Great Britain* (1814–25), which appeared in eight volumes with 308 delightful aquatint plates drawn and engraved by William Daniell. Rudolph Ackermann (1764–1834) was the best-known publisher of books with aquatint plates, and he issued the *Microcosm of London* (1809–10) [224], the *History of the University of Oxford* (1814), and the *History of the University of Cambridge* (1815), as well as many less well-known works of this kind. Ackermann employed some of the finest draughtsmen of the day on these books, including Mackenzie, F. Nash, Pugin, Pyne, Rowlandson, and W. Westall, and also many of the best engravers, among them Bluck, F. C. Lewis, D. Havell, and Stadler.

224 *The Microcosm of London*, 1809-10. 'Mounting guard, St James's Park', engraved by J. Bluck after an original by Thomas Rowlandson. Hand-coloured aquatint. 210 × 258 mm. *Victoria & Albert Museum.*

While interest in English scenery was encouraged by improvements made in road communications in this country, the popularity of foreign views was the direct result of the growth of continental travel and the great era of exploration and colonisation. Numerous English draughtsmen, including Samuel Prout, J. D. Harding, Richard Parkes Bonington, Thomas Shotter Boys, and Louis Haghe, were attracted to the continent when peace was established after the Napoleonic Wars and made drawings of their favourite cities and landscape views which they later had published as prints. Official draughtsmen were often appointed to accompany explorers on their voyages of discovery and produced visual records of the landscape, vegetation, people, and customs of far away lands which were later worked up at home, engraved, and published.

Lithography began to be a serious competitor with aquatint in the field of topography when C. J. Hullmandel published his own *Twenty-four views of Italy* in 1818. In the next few decades hundreds of collections of views at home and abroad were published with lithographs drawn by Prout, Nicholson, Harding, Westall, and Bonington in the 1820s, and Haghe, Harding, J. Nash, Boys, and J. F. Lewis in the 1830s and 1840s. One of the finest of the early lithographed publications was *Britannia delineata* (1822–3), which was an attempt to emulate the now famous French publication *Voyages pittoresques et romantiques dans l'ancienne France* (1820–78) by recording the whole of Britain

225 C. J. Hullmandel, 'Reculver', from *Britannia delineata*, 1822-3. Lithograph, printed by Hullmandel. 257 × 301 mm. *Cambridge University Library.*

226 David Roberts, *The Holy Land*, 1842-9. Lithograph by Louis Haghe after a drawing by Roberts, printed in black and two tints by Day & Son. 330 × 540 mm.

county by county. Only the first volume on Kent was ever produced, but the twenty-five plates by Hullmandel [225], Prout, Harding, and Westall include some of their best lithographed work. The most ambitious of all these lithographed publications was David Roberts's *The Holy Land* (1842-9), which consists of 248 lithographs drawn on stone by Louis Haghe after original drawings made on the spot by Roberts [226]. The lithographs were printed with one or more tint stones and in the more expensive versions were coloured by hand. Roberts describes in the introduction to the publication something of the hazards such a draughtsman had to contend with, and records how he was supplied with a guard to protect him from 'interruption or insult whilst' sketching' and was only permitted to work in the mosques on condition that he used no brushes made with hog's bristles. Roberts's *The Holy Land* was printed by Day & Son, the most important lithographic printing firm in the country for this kind of work. By the middle of the century Day & Son employed a large team of draughtsmen who specialised in various kinds of subjects, and the work was shared out according to their particular skills.

As with aquatint, lithographic prints of this kind were intended to look like water-colour paintings, and various techniques of lithographic drawing were introduced in an attempt to keep pace with changes in water-colour painting. The introduction of the dabbing style in the 1820s, improvements to the tinted style after 1835, and the invention of lithotint in 1840 were all the result of efforts to match the methods of the water-colour painter. Like aquatint, too, the lithographic print was only consummated when coloured by hand in imitation of the original from which it was copied; and in the long run many such prints found their way into frames to serve as substitutes for paintings on the walls of Victorian homes.

Political and social satire was another rich field in printmaking in this country, and draughtsmen of penetration and skill mocked the personal, cultural, social, and political weaknesses of their times, unhampered by the kinds of legal restrictions which existed abroad. Hogarth had prepared the way earlier in the eighteenth century, but at the beginning of our period two great satirists began to have their drawings published: Thomas Rowlandson (1756-1827) and James Gillray (1757-1815) [227]. Both worked primarily in etching by drawing directly on to the plate themselves, and this process had the value of speed of execution as well as the feeling of immediacy and improvisation so essential in caricature. Rowlandson was the less committed of the two to satire, and was much less incisive in his approach to it. Most of his best caricatures are of social life, and his full-blooded draughtsmanship

227 James Gillray, 'A voluptuary under the horrors of digestion', 1792. Hand-coloured etching. 343 × 280 mm. *Victoria & Albert Museum.*

228 HB, 'Stop thief!', 1831. Lithograph, printed by Charles Motte, London. 263 × 364 mm.

229 *Punch*, vol. 1, no. 1, July 1844, showing a cartoon drawn by A. S. Henning and engraved on wood by Ebenezer Landells. Page size 268 × 204 mm.

230 *The Looking Glass or Caricature Annual*, vol. 1, no. 1, January 1830, drawn and etched by William Heath. Page size 397 × 270 mm. *Reading University Library.*

captured the coarser sides of human nature to perfection; but he was also a draughtsman of pastoral scenes and an illustrator, and he turned more to these activities in later life. Gillray was much more prolific as a caricaturist than Rowlandson and etched about 1,500 plates of political and social satire, some of them after other artists' drawings. He worked equally well in both fields, but the invention and venom he displayed in his unbridled attacks on royalty and politicians in a period of uncertainty and unrest make him the father of modern caricature.

The political role of Gillray was taken up in the reign of William IV and after by John Doyle (1797–1868) whose caricatures appeared under the pseudonym HB [228]. He worked with more detachment than Gillray and with markedly less visual penetration, but his lithographed caricatures were still provocative and powerful enough to cause considerable concern in their day. They were issued by M'Lean in batches of four or five at a time during parliamentary sessions from 1829 to 1851, first as monochrome chalk drawings and later with tinted backgrounds. HB's caricatures rely much more on their textual commentaries than Gillray's, and in tempering the viciousness of earlier caricatures he set the style for the rest of the century. The caricatures drawn by Rowlandson, Gillray, Doyle, and many others were issued by the print-sellers of the day and sold at the price of prints. Doyle's, for instance, were sold individually at two shillings each by M'Lean, and the set of six volumes of prints issued between 1829 and 1834 was published in 1835 at thirty guineas. The caricatures by Heath, Seymour, and Doyle which appeared in *The Looking Glass or Caricature Annual*, which M'Lean began publishing in 1830, were sold in single monthly sheets at three shillings plain and six shillings coloured [230]. Cheaper satirical prints were published by Spooner and others, but satire for the masses had to wait until the appearance in the 1840s of *Punch* [229] and other satirical journals which were illustrated with wood-engravings.

One branch of nineteenth-century drawing which warrants rather more attention than it has so far received is documentary and scientific illustration. There is a fine tradition for this kind of work in printing which goes back to the woodcuts in early herbals and zoological books and in Vesalius's famous treatise on anatomy. Copper-engraving continued this tradition and was used to give greater precision and more detailed information. But with the rapid growth of the natural sciences and the study of mechanics the need for easier and cheaper methods of printing became more urgent, and in the nineteenth century wood-engraving and lithography gradually replaced copper-engraving and became the usual processes by which illustrations for both serious scientific treatises and simple books for the lay public were reproduced. Some of the botanical, zoological, and mechanical drawings found in nineteenth-century books and journals are models of clarity and economy of statement and, in general, present-day equivalents compare most unfavourably with them.

231 W. H. Fitch, 'Fortune's double yellow rose', from *Curtis's Botanical Magazine*, vol. 78, 1852. Hand-coloured lithograph, printed by F. Reeve. Page size 245 × 155 mm.

232 John Phillips, drawing from his own *Illustrations of the geology of Yorkshire*, 1829. Lithograph, printed by T. Inchbold, Leeds. Image 213 × 152 mm.

[34] G. Edwards, *Gleanings of natural history* (London, 1758), pp. xi-xii

Many of the draughtsmen who undertook such work are unknown, but one botanical artist might serve as an example of a type which probably existed in other fields. He is Walter Hood Fitch (1817–92), who worked as a draughtsman and lithographer for *Curtis's Botanical Magazine* from 1834 to 1877 [231], besides producing plates for very many other horticultural and botanical publications. Fitch moved to Kew Gardens as official draughtsman when Sir William Hooker became its director in 1841, and was responsible for the drawings in almost every illustrated publication issued from Kew while he was there. He was reputed to have been a remarkably rapid worker – as well he may have been, for he produced 2,500 lithographs for *Curtis's Botanical Magazine*, or over one a week for forty years, as well as more than 7,000 plates for other publications. Fitch's nephew, John Nugent Fitch (1840–1927), was almost as prolific; he took over his uncle's role as lithographer for *Curtis's Botanical Magazine*, producing nearly 2,500 plates for it.

Many scientists, such as William Hooker, who illustrated the *Botanical Magazine* on his own for a period of ten years, were competent enough as draughtsmen to make their own illustrations; and what technical skills they may have lacked in drawing were often compensated for by their greater understanding of the subject. As early as 1758 the argument for the author-illustrator in scientific works was expressed by the natural historian George Edwards in the preface to his *Gleanings of natural history*. While Edwards agreed that professional engravers might manage to give drawings greater finish, he maintained that 'they generally fall short of the spirit of the originals: so that it is always a great advantage, in any work of Natural History, when the author can perform both the drawing and engraving parts with his own hand'.[34] A list of scientists who made their own drawings in the nineteenth century would be extensive, and in natural history the tradition survives to this day.

The introduction of lithography provided an ideal opportunity for the scientist to become involved in the making of his own plates, and a number did so. The geologist John Phillips, for instance, made his own experiments in lithography and drew on stone the plates for the first edition of his *Illustrations of the geology of Yorkshire* (1829) [232], and William Swainson made lithographs for his *The naturalist's guide for collecting and preserving all subjects of natural history and botany* (1822). But it was the important zoological publications of the Ray Society, and particularly the superb lithographed plates drawn by Joshua Alder and Albany Hancock for their standard work, *Monograph of the British nudibranchiate mollusca* (1845–55) [233], that showed the possibilities of this method of working. Some of Alder and Hancock's plates appear to have been drawn on the stone by themselves, though many of the plates produced by the rather tricky lithotint process were drawn on stone after their originals by Mrs H. Holmes and W. Wing, who were probably professional lithographers.

Some rather splendid natural history books were published in our period: Thornton's *Temple of Flora* (1797–1807), Audubon's *The birds of America* (1827–38), Lear's *Illustrations of the family of psittacidae, or parrots* (1830–2), Gould's *The birds of Europe* (1832–7) and his many other ornithological publications, Moore's *The ferns of Great Britain and Northern Ireland* (1855–7), and Johnstone's *British seaweeds* (1859). But though the plates of such books were in some cases of considerable value from a scientific point of view, they were produced as much for the drawing room as for the study and were very expensive.

The practice of making engraved reproductions of paintings, which was put on a commercial footing by Marcantonio Raimondi in Italy in the early sixteenth century when he began publishing copies of Raphael's work, continued to flourish until the advent of the photo-mechanical processes in the

233 Joshua Alder and Albany Hancock, *A monograph of the British nudibranchiate mollusca*, part 4, 1848, 'Aegires Punctilucens', drawn by Hancock and lithographed by H. Holmes. Hand-coloured lithotint, printed by C. J. Hullmandel. Image 277 × 150 mm.

234 Valentine Green, mezzotint after Joshua Reynolds's painting of Georgiana, Duchess of Devonshire, 1780. 632 × 387 mm. *Victoria & Albert Museum.*

late nineteenth century. The complex methods which Raimondi evolved for this kind of work, which involved laying in parallel swelling and tapering lines, and then cross-hatching them with a similar system of marks, were developed further by numerous professional copper-engravers who devised a complete repertoire of marks to reveal form, indicate tone, and suggest textures. This remained the staple method used by engravers to reproduce paintings up to the end of the nineteenth century, though later on it was applied with less intelligence and sensitivity. All kinds of images were translated by these means, from the acknowledged masterpieces of the High Renaissance, for which they were originally devised, to the latest sentimental allegory of Victorian painting. Some images were reproduced on a vast scale, and would have taken years to engrave and perhaps half an hour or more to ink up and print each copy. Steel was used for some of the smaller images from the 1820s onwards, but the usual practice later in the century was to have the copper plates steel-faced by electrolysis, which made them more durable.

The tonal processes of engraving were also taken up for the reproduction of paintings. As we have seen, aquatint was primarily used for translating the landscape views of water-colour painters. Mezzotint, too, was almost exclusively used as a reproductive process, and skilled craftsmen such as John Raphael Smith, Valentine Green, and Samuel Reynolds made very successful interpretations of the work of the leading portrait painters of the late

235 David Lucas after John Constable, 'A Summerland', from Constable's *Various subjects of landscape*, 1833. Mezzotint. 150 × 225 mm. *Victoria & Albert Museum.*

236 Richard Lane, *Studies of figures, selected from the sketch books of Thomas Gainsborough*, 1825. Tinted lithograph, printed by C. J. Hullmandel. 152 × 118 mm.

237 Arundel Society print, 'Philosophy', from a fresco by Raphael on the ceiling of one of the Stanze in the Vatican, 1871. Chromolithograph, drawn by Mariannecci and chromolithographed by Storch & Kramer in Berlin under the direction of Professor L. Gruner. 352 × 350 mm.

eighteenth and early nineteenth centuries [234]. William Ward also made copies of portraits in mezzotint, though he is best remembered for his mezzotint reproductions of the popular rustic paintings of his brother-in-law George Morland, some of which were printed by inking up the plate in a limited number of colours. Some landscape paintings were also reproduced by mezzotint. J. M. W. Turner showed the possibilities of the process for this kind of work when he engaged Charles Turner and others to mezzotint his own landscape compositions for the *Liber studiorum* (1807–19); but this was not reproductive engraving in the normal sense as Turner designed the images expressly for the publication and even etched some of the outlines on the plates himself. The other important set of mezzotint reproductions of landscape paintings was Constable's *Various subjects of landscape* (1833) [235], which was a collection of twenty plates Constable himself published to demonstrate his approach to landscape painting. The mezzotinting was done by David Lucas under the very careful surveillance of Constable, but the plates were really too small to give anything but a general indication of the tonal qualities of Constable's paintings. David Lucas also engraved five large landscape prints in mezzotint after paintings by Constable which, though less powerful and dramatic, are more faithful reproductions.

Though widely used in Germany for reproducing collections of paintings, lithography was not often used in this way in England during the first half of the nineteenth century. Many topographical lithographs were copies of water-colour paintings, but lithography was probably not regarded highly enough in this country to have been considered suitable for reproducing major works of art. Richard Lane, whose mother was a niece of Gainsborough, made a set of lithographed *Studies of figures, selected from the sketch books of Thomas Gainsborough* (1825) which were effectively reproduced in the tinted style with the highlights removed in imitation of drawings touched up with white [236], and J. D. Harding lithographed *A series of subjects from the works of the late R. P. Bonington* (1829–30) shortly after the artist's untimely death from tuberculosis in 1828. But lithography had to wait until the commercial development of colour printing before it came into its own for this sort of work. Noel Humphreys had shown the possibilities of chromolithography for reproducing paintings in his *The illuminated books of the Middle Ages* (1844), but the great era of colour-printed reproductions was the second half of the nineteenth century when works of all kinds, from the most trivial anecdotal picture to the finest images of the great masters, were translated with equal devotion by the chromolithographers for as many as twenty or thirty successive printings. Such reproductions were often given a texture and varnished to make them superficially similar to the original paintings from which they were copied, and were known as oleographs.

The finest chromolithographic reproductions of paintings were those issued by the Arundel Society, a body founded in 1849 under the auspices of Ruskin, Samuel Rogers, and others to promote an understanding and appreciation of early Italian painting. The first prints to be issued were line engravings, but between 1856 and 1897 nearly two hundred chromolithographs of paintings were published [237], many of them being works by early Italian masters. Vincent Brooks began doing the printing, but his role soon passed to some of the leading German chromolithographic firms whose work in this field was unsurpassed. Though tainted with nineteenth-century sentiment, and often demonstrably inaccurate, the Arundel prints were an important venture in bringing convincing reproductions of great works of art into the middle-class Victorian home.

Long before the Arundel Society ceased publishing such prints works of art were being reliably reproduced by photography and the firms of Anderson and Alinari had begun their vast programme of photographing all the important works of art in Italy. With the introduction of the photo-mechanical processes the work of the draughtsman, lithographer, and engraver in this field was virtually finished. Paintings which were once the province only of those who could afford to travel the length and breadth of Europe are now conveniently reduced to fit on to a picture postcard or postage stamp, and dramatically photographed in detail to reveal every brush stroke or trace of cracking paint or plaster.

Caricatures, topographical prints, reproductions of paintings, and similar rather expensive prints made their impact on the population at large only through the windows of printsellers' shops. Pictures for the poorer classes at the turn of the eighteenth and nineteenth centuries took the form of broadsheets illustrated with crude but lively woodcuts depicting the latest execution, act of violence, disaster, or royal event. Such prints continued to be issued in their thousands in the nineteenth century by J. Catnach, J. Pitts, W. S. Fortey, and others, with a healthy disregard for the accuracy of the images used. Executions were a favourite subject, and the fate of the poor victim was usually described and committed to wood in advance of the occasion so that the broadsheet could be sold to the eager crowds who gathered to witness the event. It was common practice for the same wood block to be used over and over again, and some even incorporated a section which could be varied according to the number of men being hanged [238, 239]. Other popular prints which were sold on the streets were ballads, which often carried an impression from any old wood block the printer could lay his hands on at the time, providing it did not actually contradict the text [240, 241].

238, 239 Two execution broadsheets of the nineteenth century in which the same woodcut has been used but with different inserts for the actual scene on the gallows. *Left*, printed at the Catnach Press, London, 502 × 370 mm; *right*, printed by W. S. Fortey, London, 1867, 504 × 378 mm. Both items are in the *St Bride Printing Library*.

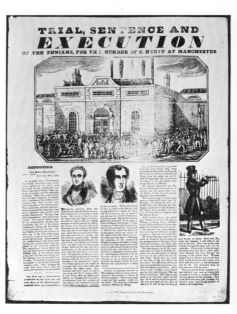

240, 241 Two popular ballads of the first half of the nineteenth century in which the same wood block has been used. *Left*, 'Blackbird', printed by Pitts, 254 × 95 mm; *right*, 'Home sweet home', printed by Pitts, 235 × 95 mm. Both items are in *Reading University Library*.

Illustrations in newspapers were very rare in the eighteenth century, and were not much more frequent in the nineteenth century. The *Observer* (founded 1791) was the first newspaper to make more than the occasional use of illustrations, and it began to print wood-engravings of outstanding events around 1820. In that year it went to town with some illustrations of the Cato Street conspiracy, and in the following year its special number for the coronation of George IV included four engravings and had a sale of 60,000 copies. Thereafter, along with the *Morning Chronicle*, *Weekly Chronicle*, and *Bell's Life in London*, it began to make use of pictures from time to time to record crimes, coronations, royal weddings and funerals, and similar important events. The difficulty of preparing illustrated news for even a weekly paper must have been formidable, and the editor of the *Observer* apologised in advance for any imperfections readers might find in the engravings of

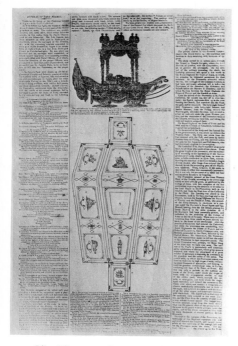

242 *The Times*, 10 January 1806, showing a wood-engraving by Richard Austin of Nelson's funeral car and a diagrammatic representation of his coffin.

243 *Gentleman's Magazine*, July 1770. Page size 216 × 126 mm.

[35] M. Jackson, *The pictorial press: its origin and progress* (London, 1885), p.263

the special issue produced to celebrate Queen Victoria's coronation, explaining that 'the whole of the labours of the artists and the engravers have been accomplished in less than a week, and this under circumstances of difficulty in obtaining admission to the scenes to be sketched, almost insurmountable'.[35] *The Times* had already experienced something of the hazards of visual reporting when it included a wood-engraving of Nelson's coffin and funeral car in 1806 [242]. The original intention was that the pall and coronet should appear on the coffin, and the engraving produced by Austin followed this arrangement; but on the day the pall was thrown into the back of the car to give the public a better view of the coffin, and the coronet was carried in another coach. All *The Times* could do was to state rather apologetically that there was not time to make the alteration.

Something of the functions of all the kinds of images that we have considered so far – caricature, topography, scientific illustration, the reproduction of works of art, and news reporting – were assumed by the illustrated journals. They brought pictorial images to the masses very cheaply, and probably exercised as important an influence on public taste in the nineteenth century as the visual images of television do today. Illustrated journals were not new in the nineteenth century, but periodicals like the *Gentleman's Magazine* (founded 1731) catered for educated tastes and were expensive [243]. The first of the new kind of periodical was called, appropriately enough, the *Cheap Magazine*, and it ran from 1813 to 1814 with just a single wood-engraving on its first page [244]. In the 1820s a number of illustrated journals were founded, the most influential being the *Mirror of Literature, Amusement, and Instruction* (1822) which appeared weekly with one wood-engraving on the first of its sixteen pages and sold for twopence [245]. But the real success of illustrated journals of this kind dates from the early 1830s and the founding of two weeklies costing a penny, the *Penny Magazine* (1832) of the Society for the Diffusion of Useful Knowledge and the *Saturday Magazine* (1832) of the Society for Promoting Christian Knowledge [246, 253]. Both were attempts to promote public learning and taste with the help of illustrations, and all kinds of instructive and elevating images were scattered throughout the eight pages of each issue. The success of these journals was prodigious, and by the end of 1832 the *Penny Magazine* could claim a circulation of 200,000 – a figure not achieved by the leading daily papers until about 1870.

With the success of these publications the future of illustrated journalism was assured, and hundreds of other periodicals appeared later in the century, some of a general nature and others catering for specialised interests. In 1841 *Punch* was founded and, along with numerous other satirical journals, began to capture the market which had previously been the monopoly of the print-sellers. The most influential of all the weekly journals was undoubtedly the *Illustrated London News*, which was founded in 1842 by Herbert Ingram [247]. It appeared in a format twice as large as that of the *Penny Magazine* and *Saturday Magazine* and its sixteen pages carried numerous wood-engravings of all shapes and sizes. The *Illustrated London News* soon became the principal purveyor of visual news; it trained a whole school of draughtsmen and engravers and remained unrivalled in this field until the foundation of the *Graphic* in 1869. The next important development was the printing of daily news with illustrations, and this really depended on the replacement of the slow manual process of wood-engraving by process engraving. The first illustrated daily paper in this country was the *Daily Graphic*, which appeared with both process line blocks and wood-engravings in 1890 and began using half-tones in 1894. The *Daily Chronicle* also started printing line illustrations in 1895, but daily newspapers were not generally illustrated until the twentieth century when half-tone blocks from photographs were popularised by the *Daily Mirror* in 1904 and the *Daily Sketch* in 1909 [248]. The photo-engraving department of the *Daily Mirror* was regularly producing zinc half-tones in

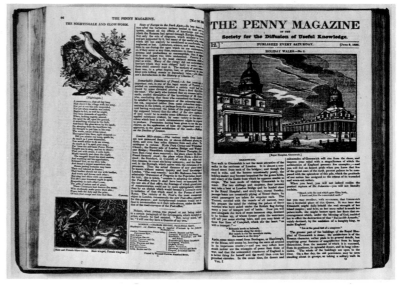

244 *Cheap Magazine*, vol. 2, 1814. Page size 164 × 100 mm.

245 *Mirror of Literature, Amusement, and Instruction*, vol. 1, 1822-3. Page size 215 × 133 mm.

246 *Penny Magazine*, vol. 1, 1832. Page size 280 × 180 mm.

247 *Illustrated London News*, vol. 1, 1842. Page size 420 × 280 mm.

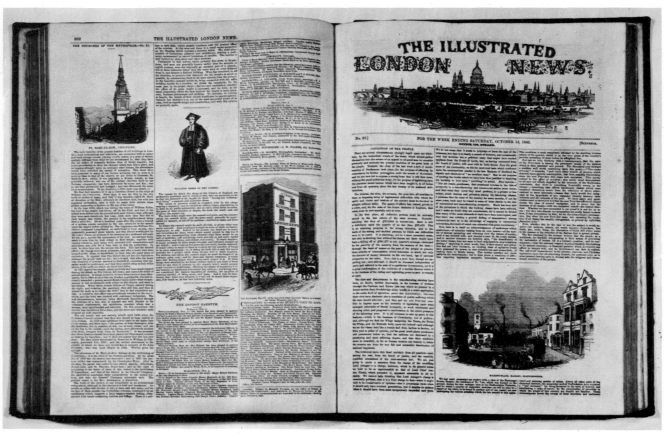

248 *Daily Sketch*, 15 March 1909. Letterpress, with half-tone illustrations. 442 × 318 mm. *St Bride Printing Library.*

this period within half an hour of receiving photographs. Other newspapers soon realised the advantages in speed of the half-tone process, and within a few years hardly any newspaper office of any importance was without its photo-engraving department.

Initially, however, illustrated journalism depended on a flourishing school of wood-engraving, and the number of wood-engravers in London grew rapidly to cater for this market from a mere handful at the beginning of the century to around 200 in 1840. In the second half of the century the numbers continued to increase and the craft of wood-engraving developed into a veritable industry to cater for the demands of the public for illustrated news. Wood-engraving was already a firmly established trade when M. U. Sears issued a set of specimens for the guidance of publishers in 1833 [249], in which he gave his charges for engraving vignettes and initial letters on the basis of the style, size, and complexity of the image. By this time the vignette form popularised by Bewick had become a familiar ingredient of the printer's style, and the typefounders responded by supplying metal casts of wood-engravings of ships, coaches, animals, rural scenes, coats of arms, and similar common images [250]. By 1840 there were already many very fine facsimile engravers, among them John Jackson, Robert Branston, Mary Byfield, Orlando Jewitt, Orrin Smith, W. J. Linton, John Thompson, and the brothers Samuel and Thomas Williams, most of whom worked for both book and journal publishers. Thereafter, the *Illustrated London News* was paramount in the development of wood-engraving; it was largely responsible for creating a new kind of illustration based on news reporting and provided something of a training ground for the next generation of engravers. In addition to the familiar vignettes and other small illustrations similar to those found in the older journals, the *Illustrated London News* also printed some very large illustrations, and the panoramas which it issued as supplements in the 1840s were over four feet long [251]. At a later stage, in order to speed up the engraving of large blocks, it pioneered the technique of bolting small units together from behind so that they could be divided up amongst a number of craftsmen to be engraved and then fitted together again afterwards.

It scarcely needs stating that the wood-engravers who worked for the journals did so under great pressure. The firm of Swain, for instance, which engraved

249 M. U. Sears, *Specimen of historical, topographical, and emblematical engravings on wood*, 1833. Image 230 × 170 mm. *Bibliothèque Nationale.*

250 Cast ornaments. From Caslon & Livermore, *Specimen of printing types*, 1825. Page size 218 × 140 mm. *St Bride Printing Library.*

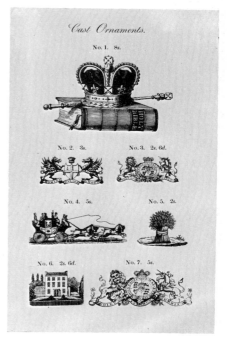

ILLUSTRATED LONDON NEWS

251 'London in 1842 taken from the summit of the Duke of York's Column', Supplement to the *Illustrated London News* of 7 January 1843. Wood-engraving. 815 × 1800 mm.

252 'View of the conflagration of the city of Hamburgh'. Wood-engraving, published in the *Illustrated London News*, vol. 1, no.1, 14 May 1842. 100 × 153 mm.

the blocks for *Punch* from 1843 until they were finally replaced by process engravings towards the end of the century, had to engrave the main cartoon for *Punch* within twenty-four hours of receiving the drawing on the block; and Joseph Swain claimed with justifiable pride that he was never once late over a period of fifty years.[36] Naturally enough, the engravers received many complaints from draughtsmen who claimed that their work had been ruined, but similar reactions are not unheard of in the days of photo-mechanical processes, and such comments should not obscure the incredible powers of interpretative draughtsmanship and technical virtuosity displayed by many facsimile engravers. The best known, and certainly one of the finest of such firms in the second half of the century was that of the brothers George and Edward Dalziel. Their working lives spanned the period defined at one end by the birth of *Punch* and the *Illustrated London News* and at the other by the virtual disappearance of wood-engraving as an industrial craft, and they engraved the work of hundreds of draughtsmen including Gilbert, Birket Foster, Millais, Hunt, Rossetti, Pinwell, Houghton, and Tenniel for thousands of books and periodicals.

In the early days of pictorial journalism illustrations were often copied from other prints. In 1834 the *Saturday Magazine* ran a series of views of cathedrals [253], many of the French ones being copies of lithographs in a well-known set of monographs on French cathedrals [254]; and the first number of the *Illustrated London News* contained an illustration of the recent conflagration of Hamburg which was made by copying a view of the city from an old print in the British Museum and adding the necessary flames, smoke, and human activity [252]. In the case of events for which there was prior notice, drawings were usually made in advance, and a number of stories are recorded of inaccuracies that resulted from this practice. One reliable instance is described by Vizetelly[37] and again concerns the illustrations for the first number of the *Illustrated London News* which he helped to engrave. John Gilbert prepared some drawings of a fancy-dress ball which was to be held at

[36] M.H.Spielmann, *The history of 'Punch'* (London, 1895), p.250

[37] H.Vizetelly, *Glances back through seventy years*, 2 vols (London, 1893), vol. i, pp.231–2

253 *Saturday Magazine*, 11 October 1834. Wood-engraving by J. W. Whimper of the Cathedral of Orleans. Page size 282 × 180 mm.

254 F. T. de Jolimont, *Vues pittoresques de la Cathédrale d'Orléans*, 1826. Lithograph, drawn by Chapuy and printed by Engelmann. 262 × 170 mm.

255 John Gilbert, illustration of a fancy-dress ball at Buckingham Palace. Wood-engraving, published in the *Illustrated London News*, vol. 1, no. 1, 14 May 1842. 130 × 248 mm.

256 E. A. Goodall, 'The Redan at sunrise', a sketch from the Crimea. Wood-engraving, published in the *Illustrated London News*, 6 October 1855. 235 × 354 mm.

Buckingham Palace, and he followed to the best of his ability information provided beforehand that Prince Albert was to wear a coronal of pearls; he interpreted this as a string of pearls, instead of a tiara, and it appeared as such in one of the published engravings [255].

There was clearly no tradition of reliable pictorial journalism at the outset of the *Illustrated London News*, and in its early years it was largely kept alive by the fertile imagination and busy pencil of John Gilbert, with the help of William Harvey and Kenny Meadows. But along with other journals concerned with news reporting it soon built up a team of special draughtsmen who made rapid on the spot sketches of events as they took place. Royal occasions, openings of new railway lines, international exhibitions, trials, wars, and revolutions were all thoroughly recorded by its visual reporters of the second half of the nineteenth century, and particularly good work of this kind was produced by A. Forestier, Walter Wilson, and R. Caton Woodville.

The role of the special war artist dates from the Crimean War when J. A. Crowe and E. A. Goodall sent back sketches for the *Illustrated London News* [256], William Simpson made drawings on the spot for *The seat of war in the*

H

257 Front page of the *Illustrated London News*, 17 September 1870, showing a wood-engraving adapted from the extreme left-hand side of the sketch reproduced in Plate 258. Page size 405 × 282 mm.

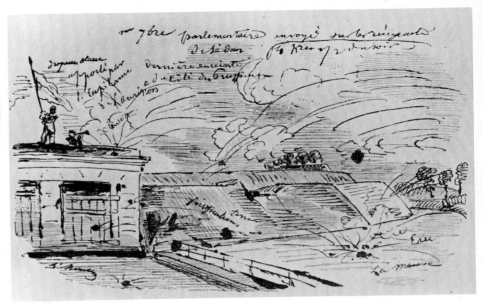

258 Sketch of the surrender of Sedan done on the spot in 1870. From a wood-engraved facsimile in Mason Jackson, *The pictorial press: its origin and progress*, 1885.

259 Sydney Hall, sketch made in court during the Parnell case. Wood-engraving published in the *Graphic*, 13 April 1889. 104 × 124 mm.

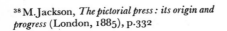

38 M. Jackson, *The pictorial press: its origin and progress* (London, 1885), p.332

East (1855–6) [262], and Roger Fenton took his well-known photographs. From then onwards the war artist was not often unemployed. The Franco-Prussian War was the first war to be brought home to the British public as really topical news [257, 258]; the *Illustrated London News* alone had five artists in the field, among them Jules Pelcoq and William Simpson, and during the siege drawings were photographed and sent out of Paris in four different balloons to ensure that at least one set arrived safely. The hazards of illustrating this kind of event were obviously considerable, and one special war artist described how he made his drawings on tiny pieces of tissue paper which he rolled into pills ready to swallow should this be necessary.[38]

The position of the *Illustrated London News* began to be seriously challenged with the founding of the *Graphic* in December 1869, just in time to take advantage of the newsworthy events of the Franco-Prussian War. Very soon this new journal took the lead in pictorial journalism and trained a highly successful team of illustrators and wood-engravers of its own. Its draughtsmen were paid very highly, and advertisements claimed that the best of them could earn annual salaries of as much as £2,000. Considering the difficulties of working under pressure which they had to contend with, some of the drawings for the *Graphic* produced by such draughtsmen as Sydney Hall [259], Paul Renouard [260], and William Hatherell were quite outstanding.

In order to cater for the needs of pictorial journalism the pattern of training draughtsmen began to change, and the practice of drawing moving figures from memory became popular in the schools for press illustration. With the appearance of illustrated daily papers the draughtsman had to work even more quickly [261], and an article in the *Dublin Daily Express* (September 1900) claimed that on average only ten minutes was allowed for the artist to produce a drawing which had to appear in the same evening's paper. The development of fast-speed photography was an enormous boon to the artist and, towards the end of the century, process blocks were quite often made from drawings which had been copied or traced from photographs.

Before the *Illustrated London News* and the *Graphic* absorbed its market, there existed a flourishing branch of visual reporting in lithography. This was in its hey-day around the middle of the nineteenth century when the openings of new railway lines, the Great Exhibition, Wellington's lying in state and

A CORNER AT THE DANCING CLASS

THE EMPLOYMENT OF CHILDREN IN PANTOMIMES

260 Paul Renouard, cover illustration for the *Graphic*, 30 March 1889. Wood-engraving. Page size 401 × 293 mm.

261 W. Fitzwater Wray, 'Warehouse fire at Bradford'. Process engraving produced by the *Bradford Observer*, 30 March 1896. From *Process Year Book*, vol. 3, 1897.

262 William Simpson, 'Charge of the Light Cavalry Brigade', from his *The seat of war in the East*, 1855-6. Hand-coloured lithograph, drawn on stone by E. Walker and printed by Day & Son. 274 × 460 mm.

263 Photographic van used by Roger Fenton during the Crimean War. From a wood-engraving in the *Illustrated London News*, 10 November 1855.

39 W. Simpson, 'Lithography: a finished chapter in the history of illustrative art', *Journal of the Royal Society of Arts*, vol. 39, 1890-1, p.195

40 W. Simpson, *The autobiography of William Simpson*, edited by G.E.Todd (London, 1903), p.35

funeral, the Crimean War, and similar important events attracted enormous public attention. The leading lithographic printer in this field was the firm of Day & Son, which employed a team of specialist draughtsmen to take on a wide range of pictorial work. One of these draughtsmen was William Simpson (1823–99), who joined the firm just as it was being submerged by work connected with the Great Exhibition; in fact, he claimed that he was kept so busy recording the exhibition for others that he could scarcely get a day off to go to see it for himself.[39] Simpson was soon to become Day & Son's principal draughtsman, and in 1854 he was commissioned by Colnaghi's to go to the Crimea to make drawings of the fighting there. He remained in the field throughout the war, sending back pictures which were lithographed in the studios of Day & Son and published in the form of two sets of tinted lithographs as *The seat of war in the East* (1855–6) [262]. Propriety was of paramount importance, and Simpson describes how his drawings had to be submitted to Lord Raglan on the spot, and to the War Minister and Queen Victoria at home, before they could be placed in the hands of the lithographers.[40] Simpson also undertook a similar trip to India in 1859 to record the aftermath of the mutiny there, but the firm of Day & Son ran into financial difficulties and no effective publication of his drawings appeared. He later became a successful special artist for the *Illustrated London News*, recording the Abyssinian expedition, the opening of the Suez canal, and, as we have seen, the siege of Paris. By turning to work for an illustrated journal Simpson was acknowledging the obvious economic reality that wood-engraving was fast supplanting lithography in the field of news reporting.

Not long afterwards, however, the position of the special artist was itself being seriously threatened by photography [263]. In topography and portraiture, where the subject remained more or less still, the photographer began to replace the draughtsman very soon after the announcements of the invention of photography by Fox Talbot and Daguerre in the late 1830s. But visual recording of actual events remained beyond the scope of the camera until Frederick Scott Archer's invention in 1850 of the wet collodion process, which allowed much faster exposures than all previous methods. A further improvement came with the development of dry plates which could be prepared in advance. A number of dry collodion processes were developed from the mid-1850s, but it was not until the large-scale commercial production of gelatine dry plates after 1878 that the old wet collodion processes began to be superseded and the era of the snapshot really began. Apart from their convenience, gelatine dry plates opened up the possibility of instantaneous photography of moving scenes as they led to very much faster exposures.

264 Lottery poster, 1826. Woodcut, hand-coloured, printed by Thorowgood, London. 733 × 503 mm. *John Johnson Collection.*

By 1880 photographs were being faithfully engraved on wood for the *Illustrated London News* and the *Graphic*, and photographic images of all kinds became much more common as half-tone blocks began to oust wood-engravings from the pages of these journals in the 1880s and 1890s. The speed of photography alone gave it an enormous advantage over the draughtsman, and this was an important factor in the emergence of illustrated daily papers at the beginning of this century. Though the *Illustrated London News* continued to use drawn illustrations regularly for some purposes until as late as the mid-1960s, the photographer had almost entirely replaced the draughtsman long before this. Journalism has been the principal patron of photography, and some of the finest photographs of this century must fall into the category of news reporting. The news photographs which appear day by day in our papers and magazines show the same high level of professionalism (often in the face of similar difficulties) as the drawings of the special artists who worked for the journals of the second half of the nineteenth century.

Another new kind of popular imagery was brought into being with the rapid expansion of advertising in the early nineteenth century. Before then a few pictorial advertisements had begun to appear in newspapers, directories, and guides [265]; and tradesmen's cards occasionally bore pictorial images which served as advertisements. Some eighteenth-century posters and handbills were engraved on copper or carried small woodcuts, though, as far as is known, most of them were purely typographical. As competition in advertising increased, however, pictorial images began to assume more importance, and by the middle of the nineteenth century were being widely used in advertising campaigns, sometimes in most inventive ways. Not until the last two decades of the nineteenth century did pictorial advertising make much of an impact in the journals, and a comparison of advertisements in the *Illustrated London News* and the *Graphic* in the 1870s with those in the 1880s and 1890s reveals a tremendous increase in the use made of pictorial imagery to persuade potential buyers.

Some of the earliest promoters of pictorial advertising were the agents for the national lotteries, such as Bish, Swift, and Hazard. Pictorial images appeared frequently on their handbills, and some of their lottery posters that have survived also contain large woodcuts. For the important campaign he launched on the occasion of the final state lottery held in England in 1826 Bish issued at least one poster which was predominantly pictorial [264]; it consists of a hand-coloured woodcut figure of a Negro boy-trumpeter which fills most of the imperial (30 × 20 in.) sheet. It was for this 'Last of all lotteries' too that Bish introduced a special hexagonal advertising hoarding which was drawn by horse through London [266].

Though few of the millions of items issued by the most enterprising advertisers of the nineteenth century have survived, it is quite clear that pictorial images figured largely in some of them. Rowland, of Macassar oil fame [267], Holloway, who sold pills and ointments, and the New Adelphi Theatre in London are known to have advertised widely around the middle of the nineteenth century. Thomas Holloway, who began advertising in a big way in 1837, was reputed to have spent as much as £20,000 a year on it in 1851 and £40,000 in 1862.[41] Apart from advertisements in newspapers and journals, which were considered the most effective means of reaching a wide public, handbills were distributed at street corners, sandwichmen paraded the streets, posters were plastered on every available wall, bills were slipped under doors or through letterboxes, and by the early 1860s even direct mailing techniques were being considered. One of the most ambitious and successful advertising campaigns of the middle of the nineteenth century was devised by William Smith, the acting manager of the New Adelphi Theatre, for Watts Phillips's play 'The dead heart' in 1859. In his book

265 Pictorial advertisements engraved by Hancock for James Bisset's *Magnificent directory*, Birmingham, 1800. 190 × 107 mm. *John Johnson Collection.*

[41]W.Smith, *Advertise. How? When? Where?* (London, 1863), pp.145–7

266 Advertising perambulator used by Bish for the last state lottery, 1826. Wood-engraving from W. Smith, *Advertise. How? When? Where?*, 1863.

267 Advertisement of A. Rowland & Sons, mid-nineteenth century. Relief print. 217 × 143 mm. *John Johnson Collection.*

about advertising published in 1863 Smith lists the printed publicity which was produced for him during the run of the play by W. S. Johnson's Nassau Steam-Press:

'10,000,000 adhesive labels,
30,000 small cuts of the Guillotine scene,
5000 reams of note-paper,
110,000 business envelopes,
60,000 pence envelopes,
2000 six-sheet cuts of Bastile scene,
5,000,000 hand-bills,
1000 six-sheet posters,
500 slips,
1,000,000 cards, the shape of a heart,
100 twenty-eight sheets,
20,000 folio cards for shop-windows'[42]

268 Sandwichmen advertising 'The dead heart'. Wood-engraving from W. Smith, *Advertise. How? When? Where?*, 1863.

Sandwichmen carried heart-shaped boards through the streets [268], and adhesive labels in the form of hearts were freely distributed. These hearts became something of a craze, as have similar advertising gimmicks since, and the public itself unwittingly became the means of promotion and began sticking them on to the clothes of unsuspecting people, on cabs, and every conceivable kind of object. This campaign alone gives some indication of the ephemeral nature of such printing, for I have been able to trace only a few examples of the sixteen million items which were produced. During the second half of the nineteenth century novelty advertising of this kind was very highly developed [269, 270]. Great originality was often shown in the use

269-70 Hudson's soap advertisement of the 1880s (front and back views). Chromolithograph, signed JBB. 153 × 226 mm.

[42]W. Smith, *Advertise. How? When? Where?* (London, 1863), p.72

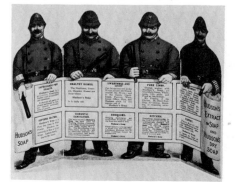

271 Advertisement for Crawford's biscuits, to be made up into three dimensions. Chromolithograph. *John Johnson Collection.*

272 London poster hoardings at the end of the last century. Photograph. *Reproduced by kind permission of Aero Films and Aero Pictorial Ltd.*

273 Dudley Hardy, 'A gaiety girl', theatre bill for the Prince of Wales' Theatre. Colour lithography, printed by Waterlow & Sons Ltd, London. 2210 × 990 mm. *Victoria & Albert Museum.*

274 'Wall-posting as it is.' Wood-engraving from W. Smith, *Advertise. How? When? Where?*, 1863.

275 'Wall-posting as it ought to be.' Wood-engraving from W. Smith, *Advertise. How? When? Where?*, 1863.

of folding and cut-out images, such as a soap advertisement in which a cherubic baby pops up from its tub as you open it and a biscuit advertisement which was designed to be made up into a three-dimensional model [271], and hardly a trick of the present-day advertiser was not anticipated in this period.

Of all advertising media the pictorial poster deserves special mention because of its enormous impact on the urban environment. It was not an invention of the late nineteenth century, as is often implied in books on the poster; as we have already seen, pictorial posters existed in this country even before the lotteries were closed in 1826. Whether this tradition continued uninterrupted is not known, but by the middle of the century woodcut and lithographed pictorial posters were certainly being produced for theatres, circuses, and other entertainments. The list of items issued for the New Adelphi Theatre which is printed above is sufficient evidence alone, but a number of fully pictorial posters from the middle of the century have survived. One lithographic printer in London, G. Webb, seems to have specialised in this kind of work; several of his pictorial posters have survived and one of them, a hand-coloured ink lithograph advertising Vauxhall Gardens, was printed on four sheets and measures about 6 × 5 ft [278].

All the same, a comparison of illustrations showing posters of the middle of the century [8,274] with photographs of hoardings in the late 1890s [10,272] reveals a distinct change from the predominantly verbal to the predominantly pictorial. The change was brought about by the need for greater impact and was made possible by technical improvements in chromolithography and machine printing; but it may also have been assisted to some extent by the change-over from an indiscriminate system of billposting which prevailed in the middle of the century [274] to a system introduced some twenty years later of orderly hoardings hired out by contractors [275]. Posters began to be seen as pictures; hoardings were frequently built with surrounds like picture frames and some posters, such as Millais's well-known 'Bubbles' advertisement, were merely adaptations of existing paintings. In the 1890s Dudley Hardy [273] and the Beggarstaff Brothers, inspired by the example of Chéret, Lautrec, and others in France, began to design posters to suit the needs of street advertising. Their posters were conceived in simple and striking silhouettes and the copy was fully integrated with the images.

Such posters were the exception, however, and the majority of pictorial posters conceived and printed by specialist firms, like the lithographers David Allen & Sons of Belfast, Manchester, and London, were hack paintings with lettering added [276]. In their catalogue of posters for 1900 David Allen & Sons offered over 700 examples of what might be called off-the-peg lithographic posters for theatrical and similar performances embracing 'such a wide range and variety of subjects that suitable pictorials for almost any piece are practically certain to be found among our stock'. They also provided letterpress slips, printed from type to imitate lithography, for pasting on top of the posters to give the appropriate copy 'in such an artistic manner' as to appear to have been printed with the picture.

An attempt to redeem the quality of poster designing was made by Frank Pick when he was appointed to the London Underground just before the First World War, first as development officer (1909) and then as commercial manager (1912). After the war Pick rose to become managing director, but he continued to take an active interest in all aspects of design. He began to use the hoardings of the Underground as picture galleries for the people and commissioned artists of repute to design posters for them. The most influential of these was E. McKnight Kauffer, whose strong geometric designs brought the first breath of modern European art to the general public in the 1920s [277]. Many other artists, including Frank Brangwyn, Edward Bawden, Graham Sutherland, and Jacob Epstein, designed posters for the London Transport Board in the period between the two world wars.

Since the Second World War some of the most effective poster advertising has been the work of the agencies, where teams consisting of art directors, market researchers, copywriters, photographers, and typographers combine their talents to produce posters and other persuasive literature with a view to getting an idea across as powerfully as possible to the particular section of the public they are aiming at. Superbly-produced large-scale photographs are now the order of the day and have virtually replaced the drawn images of the artist. Such posters have made a significant contribution to the urban scene and have also helped to influence the painting of our time by showing the power of ordinary objects when blown up to an enormous scale.

The introduction of a cheap postal system in this country in 1840 opened up the possibility of other kinds of mass picture printing – greeting cards of all kinds and picture postcards. Unlike posters, which were rarely preserved, these humble forms of popular printing must have survived from the nineteenth century by the million, largely because of the fashion in late Victorian times for pasting or slipping them into specially-made albums [279].

276 Theatre bill, *c.* 1895. Colour lithography, printed by S. C. Allen & Co., London. 508 × 762 mm. *Victoria & Albert Museum.*

277 E. McKnight Kauffer, London Underground poster, 1924. Colour lithography, printed by Johnson, Riddle & Co. Ltd, London. *London Transport Board.*

107

278 Poster advertising Vauxhall Gardens,
c. 1850. Lithograph, hand-coloured,
printed on four sheets by G. Webb.
1960 × 1480 mm. *John Johnson Collection.*

279 Chromolithographed greeting cards mounted in an album of about 1882. Page size 291 × 228 mm.

280 J. C. Horsley, the first Christmas card, designed in 1843 for Sir Henry Cole. *Victoria & Albert Museum.*

281 The manufacture of valentines. Wood-engraving from the *Illustrated London News*, 14 February 1874. 335 × 236 mm.

282 Pictorial envelope, 1866. Engraved by W. Dickes, London. 90 × 145 mm. *John Johnson Collection.*

The first Christmas card is generally considered to have been a private one designed by J. C. Horsley for Henry Cole, one of the founders and the first director of the Victoria and Albert Museum, for Christmas 1843. Three years later Cole had one thousand copies printed lithographically and sold them at his own art shop in Bond Street [280]. The fashion for sending Christmas cards did not really get under way until the 1860s, but by 1880 the Post Office felt it necessary to issue the first of its now familiar appeals to post early for Christmas. The history of the valentine goes back much further, though its commercial development was more or less in line with that of the Christmas card. Both were dependent on technical improvements in colour printing, and particularly in lithographic machine printing, and on a plentiful supply of cheap female labour for the hand work [281]. The leading publishers of such greeting cards were Raphael Tuck, De la Rue, and Marcus Ward and, as with high-class reproductions of pictures, most of the actual printing was done by leading German chromolithographic firms.

The picture postcard came rather later, and is usually considered to have evolved from the pictorial envelope [282] which flourished at the outset of the postal system. What are often regarded as the earliest picture postcards were developed for the special use of the French army during the Franco-Prussian War of 1870. But picture postcards seem to have achieved widespread success as a result of the publication at the Paris Exhibition of 1889 of a card bearing a lithograph of the Eiffel Tower which could be bought and posted from the top of the tower itself. Thereafter, the future of the picture postcard was assured on a world-wide basis, and there developed an almost incredible craze for writing and collecting them which lasted well into this century. In 1903 alone 600 million postcards passed through the hands of the Post Office.

Pictorial cards of all kinds can be seen as a barometer of public taste over the last hundred years; they reveal very clearly both the all-pervading over-sentimentalisation of Victorian taste and the incredibly catholic attitudes of recent years. A few well-known artists, such as Walter Crane and Kate Greenaway, designed Christmas cards in the late nineteenth century, and the twentieth-century picture postcard has produced its own minor master of seaside fun in the person of Donald McGill; but otherwise, no individual figures single themselves out.

There were, of course, many other applications of picture printing in the nineteenth century, some of which can just be touched upon. The Victorians had their equivalent of the laminated record sleeve in the form of colourful

283 Alfred Concanen, music cover of the 1860s. Lithographed in five colours and printed by Stannard & Son. 346 × 205 mm.

pictorial music covers. These began to be produced in the 1840s, and some of the lithographers who designed them – Robert Brandard in the 1840s and 1850s, and particularly Alfred Concanen in the 1860s [283] – were minor masters in portraying their own times. A thriving tradition of illustrated music covers continued almost to the end of the nineteenth century and it provides a vivid record of the changing interests and tastes of the period.

By the second half of the nineteenth century illustrated trade catalogues were common, shopkeepers often had their own paper bags with perhaps a view of their premises printed on them, and groceries and other commodities were also being sold in boxes, packs, bottles, or tins which bore printed images. Cards, or stiffeners as they were called, were introduced by cigarette manufacturers to strengthen their paper packets and were soon printed with sets of related images by chromolithography. Some firms, and particularly the biscuit manufacturers, were not slow to see some of the long-term uses of their tins [284] and had them made in all kinds of ornamental shapes and printed with decorative designs and popular images by offset lithography. In this century, the bombardment of printed images in the form of advertisements, dust wrappers of books, magazines, paperback covers, record sleeves, packages, and catalogues continues unabated.

284 Huntley & Palmers' biscuit tins, 1892 and 1893. Offset lithography, printed on tin by Huntley, Boorne & Stevens Ltd, Reading. *Huntley & Palmers.*

Chapter 7
Design: survivals and new approaches

Nineteenth-century printing shows a strange blend of the old and the new: though great innovations were made in printing technology and many new kinds of work issued from the machines, very little fresh thought was given to matters of design. The predominant concern was with style, and in many branches of printing stylistic mantles were assumed according to prevailing interests and tastes without much concern for their suitability for the particular job in hand. Most such styles were either historically based or, particularly after the Great Exhibition, derived from foreign sources. This kind of approach to designing is particularly evident in fine books and prestige printing generally where style often served as a trimming to disguise unthinking use of traditional formulas. Hardly any branch of printing entirely escaped such influences in the second half of the nineteenth century. Only when the printer or designer was faced with new kinds of work to produce, where there were no real models to follow and where practical considerations were often paramount, did he begin to break away from his own conventions and design in order to solve particular problems.

A parallel situation is seen very clearly in nineteenth-century architecture and engineering. On the one hand there are the mock Gothic towers and classical façades of town halls, museums, and hospitals, which were built in known styles in order to impress; on the other, the unprecedented and often exciting forms of bridges and railway terminuses, which resulted from the solution of rather specific problems using, for the most part, basic engineering structures. There is little in nineteenth-century printing to compare with such masterpieces of engineering, but they certainly had their modest counterparts, and the illustration overleaf may serve as an example [287].

One of the reasons for the sterility of design in many areas of printing in the later nineteenth and early twentieth centuries was the strength of the book tradition. Some practices established in manuscript and early printed books have persisted with great consistency to this day, largely because human beings and their methods of reading have not changed significantly. Line length, for instance, may vary from one book to another according to its size and purpose, but generally speaking the number of words on a line has remained remarkably constant; and research this century has tended to confirm what printers have determined pragmatically over the centuries. There can be little to challenge in such customs; indeed, contemporary typographers might well learn something from them.

Other traditional practices in book design seem to have less general validity. Large initial letters, which originally served to decorate a manuscript or printed page as well as to identify a chapter opening or help the reader to find his way around the text [285], are now more often used as stylistic conventions and usually serve neither purpose. Contents pages of books continue to be set to the full width of the text with the items ranging to the left and the page numbers to the extreme right [286] – a practice which might satisfy some rational visual or technical structure but, especially when the entries are short, can lead to difficulties in reading. These are just two of the

285 An example of the use of large initial letters to help the reader find his way around the text. *Dictionaire Francoislatin*, Paris, 1539. Letterpress, with *manière criblée* relief blocks, printed by Robert Estienne. Page size 292 × 200 mm. *Reading University Library*.

CONTENTS

286 Contents page of a research report published in 1951. 245 × 175 mm.

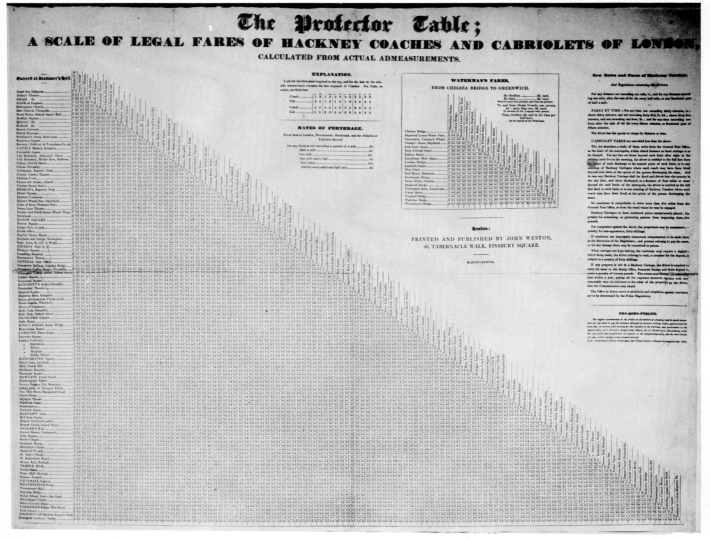

287 Notice of legal fares of Hackney coaches and cabriolets of London, 1837. Letterpress, printed and published by John Weston, London. 467 × 597 mm. *John Johnson Collection.*

conventions of book typography which still flourish and, so far as I am aware, they continued unchallenged until the late nineteenth century.

No tradition in English printing has been quite so powerful as that of the roman letter and, in particular, the letterforms used for text composition in books. Fifteenth- and sixteenth-century Italian type designs, which were themselves modelled on contemporary scripts, have survived with only minor modifications and have been adapted to suit the needs of hot-metal composing machines, photosetting, and direct impression composition. Reading rests on the understanding of conventions, and so strong has the hold of the traditional forms of the Latin alphabet been that no new designs of letters for text composition have departed radically from the shapes and proportions of the earliest roman types. Research has shown that we prefer reading, and also read most easily, those types we are most familiar with; and there can be no stronger force in maintaining traditional forms.

The basic arrangement of the printed book was also established in Renaissance Italy, and by the end of the eighteenth century even special problems in book production had come to be solved in predictable and generally accepted ways. Basic solutions were usually adapted to suit new needs and methods of production as they arose, or were changed in style to conform with current tastes. As it happens, however, crafts often flourish under such circumstances – and printing was no exception. Compliance with conventions encourages the full exploration of possibilities within the prescribed system and leads to a continual refinement of them; critical awareness can be sharpened through repeated experience in similar fields; and, what is more, the very limitations imposed by tradition can prevent the inept from making gross blunders. Instances of this from the past are numerous and can be found in many areas of human endeavour, but the example of Georgian domestic architecture may be mentioned because of the qualities it shares with the typography of the same period. The books printed by Bensley, Bell, and Bulmer [288, 289] during the decades immediately before and after the year 1800 show much the same sense of inevitability and propriety as Georgian architecture and helped to create what Stanley Morison has described as the finest period of English typography.

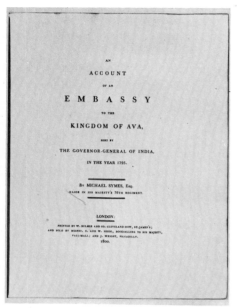

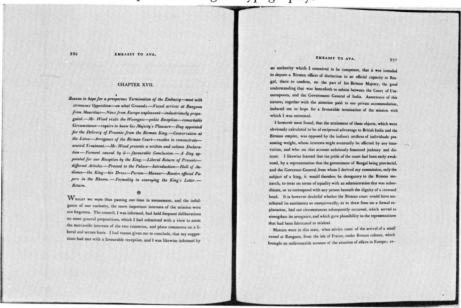

288,289 Title-page and chapter opening of M. Symes, *An account of an embassy to the kingdom of Ava*, 1800. Letterpress, printed by William Bulmer. Page size 326 × 255 mm.

Since the late eighteenth century, book designers have mostly followed this traditional pattern, adapting it to new purposes and endowing it with different associations through the use of appropriate papers, types, and decorations. Charles Whittingham and William Morris in the nineteenth century, and Francis Meynell and Stanley Morison in this century, though they produced books which often look very different from one another, were all basically working within the established conventions of book design. All made major contributions to printing, but they do not appear to have questioned the centuries-old conventions of book design – or, if they did question them, they must have decided that they were worth preserving. When Charles Whittingham printed an extraordinary edition of Euclid's geometry for the mathematician Oliver Byrne in 1847, which was a most forward-looking book in its visual approach to teaching geometry through colours, and a remarkable technical achievement in letterpress printing as well, he handled the text in a thoroughly traditional manner and included large wood-engraved letters in the *manière criblée* style popular in the sixteenth century [290, 291].

290, 291 Oliver Byrne, *The first six books of the elements of Euclid in which coloured diagrams and symbols are used instead of letters for the greater ease of learners*, 1847. Letterpress, printed in four colours by Charles Whittingham for the publisher William Pickering. Page size 235 × 188 mm.

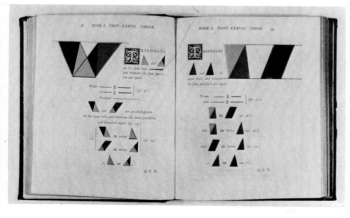

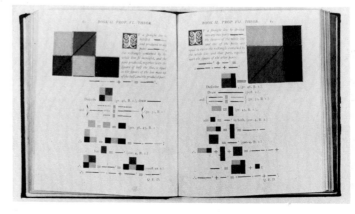

It must be admitted that there were often very good reasons for preserving some of the conventions of book typography. After all, even such an apparent anachronism as the numbering of the preliminary pages of a book in roman numerals and those of the rest in arabic numerals is soundly based on practical grounds. It allows the preliminary pages, which can often be written only after the main body of the book has been set, to be paginated and printed later. Nevertheless, traditional practices have inhibited the development of book design in some respects and have been so powerful that their influence on typography has extended well beyond the field of book production.

Even posters were once conceived in a form which stemmed from book typography. In the late eighteenth and early nineteenth centuries, before the introduction of bold display types, many posters or window bills were designed according to book conventions with the main text matter set in paragraphs with their first lines indented [292]. A large initial letter was frequently used for the opening line, together with capitals for the first word or so, and the equivalent of a running headline was often placed at the top of the sheet and separated from the main text by a rule. It may be that the copy was written by the client in a formal manner, and that the style of writing was even modelled on the form of language found in other kinds of printing, but typographic design and matters of linguistics cannot really be considered separately.

As methods of writing copy changed and large bold types were introduced, posters began to break away from the book tradition [293, 294]. It is impossible to say which of these innovations came first, but during the second and third decades of the nineteenth century a new kind of typographic poster began to be produced which made use of bold display letters to emphasise individual words or lines. In turn this too developed into a tradition which continues to this day in a rather watered-down form in the auction bills of estate agents. The ingredients of this tradition were formed from the practice of the craft itself, and are not primarily the result of the application of aesthetic principles. The need to convey information as powerfully as possible was clearly uppermost in the printer's mind, and his instinctive reaction was to use the maximum size letterforms that would fit into the available space. He would almost certainly have designed his poster in the chase, and probably on the bed of the press, and as a result many typographical posters of the nineteenth century show very clearly the limits of the rectangular shape into which the letters were fitted like children's bricks [294]. The use of condensed letters to give maximum effect to long words in narrow formats, and of expanded letters for short words in wide formats, arises quite naturally

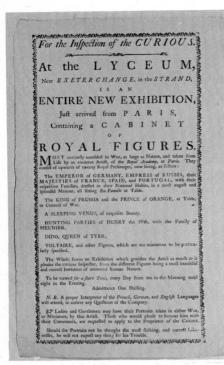

292 Exhibition notice, late eighteenth century. Letterpress, anon. 315 × 198 mm. *John Johnson Collection.*

293 Auction bill, 1850. Letterpress, printed by J. Diplock, Trowbridge. 500 × 380 mm. *Wiltshire County Record Office.*

294 Notice of entertainment, 1874. Letterpress, printed in green and black by H. Collings & Co., Bishop's Stortford. 502 × 380 mm. *Essex County Record Office.*

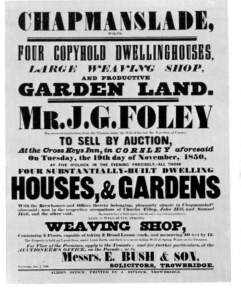

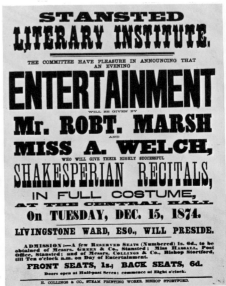

from this practice. The use of a variety of different types on the same poster may also have been determined initially by practical considerations – in this case by the limited sizes of the founts of large display letters held by the printer. Repetition of the same letter even only two or three times on the same poster may well have presented a real embarrassment to the small jobbing printer who undertook this sort of work, and an obvious solution to the problem was to turn to a different type of a similar size. No doubt the visual possibilities of variety were soon exploited for their own sake, but the fashion for using a medley of types on posters in the nineteenth century may well have had its roots in technical problems.

The history of printing reveals many similar cases in which features originally derived from technical limitations or the characteristics of a particular process survived for purely aesthetic reasons or because of their associations. In the course of time their original significance often ceased to be understood and, as a result, they usually became debased. The survival of such forms can be seen as a symptom of uncreative designing, yet it is not without its value. Continuity of style in certain fields of printing does at least mean that categories of work can be identified by their general flavour even before their contents can be read. An auction sale poster can usually be distinguished at a glance from a poster for a concert in the Royal Festival Hall, and so can a legal document from a piece of sales literature. This is an important function of design in printing, and the value of conventions as an aid to recognition should not be underestimated. In spoken language the linguist distinguishes a variety of registers which are commonly used in different circumstances – when presenting a scientific paper, reprimanding children, talking to one's lover, and so forth – and these too must depend on a residue of convention in order to have the desired effect.

Examples of the survival of conventions in printing outside the book field are plentiful in the nineteenth century, and some have lasted well into the twentieth century. One of the strongest of these is the survival of the engraved style in work such as letterheads, invoices, invitations, and music titles. It was already firmly established in the latter part of the eighteenth century, and is typified by the curving and swelling lines which arise from the way in which the lozenge-shaped burin is worked across the copper, making wider marks as it cuts deeper into the metal [295]. The shapes of the letters were mainly based on those of the great writing masters of the eighteenth century, and their ornate flourishes were easily adapted to engraving. The burin lent itself to the translation of this style as it moves most naturally in wide sweeping curves in much the same way as figure skaters on ice. This method of working lasted well into the present century for the production of many

295 Billhead of Henry Barnett, copper-plate printer, 1835. Copper-engraved. 126 × 157 mm. *John Johnson Collection.*

296 Billhead of R. Cartwright, law stationer, 1834. Lithographed. 114 × 187 mm. *John Johnson Collection.*

297 Billhead of the London Wine Company, 1826. Wood-engraving, with type. 243 × 200 mm. *John Johnson Collection.*

298 Invoice of George Hadfield & Co. Ltd, 1930. Lithographed heading, the text overprinted letterpress. 262 × 206 mm.

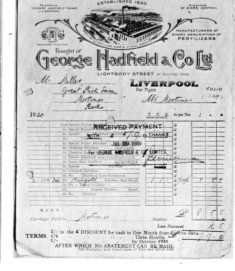

kinds of prestige jobbing printing and still continues on a very limited scale, but by the middle of the nineteenth century copper-engraving could no longer compete commercially with letterpress and lithographic printing. Consequently, these other processes entered the field which had hitherto been virtually the province of copper-engraving and, naturally enough, craftsmen adapted the traditional style of working to their own purposes. Lithographers found little difficulty in copying the style of copper-engraved lettering and ornament [296]. Letterpress printers had greater technical problems [297], but the typefounders issued types and decorative units which enabled them to emulate the style created in the late eighteenth century, and similar designs are still used by jobbing printers for invitations and business cards.

The practice of printing an engraved vignette of a tradesman's shop, workshop, or factory on his notepaper and invoices also continued as a general convention right through the nineteenth century, and was only really abandoned after the Second World War [297, 298]. The familiar custom in such work of using an integrated design consisting of both picture and words was originally evolved in copper-engraving, but was later taken over in lithography and, with rather more difficulty, in wood-engraving.

The engraved tradition also left its mark on security printing and postage stamps. The engraved patterns and copper-engraved styles of lettering used in the early nineteenth century for bank-notes, promissory notes, and passports had a very wide influence, and they still survive in emasculated and rather unconvincing forms in similar work produced today. A particularly

299 Exchequer bill, with instructions for cutting 'indentwise' through the flourishes, 1695. Copper-engraving. 247 × 206 mm. *John Johnson Collection.*

300 Set of three exchequer bills, cut indentwise, 1697. Copper-engraved. 277 × 170 mm. *John Johnson Collection.*

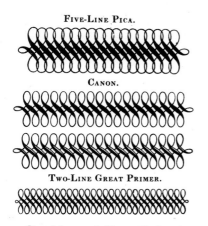

FIVE-LINE PICA.

CANON.

TWO-LINE GREAT PRIMER.

301 Cast 'cheques'. From Caslon & Livermore, *Specimen of printing types*, 1825. *St Bride Printing Library.*

302 Coupon for Outline low fat spread from a Ryvita wrapper showing the use of the 'cheque' motif in the border, 1969. Photogravure, printed in red and blue. 50 × 123 mm.

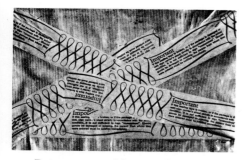

303 Paper tape used by a mail-order firm for sealing its parcels, 1969.

304 Penny Black postage stamp, issued on 6 May 1840. Engraved on steel by Frederick Heath and printed by Perkins, Bacon & Co. *British Museum.*

persistent example of this is the elaborate scroll work found on copper-engraved exchequer notes of the seventeenth century [299]. Such documents were designed to be cut down the middle of the patterns and separated, and both the line of the cut and the complex and varied patterns had then to be matched exactly. The forms of such patterns derived from pen work and were reinforced by the copper-engraver's burin. They were widely used on copper-engraved notes and cheques for a century or more [300], and from the end of the eighteenth century the typefounders produced similar designs for letterpress printing which were known as 'cheques' [301]. In the course of time these cheque patterns ceased to have any practical value as a means of preventing forgery and came to be used merely for their association with security printing [302, 303].

When Frederick Heath engraved the designs for the Penny Black postage stamp, which was issued in 1840, he adopted as a matter of course the familiar swelling lines and dot-and-lozenge techniques of copper-engraving to model the young Queen Victoria's head [304]. Later designers of postage stamps were even more influenced by copper-engraving and placed the sovereign's head within an oval, which was a practice that had flourished in portrait engraving for centuries. The placing of a profile portrait within some kind of oval framework continued in British stamps until recently, and so too did the method of hatching used to model the head. A tradition of this kind could hardly survive in a very vital form for over a century and, as with bank-notes, there has been a gradual but progressive decline in the standard of such work.

One very persistent graphic idiom which has survived for over 400 years is the chiaroscuro print – a method of printing one or more tones of the same colour (usually buff or straw) either with or without a black working. It was originally developed in woodcutting in the early sixteenth century as a means of reproducing tonal drawings, but it was revived and adapted by John Baptist Jackson and Elisha Kirkall in the eighteenth century and used for other purposes as well. From then on the chiaroscuro print had an enormous influence and became one of the accepted idioms in which printed images of all kinds could be conceived. In this country its popularity was assured when William Gilpin began to produce books based on his picturesque tours which contained aquatint plates tinted by hand with monochrome washes of water-colour, usually buff or straw in colour. Gilpin explained his recourse to these tints as a means of counteracting the glaring whiteness of the paper – though he must also have been influenced by the current use of the Claude glass, which was a piece of amber-tinted glass which the eighteenth-century connoisseur used to hold in front of an English view to give it the golden glow of the Italian campagna as seen in Claude Lorraine's paintings. Right from the early days of lithography a tint stone was used in Germany to support the black printing, partly because of its association with German chiaroscuro woodcuts, and partly because the tone could be used to give the paper much the same colour as the lithographic stone on which the drawing was made. In addition, when highlights were scraped away from the tint stone, it could be used as a means of imitating drawings on tinted paper touched up with white. The chiaroscuro method was very popular with German lithographers and for a short period after 1817 it began to be used in this country too; then, as a result of technical improvements made in the mid-1830s, it became almost the accepted idiom for making lithographs all over Europe. The style was also taken up in wood-engraving in the nineteenth century, first of all in the *Illustrations to Puckle's Club* (1820), then by Savage, Baxter, and others, and later in some of the large wood-engraved plates of the *Illustrated London News* and the *Graphic*. The style was again adapted to new purposes when process engraving was perfected, and the printing of double-toned half-tone blocks in black and buff was extremely popular for a long time, and before the Second World War even warranted a special classification in process engravers' price lists.

The technique of compound-plate printing, which is described in the chapter on colour printing, also had a lasting influence. It was originally invented in an attempt to prevent the forgery of bank-notes and other security printing, but it very soon began to be copied. An important early use of the process was for the coronation of George IV in 1821; and for that occasion, while the tickets to view the ceremony in Westminster Abbey and Westminster Hall were printed by the genuine compound-plate method [397, 398], the less important pass tickets were merely printed in two colours in imitation of the style of compound-plate prints [348–50]. By this time the style had already become associated with a particular kind of printing. Some firms, such as Stephens, the ink makers, began by using the process for their labels as a means of assuring the public of the authenticity of their products, but ended by copying only the appearance of such prints.

A few more examples may help to emphasise the persistence of conventions in printing. A familiar feature of estate agents' auction bills is the reversed-out logotype [305–7], which stems from a technique frequently used in the second quarter of the nineteenth century [308]. The traditional estate agents'

305 Auction bill, Martin & Pole, Reading, 1969. Letterpress, printed in blue on yellow paper by the Creative Press, Reading. 890 × 572 mm.

306 Auction bill, Hampton & Sons, London, 1969. Letterpress, printed in blue and black by Rawlinsons Ltd, Northwood. 894 × 572 mm.

307 Auction bill, A. C. Frost & Co., Burnham, 1969. Letterpress, printed in red and black by Rawlinsons Ltd, Northwood. 763 × 509 mm.

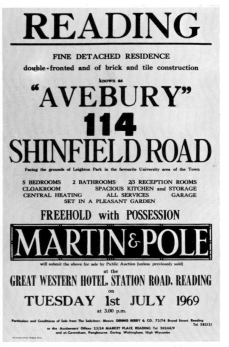

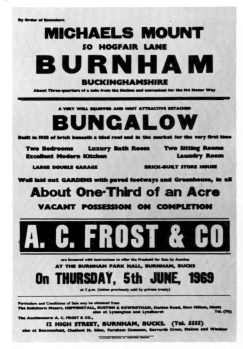

308 Auction bill, Elliot Smith, Cambridge, 1829. Letterpress, printed by Weston Hatfield, Cambridge. 445 × 370 mm. *Trumpington Parish Church.*

309 Sale catalogues: *left*, 1808, page size 333 × 210 mm; *right*, 1934, page size 330 × 205 mm.

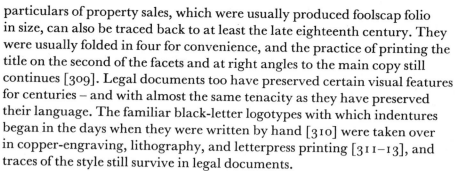

particulars of property sales, which were usually produced foolscap folio in size, can also be traced back to at least the late eighteenth century. They were usually folded in four for convenience, and the practice of printing the title on the second of the facets and at right angles to the main copy still continues [309]. Legal documents too have preserved certain visual features for centuries – and with almost the same tenacity as they have preserved their language. The familiar black-letter logotypes with which indentures began in the days when they were written by hand [310] were taken over in copper-engraving, lithography, and letterpress printing [311–13], and traces of the style still survive in legal documents.

310		
311	312	313

Indenture logotypes. Examples of style surviving changes in methods of production:

310 Manuscript, 1786. *Essex County Record Office.*

311 Copper-engraved, 1841. *Museum of English Rural Life, Reading University.*

312 Lithographed, 1851. *Essex County Record Office.*

313 Letterpress, cast logotype from V. & J. Figgins, *Epitome of specimens, c.* 1850. *St Bride Printing Library.*

Sufficient examples have been given to show the extent to which printing styles and conventions have been influenced by technical considerations, and how some of the conventions survived for a long time even after the original methods of production had changed. These were the main forces that worked from within the printing and allied trades to shape the appearance of printing; but other influences, both social and artistic, were brought to bear from outside.

Art and architecture have played a significant part in the appearance of printing and from time to time have been responsible for major waves of change, the ripples of which eventually spread far and wide to become absorbed in the mainstream of printing. An account of such changes would be a record of the history of the art of the period and must be looked for elsewhere, but it is worth mentioning that the appearance of printing, at least in the nineteenth and twentieth centuries, seems to have been the result of a continual tug-of-war between the influences of function, technique, and convention on the one hand and the forces of current fashion on the other. Of course, these influences need not be in conflict with one another, and sometimes there does seem to have been a basic harmony between them. As examples of this we may take the charming embossed designs of Dobbs and others of the 1820s [314] which lent themselves naturally to the translation of the stucco ornaments made fashionable in the previous century by Robert Adam [315], or the striking poster designs of E. McKnight Kauffer of the

314 Trade card of Dobbs & Co., *c.* 1821. Copper-engraving with embossed border. 116 × 165 mm. *John Johnson Collection.*

315 Robert Adam, detail of stucco ceiling in the dining room in Hatchlands Park, Worsley, 1758-9.

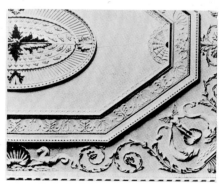

1920s and 1930s [316] which owed a great deal to contemporary abstract painting in their use of powerful shapes and colours [317]. For the most part, however, the real value of the artist in relation to printing has been as a catalyst, sowing seeds of discontent with the established order, rather than mapping out sure paths for the future.

316 E. McKnight Kauffer, London Underground poster, 1923. Colour lithography, printed by Vincent Brooks, Day & Son Ltd, London. *London Transport Board.*

317 Wassily Kandinsky, 'Battle', 1910. Painting in the Tate Gallery. 945 × 1300 mm. *Tate Gallery.*

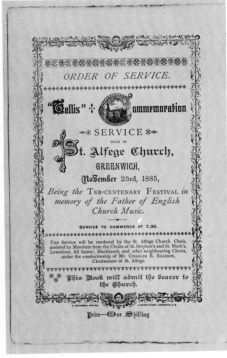

318 Order of service to commemorate the tercentenary of the death of Thomas Tallis, 1885. Letterpress, printed by H. Richardson, London. 242 × 155 mm.

The Gothic Revival (the only important revival of the nineteenth century that printing could legitimately share with architecture) produced its pioneers who designed for printing, and Henry Shaw, Owen Jones, and Noel Humphreys produced impressive work in this style because of their genuine enthusiasm for the art of the Middle Ages. But a private indulgence of this kind provided no long-term alternative to the less idiosyncratic and self-conscious typography of the Georgian era, and eventually led to half a century of derivative work [318]. Similarly, William Morris's return to the past, though it had its imitators for a decade or so, and though it was more fundamental in its objectives, provided no real answer for the future. Art Nouveau, Futurism, Cubism, de Stijl, and Dada have all left their mark on printing, and so too have the numerous post-war art movements. Like the Gothic Revival, however, their role has been to provide a visual repertoire of style, and for the most part they have only affected advertising, magazines, and similar categories of printing. Even the work of the Bauhaus in Germany, which of all movements had the most to offer printing and other areas of design, tended to be seen in England at the time only for its superficial qualities of modernity, such as clean-looking lines, and its essential message was at first overlooked.

New approaches to design in printing grew out of the social and economic necessity in an industrialised society of communicating clearly, widely, and persuasively. They began to make themselves felt in the first half of the nineteenth century in fairly routine work, such as road and railway guides, timetables, directories, plans, accounts, catalogues, and price lists, and later on in advertising and packaging as well. Numerous examples of work of various kinds can be found among the illustrations in the second part of this book. The originality and effectiveness of the ordering of the information in such printing is often taken for granted because it works so well. Bradshaw's first railway timetables, for instance, which were produced small enough to fit easily into the pocket or purse, are masterly examples of sensible designing [319]. Complex information about times, distances, stations, and fares is organised in a form which is easily intelligible, and this general pattern has been followed for over a century. Some surprisingly graphic methods of presenting information were also developed in the nineteenth century. As examples we may take the popular broadsheets showing in pictorial form

319 *Bradshaw's railway companion*, 1842. Letterpress. Page size 115 × 75 mm. *John Johnson Collection.*

4 **GREAT WESTERN.**

Distance.	DOWN TRAINS. STATIONS.	8¾ a.m.	6 a.m. mail.	11 a.m.	8 a.m.	9 a.m.	10¼ a.m. mail.	11 a.m.	12 noon.	1½ p.m.	2 p.m.	4 p.m.	5 p.m.	5½ p.m.	7½ p.m.	8 55 p.m. mail.	GOODS. a.m.	GOODS. p.m.
Mls.	PADDINGTON ..	..	6 0	..	8 0	9 0	10 15	11 0	12 0	1 30	2 0	4 0	5 0	5 30	7 30	8 55	4½	9½
5½	Ealing	..	..	..	..	9 11	..	11 11	..	1 41	..	4 11	..	5 41	7 41	..	..	..
7¼	Hanwell	..	..	..	..	9 15	..	11 15	..	1 45	..	4 15	..	5 45	7 45	..	..	..
9	Southall	..	A	..	..	9 20	..	11 20	..	1 50	..	4 20	..	5 50	7 50	..	D.	..
13	West Drayton	..	..	..	B	9 29	..	11 29	..	1 59	..	4 29	..	5 59	7 59	9 20	5 24	..
18	SLOUGH	..	6 35	..	8 40	9 40	10 50	11 40	12 40	2 10	2 38	4 40	5 53	6 10	8 10	9 30	5 44	10 30
22½	MAIDENHEAD ..	..	6 45	..	B	9 50	11 2	11 50	..	—	2 50	4 50	..	6 20	8 20	9 40	6 0	..
30¾	Twyford	..	..	..	9 5	—	..	—	1 12	..	3 8	5 8	..	—	8 38	..	6 30	..
35¾	READING	..	7 15	..	9 20	..	11 35	..	1 25	..	3 22	5 20	6 15	..	8 50	10 10	6 50	11 36
41¼	Pangbourne	..	..	..	9 35	..	..	..	1 42	..	..	—	6 27	..	9 5	..	7 40	..
44½	Goring	..	7 34	..	..	..	..	..	..	..	..	..	..	..	9 12	..	..	..
47½	Wallingford Road..	..	..	..	9 49	..	..	..	1 56	..	3 45	..	6 40	..	9 20	10 35	..	12 19
56¼	STEVENTON	..	7 55	..	10 8	..	12 18	..	2 15	..	4 3	..	6 58	..	9 35	10 50	8 30	12 50
63¾	Farington Road	..	8 10	..	C	..	12 33	..	..	..	4 18	..	7 14	..	9 50	11 5	..	1 19
71¼	Shrivenham	..	..	..	10 38	..	..	..	2 45	..	4 36	..	..	..	10 5	..	..	1 49
77	Swindon (Junction.)	..	8 35	..	10 50	..	1 0	..	2 58	..	4 50	..	7 40	..	10 20	11 30	10 0	2 15
	Dep. for Cheltenham	..	8 55	..	11 0	..	1 10	..	3 8	..	5 0	..	7 50	..	..	11 40	11 0	8 55
	81¼ Purton	..	9 5	..	11 10	..	..	..	3 18	..	5 8	..	..	..	..	..	11 10	9 5
	85¼ Minety	..	9 15	..	11 20	..	1 30	..	..	..	5 18	..	8 5	..	..	..	11 20	9 15
	95 Cirencester	..	9 50	..	11 40	..	1 55	..	3 48	..	5 40	..	8 30	..	..	12 25	11 40	9 50
77	Swindon, Junc.(depr	..	8 45	..	11 0	..	1 10	..	3 8	..	5 0	..	7 50	..	..	11 40	10 20	2 30
82¾	WOOT. BASSET..	..	8 58	..	..	..	..	..	3 20	..	5 13	..	8 2	..	..	..	11 50	3 0
93¾	CHIPPENHAM ..	..	9 23	..	11 32	..	1 40	..	3 45	..	5 35	..	8 25	..	..	12 10	12 40	3 45
98¼	Corsham	..	9 33	..	11 42	..	..	..	3 55	..	..	..	8 35	..	..	..	..	..
101¾	Box	..	9 43	..	..	p. m.	..	..	..	..	5 55	..	..	..	..	..	..	..
106¾	BATH	8 45	9 55	11 0	12 3	1 0	2 5	..	4 15	5 0	6 10	8 30	9 0	..	..	12 40	1 20	5 0
108¼	Twerton	..	10 0	..	..	1 5	..	..	..	5 5	..	..	..	..	..	..	..	..
111¼	Saltford	8 58	..	11 13	..	1 13	..	..	..	5 13	..	..	..	..	..	..	..	..
113¼	Keynsham	9 5	10 15	11 20	..	1 20	..	..	..	5 20	..	8 50	..	..	..	..	..	..
118¼	BRISTOL, arrival..	9 15	10 30	11 30	12 30	1 30	2 30	..	4 45	5 30	6 40	9 0	9 25	..	..	1 5	2 0	5 40
	BRISTOL, depart. .	9 25	10 50	..	12 40	—	2 40	..	5 0	—	7 0	—	—	..	..	1 15	7 0	9 25
126¼	Calling at Nailsea ..	9 45	11 8	..	..	..	..	..	5 18	..	7 18	..	..	..	..	..	7 18	9 45
130¼	Clevedon Rd. at Yatt	9 55	11 18	..	1 5	..	3 3	..	5 26	..	7 27	..	..	..	..	..	7 27	9 55
133¾	Banwell	..	11 25	..	..	..	..	..	..	..	7 35	..	..	..	..	..	7 35	..
136¾	WESTON SUPER.	10 15	11 35	..	1 20	..	..	..	5 40	..	7 42	..	..	..	..	..	7 42	10 15
145¾	Highbridge	10 35	11 53	..	..	..	3 30	..	5 56	..	8 10	..	..	..	..	..	8 10	10 35
151¼	BRIDGEWATER .	10 50	12 10	..	1 50	..	3 45	..	6 10	..	8 30	..	..	..	..	2 25	8 30	10 50

N.B.—Trains will stop on particular days as indicated by the letters A Wednesdays, B B Saturdays, C Mondays, D Wednesdays, and E Tuesdays.

On Sundays.—From Paddington and Cirencester to Bridgewater, mail, at 10 15 a.m., 2, and mail 8 55 p.m.; from Paddington to Reading, at 9 a.m. from Paddington to Maidenhead, at 5 p.m.; from Paddington to Slough, at 9 30 a.m.; from Swindon Junction to Bridgewater, at 8 45 a.m.; from Bath to Bridgewater, at 8 45 a.m.; from Bath to Bristol, at 5, and 8 30 p.m.

N.B. Bridgewater is 11 miles from Taunton, 42 from Exeter, and 90 from Plymouth: Cirencester is 15 miles from Cheltenham, 12 from Stroud, and 17 from Gloucester. Goods' Trains on Sunday will leave Swindon at 1 10, instead of 8 55 a.m., or 11 a.m.

the sequence of carriages in coronation and funeral processions [394], the colour-printed column chart displaying statistical information relating to attendance, publications sold, and refreshments consumed during the course of the Great Exhibition [320], or the diagrams mentioned above which were printed in four colours as an aid to the understanding of geometry [290, 291].

Such typographic and graphic work had to be planned from scratch; fresh approaches were inevitable as there were no real models to follow. The book printer, on the other hand, knew from his experience of past jobs just how a book should be organised, and the accepted conventions of book production were described by the authors of printers' manuals for a century or more. The only major decisions which remained to be taken by the printer concerned type size and spacing between the lines; and these decisions were made, if we are to judge by the manuals, on the basis of the number of pages a book should make. I can find no reference in such manuals to designing or planning a book in advance, beyond casting off the copy to calculate the number of pages. The designing was presumably done on the shop floor by the compositor or the overseer, with perhaps just the client's instruction to follow a particular precedent – and, of course, a great deal of designing is still done this way. Such methods would have been of little avail, however, where there were no precedents to follow and where the material was not straightforward; and at some stage, and I suspect in the nineteenth century, it became common practice for designs to be tried out in advance on paper.

A number of drawings which appear to be layouts for the famous *Nuremberg Chronicle* of 1493 have recently been published,[43] and some rough sketches for Plantin's title-pages have also survived. The first English printer who is recorded as having prepared layouts seems to have been T. C. Hansard, though he makes no mention of the practice in his extensive manual, *Typographia*, which was published in 1825. Though little seems to be known about the origins of the practice of working out typographic designs on paper, it proved to have great significance because it released typography from the tyranny of some of its craft-based conventions. Like so many radical changes, however, it has had some unfavourable repercussions, and in this century has led to the emergence of a new kind of designer, often working independently of the printing trade, who only too frequently knows less than he needs to about the industrial processes he is designing for.

[43] A. Wilson, *The design of books* (New York & London, 1967)

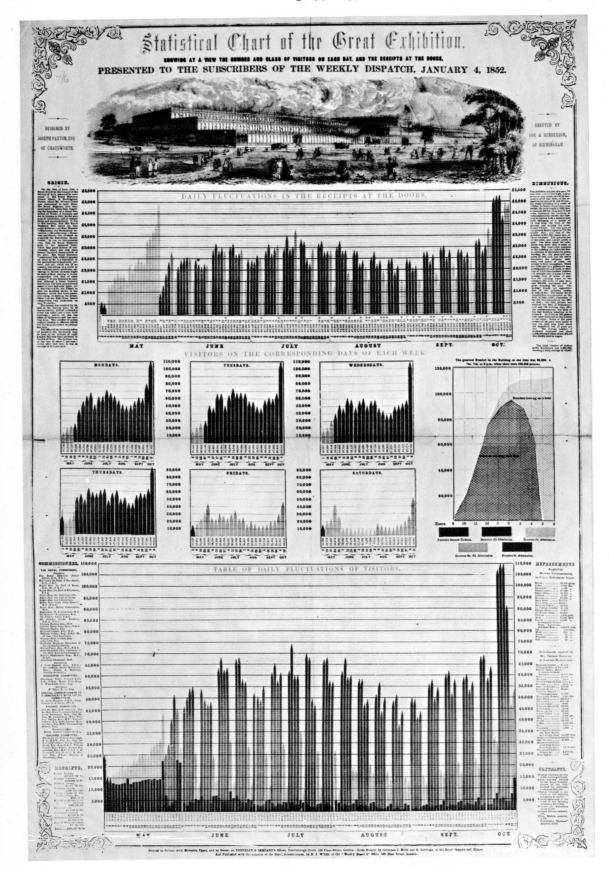

320 Statistical chart of the Great Exhibition, published by the *Weekly Dispatch*, 1852. Letterpress, printed in blue, red, yellow, and black by Vizetelly & Co., from designs by Corporals J. Mack and A. Gardener of the Royal Sappers and Miners. 750 × 510 mm. *Reading University Library*.

The first important break with one of the most enduring traditions of printing came with the challenge to the principle of symmetry. This tradition, which is rooted in the ideas of Renaissance humanism, began to be undermined in the nineteenth century as a result of various stylistic and technical influences. The Gothic Revival had drawn attention to the great variety of medieval manuscripts, many of which were not organised within such a strict geometrical framework as printed books. While manuscripts were usually written within some kind of grid, which was repeated from page to page for the sake of convenience, it did not impose nearly such rigid limitations as those demanded by the craft of printing and was modified as occasion demanded according to linguistic and decorative needs. It is also a characteristic of the Western tradition of writing that it is easier to start lines at the left-hand margin than to centre them, as centred lines involve very careful planning. In letterpress printing, on the other hand, any break with the overall rectangular structure of a type area presents considerable technical problems, though either method of composing lines can be adopted with equal ease.

The study of medieval manuscript books in the nineteenth century revealed a structural freedom which, for both technical and philosophical reasons, was not found in early printed books; and it upset the well-established convention of symmetry. But though some printers were prepared to abandon symmetry from around the middle of the nineteenth century as a means of producing books in a medieval style, the positive practical advantages of the change were not appreciated at this stage. Later on in the century the widespread interest in the intuitive and, to Western eyes, unorthodox aspects of Japanese art left its mark on printing, and led Whistler to experiment with asymmetric typography in a more enlightened and original way in a few of his manifestoes and exhibition catalogues [321].

The rapid commercial growth of lithography in the jobbing field with the introduction of powered machines shortly after the middle of the nineteenth century was another reason for the movement away from symmetrical design. Lithography imposed very few technical limitations on the appearance of printing and lithographic artists and letterers explored its possibilities to the full, deriving their inspiration from all kinds of sources and combining images and words in every conceivable way. In face of this threat from lithography the letterpress jobbing printer developed a similar style in the 1880s [322] which became known as Artistic Printing or the Leicester Free Style (as it was particularly popular among Leicester printers). It is typified by the rejection of many of the conventions which stemmed from the traditional craft of letterpress printing: symmetry was abandoned, words and ornaments were irrationally placed, decorative rules and flowers were used with great abandon, and jobs were frequently printed in close register in many colours. Such virtuoso pieces of typography were made easier by the invention of a machine which could bend plain or patterned rules into all sorts of shapes for decorative purposes, and by the invention of the small jobbing platen machine which gave accurate register. All the same, the time spent in setting work of this complexity could only be justified economically because of the greater output of the new machines and the longer runs which were needed to meet growing markets.

Though William Morris and some of his followers in the Private Press Movement took up the practice of ranging their text to the left on title-pages, book typography of the nineteenth and early twentieth centuries for the most part held firmly to the principle of symmetry. It was only in jobbing printing that the tradition was seriously challenged. There was no real dogma behind the change, however, and symmetry was abandoned at first in the course of producing novel and exciting visual effects, without any serious alternatives being explored.

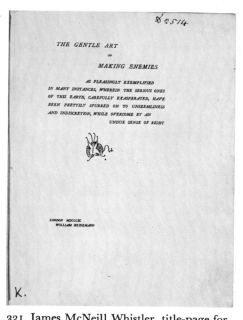

321 James McNeill Whistler, title-page for his *The gentle art of making enemies*, 1890. 201 × 153 mm.

322 Raithby & Lawrence, *Specimens of printing*, Leicester, 1884. Letterpress, printed in crimson. 111 × 166 mm. *St Bride Printing Library*.

323 F. T. Marinetti, *Les mots en liberté futuristes*, 1919.

324 El Lissitzky, cover for *Merz*, 8/9, 1924.

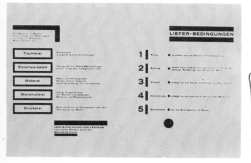

325 Herbert Bayer, Bauhaus catalogue, 1925.

44 B.Evans, 'A note on modern typography', in J.C.Tarr, *Printing to-day* (London, 1945), p.168

The real break with symmetry, and other aspects of the typographic tradition as well, came in the twentieth century; and it formed part of a much wider movement in art, architecture, and industrial design which challenged accepted concepts and sought to find new forms more suited to the machine age. Isolated pleas for a new approach to design which openly embraced the machine were made in America and Europe around the turn of the century by Frank Lloyd Wright, Henri van de Velde, and other architects. By the outbreak of the First World War the movement had taken root on the continent and had begun to find enthusiastic support from groups of impassioned artists. Typography began to be affected by these new ideas just before the war when the Italian Futurist leader, Marinetti [323], used a more dynamic approach to typography in some of the movement's manifestoes 'to give words all the speed and power of aeroplanes, trains, waves, of explosives, of the sea spray, of atomic energy'.[44] Soon after the war the Russian El Lissitzky, who came under the influence of the Suprematist painter Malevich in Russia, began exploring the visual possibilities of words in some of his own paintings and, later on, in printed work as well. He moved to Berlin in 1921, where he met many of the most advanced thinkers in the arts and took advantage of the better printing facilities to produce some of his most original typography [324]. Thereafter, he travelled widely in Europe and became one of the main channels through which the new ideas about typography and graphic design were spread.

New approaches to typography were explored more systematically at the art school, known as the Staatliches Bauhaus, which was founded by the architect Walter Gropius at Weimar in 1919. Though Gropius did not lay down any firm policy at the Bauhaus, he tried to reconcile some of the ideals of the English Arts and Crafts Movement, which had influenced him strongly, with the needs of industrial production; and by the time he came to set up the Bauhaus he had already completed the buildings which form the cornerstone of twentieth-century architecture and bear witness to an approach which has since become central to the development of design theory. Typography became part of the Bauhaus curriculum only after the school's move to Dessau in 1925. Like other areas of design taught there, it was approached with a real regard for function, an understanding of production methods, complete freedom from the fetters of tradition, and an underlying modernity of style. The typography produced by Herbert Bayer [325] and others at the Bauhaus in the 1920s marks the most profound change in the appearance of printing since its invention, and represents the first serious attempt to develop an approach which came to terms with the needs of both the user and the machine.

The traditional centred approach catered reasonably well for most problems encountered in book design, but it was not nearly adaptable enough to cater for the needs of advertising and business printing and took no account of the advent of the typewriter. In answer to these new requirements the typographers of the Bauhaus abandoned the symmetrical layout and placed their type in meaningful groups of words or sentences; and in doing so often arrived at striking visual arrangements. They frequently set words or lines of type at right angles to one another and used heavy rules and simple geometrical shapes to produce powerful abstract arrangements. They also used space as a positive factor in their designs and made great play with contrasts of scale, setting a single word or line of type in a very large size in close proximity to passages of text in composition sizes. The sanserif was regarded as the type most in keeping with the spirit of the machine age; its clean lines and geometrical shapes harmonised well with the prevailing style, and it marked the most obvious break with the black-letter tradition of German printing. The pictorial equivalent of the sanserif letter was photography, which was seen by Bauhaus designers as the most objective, powerful, and immediate means of pictorial communication.

As so often happens, however, there appears to have been a discrepancy between theory and practice. Much of the work of the Bauhaus typographers reflects a struggle between their desire to express the meaning of a message and their instinctive tendency to produce visually stimulating patterns. The two need not be in conflict, of course, but in Bauhaus typography which falls short of the highest standards they sometimes were, and on occasions words were arbitrarily broken or squeezed into geometrical shapes for the sake of effect and at the expense of ease of reading.

A similar break with the past was made in Germany in the late 1920s by Jan Tschichold. Though he never worked at the Bauhaus, he shared many of the same ideals and became the publicist of the new movement in typography. In 1928 he published his *Die neue Typographie* [326] and in 1935 his *Typographische Gestaltung*, in both of which he described the new asymmetrical approach to design for printing and demonstrated some of its applications. Tschichold's work was more restrained than that of the Bauhaus typographers and shows a greater respect for the meaning of the text and the method of production; and it is probably for these reasons that it has had a more lasting influence on the printing trade.

326 Jan Tschichold, *Die neue Typographie*, 1928.

The ideas promoted with such enthusiasm on the continent met with little favour in this country, where printing was still dominated by the book tradition. English typography was undergoing its own quiet revolution, and Stanley Morison, Francis Meynell, Bernard Newdigate, Harold Curwen, and Oliver Simon showed their dissatisfaction with the muddle of Victorian and Edwardian printing by reviving a straightforward approach to typography based on the finest examples from the past. Most of the examples they turned to were books, and the lessons learned from book production were applied with great discrimination by the Curwen Press and other quality printers to the field of jobbing work.

The German magazine *Gebrauchsgraphik*, founded in 1925, was one of the earliest channels through which the *avant-garde* graphic designer in England came to hear about the new continental ideas. In the first place, as might be expected, the influence of continental design made itself felt in advertising. In the 1920s the posters and other publicity designs of McKnight Kauffer and the work of the most enterprising agencies, such as Crawford's, where Ashley Havinden was designer, and Greenly's, began to take on exciting new visual forms [327]. The change revealed a new freedom of spirit in design rather than any particular dogma, but the trappings of continental design and painting were taken up with great verve. Many of the visual images derived in a general way from cubist painting and other forms of modern art, and the use of bold lettering, often set on the slant, stems from German typography. It was the advertisers too who abandoned for a time the practice of beginning proper nouns with capital letters and used German types, such as Erbar, Kabel, and Futura.

327 Ashley Havinden, poster for Eno's fruit salt, 1927. Colour lithograph, designed and produced by W. S. Crawford Ltd, printed by Haycock, Cadle & Graham Ltd, London. 762 × 508 mm. *Victoria & Albert Museum.*

In the early 1930s the ideals of the New Typography began to be set out for all the British printing trade to read in articles in *Commercial Art*, *Printing Review*, and *Penrose Annual*. Tschichold wrote an article entitled 'New life in print' which appeared in *Commercial Art* (July 1930), and in 1935 an exhibition of his work was held in the London offices of the printing and publishing firm of Percy Lund, Humphries, for which he worked for a time as consultant typographer [328, 329]. However, there were far fewer advocates of the New Typography than there were opponents, and even those typographers who did attempt to practise it did so with little real understanding. With the exception of the *Penrose Annual* for 1938, which was designed by

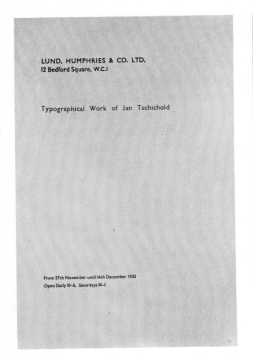

LUND, HUMPHRIES & CO. LTD.
12 Bedford Square, W.C.1

Typographical Work of Jan Tschichold

From 27th November until 14th December 1935
Open Daily 10-6, Saturdays 10-1

These are the fundamental ideas of my typography:

To-day the production and use of printed matter have increased enormously, yet anyone who publishes anything, whether an announcement, a prospectus, or a book, expects that it shall be read. Not only the buyer, but still more the reader of printing, unconsciously demands that it should be printed clearly and in an orderly fashion. For he is not at all willing to read everything. At best he does not read what is uncomfortable, and he prefers printing which looks orderly. He is pleased when something is set suitably and clearly, because his effort to understand what is printed is less than would otherwise be the case. Therefore the important parts must be brought out clearly; the unimportant must fall into the background. The resulting contrasts of black and white are not possible within the confines of the old laws of typography. These laws demand an appearance of more or less even grey: hence bold and extra bold types which primarily make possible a clear arrangement appear ugly in a traditional setting. Also, the sentence must be concentrated centrally, which is not always the best form, and does not always give an appearance which is easily understandable. Moreover, it has a tendency to make for a sameness in treating subjects which by their nature and purpose are different, and which therefore demand a difference in layout and treatment.

I attempt, therefore, to cultivate an asymmetrical form of make-up and setting, and believe this form is capable of improving present-day typography considerably. An asymmetrical style gives scope for greater variety and is better suited to the practical and aesthetic requirements of modern mankind.

This present age of speed demands that the technique of typography comes into line with it. We can only afford to spend a fraction of the time over a letter-heading or other jobbing work which was spent on this subject in the 'nineties'. We therefore need new rules to work to, simpler than the old, which none the less result in an efficient layout. The number of these rules must be reduced and the new ones must offer, in spite of their simplicity, possibilities comparable with the old. These rules must harmonise exactly with the technique of machine composition, which to-day is gaining in importance in the setting of jobbing work. The old hand-setting and the modern machine work must be used in co-operation, for any variation of typographical technique between the two would only make for discord. Primarily, the rules must allow for machine setting throughout all jobbing work. I do not, however, belong to those who

328,329 Guide published in connection with the exhibition of typographical work of Jan Tschichold at the offices of Lund, Humphries & Co. Ltd, London, 1935. Letterpress, set in Gill Sans and printed by Lund, Humphries in black and red on grey antique laid paper. Page size 212 × 113 mm. *John Johnson Collection.*

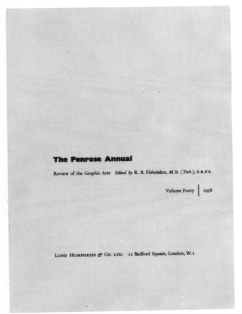

The Penrose Annual

Review of the Graphic Arts   *Edited by* R. B. Fishenden, *M.Sc. (Tech.),* F.R.P.S.

Volume Forty | 1938

LUND HUMPHRIES *& CO. LTD.*   12 Bedford Square, London, W.1

330 *Penrose Annual*, vol. 40, 1938, title-page. Letterpress, designed by Jan Tschichold and printed by Lund, Humphries & Co. Ltd. 279 × 203 mm.

Tschichold himself [330], the book seems to have escaped its influence almost entirely in the inter-war years; and when Stanley Morison declared in his *First principles of typography* that book typography 'requires an obedience to convention which is almost absolute'[45] he was almost certainly echoing majority current opinion.

Nevertheless, the New Typography did leave its mark on jobbing printing in this period, and the popularity of Gill Sans, which was often used in the 1930s as a means of giving printing a modern look, must be partly seen as a product of German influence. Stanley Morison's arresting book jackets for the publisher Gollancz and Francis Meynell's press advertisements of the 1930s also show a refreshing new outlook which seems to owe something to continental influences. Some English printing can be more specifically related to the new approach to design for printing. The catalogue of Greenly's second exhibition of modern advertising (1930) is a vigorous pastiche of Bauhaus typography [331–4]; the use of heavy rules and juxtaposed rectangles of type clearly relates to their style, and so too does the visual impact gained by printing in black and green on silver card. The publicity booklet of the match maker Bryant & May Ltd, which was printed in the early 1930s by the Curwen Press with a cover design by Paul Nash and photographs by Bruguière, is a more restrained example of the influence of the new approach to typography and graphic design [335, 336]. The narrow margins of the text pages and the use of photographs which bleed off the page are deliberate breaks with traditional practice, though it will be noted that the headings are centred on the page. For the most part English typographers of the inter-war years did not understand the full significance of the New Typography, and certainly did not see its implications in the fields of business and information printing.

Not until after the Second World War were the possibilities of the New Typography really explored widely in this country, first by a few pioneers, such as Anthony Froshaug, Ernest Hoch, and Herbert Spencer, and then more generally in the 1950s as a result of the influence of Swiss typography. What was originally seen in England as an experiment with visual elements began to be taken for its important design implications – as an approach to typography more widely adaptable to a range of requirements than the traditional symmetrical approach.

[45] S. Morison, *First principles of typography* (Cambridge, 1936), p.8 (originally published in *The Fleuron,* no. 7, 1930)

331–334 Catalogue of *Greenly's exhibition of modern advertising*, 1930. Letterpress, printed in emerald green and black, the cover on silver card with blind printing. Page size 172 × 229 mm. *John Johnson Collection.*

335, 336 E. P. Leigh-Bennett, *Match making*, c. 1930. Letterpress, designed and printed by the Curwen Press, London, with photographs by Bruguière. Page size 236 × 175 mm.

337 Petrus de Crescentiis, *Ruralia commoda*, Augsburg, 1471. Letterpress, printed by Johann Schüssler. Page size 298 × 215 mm. *Reading University Library.*

338 *Penrose Annual*, vol. 62, 1969. Letterpress, designed by Herbert Spencer and printed by Lund, Humphries, London and Bradford. Page size 295 × 210 mm.

The increasing use during the last decade of text set with even spacing between words and a ragged edge to the right, which was itself partly the consequence of the widespread acceptance of the typewriter, must also be seen as a contributory factor in the relaxation of the hold of symmetry. It is a practice which encourages the ranging of headings to the left and, of course, results in an arrangement of type which has an irregular profile to the right and is therefore asymmetric. The introduction of ragged-edge setting has also begun to modify the traditional view that facing pages of a book should be considered together as a balanced arrangement of two parts which are virtual mirror images of one another [337]. Though the individual pages of a traditional book may or may not be more or less symmetrically arranged, the placing of items such as page numbers and running headlines off-centre has been accepted traditionally only when they conformed to an overall scheme of symmetry which applied to both pages, that is, when they were placed to the extreme left and right respectively of opposite pages. Ragged-edge setting cannot be accommodated by such a scheme of symmetry, and its widespread use has led to a breakdown of the monopoly of the traditional view of the book and to an acceptance that facing pages may equally well be considered as two separate but related parts arranged side by side [338].

The long-term significance of the New Typography does not lie in determining whether or not type should be symmetrically disposed on a page, any more than the modern architect is concerned as a matter of principle with whether to place the front door in the centre of a house. Symmetry has come to be regarded as just one of a number of possibilities. The real contribution of the New Typography is that it brought about a new approach to design for printing based neither on outmoded craft conventions nor on preconceived aesthetic principles, but one in which the principal concern is to find an appropriate solution to a particular problem which has as a prime consideration the needs of the reader. It is only fair to say that we do not yet know exactly what these are, and, of course, any piece of printing is likely to be read by thousands of very different individuals; but there has been a growing feeling in this country and elsewhere in the last decade that design for printing should be approached by first asking the question, 'How can what we want to communicate be ordered so as to be most easily understood?'

New approaches to the design of printed material have really been forced upon the typographer by developments in society as a whole. The growing demands of business, government, and scholarship have made it essential that printing is read as quickly, effectively, and with as little physical strain as possible. Information may need to be read at different levels so that some readers can skip through and pick up the essence of the contents just by reading the headings; other information might perhaps be better expressed in simple diagrammatic form. The very quantity of printing produced in the last few decades taxes others besides the reader; if printing is not consigned to the wastepaper basket it has to be classified, catalogued, and stored. This has led to an increasing use in a number of countries of a rational system of standard formats for information printing based on a national standard which was adopted in Germany in the 1920s. Methods of learning and transmitting information have also brought about changes in printing. The growth of programmed learning techniques has led to new kinds of printing which are not sequential in the normal sense, but are designed to be followed by readers in many different ways. The use of diagrammatic methods for presenting orderly sequences of operations, known as algorithms, which have been used by scientists for the purposes of problem solving and communication for some time, have also begun to be applied more generally in order to simplify instructions for the general public [339]. The advent of television and the widespread use of photographic imagery have helped to create a generation much more reliant on visual means of communication than ever before, and have led to an increasing use of pictures and diagrams in printing both to stimulate and to inform. All these changes call for new approaches to the design of printing where reference to examples from the past can be of little immediate help.

The challenge to traditional practices in typography has been encouraged by recent technical developments. The widespread use of offset lithography, which allows a greater freedom in arranging text in relation to illustrations on a wide range of papers, has helped to break down the convention of printing images separate from the text which stemmed from the days when copper plates were used for illustrations. The increasing use of high-quality typewriters has made us more accustomed to text set with a ragged edge to the right, and has led to the questioning of the need for the extensive founts of type used in traditional printing which normally include lower-case letters, capitals, small capitals, italics, figures, superior figures, and a variety of other symbols, as well as related bold alphabets. New methods of reproducing graphic material, such as xerography and microfilm, have drawn attention to the need for letterforms, illustrations, and overall design which satisfy a variety of purposes.

Above all, the increasing use of computers in connection with traditional composing machines and cathode-ray tubes has forced the typographer to reconsider some of his conventions. While computers can be programmed to copy most features of traditional typography, they can do some things very much cheaper than others. The most subtle letter designs of the past and the most complex typographical arrangements can already be simulated reasonably well on a cathode-ray tube in response to purely numerical data from a computer [340], but the cost in computer time is at present extremely high. Though it is almost certain that costs will come down gradually, the expense of implementing complex traditional designs compared with others planned with the machine function in mind is bound to remain high. What may be a simple mental and manual activity for the compositor is not necessarily easy for the programmer nor good use of computer time. The introduction of computers into the field of printing in the last decade has merely emphasised the already existing need in a complex industry for

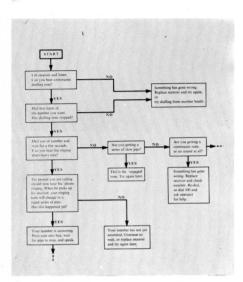

339 An algorithm for making a local telephone call. From B. N. Lewis, I. S. Horabin, and C. P. Gane, *Flow charts, logical trees and algorithms for rules and regulations*, CAS occasional paper, no. 2, 1967.

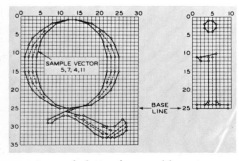

340 A sample letter drawn with vectors on a cathode-ray tube in imitation of a Baskerville design. From the *Journal of Typographic Research*, vol. 1, no. 4, 1967.

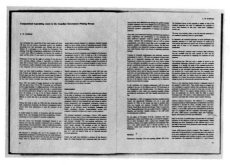

341 Institute of Printing, Proceedings of the 1966 International Computer Typesetting Conference, *Advances in computer typesetting*, 1967. Designed by Maurice Goldring, computer typeset by Southwark Offset Ltd, London, and printed offset lithography by Fletcher & Son Ltd, Norwich. Page size 297 × 210 mm.

342 Maurice Goldring, one of the master layouts for *Advances in computer typesetting*, prepared in advance of receiving details of the copy, 1966. Sheet size 420 × 594 mm.

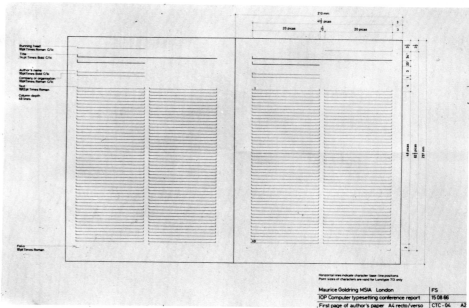

343 *The Bible*, Revised Standard Version, with illustrations by Horace Knowles, published by Wm. Collins Sons & Co. Ltd for the British & Foreign Bible Society, 1968. Letterpress, composed at Stephen Austin and Sons Ltd, processed by an ICT 1500 computer at Rocappi Ltd, printed by Collins Clear-type Press. Page size 189 × 135 mm.

[46] From her notes to *Taylor's scientific memoirs*, vol. iii, p.360. Quoted B.V.Bowden (ed.), *Faster than thought; a symposium on digital computing machines* (London, 1953), p.398

typographic designers who are able to understand the limitations and possibilities of the technology at their disposal. The typographer of today, like his counterpart in the late eighteenth century, is concerned with planning; but his problems are more varied, the tools at his disposal are infinitely more complex, and he has to specify accurately so that others who may not even speak the same language can understand his intentions [341, 342].

For all the technological developments in printing in recent years, the hold of tradition has been very strong. The printing industry, with its long-standing trade and craft traditions, has a great sense of history. Reading is one of the most conventional of human activities and, despite recent trends, many still believe that the printed word is the surest and most effective means of communication, particularly from one generation to another. Yet if radical changes are ever to be made in our letterforms and the conventions we adopt for organising them, no greater opportunity is likely to arise than in this present period of transition from mechanisation to automation. The technological advances of the last decade are of even greater significance for printing than those of the nineteenth century, but the very necessary experimental work in the use of words and pictures for purposes of communication has lagged far behind. When all is said and done, a computer can only do what it is instructed to do. This axiom was phrased very precisely by Lady Lovelace in 1842 with regard to the first real digital computer, Charles Babbage's newly invented analytical machine, when she stated that 'It has no pretensions whatever to *originate* anything. It can do whatever *we know how to order it* to perform'.[46]

At the time of writing, it seems that engineers are ordering the machine to perform in printing what years of experience have shown works reasonably well. Conventions and the desire to emulate the finest and most complex productions of traditional printing are still such powerful forces that the introduction of computers into the field of printing during the last decade has had little influence on its appearance. The first computer-set Bible, published for the British & Foreign Bible Society by William Collins in January 1968, is a case in point [343]. Large initial letters, which were something of an anachronism when they were taken over into printing from the manuscript tradition, have been used for its chapter openings and a computer was programmed to instruct 'Monotype' composition casters to leave the appropriate spaces in the text so that the letters themselves, as well as illustrations of various shapes, could be dropped in by hand afterwards. Many other works which have been set with the help of computers, such as telephone directories, bibliographies, and newspapers, have also been made indistinguishable from conventionally produced printing both as a point of honour and as a commercial expedient. History records many precedents of this kind, and it is worth recalling that when the first printers experimented in the mid-fifteenth century by casting metal units and assembling them into lines of words they took for their models the contemporary manuscript books they saw around them.

Part II Illustrations

Ceremony

133

Coronation tickets and invitations
George IV's coronation
Queen Victoria's coronation
Public celebration of royal occasions
Nelson's funeral
Wellington's funeral
Announcements of royal deaths
Queen Victoria's death and funeral
Special issues of newspapers
Royal openings
Banquets, balls, and special performances

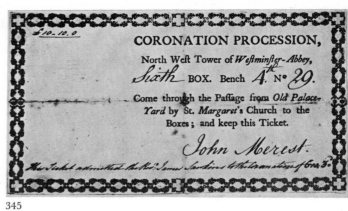

345

344

347

346

350

348

349

344 Ticket for the coronation of George III, 1761. Engraved on copper by G. Bickham. 204 × 230 mm. *John Johnson Collection.*

345 Ticket to view the coronation procession of George III, 1761. Letterpress, printed in red, with blind-stamped coat of arms. 100 × 178 mm. *John Johnson Collection.*

346 Ticket to view the coronation procession of George IV, 1821. Etching and engraving by Jones & Barriff, London, printed in Indian red. 157 × 186 mm. *John Johnson Collection.*

347 Ticket to view the coronation procession of George IV, 1821. Etching and engraving with gold-blocked wreath, designed and engraved by R. Scott, London. 140 × 195 mm. *John Johnson Collection.*

348 Pass ticket to Westminster Abbey for the coronation of George IV, 1821. Letterpress, with machine-engraved patterns, printed in black and blue. Embossed border by Dobbs. 210 × 160 mm. *John Johnson Collection.*

349 Pass ticket to Westminster Hall for the coronation of George IV, 1821. Letterpress, the centre pattern machine-engraved, printed in red and blue. Embossed border by Dobbs. 188 × 134 mm. *John Johnson Collection.*

350 Pass ticket to view the coronation procession of George IV, 1821. Letterpress, with machine-engraved patterns, printed in red and blue. Embossed border by Dobbs. 213 × 170 mm. *John Johnson Collection.*

351 Ticket to Westminster Abbey for the coronation of William IV, 1831. Copper-engraved. 193 × 268 mm. *John Johnson Collection.*

351

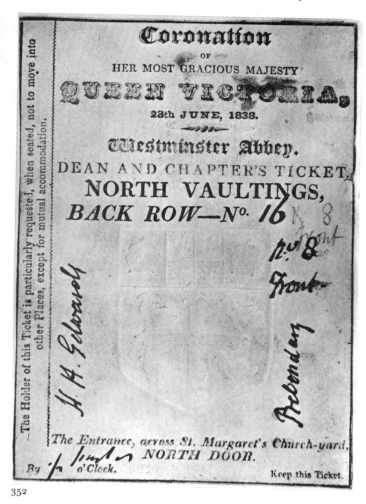

353

354

352

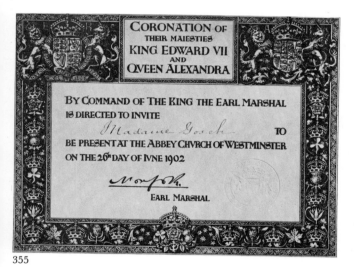

355

356

352 Ticket for the coronation of Queen Victoria in Westminster Abbey, 1838. Letterpress, printed in red and black, with blind-stamped coat of arms. 127 × 90 mm. *John Johnson Collection.*

353 Ticket for the coronation of Queen Victoria in Westminster Abbey, 1838. Engraved, printed in black on cerise coloured paper. 163 × 225 mm. *John Johnson Collection.*

354 Ticket to view the coronation procession of Queen Victoria, 1838. Lithographed, probably engraved on stone, printed in black on green card by Reynolds, London. 91 × 122 mm. *John Johnson Collection.*

355 Invitation to the coronation of Edward VII and Queen Alexandra, 26 June 1902 (postponed to 9 August 1902). Etched by G. W. Eve and printed in brown. 212 × 257 mm. *John Johnson Collection.*

356 Invitation to the coronation of George VI and Queen Elizabeth, 1937. Letterpress. 221 × 266 mm. *John Johnson Collection.*

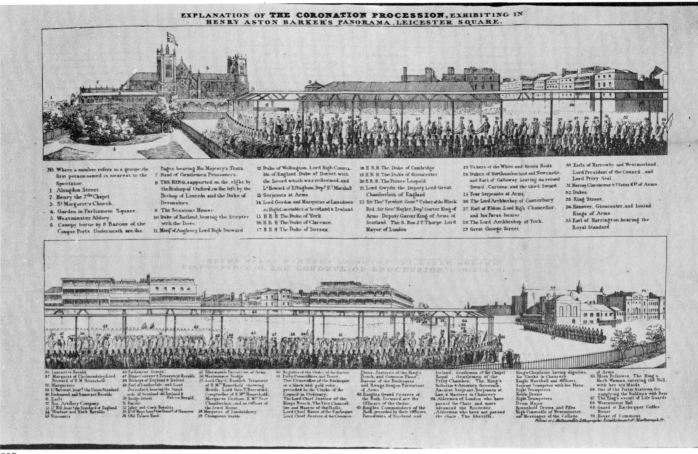

357

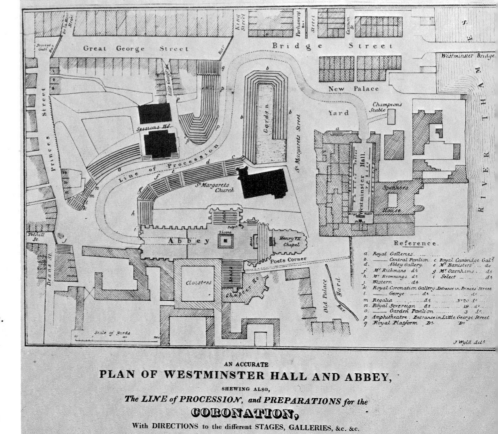

357 Explanation of Barker's panorama of the coronation procession of George IV. Lithograph, printed by C. J. Hullmandel. From *Description of the procession on the coronation of George the Fourth*, London, 1822. Size of folding plate 312 × 492 mm. *John Johnson Collection.*

358 Plan showing the route of the coronation procession of George IV, 1821. Hand-coloured lithograph, drawn by J. Wyld, printed and published by Wyld & King, London. The text at the foot was printed letterpress and pasted down. Total size 260 × 278 mm. *John Johnson Collection.*

358

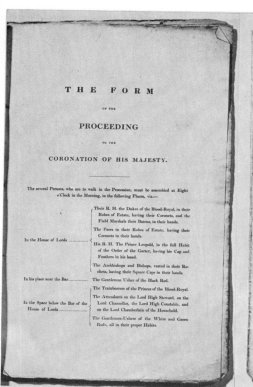

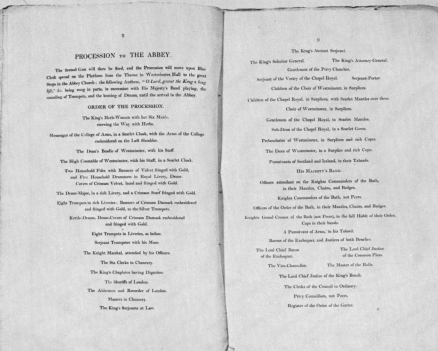

359

360

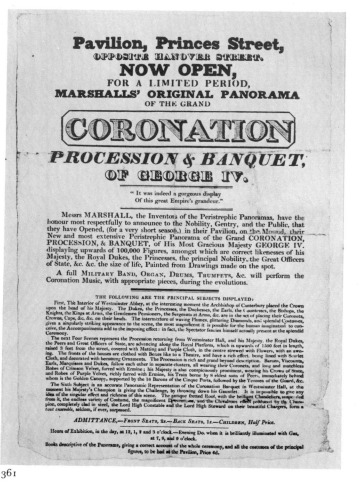

361

359 Pages from *The ceremonies to be observed at the royal coronation of His Most Excellent Majesty King George the Fourth*, 1821. Letterpress, printed by Samuel and Richard Bentley. Page size 343 × 216 mm. *John Johnson Collection.*

360 Profile portrait of George IV. Embossed on pink card by Dobbs, London. 252 × 225 mm. *John Johnson Collection.*

361 Notice of exhibition of Marshalls' panorama of the coronation procession and banquet of George IV. Letterpress, with wood-engraved logotype for the word 'coronation'. 262 × 180 mm. *John Johnson Collection.*

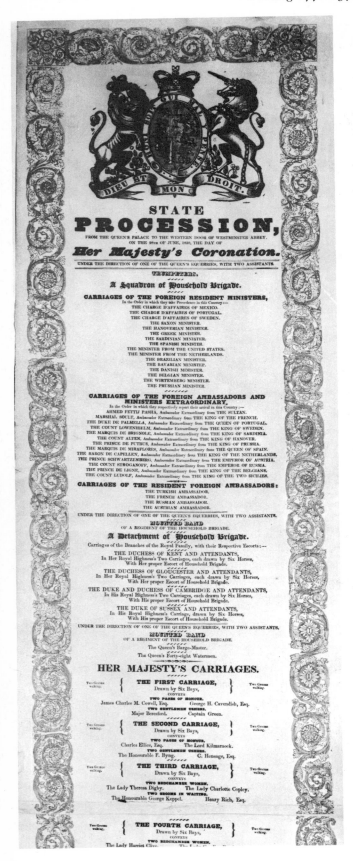

362 Order of the state procession on the day of Queen Victoria's coronation, 1838. Letterpress, printed in red and blue by J. Hartnell, London. 1345 × 273 mm. *John Johnson Collection.*

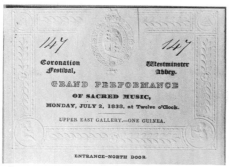

363

364

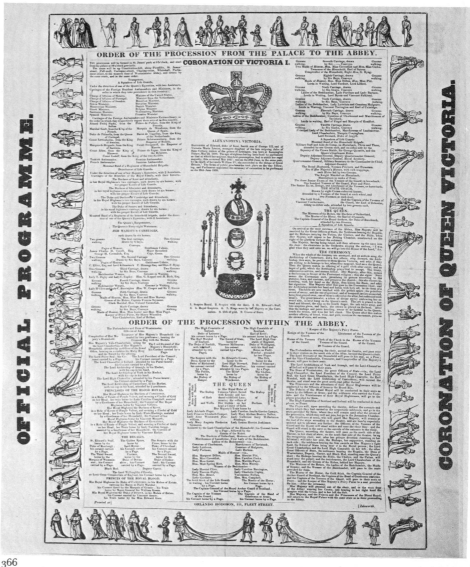

366

367

365

363 Ticket for a performance of sacred music, 1838. Letterpress, printed in blue on white card, with embossed border by Whiting. 90 × 123 mm. *John Johnson Collection.*

364 Ticket for a rehearsal of sacred music, 1838. Letterpress, printed in blue on white card. 92 × 124 mm. *John Johnson Collection.*

365 Profile portrait of Queen Victoria, *c.* 1838. Embossed on white card by Dobson, London. 212 × 158 mm. *John Johnson Collection.*

366 Official programme of the coronation of Queen Victoria, 1838. Letterpress, printed at Isleworth and published by Orlando Hodgson, London. 502 × 400 mm. *John Johnson Collection.*

367 The coronation of Queen Victoria. Engraved by H. T. Ryall after a painting by Sir George Hayter. 560 × 865 mm. *Victoria & Albert Museum.*

368

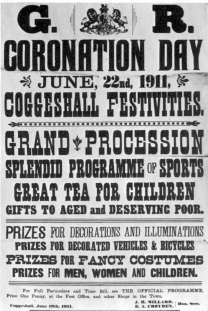

369

370

368 Notice of rustic sports in Cambridge in
celebration of Queen Victoria's coronation,
1838. Letterpress, printed by S. Wilson.
765 × 250 mm. *Cambridge Folk Museum.*

369 Notice of Festivities in Coggeshall on the occasion of the
coronation of George V, 1911. Letterpress, printed in red and
blue by J. A. Dodds, Coggeshall. 890 × 570 mm. *Essex County
Record Office.*

370 Notice of celebrations in Oxford on the occasion of the
coronation of George VI, 1937. Letterpress, printed in red and
blue by the Hollywell Press, Oxford. 752 × 500 mm. *John
Johnson Collection.*

RUSTIC SPORTS

ON SAFFRON WALDEN COMMON,

IN CELEBRATION OF THE

MARRIAGE

OF H. R. H.

ALBERT EDWARD, PRINCE OF WALES,

On Tuesday, March 10th, 1863.

PROGRAMME OF SPORTS,
TO COMMENCE AT THREE O'CLOCK.

A DONKEY RACE,

First Prize, Five Shillings; Second Prize, Half-a-Crown.

HURDLE RACE,

over 12 Hurdles. First Prize, Five Shillings; Second Prize, Half-a-Crown.

FOOT RACES,

100 yards, for Boys under Nine Years of Age, First Prize, a New Knife; Second Prize, Ditto. 100 Yards, for Boys under Twelve Years of Age, First Prize, a New Knife; Second Prize, Half-a-Crown. 400 Yards, First Prize, Five Shillings; Second Prize, Half-a-Crown. 200 Yards, First Prize, Half-a-Crown. 800 Yards, First Prize, Five Shillings, Second Prize, Half-a-Crown.
The 200, 400, and 800 Yard Races are open to Men and Boys.

JUMPING IN SACKS,

a distance of 50 Yards. Each Man to jump in a 4-bushel Sack, (to be provided by himself for the occasion.) First Prize, Three Shillings; Second Prize, Two Shillings.

THE LONG JUMP.   THE HIGH JUMP.
Prize, One Shilling.   Prize, One Shilling.

A JINGLING MATCH,
Or, Blind Buff and the Bellman.

Sixpence will be given for each catch. The time allowed for this Match is 15 minutes; and the Bellman will not be allowed to silence his Bell longer than 30 seconds at a time.

CLIMBING A GREASY POLE,
For Sundry Prizes.

SCRAMBLING AND BOBBING FOR ORANGES.

DONKEY RACE,

in which no man will be allowed to ride his own Donkey. The last Donkey in will be declared the Winner.

WHEELBARROW RACE,

Blindfolded. Every Man to bring his own Wheelbarrow. Prize, Five Shillings.

Entries for the Donkey Races to be made at the Corn Exchange, on Monday Evening March 9th, between 6 and 7 o'Clock. The Riders to appear in Jackets and Caps.

HART, PRINTER, SAFFRON WALDEN.

HER MAJESTY'S JUBILEE.

FELLOW BURGESSES,

Thanks to the exertions of hard-working Dinner and Tea Committees and of an indefatigable Honorary Secretary, the arrangements for Her Majesty's Jubilee on Monday, 20th inst., are complete. Two thousand three hundred will dine together in Bridge Street at 56 tables; no applications have been refused, and the list is necessarily closed.

I respectfully invite you to close your Shops, hang out your bunting, and illuminate with gas, or candles in your windows. The gas will be supplied gratuitously, on application, by the Corporation.

Tea will be supplied to two thousand children, more or less, under the age of 14, and under the direction of a Committee of Ladies and Gentlemen, who have kindly undertaken to carry out this part of the Jubilee Programme.

To avoid confusion, and to provide for your comfort and convenience, I have, in accordance with the unanimous wish of the General Committee, given instructions that the traffic shall be stopped in Bridge Street and diverted by way of Guild Street and the Water-side.

I have the fullest confidence in your loyalty and good-feeling.

GOD SAVE THE QUEEN!

ARTHUR HODGSON,
Mayor.

TOWN HALL,
JUNE 15th, 1887.

By kind permission of Colonel Perkins and the Officers of the 4th Battalion Royal Warwickshire Regiment, the Band will play in New Place Gardens on Thursday, 16th instant (to-morrow), from 4 till 6 o'clock p.m. Admission Free.

HERALD PRINTING WORKS, STRATFORD-ON-AVON.

372

GREAT & LITTLE COGGESHALL.

SILVER JUBILEE
CELEBRATIONS
MONDAY, MAY 6th, 1935.

MORNING.
HOUSE DECORATING COMPETITION & JUDGING.
AFTERNOON.   Prizes to the value of £6

COMIC CARNIVAL PROCESSION
Assemble at Market Hill, 2 p.m.   Numerous Prizes.

SPORTS for Children and Adults on Recreation Ground.
3 to 5 p.m.   6·30 to 7·30 p.m.
20 Events.   Prizes in each Event.

VARIOUS SIDESHOWS.

BABY SHOW at Lecture Hall, 3 p.m.
5 Open Classes.   Prizes in each Class.

TEA for School Children at St. Peter's Hall, 5 p.m.
with PRESENTATION OF SOUVENIRS.

EVENING.
WHIST DRIVE AT LECTURE HALL, 8 P.M.
ADMISSION 1s. (including Refreshments).

DANCE AT ST. PETER'S HALL, 9 P.M. TO 1 A.M.
MUSIC BY JUBILEE DANCE BAND.
ADMISSION 1/-   Combined Tickets for Whist Drive and Dance, 1s. 6d.
Tickets obtainable from Messrs. Amos & Palmby.

H. J. Smith & Son, Coggeshall Press.   For full details of the above events, see Programmes, price One Penny.

373

---

371 Notice of rustic sports in Saffron Walden to celebrate the marriage of the Prince of Wales, 1863. Letterpress, printed by Hart, Saffron Walden. 630 × 254 mm. *Essex County Record Office.*

372 Notice of arrangements in Stratford-on-Avon on the occasion of Queen Victoria's Jubilee, 1887. Letterpress, printed at the Herald Printing Works, Stratford-on-Avon. 429 × 267 mm. *John Johnson Collection.*

373 Notice of celebrations in Great and Little Coggeshall on the occasion of the Silver Jubilee of George V, 1933. Letterpress, printed in red and blue by H. J. Smith & Son, Coggeshall Press. 760 × 505 mm. *Essex County Record Office.*

374

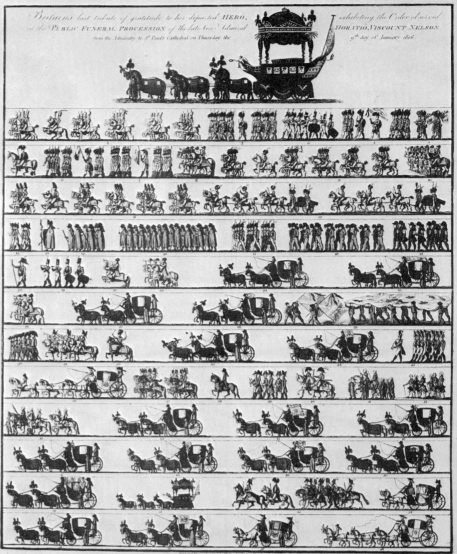

376

377

375

374 Ticket of admission into the funeral procession of Lord Nelson, 1806. Etching and engraving. 190 × 278 mm. *John Johnson Collection.*

375 Explanation of the print exhibiting the public funeral procession of Lord Nelson. Letterpress, published by John Wallis, London, 1806. 245 × 200 mm. *John Johnson Collection.*

376 Order of the public funeral procession of Lord Nelson, 1806. Copper-engraving, published by John Wallis, London, 1806. 473 × 350 mm. *John Johnson Collection.*

377 Lord Nelson's funeral procession by water. Hand-coloured aquatint by J. Clark and H. Merke after an original by Turner. From F. W. Blagdon, *History of the life, exploits, and death of Horatio Nelson,* London, 1806. 327 × 476 mm. *John Johnson Collection.*

378

379

380

381

378 Broadsheet describing Lord Nelson's funeral ceremony. Letterpress, printed on grey paper by Burbage and Stretton, Nottingham. 508 × 375 mm. *John Johnson Collection.*

379 Detail of Plate 378. 190 × 122 mm.

380 Description of the funeral car of Lord Nelson. Letterpress, with wood-engraving, printed by R. Edwards, London. 183 × 124 mm. *John Johnson Collection.*

381 Lord Nelson's funeral car. Hand-coloured engraving, published by Laurie & Whittle, London, 1806. 203 × 267 mm. *Victoria & Albert Museum.*

382

383

384

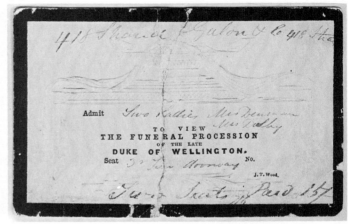

385

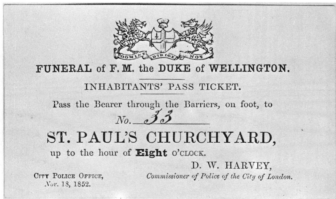

386

387

382 Ticket of admission to the funeral of the Duke of Wellington in St Paul's Cathedral, 1852. Engraved. 118 × 183 mm. *John Johnson Collection.*

383 Ticket to view the funeral procession of the Duke of Wellington, 1852. Engraved by Morrish, London. 76 × 113 mm. *John Johnson Collection.*

384 Ticket to view the funeral procession of the Duke of Wellington, 1852. Lithographed by Wiseman & Son, London. 76 × 115 mm. *John Johnson Collection.*

385 Ticket to view the funeral procession of the Duke of Wellington, 1852. Letterpress, with embossing, printed by J. T. Wood. 75 × 114 mm. *John Johnson Collection.*

386 Inhabitants' pass ticket for the day of Wellington's funeral, 1852. Letterpress. 73 × 119 mm. *John Johnson Collection.*

387 Inhabitants' pass ticket for the day of Wellington's funeral, 1852. Letterpress. 75 × 120 mm. *John Johnson Collection.*

388 Ticket to view the funeral procession of the Duke of Wellington, 1852. Letterpress. 74 × 113 mm. *John Johnson Collection.*

388

389

390

389 Funeral car of the Duke of Wellington. Tinted lithograph, printed by Day & Son and published by Day & Son and Ackermann & Co., 1852. 480 × 685 mm. *John Johnson Collection.*

390 Funerary card showing Wellington's funeral car, *c.* 1852. Embossed by J. T. Wood. 112 × 145 mm. *John Johnson Collection.*

391 Ballad, 'The sights of the Wellington funeral'. Letterpress, printed by Disley, London. 250 × 185 mm. *John Johnson Collection.*

THE SIGHTS
OF
The Wellington Funeral

What wonderful sights old Britannia did view,
In the year eighteen hundred, fifty, and two,
Four millions of persons, the great and the small,
To see the great warrior go to St. Paul's ;
The conqueror of nations—the pride of the world,
Who the standard of liberty brightly unfurled,
Who fought in the Indies, and conquered proud Spain,
We shall never behold that great soldier again.

We shall ever remember that wonderful day,
The eighteenth of November, all classes so gay,
From the peer to the peasant, the rich and the poor
Such a sight sure in London was ne'er seen befor

There's princes, ambassadors, and over the seas
Came the Frenchman, the Spaniard, and proud Portuguese ;
Tens of thousands of nobles all came from afar,
To behold the great wonderful funeral car.
There was old women, young women, weavers and snips,
Doctors, butchers, and bakers, and coalheavers tripped.
All the soldiers in Britain so mournful was there,
Queen Victoria, Prince Albert, and London's Lord Mayor.

Seven thousand policemen to keep the streets clear
And protect all the sweet pretty maidens so dear,
There was baskets and cradles to stand on to view
With stools, forms, and benches, and deal tables too
All the tops of the houses with thousands was lin'd
Every window with ladies so handsome and fine,
Such pushing, such driving—such squeezing, O la !
Ladies never did get such a shoving before.

And when down to Chelsea they bundled away,
Near one hundred thousand on every day,
Some lost their lockets, and some lost their shawls
Some fell a fainting while others did squall.
Some had their pockets picked, some wars did not mind,
Some men lost the tails of their jackets behind,
Some lost a stocking, and some lost a shoe,
There was barbers and lawyers, and quakers, and Jews.

For a week over London by night and by day,
To knock up the seats they did hammer away,
A guinea a stand to pay some had got,
While many was stuck on the chimney pots ;
The fine great procession did reach to please all,
All from the Horse Guards to the dome of St. Pauls
It was three miles in length and it dazzled each eye
And a many a blind man to see it did sigh.

When erecting the seats as the hammers home went
The sound might be heard down at Dover, in Kent
The Strand was amazing, and Fleet-street way fine
Pall-mall and St. James's-street was not behind.
And thirty old women was at Charing-cross,
All trying to get up the man on his horse,
Along Piccadilly, what grandeur now mark,
Was seen and all over St. James's green park.

Most glorious to see was the funeral car,
And splendid magnificent great Temple-bar,
Decorated with velvet, so handsome about,
It shone in great splendour within and without.
Scenes more magnificent never could be,
More brilliant in Europe none ever did see.
The laws were arranged every one to protect.
Who did the remains of that warrior respect.

The day was delightful, the ladies did sweat,
And the sight while we live we can never forget,
The fine British soldiers so grand did appear,
Which smote every heart of each lady so fair.
The loss of the Duke caused the nation much pain
On earth we shall never behold him again,
He only is gone, though Britannia droops low,
Where every mortal on earth soon must go.

He is gone, he is gone, we no more shall him view
Him who conquered all nations and great Waterloo
Recorded shall ever be Wellington's name,
He lived and he died in great honour and fame.

Disley, Printer, No. 16, Arthur-street, Oxford-street.

391

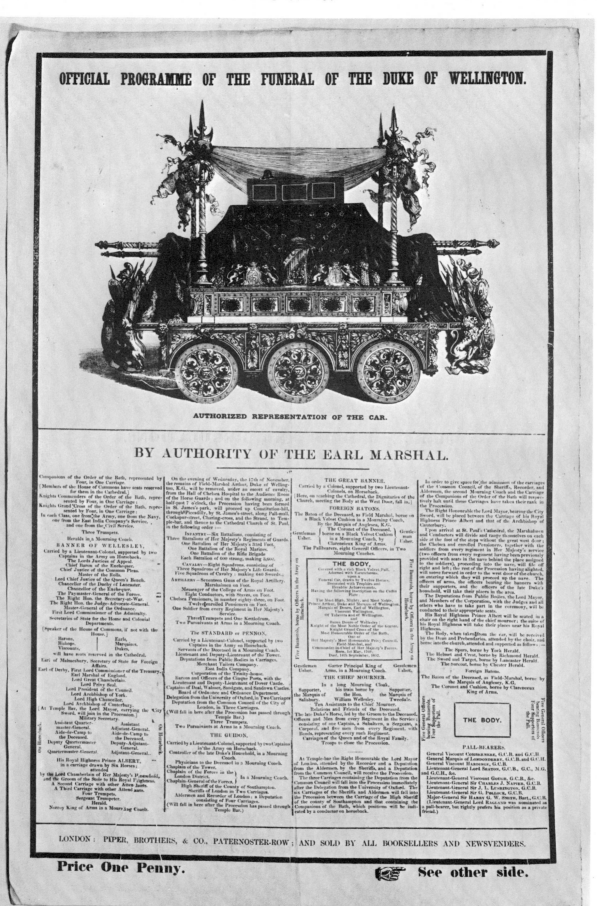

392 Official programme of the funeral of the Duke of
Wellington, 1852. Letterpress, with wood-engraving of the
funeral car. Published by Piper Brothers & Co., London.
505 × 315 mm. *John Johnson Collection.*

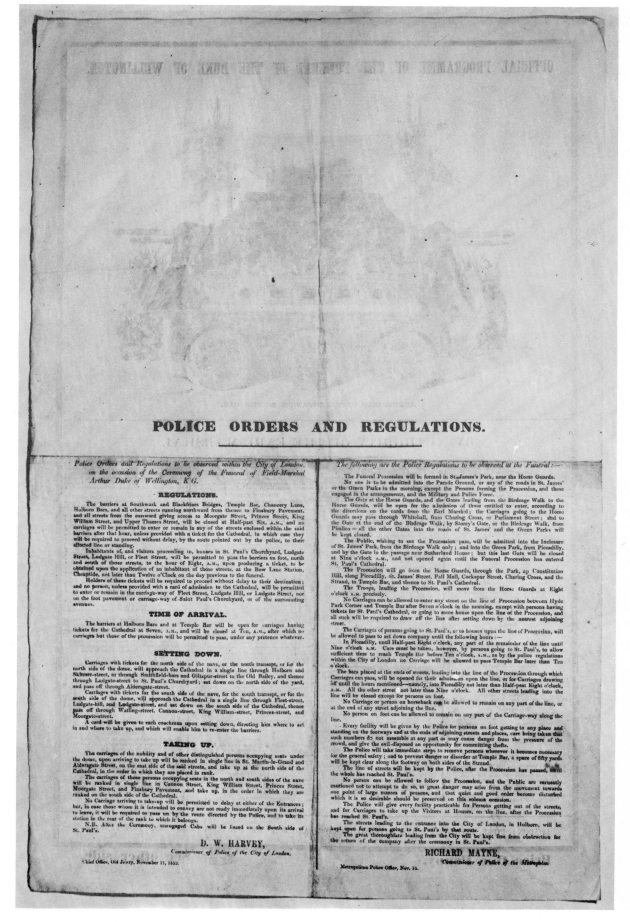

393 Official programme of the funeral of the Duke of
Wellington, 1852. Reverse of Plate 392.

394 Description of the funeral procession of the Duke of
Wellington. Letterpress, with wood-engravings, printed by
W. S. Johnson, London. 562 × 451 mm. *John Johnson Collection.*

395

395 Funeral of the Duke of Wellington,
'The funeral car passing the Archway at
Apsley House'. Colour lithograph by
T. Picken after a painting by Louis Haghe,
printed by Day & Son and published by
Ackermann & Co. and Day & Son, 1853.
405 × 547 mm. *John Johnson Collection.*

396

396 Detail of Plate 395. 98 × 123 mm.

397

397 Ticket of admission to Westminster
Hall for the coronation of George IV,
1821. Letterpress, compound-plate printing,
with an embossed border by Dobbs.
236 × 262 mm. *John Johnson Collection.*

398 Ticket of admission to Westminster
Abbey for the coronation of George IV,
1821. Letterpress, compound-plate printing,
with an embossed border by Dobbs.
240 × 261 mm. *John Johnson Collection.*

398

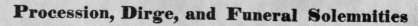

399 Broadsheet commemorating the funeral
of George IV, 1830. Letterpress, with
wood-engraving, printed by J. Catnach,
London. 350 × 212 mm. *John Johnson
Collection.*

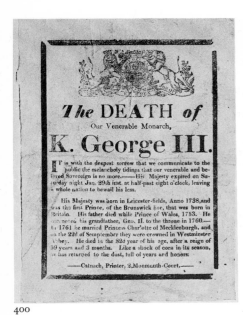

400

401

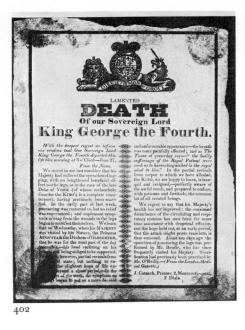

402

403

404

400 Announcement of the death of
George III, 1820. Letterpress, printed on
grey paper by Catnach, London. 255 ×
187 mm. *John Johnson Collection.*

401 Announcement of the death of Queen
Caroline, 1821. Letterpress, anon. 383 ×
251 mm. *St Bride Printing Library.*

402 Announcement of the death of
George IV, 1830. Letterpress, printed by
Catnach, London. 246 × 191 mm.
St Bride Printing Library.

403 Admission ticket for the interment of
George IV, 1830. Engraved. 90 ×
132 mm. *John Johnson Collection.*

404 Announcement of the death of
William IV, 1837. Letterpress text printed
by E. Style, Windsor, on paper headed
with a lithographed vignette drawn on
stone by G. Childs and printed by J. Graf,
London. 247 × 197 mm. *John Johnson
Collection.*

ST. JAMES'S GAZETTE

DEATH OF THE QUEEN

405

FINANCIAL NEWS

THE GREAT CITY DAILY

WEDNESDAY, JANUARY 23   PRICE ONE PENNY

DEATH OF THE QUEEN

406

GREAT WESTERN RAILWAY.

FUNERAL

OF

Her late Majesty Queen Victoria

On SATURDAY, FEBRUARY 2nd, 1901,

The Train Service throughout the Great Western Company's system will be the same as on Sundays, with the following modifications, viz.:—

The 5.30 a.m. and 5.40 a.m. Newspaper Trains from Paddington will run as usual as far as Plymouth and Swansea respectively, with connections to the Weymouth Line, Torquay, Kingswear and Penzance, and also to Oxford, Birmingham, Wolverhampton, Dudley, Worcester, Malvern, &c.

The 12.0 night Train from Paddington to Penzance, and the 12.15 night Train from Paddington to Birmingham, Chester, Birkenhead and Liverpool will run as usual.

LONDON AND WINDSOR SERVICE.

The 1.0 p.m. Sunday Train from Paddington to Windsor will not run.
The 10.30 a.m., 10.35 a.m., 1.50 p.m. and 2.20 p.m. Sunday Trains from Paddington will not convey passengers to Windsor.
Windsor Station will be closed for public traffic from 11.0 a.m. until 2.30 p.m.

LONDON SUBURBAN SERVICE.

The following Trains will run as on Week Days in addition to the usual Sunday service:—
8.0 a.m. Southall to Paddington.
7.45 a.m. Windsor to Paddington.
8.0 a.m. Reading to Paddington.
8.50 a.m. Southall to Paddington.
8.53 a.m. Uxbridge to Paddington.
A Train will run from Southall to Paddington at 10.0 a.m., calling at intermediate Stations.
The 11.25 a.m. Sunday Train from High Wycombe to Paddington will be half an hour later at all Stations.

SAILINGS—NEW MILFORD AND WATERFORD.

There will be no Steamer from Waterford to New Milford on Friday, February 1st, nor from New Milford to Waterford on Sunday morning, February 3rd.

The issue of Week-end Excursion Tickets to Windsor and the Half-day Excursion Tickets to London will be suspended.

For particulars of any additional Local arrangements on other parts of the Line, see Special announcements issued locally.

J. L. WILKINSON, General Manager.

Paddington Station, January, 1901.

Wyman & Sons, Ltd., Printers, 63, Carter Lane, Doctors' Commons, E.C.

407

405 News bill announcing the death of Queen Victoria, 1901. Letterpress. 760 × 507 mm. *John Johnson Collection.*

406 News bill announcing the death of Queen Victoria, 1901. Letterpress. 762 × 505 mm. *John Johnson Collection.*

407 Notice of Great Western Railway arrangements on the day of the funeral of Queen Victoria, 1901. Letterpress, printed by Wyman & Sons Ltd, London. 250 × 155 mm. *John Johnson Collection.*

408 Notice of mourning for Queen Victoria, 1901. Letterpress, printed by Goulding & Son, Louth. 350 × 460 mm. *John Johnson Collection.*

409 Ticket for a service of solemn supplication in St Paul's Cathedral at the hour of the funeral of Queen Victoria, 1901. Letterpress, black and purple on white card. 75 × 114 mm. *John Johnson Collection.*

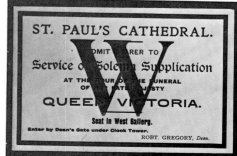

BOROUGH OF LOUTH.

FUNERAL

OF HER LATE MAJESTY

QUEEN VICTORIA.

I HEREBY REQUEST that the 2nd February may be observed as a DAY OF GENERAL MOURNING, and that ALL BUSINESS BE SUSPENDED so far as possible.

D. Pickling, MAYOR.

Town Hall, 26th January, 1901.

GOULDING & SON, PRINTERS, &c. MERCHANTS, LOUTH.

408

ST. PAUL'S CATHEDRAL.

ADMIT BEARER TO

Service of Solemn Supplication

AT THE HOUR OF THE FUNERAL OF HER LATE MAJESTY

QUEEN VICTORIA.

Seat in West Gallery.

Enter by Dean's Gate under Clock Tower.

ROBT. GREGORY, *Dean.*

409

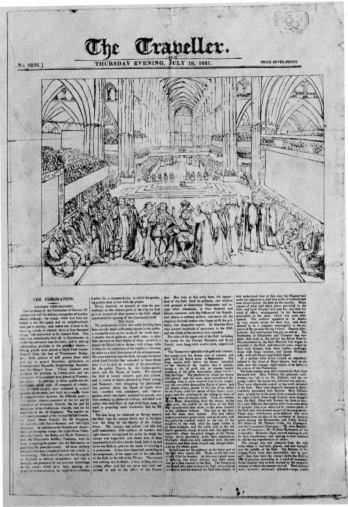

411

412

410 Special issue of the *Traveller* on the occasion of the coronation of George IV, 19 July 1821. Letterpress with lithographed illustration. 505 × 340 mm. *John Johnson Collection.*

411 Special issue of the *Sun* to mark the coronation of Queen Victoria, 13 July 1838, 15th ed. of issue of 28 June 1838. Letterpress, the text in gold and the portrait and signature in black. Printed by William Clowes & Sons and gilded by De la Rue & Co. 660 × 488 mm. *St Bride Printing Library.*

412 Silver Jubilee issue of the *Daily Mail*, 6 May 1935. Letterpress on silver-coated paper. 610 × 438 mm. *John Johnson Collection.*

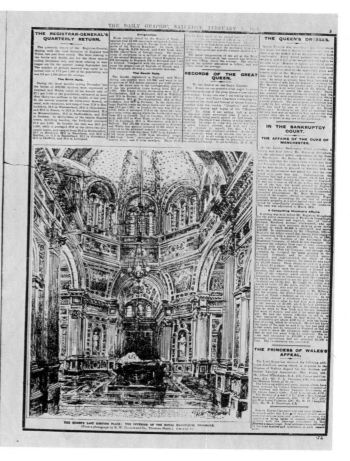

413

414

413 Issue of the *Daily Graphic* which appeared on the day of Queen Victoria's funeral, 2 February 1901. Letterpress, with process engravings of drawings made from photographs. 425 × 302 mm. *St Bride Printing Library.*

414 Issue of the *Daily Express* recording the coronation of Edward VII and Alexandra, 11 August 1902. Letterpress, with process engravings from drawings by Fred Pegram. Page size 597 × 445 mm. *Reading University Library.*

ROYAL PROCESSION
ON THE OPENING OF LONDON BRIDGE
WITH THE ARRANGEMENTS OF THE ENTERTAINMENT.----MONDAY, AUG. 1, 1831.

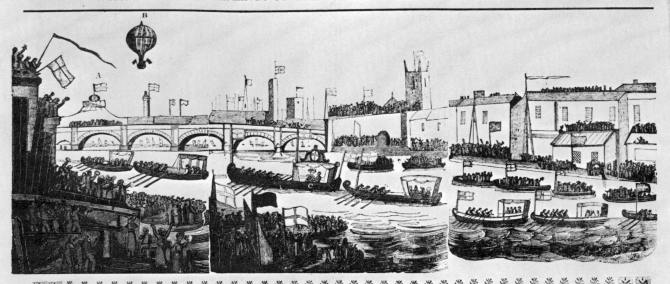

Thursday the London Bridge Committee assembled at Guildhall, for the purpose of making arrangements for the first of August, the day on which his Majesty is to open the New Bridge. Directions had been previously given by the Committee, to cover a considerable part of the Bridge with an awning, and the workmen were rapidly advancing in the necessary operations, when the Chairman and several Members of the Corporation went, at three o'clock, to judge of the probable effect of the plan upon which the ceremony is to be conducted.

The Royal tent is to be pitched at the London side of the Bridge, near to the place on which Fishmonger's Hall stood, and will command an unobstructed view of the whole line of road to the Southwark side. The Royal table will be laid for about twenty persons. On the left of it, extending to one of the entrances from Thames street, will be laid two tables for the noble persons who will accompany their Majesties. One of these tables will be laid for 68, the other for 76 individuals. A large space will be left open at the right of the Royal tent, it being the intention of their Majesties to disembark at the Grand Wharf on the right of the Bridge; and the Committee having appointed that the procession shall go forward from that spot the moment their Majesties land. A double row of tables will be ranged, on each side of the wide space through which the procession is to pass, for the accommodation of the other visitors, who are to be admitted, if we may judge from the present appearance of the arrangements, to the number of 1,560. The awning, which is to be placed over the long table, will extend to the length of about 400 feet; there are to be three roofs to the large awning, so that the company will be as effectually secured against bad weather as if they were to be shut up in the Guildhall, which the art of man could never make worthy of a comparison with the scene which will be presented on the 1st of August on London Bridge, the river, and in the surrounding neighbourhood. Flags and colours, with emblems and devises, will wave above the heads of the company, and cannon will be fired at intervals. Bands of music will, in various parts of the arena, perform during the ceremony, and every thing that can contribute to render the spectacle delightful to the public will be done, at least so far as the Committee may be able to satisfy the public curiosity. The works on the Bridge are superintended by Mr. Montague, the Clerk of the Works.

The Lord Mayor has given up the authority over the river for the day of the ceremony to Sir Byam Martin, and the arrangements on the water are to be under the direction of Mr. George Ledwell Taylor, the Surveyor to the Navy. Their Majesties are to go on board the Royal Barge at Somerset House at three o'clock in the after-

noon, and the procession on the Thames is to be as follows :— First advances the Trinity barge, next the Victualling Board barge, and then follow in order the Navy Board barge, the Treasurer of the Navy's barge, the Board of Ordnance barge, the Commander-in-Chief of the Army's barge, the Admiralty barge, the Lords of the Treasury barge, the Royal barge, the Royal Family's barge, the barge of the Lords and others in attendance upon his Majesty.

From Somerset House to London bridge barges splendidly decorated will be moored on each side of the river, and between the barges so moored, room will be left for the small boats, so that immense numbers of persons will be enabled to see the water procession, which, it is expected, will be infinitely more grand, as it will be infinitely more extensive than the procession on the bridge. The barges of all the Companies will be ranged near the bridge, splendidly decorated. The river will, during the whole ceremony, present the most brilliant exhibition. Not a vessel or boat will be seen to move in tha line of procession, with the exception of those which are to perform the procession itself. In the barges moored along the line of procession, seats are to be fixed one above another for the accommodation of the public.

Barriers are to be fixed at Fish-street-hill, at Little East-cheap, Gracechurch-street, in Cannon-street, in Mile's-lane, and in Upper Thames-street.

The Thames Police are to take their station on the river to prevent accidents. It has not yet been determined in what dress the Corporation are to receive their Majesties, but it is supposed that the Lord Mayor and Aldermen will appear in their robes, and the Members of the Court of Common Council in their gowns.

Much as had been expected from the splendid preparations at Guildhall, it is impossible that the spectacle could, if the entertainment had taken place, been at all comparable to that which will be displayed on the 1st of August.

The Landing of

ROYAL WILLIAM and ADELAIDE at London Bridge.

HORSE to horse, and man to man,
To London City leads the van,
To welcome on a glorious plan,
The Queen and Royal William.

Chorus.

Welcome WILLIAM from the THAMES,
On all our hearts you have just claims,

And joyfully we'll bless those names
Of ADELAIDE and WILLIAM.
His very presence hope instils,
And drives afar the thought of ills,
True courage every bosom fills,
At sight of ROYAL WILLIAM.

Welcome William, &c.

Behold him leave the subject tide,
And Adelaide around his side,
He opens London Bridge with pride,
All cry, Live Royal William.

Welcome William, &c.

The thistle, shamrock, and the rose,
The brilliant flags above disclose,
And sounds of cannon interpose,
To honour Royal William.

Welcome William! &c.

This Bridge, upon a strong built form,
Will weather many a wintry storm,
Coeval with that great Reform,
Brought on by Royal William.

Welcome William, & c.

Peace and joy attend his way,
Justice marks his Sovereign sway,
He's dearest friend, in truth, is Grey,
Hurrah for Royal William.

Welcome William, &c.

Commerce hails this happy day,
Keels shall cut the watery way,
Trade once more be brisk and gay,
Hurrah for Royal William.

Welcome William, &c.

Breathes there a degenerate son,
Who would not to his standard run,
The battle of Reform is won,
And that by Royal William.

Welcome William, &c.

The father of his people he,
Lord of the isles and every sea,
Then let us toast with heartfelt glee,
The Queen and Royal William.

Welcome William, &c.

London Bridge is opened wide,
The Citszens may shout with pride,
"Often may we from the tide,
Welcome Royal William.

Welcome William, &c.

King of a nation without stain,
Our rights he'll manfully maintain,
Supreme upon the land and main,
Long life to Royal William.

Chorus.

Welcome, Welcome, from the Thames,
Every tongue the praise proclaims,
Of those beloved and honoured names,
Queen Adelaide and William.

New London Bridge and King William for ever !

THE glory of England begins to appear,
Our King has gone forth, unto every one dear;
And dear is the Queen, who in all her just ways,
Demands from her people attention and praise.

Chorus.

Heart of Oak is our King,
Long may he preside,
To reign and command
On the land and the tide.

Father THAMES to the monarch his Trident resigns,
And COMMERCE with him obedience combines;
With the hearts of his subjects the NAIDS agree,
To hail him the Lord of the land and the sea.

We see London Bridge a proud structure expand,
Connecting a portion of this happy land;
The King gives the word, there is no toll to pay,
And blest are the people upon this happy day.

Chorus.—Heart of Oak is our King, &c.

The thunder of cannon re-sounds through the skies,
And God save the King in a thousand tones rise;
As over the Bridge, he moves on with his Queen,
A happier sight has old England ne'er seen.
For the good of the nation the Sovereign attends,
With his people he mixes, and thus he makes friends;
No feasting he wants, and would rather endure
A fast, and give every thing to the poor.

London Bridge now will stand on a solid foundation,
Reflecting both honour and pride on the nation;
And Reformers who pass it, will say with three cheers,
It's strength's in the people and not in the PEERS.

Chorus.—Heart of Oak is our King, &c.

J. Catnach, Printer, 2, Monmouth-Court, 7 Dials.

415 Account of arrangements on the occasion of the opening of
London Bridge, 1831. Letterpress, printed by J. Catnach,
London. 508 × 382 mm. *St Bride Printing Library.*

416

416 Ticket for the opening of the Tower Bridge by the Prince of Wales, 1894. Designed and chromolithographed in twelve colours by Blades, East & Blades, London. 223 × 308 mm. *John Johnson Collection.*

417 Ticket for a ball at the Guildhall on the occasion of the visit of the Prince and Princess of Wales to the City of London, 1863. Chromolithographed in ten colours with additional printing in gold and silver, hand-colouring, and embossing. 260 × 320 mm. *John Johnson Collection.*

417

418

419

420

418 Menu for the reception of the Shah of Persia by the Corporation of the City of London, 1873. Chromolithograph, printed in four colours by Blades, East & Blades, London. 284 × 183 mm. *John Johnson Collection.*

419 Menu for the banquet given by the Corporation of the City of London for the Prince of Wales, 1876. Chromolithograph, printed in six colours by Jones & Cuthbertson, London. 265 × 192 mm. *John Johnson Collection.*

420 Detail of a sheet of 18 pairs of embossed and cut-out oval portraits of Edward VII and Alexandra, *c.* 1902. Chromolithograph, printed in ten colours in Germany. Size of one pair of ovals and crown 73 × 57 mm. *John Johnson Collection.*

421 Programme for the Royal Opera, Covent Garden, in honour of the visit of the President of the French Republic, 1903. Printed on silk, the brown working by letterpress and the other colours by lithography. 430 × 320 mm. *John Johnson Collection.*

422

423

424

422 Notice of a fancy-dress ball and concert in celebration of George IV's birthday, 1828. Letterpress, with a machine-engraved border, printed in grey-blue and brown by James Whiting, London. 427 × 275 mm. *John Johnson Collection.*

423 Souvenir programme of the state performance at Covent Garden in honour of the marriage of the Duke of York and the Princess May of Teck, 1893. Printed on silk in two brown workings, the text letterpress and the portraits and border probably collotype. Designed by J. Walery. 530 × 360 mm. *John Johnson Collection.*

424 Cover of the programme for the reception and luncheon at Guildhall to the King of the Belgians, 1937. Photogravure, with hand-working on the plate and hand-colouring, produced by Raphael Tuck & Sons Ltd. 289 × 208 mm. *John Johnson Collection.*

425

425 Invitation to the opening of the new Royal Exchange by Queen Victoria, 1844. Steel-engraved and embossed by De la Rue & Co., the vignette of the Royal Exchange engraved by Thomas Higham after an original by William Tite. 264 × 185 mm. *John Johnson Collection.*

426 Order of the state procession from Buckingham Palace to the Royal Exchange, 1844. Letterpress, printed in red and blue for Her Majesty's Stationery Office. 972 × 330 mm. *John Johnson Collection.*

426

Rural life

Associations for the prevention of crime
Reward notices
Game and poaching
Public notices
Friendly societies
Poor relief
The country labourer
Horticultural shows
Agricultural shows and fairs
Livestock sales
Farms and produce
Cultural activities

1836.

CHIPPENHAM ASSOCIATION

FOR THE PREVENTION OF

Robberies and Thefts,

AND

Protection of the Persons and Property of the Members:

HELD AT THE DUKE OF CUMBERLAND INN.

Established the 24th of February, 1809.

MEMBERS.

ASHE, REV. R., LANGLEY HOUSE.
ALEXANDER, R. H., CORSHAM.
ALEXANDER, RICHARD, CHIPPENHAM.
ALEXANDER, THOMAS, CHIPPENHAM.
BLAKE, WILLIAM, BIDDESTONE.
BUTLER, JOHN, FOWLSWICK.
BRYANT, FRANCIS, ALLINGTON.
BETHELL, JOHN, KELLAWAYS.
BEWLEY, WILLIAM, BROAD'S GREEN.
BAYLIFFE, HENRY, SEAGRY.
COTES, REV. C. G., STANTON St. QUINTIN.
COLEMAN, W., LANGLEY-FITZHURST.
COLLETT, THO.'S. EXECUTORS, CORSHAM.
COLBORNE, WILLIAM, CHIPPENHAM.
CARPENTER, WILLIAM, CHIPPENHAM.
DAY, THOMAS, SOUTHSEA FARM.
DARLEY, JOHN, CHIPPENHAM.
GALE, WILLIAM, PEWSHAM.

GALE, WILLIAM, CHIPPENHAM.
GALE, WILLIAM, BIDDESTONE.
GARNER AND PERRIN, WEAVERN MILL.
GIBBS, JOHN, SLAUGHTENFORD.
GOLDNEY, HARRY, CHIPPENHAM.
HULBERT, MESSRS. W. & R., PICKWICK.
HULBERT, JOHN, LYPIATT.
KNIGHT, THOMAS, LANGLEY BURRELL.
KNIGHT, THOMAS, JUN., DRAYCOT.
LIFELY, BENJAMIN, CHIPPENHAM.
LOCKE, F. A. S., PEWHILLS.
LITTLE, THOMAS, BIDDESTONE.
LITTLE, JOHN, BIDDESTONE.
LEA, JOHN, SUTTON BENGER.
LANE, ISAAC, DUNLEY FARM.
LANE, WILLIAM, LANGLEY-FITZHURST.
MOORE, JOSEPH, CHIPPENHAM.
MAILLARD, MRS., LANGLEY BURRELL.

MITCHELL JOHN, SHELDON.
NEELD, JOSEPH, GRITTLETON HOUSE.
NOYES, GEORGE, CHIPPENHAM.
NOYES, JAMES, CHIPPENHAM.
PINNIGER, BROOME, CHIPPENHAM.
PLUMMER, WILLIAM, CORSHAM.
PAINTER, DANIEL, WEST YATTON.
PINNIGER, BROOME, TYTHERTON.
RUSS, HARRY, SHELDON.
RUGG, WILLIAM, CHIPPENHAM.
RUSS, JOHN, SUTTON-BENGER.
SPENCER, HENRY, CHIPPENHAM.
SMITH, JAMES, CHIPPENHAM.
TAYLER, W. A., CASTLE COMBE.
WITTS, JOHN, LANGLEY BURRELL.
WRIGHT, THOMAS, SWINLEY.

The following Rewards

Will be paid on the apprehension and conviction of Offenders committing any of the Offences undermentioned.

	£	s	d
Murder, Burglary, Highway Robbery, Setting Fire to any House, Stable, Outhouse, Shop, or Granary, or any Building used in carrying on any Trade or Manufacture, or to any Stack of Corn, Grain, Hay, or Wood; or committing any other offence punishable with death.	15	0	0
Stealing from the Person of any Member, or assaulting him with an intent to do so; stealing, or embezzling, by any Clerk, Servant, Agent, or Factor, of any Goods or Merchandize intrusted to his or her care; or stealing any Horse, Cow, Calf, or Sheep; or committing any other offence punishable by law with transportation for life, or for fourteen years.	10	0	0
Robbery in any Building not privileged as part of the Dwelling-House, or in any Shop, Warehouse, or Counting-House; or Stealing to the value of Ten Shillings, any Goods of Woollen or Cotton, in process of manufacture, exposed in any field or other place; or stealing or maliciously destroying or injuring any Tree, Sapling, or Shrub, growing in a Garden, Orchard, or Ground, adjoining or belonging to any Dwelling-House, exceeding the value of One Pound, or in any other place, exceeding the value of Five Pounds; or any Glass, Woodwork, or Fixture, belonging to any Building or other place; or obtaining Money or Goods under false pretences; or setting Fire to any Crop of Corn or Grain, either standing or cut down, or committing any other offence punishable by law with transportation for seven years.	7	10	0
Stealing or maliciously Damaging or injuring any Timber-Tree, Sapling, or Underwood; or stealing or breaking any Gate, Fence, Pales, Stile, Posts, or Iron-work, or any Tools used in Trade, or Husbandry; or pulling up or destroying any Turnips, Roots, or Vegetable production, in any Garden, Field, or other place; or committing any other offence punishable on Summary Conviction, whereby the loss or damage sustained shall exceed the value of Five Pounds.	5	0	0
And to any amount or value exceeding Two Pounds and less than Five Pounds.	2	0	0
And to any amount or value less than Two Pounds.	0	10	6

ALEXANDER, PRINTER AND BOOKBINDER, CHIPPENHAM.

427

428

429

430

431

427 Notice, Chippenham Association for the prevention of robberies and thefts, 1836. Letterpress, printed by Alexander, Chippenham. 564 × 447 mm. *Wiltshire County Record Office.*

428 Notice, Ulverston Association, 1808. Letterpress, printed by John Soulby (senior), Ulverston. 330 × 193 mm. *Barrow Public Library.*

429 Notice, Ulverston New Association, 1823. Letterpress, printed by John Soulby (junior), Ulverston. 440 × 265 mm. *Museum of English Rural Life, Reading University.*

430 Public submission, Ulverston, 1806. Letterpress, printed by John Soulby (senior), Ulverston. 221 × 179 mm. *Barrow Public Library.*

431 Reward notice, Ulverston, 1808. Letterpress, printed by John Soulby (senior), Ulverston. 210 × 170 mm. *Barrow Public Library.*

25 GUINEAS
REWARD.

Henfield Prosecuting Society.

WHEREAS some evil disposed Person or Persons, did, in the Night of Tuesday, the 8th Instant, break open the Stable on Furzefield Farm, in the Parish of Shermanbury, in the occupation of Mr. **THOMAS PAGE**, and maliciously **CUT OFF** and carry away

THE HAIR

FROM THE

TAILS OF 3 CART HORSES

the property of the said THOMAS PAGE.

A REWARD OF
FIVE GUINEAS

will be given to any Person or Persons giving Information of the Offender or Offenders, so that he or they may be Convicted thereof; such Reward to be paid by the Treasurer of the said Society, immediately after such Conviction.

THOMAS COPPARD, Clerk.

HORSHAM, 9th MAY, 1838.

A FURTHER REWARD OF
20 GUINEAS

will be paid on such Conviction as aforesaid, by me

THOMAS PAGE.

Printed by Charles Hunt, West Street, Horsham.

432

433

STEEPLE-ASHTON,
Twenty Guineas
REWARD.

THE practice of STEALING HAY from the Ricks, ROBBING CATTLE of their FODDER, CUTTING and LOPPING TREES, &c. having increased to such an extent that the depredators (from the lenity with which they have been hitherto treated) seem to carry on their work of Plunder, almost with impunity.

And in order to check the evil, or severely punish the Offenders. We the underfigned, do hereby jointly agree to pay a Reward of

TWENTY GUINEAS,

to any Person, or Persons, who shall give such Information, as shall lead to the Conviction of any one or more of such Miscreants, who shall be detected in *any of the above Malpractices* to the detriment of either.

A REWARD OF
Three Guineas,

Will also be paid for such Information as shall Convict any Person or Persons of CUTTING LIVE WOOD, FROM HEDGES, carrying away POSTS OR RAILS, STEALING RICK-BOUNDS, &c.

And for the more effectually obtaining the ends of Justice, and that the severest penalties of the Law, may be inflicted, we also resolve to assist and support each other, in the Expences attending all and every Prosecution for such Offences, as witness our Hands 29th, day of December, 1807.

George Ball
Walter Newman
John Bull
Mary Hall.
John Adams
Francis Long
Thomas Stillman

Sweet, Printer, Trowbridge.

434

100
GUINEAS
REWARD.
Whereas some Person or Persons did Wantonly and Maliciously
KILL A MARE
In the Tything & Parish of Steeple Ashton,
THE PROPERTY of Mr. ISAAC LINE,
BY STABBING HER,
In the Night of the 17th Day of September last ; and did also in the Night of the 29th Day of the same Month,
WANTONLY AND MALICIOUSLY
MAIM & KILL
A GELDING,
HIS PROPERTY.

The principal Inhabitants of the said Tything being desirous to discover the Offender or Offenders, do hereby offer

A Reward of 100 Guineas
to any Person or persons who will in either case, give such information as will lead to such discovery.
And they also hereby offer a further Reward of
100 Guineas
to any Person or Persons who shall give such information as will lead to the discovery of any Offender or Offenders who shall or may within the term of One Year from the date hereof, wantonly and maliciously kill, or maim with intent to kill, or disable any Cattle belonging to them, the said inhabitants, or who shall or may wilfully and maliciously set on Fire any of their Ricks, Houses, or Outbuildings.

The above Rewards to be paid by the Churchwardens and Overseers of the Poor of the said Tything on Conviction of the Offender or Offenders.

An Accomplice or Accomplices will be entitled to the above Rewards, and every exertion used to obtain a free pardon.

Dated the 3rd day of October, 1825.

SWEET, PRINTER, TROWBRIDGE.

435

20 GUINEAS
REWARD.

Whereas some person or persons, did on Thursday Evening last, or early the following Morning, Steal and Carry away, from and out a Close of Pasture Land, called THE MIDDLE DOWN, situate near the Dwelling-House of the late Mr. JAMES BETHELL, of *Lady-Down*, in the Parish of Bradford, Wilts,

An Unshorn Fat Wether

The Property of the Representatives of the said *JAMES BETHELL.*

The Society for the better protection of Live and Dead Stock, established in Trowbridge and its Neighbourhood, (of which Mr. Bethell was, and his Representatives are now Members ;) do hereby offer the above Reward to any Person or Persons who shall apprehend and bring before a Magistrate the Person or Persons guilty of the above Offence. The Reward to be paid on his, her, or their Conviction.

THOMAS TIMBRELL,
Solicitor to the said Society.

Trowbridge, 31st May, 1831.

E. Sweet, Printer, Trowbridge.

432 Reward notice, Henfield Prosecuting Society, 1838. Letterpress, printed by Charles Hunt, Horsham. Approximately 415 × 325 mm. *Museum of English Rural Life, Reading University.*

433 Reward notice, Steeple-Ashton, 1807. Letterpress, printed by Sweet, Trowbridge. 312 × 188 mm. *Wiltshire County Record Office.*

434 Reward notice, Steeple-Ashton, 1825. Letterpress, printed by Sweet, Trowbridge. 437 × 280 mm. *Wiltshire County Record Office.*

435 Reward notice, Trowbridge, 1831. Letterpress, printed by E. Sweet, Trowbridge. 285 × 223 mm. *Wiltshire County Record Office.*

GAME.

Abstract from an Act of Parliament passed in the Year 1787.

" That every Person who shall trace any Hare, or other Game in the Snow, shall for every such offence forfeit the Sum of 5l. upon conviction before a Magistrate."

I am determined to enforce the above Act in every instance.

PIERCE MEADE.

Dromore House,
December 20, 1808.

436

GAME.

WHEREAS the GAME within the Manor of *Heyham*, in the County of *Lancaster*, has of late Years been very much destroyed.

WE whose Names are hereunto subscribed being respectively the Owners or Occupiers of Lands,

Do hereby give Notice,

That all PERSONS found Trespassing thereon, will be Prosecuted as the Law Directs.

AUGUST 26th 1802.

Thomas Clarkson.	Matthew Hadwen.
Samuel Bayley.	Richd. Shiers.
Jacob Ridley.	Jonas Middleton.
Rd. Cuton.	Robt. Mount.
Thomas Hadwen.	T. Blake.
Richard Mashiter.	Thos. Jackson.
John Hadwen, Senior.	Thos. Drinkall.
John Hadwen, Junior.	Rd. Thompson.
Joseph Banks.	Jno. Jackson.

H. WALMSLEY, Printer, New-Street, Lancaster.

437

GAME.

Gentlemen Sportsmen

Are requested not to Hunt, Course or Shoot upon the Lands or Grounds in the Parish of Pennington, in the County of Lancaster, belonging to or in the occupation of the Persons whose names are hereunto subscribed:—All other Persons found trespassing on such Lands or Grounds, will be prosecuted as the Law directs.

James Park	William Fleming
William Town	Isaac Dickinson
William Townson	Thomas Fell
Thomas Fisher	John Huddleston

Ulverston, September 20th 1825.

[J. Soulby, Printer, Market-place, Ulverston.]

438

NOTICE.

We whose Names are hereunto subscribed, being Owners & Occupiers of the different Estates in the ISLAND of WALNEY, do hereby give Notice that no Qualified PERSON will be allowed to beat for GAME, upon any of our Lands—And all unqualified Persons found Trespassing thereon will be PROSECUTED,

John Postlethwaite	Rev. Mr. Troughton	John Heslam
William Simpson	James Robinson	John Phizackley
Miles Gibson	W. Greenwood, Jun.	Francis Whithers
George Gibson	Thos. Greenwood	Richard Clark
W. Greenwood, Sen.	Thos. Walton	Samuel Redhead
Robert Greenwood	Joseph Walton	Jane Strickland

Ulverston, August 13th, 1824.

J. Soulby, Printer, Market Place, Ulverston.

439

436 Game notice, Dromore House, 1808. Letterpress, anon. 380 × 190 mm. *John Johnson Collection.*

437 Game notice, 1802. Letterpress, printed by H. Walmsley, Lancaster. 245 × 190 mm. *Barrow Public Library.*

438 Game notice, Ulverston, 1825. Letterpress, printed by John Soulby (junior), Ulverston. 275 × 220 mm. *Museum of English Rural Life, Reading University.*

439 Game notice, Ulverston, 1824. Letterpress, printed by John Soulby (junior), Ulverston. 333 × 210 mm. *Museum of English Rural Life, Reading University.*

440 Form of summons relating to poaching, *c.* 1824. Letterpress, printed by John Soulby (junior), Ulverston. 315 × 197 mm. *Museum of English Rural Life, Reading University.*

Lancashire TO WIT.

To the Constable of County of Lancaster in the

WHEREAS Information and Complaint hath been made before me Esquire one of his Majesty's Justices of the Peace for the said County that on the Day of in the year of our Lord one Thousand Eight Hundred and one of in the County aforesaid being a Person not then having Lands or Tenements or any other Estate, of Inheritance in his Own right, or in his Wife's right of the clear yearly value of one Hundred Pounds, or for term of Life; nor then having Lease or Leases, for Ninty Nine years, or for any longer term, of the clear yearly value of one Hundred and Fifty Pounds, nor then being the Son and Heir apparent of an Esquire or other person of higher degree; nor then being the Lord of any Manor, Lordship or Royalty; nor then being the Owner or Keeper of any Forrest, Park, Chase or Warren; nor then being the Game-keeper of any Lord or Lady of any Lordship, Royalty or Manor, duly made constituted or appointed by writing under his or her hand and Seal to take, kill or destroy the Game or any sort of Game whatsoever, in or upon any Lordship Royalty or Manor; nor then being truly and Properly a Servant of or to any Lord or Lady of any Lordship, Royalty or Manor; nor then being immediately appointed to take and kill the Game for the sole use and immediate benefit of any Lord or Lady of any Lordship, Royalty or Manor, nor then being a person in any other manner qualified, empowered licenced or authorized by the Laws of this Realm either to take, kill, or destroy any sort of Game whatsoever, or to keep or use any Dog, Gun, or other Instrument for that purpose, unlawfully did at the Parish of in the County of aforesaid keep and use to kill and destroy the Game contrary to the form of the Statute in that Case made and provided; whereby he hath forfeited the Sum of Five Pounds to be applied as the Act directs.

THESE are therefore to require you forthwith to Summon the said to appear before me at in the said County on the Day of at the Hour of in the Forenoon to Answer the said Information and Complaint, and to be further dealt with according to Law. And be you then there to certify, what you shall have done in the Execution hereof. herein fail not.

GIVEN under my Hand and Seal this Day of in the Year of our Lord one Thousand Eight Hundred and

440

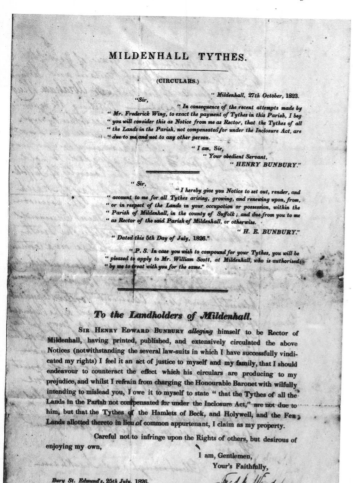

MILDENHALL TYTHES.

(CIRCULARS.)

" Mildenhall, 27th October, 1823.

"Sir,

" In consequence of the recent attempts made by
" Mr. Frederick Wing, to exact the payment of Tythes in this Parish, I beg
" you will consider this as Notice from me as Rector, that the Tythes of all
" the Lands in the Parish, not compensated for under the Inclosure Act, are
" due to me and not to any other person.

" I am, Sir,
" Your obedient Servant,
" HENRY BUNBURY."

" Sir,

" I hereby give you Notice to set out, render, and
" account to me for all Tythes arising, growing, and renewing upon, from,
" or in respect of the Lands in your occupation or possession, within the
" Parish of Mildenhall, in the county of Suffolk ; and due from you to me
" as Rector of the said Parish of Mildenhall, or otherwise.

" H. E. BUNBURY."

" Dated this 5th Day of July, 1826."

" P.S. In case you wish to compound for your Tythes, you will be
" pleased to apply to Mr. William Scott, at Mildenhall, who is authorised
" by me to treat with you for the same."

To the Landholders of Mildenhall.

SIR HENRY EDWARD BUNBURY alleging himself to be Rector of
Mildenhall, having printed, published, and extensively circulated the above
Notices (notwithstanding the several law-suits in which I have successfully vindi-
cated my rights) I feel it an act of justice to myself and my family, that I should
endeavour to counteract the effect which his circulars are producing to my
prejudice, and whilst I refrain from charging the Honourable Baronet with wilfully
intending to mislead you, I owe it to myself to state " that the Tythes of all the
Lands in the Parish not compensated for under the Inclosure Act," are not due to
him, but that the Tythes of the Hamlets of Beck, and Holywell, and the Fen
Lands allotted thereto in lieu of common appurtenant, I claim as my property.

Careful not to infringe upon the Rights of others, but desirous of
enjoying my own,

I am, Gentlemen,
Your's Faithfully,

Bury St. Edmund's, 25th July, 1826.

Fred.t Wing

441

NOTICE to the PUBLIC,

(The Poor as well as the Rich.)

At a special MEETING of the Inhabitants of the Parish of
CHISLEHURST, on Monday, the 23rd Day of *March*, 1807,
it was proved, by the incontestable Evidence of several very
old and respectable Persons, viz.—

Mr. GEORGE MACE, Mr. RICHARD TURNER, Mr. GEORGE SCUDDER,
AND OTHERS,

THAT, from *Scadbury Gate, St. Paul's-Cray Common*, down the Avenue of the Park
to a Lane on the Right-Hand Side, near the Farm House, and then down that
Lane to *St. Paul's-Cray*, is

A common Foot Path, Bridle Way, and Cart Way,

AND HAS UNINTERRUPTEDLY BEEN SO

For FOUR SCORE YEARS,

According to the Testimony of the FIRST WITNESS ;
And who added, that he frequently met in the Park, Sir EDWARD BETTENSON, the
then Proprietor of the Estate, who never molested him on his Way throught it.
Mr. TURNER, Mr. SCUDDER, and other Evidences, went back to FIFTY and
SIXTY YEARS.

It is true (for certain Reasons) the *Higher Order* of Inhabitants have not been
refused Admittance at *Scadbury Gate*, but many of the lower Class have been insolently
TURNED BACK by the Man at the LODGE.

Inhabitants of Chislehurst,

But more particularly I address myself to those of my Fellow
Creatures who happen unfortunately to be POOR,

An Attempt has been made to deprive you of your JUST RIGHTS, &c.—be not
afraid to tread the common Path as often as you please ; and if you walk in the Paths of
Virtue and Honesty, I hope you will always find, among the higher and middling Classes,
some Men of Independence and Integrity who will consider it their Duty to be

Protectors of your Just Rights and Privileges.

N.B. Other Public Paths through the PARK are STOPPED up, which OUGHT TO
BE THROWN OPEN AGAIN.

Keep this as a Memorandum, it may be of Use hereafter when I am dead and gone.

442

Whereas,

Some evil disposed Person or
Persons, have done considerable
damage in the Wood & Grounds
near Low Wood, belonging to
MR. RALPH BREWER;

NOTICE

IS THEREFORE HEREBY GIVEN,

That whosoever is found Trespassing after the date hereof,
will be prosecuted to the utmost
rigour of the Law.

Ulverston, April 29th 1826.

J Soulby Printer Market Place Ulverston.

443

CAUTION
TO
Trespassers.

An Act of Parliament passed 15th July, 1820, for the summary Punishment
in certain Cases, of Persons wilfully or maliciously damaging or committing
Trespasses on public or private Property.

The first clause enacts, that if any person or persons shall wilfully or
maliciously do or commit any damage, Injury or Spoil, to or, upon any Building,
Fence, Hedge, Gate, Stile, Guide Post, Milestone, Tree, Wood, Underwood, Orchard,
Garden, Nursery Ground, Crops, Vegetables, Plants, Land, or, other Matter or
Thing growing or being thereon, or to or upon real or personal property, of any
Nature or kind soever, and shall be thereof convicted within four Calendar Months,
before a Justice of the Peace, shall forfeit and pay to the party aggrieved, such sum of
Money not exceeding Five pounds as shall appear to such Justice, a reasonable
compensation; but if the conviction is on the sole evidence of the party aggrieved, the
compensation then to be paid to the Overseers of the Poor, &c. And if any such
Damage, Injury, or Spoil, shall have been done or committed as aforesaid, to or upon
any Church, Chapel, Bridge, Building, Common Way or other Property whatsoever,
whether real or personal of a public Nature, it shall be lawful for such Justice to
proceed against and convict the offender or offenders, within the time aforesaid, and
in the manner aforesaid, in any sum not exceeding Five Pounds, one moiety to be
paid to the party prosecuting, and the other for the use of the Poor. In default of
immediate Payment in either case with Costs, Offenders may be committed to
the Common Gaol or House of Correction, there to be kept to hard Labour, for any
time not exceeding Three Months unless sooner paid.

The second clause provides that if any Male Person under the Age of Sixteen, shall
offend against any of the provisions of the Act, he shall in default of payment of the
sum awarded against him with costs, be committed to the House of Correction, for
any time not exceeding Six Weeks.

And the third Clause enacts. That it shall be lawful for any Constable, and
for any Owner of any property damaged, his Servant or other Person acting under
his Authority and for such Person as he may call to his Assistance without any
Warrant or other Authority than by this Act, to seize, apprehend and detain, any
Person or persons who shall have actually committed, or be in the Act of committing
any Offence or Offences against any of the provisions of this Act, and to take him
before any Justice of the Peace.

John Soulby, Printer, Market Place, Ulverston.

444

441 Tythe notice, Bury St Edmunds, 1826. Letterpress, anon.
320 × 203 mm. *Museum of English Rural Life, Reading University.*

442 Notice, Chislehurst, 1807. Letterpress, anon. 242 × 199 mm.
John Johnson Collection.

443 Notice, Ulverston, 1826. Letterpress, printed by John Soulby
(junior), Ulverston. 164 × 208 mm. *Museum of English Rural
Life, Reading University.*

444 Notice, c. 1820. Letterpress, printed by John Soulby (junior),
Ulverston. 440 × 270 mm. *Museum of English Rural Life,
Reading University.*

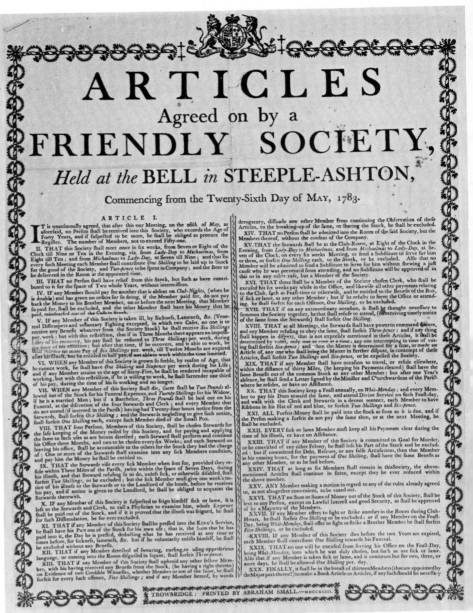

445

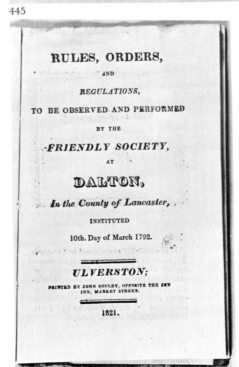

446

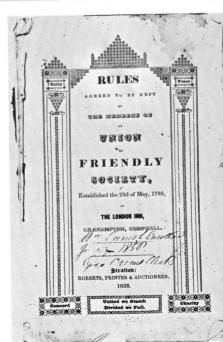

447

445 Articles agreed on by Steeple-Ashton Friendly Society. Letterpress, printed by Abraham Small, Trowbridge, 1793. 515 × 380 mm. *Wiltshire County Record Office.*

446 *Rules, orders, and regulations, to be observed by the Friendly Society, at Dalton*, Ulverston, 1821. Letterpress, printed by John Soulby (junior). Page size 150 × 95 mm. *Museum of English Rural Life, Reading University.*

447 *Rules agreed to be kept by the members of an Union or Friendly Society, at Kilkhampton, Cornwall*, Stratton, 1838. Letterpress, printed in green and blue by Roberts. 226 × 143 mm. *Museum of English Rural Life, Reading University.*

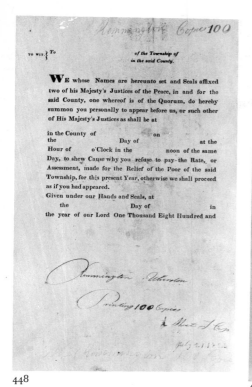

448

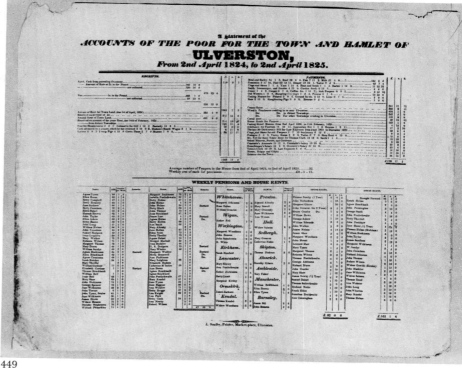

449

450

451

448 Form of summons relating to non-payment of poor relief, *c.* 1824. Letterpress, printed by John Soulby (junior), Ulverston. 325 × 203 mm. *Museum of English Rural Life, Reading University.*

449 Statement of accounts of the poor for Ulverston, 1825. Letterpress, printed by John Soulby (junior), Ulverston. 430 × 535 mm. *Museum of English Rural Life, Reading University.*

450 Indenture of apprenticeship of an eight-year old poor child in the parish of Saint Dominick, Cornwall, 1803. Letterpress, printed for His Majesty's Stationery Office by J. Hayes, London. 235 × 384 mm. *Museum of English Rural Life, Reading University.*

451 Poor's Rate receipt, Bishop's Tawton, 1847. Letterpress, anon. 85 × 217 mm. *Museum of English Rural Life, Reading University.*

452

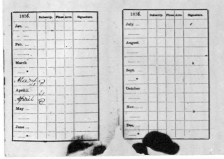

453

454

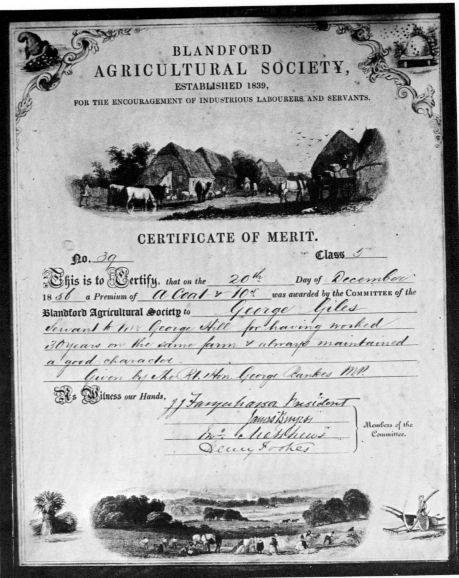

455

452, 453 Membership card of the National
Agricultural Labourers' Union, 1875.
Letterpress, printed by the 'Chronicle'
Steam Printing Works, Leamington. Page
size 120 × 80 mm. *Museum of English
Rural Life, Reading University.*

454 To let notice, early 1820s. Letterpress,
printed by John Soulby (junior), Ulverston.
157 × 190 mm. *Museum of English Rural
Life, Reading University.*

455 Certificate of merit awarded by
Blandford Agricultural Society, 1856.
Steel-engraving with letterpress text.
Designed and drawn by L. J. Wood,
engraved by Shaw & Sons, London.
285 × 230 mm. *Museum of English Rural
Life, Reading University.*

456 Certificate awarded by the Royal East
Berks Agricultural Association, 1897.
Intaglio, engraved and printed by
W. Burnham, Maidenhead. 187 ×
223 mm. *Museum of English Rural Life,
Reading University.*

456

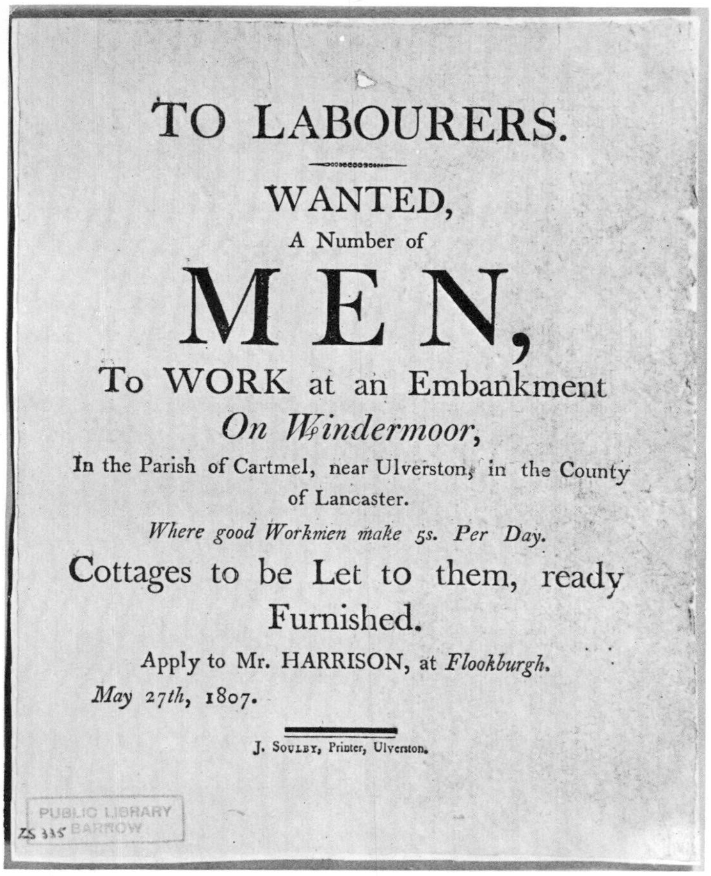

457

458

459

457 Advertisement for labourers, 1807. Letterpress, printed by John Soulby (senior), Ulverston. 213 × 170 mm. *Barrow Public Library*.

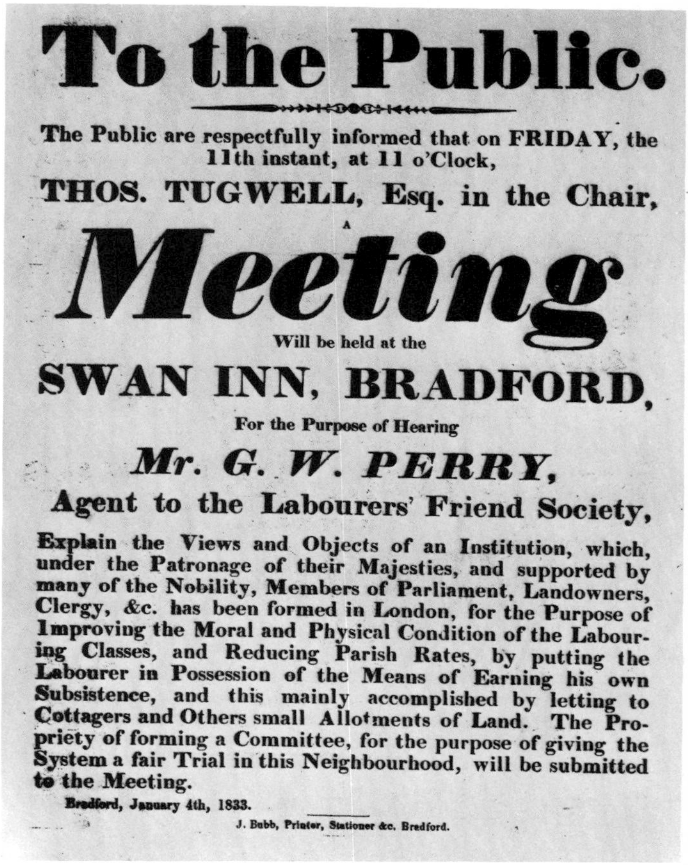

458 Notice of meeting, Bradford, 1833. Letterpress, printed by J. Bubb, Bradford. 308 × 247 mm. *Wiltshire County Record Office*.

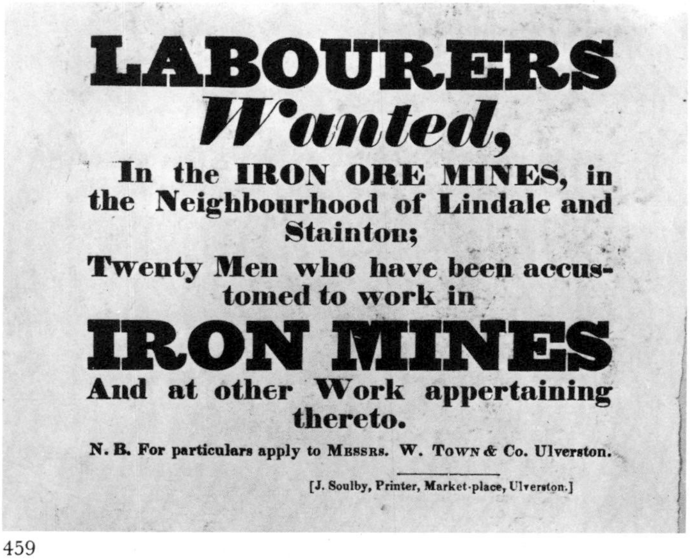

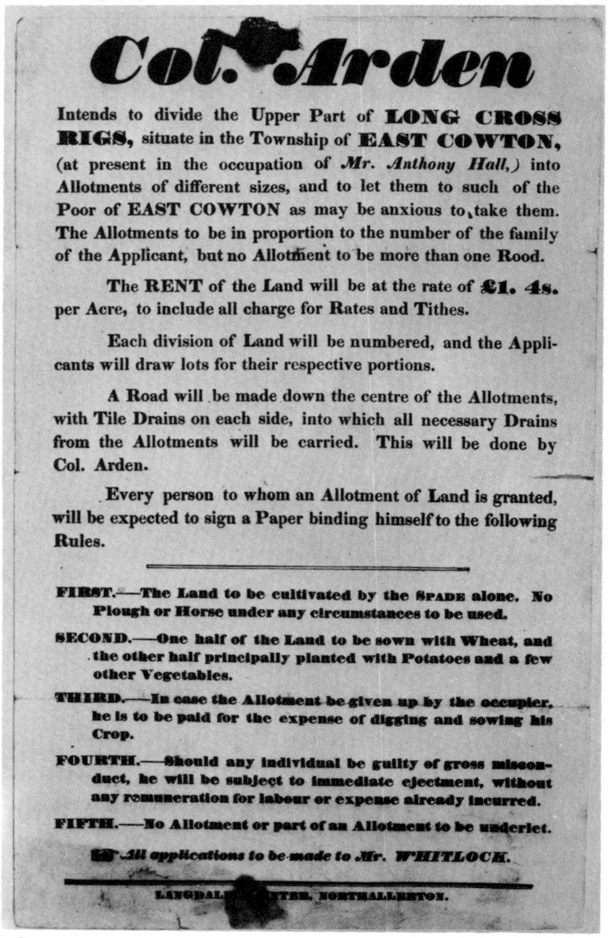

459 Advertisement for labourers, Ulverston, c.1825. Letterpress, printed by John Soulby (junior), Ulverston. 180 × 225 mm. *Museum of English Rural Life, Reading University*.

460 Notice of renting of allotments of land, East Cowton. Letterpress, printed by Langdale, Northallerton. 316 × 199 mm. *Museum of English Rural Life, Reading University*.

460

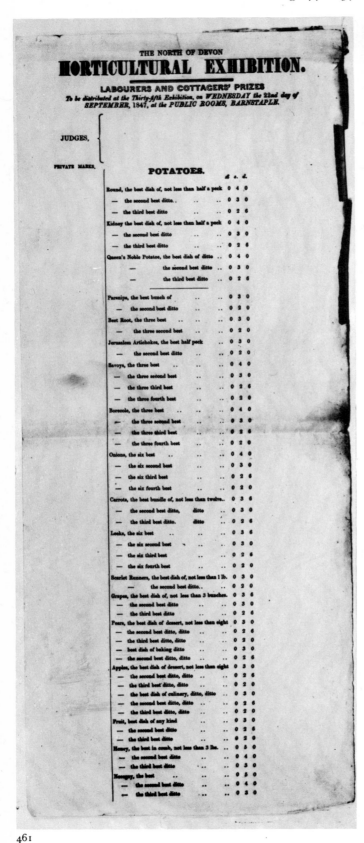

THE NORTH OF DEVON
HORTICULTURAL EXHIBITION.

LABOURERS AND COTTAGERS' PRIZES
To be distributed at the Thirty-fifth Exhibition, on WEDNESDAY the 22nd day of SEPTEMBER, 1847, at the PUBLIC ROOMS, BARNSTAPLE.

JUDGES,

PRIVATE MARKS,

POTATOES.

POTATOES
SHEW.

THE LABOURING CLASSES resident in the Parishes of AYLESBURY, HARTWELL, and STONE, are informed that the ANNUAL SHEW for the Prizes given by JOHN LEE, Esq. L.L.D. will take place at the Crown Inn, Aylesbury, on THURSDAY, *28th October* next.

Each Person must produce Six Potatoes of the same Sort, which must be placed in the Show Room before Two o'Clock on the above Day.

THOMAS FIELD,
Honorary Secretary.

Aylesbury,
October 20. 1841.

MAY, PRINTER, AYLESBURY.

462

KELVEDON
HORTICULTURAL SOCIETY.

PRIZES
FOR
VEGETABLES,
FLOWERS, & FRUIT,

Will be awarded to Cottagers resident in the Parishes of Kelvedon, Feering, Messing, Inworth, Great Braxted, and Rivenhall,

IN FELIX HALL PARK,
In JULY, 1870.

LISTS OF PRIZES WILL BE ISSUED IN DUE TIME.

W. GODFREY, PRINTER AND BINDER, KELVEDON.

463

461

461 North Devon Horticultural Exhibition, list of labourers and cottagers' prizes, Barnstaple, 1847. Letterpress, anon. 472 × 195 mm. *Museum of English Rural Life, Reading University.*

462 Notice of potato show, Aylesbury, 1841. Letterpress, printed by May, Aylesbury. 230 × 276 mm. *John Johnson Collection.*

463 Kelvedon Horticultural Society, notice of prizes, 1870. Letterpress, printed on buff paper by W. Godfrey, Kelvedon. 377 × 251 mm. *Essex County Record Office.*

KELVEDON HORTICULTURAL SOCIETY.

THE FOLLOWING PRIZES FOR

Vegetables, Flowers, Fruit, Honey,

&c., &c.,

WILL BE AWARDED

IN FELIX HALL PARK, KELVEDON,

On THURSDAY, 10th AUGUST, 1871.

VEGETABLES.

For the best peck of Kidney Potatoes, *Prize*—A steel Fork.
For the second-best ditto .... 3s. 6d.
For the third-best ditto .... 2s. 6d.
For the best peck of Round Potatoes, *Prize*—A steel Fork.
For the second-best ditto .... 3s. 6d.
For the third-best ditto .... 2s. 6d.
For the best Collection of Vegetables, *Prize*—A steel Fork, and 1s.
For the second-best ditto, *Prize*—A steel Fork.
For the third-best ditto .... 2s. 6d.
For the fourth-best ditto .... 1s. 6d.
For the best twelve Kidney Potatoes .... 3s. 0d.
For the second-best ditto .... 2s. 0d.
For the third-best ditto .... 1s. 0d.
For the best twelve Round Potatoes .... 3s. 0d.
For the second-best ditto .... 2s. 0d.
For the third-best ditto .... 1s. 0d.

	First.	Second.	Third.
	s. d.	s. d.	s. d.
Six Carrots	3 0	2 0	1 0
Six Onions (this year's growth)	3 0	2 0	1 0
Bunch of Six Turnips	3 0	2 0	1 0
Quarter-of-a-peck of Peas	3 0	2 0	1 0
Twenty pods of Windsor Beans	3 0	2 0	1 0
Twenty pods of Long-pod Beans	3 0	2 0	1 0
Three Cabbages	3 0	2 0	1 0
Thirty French Beans—dwarf	3 0	2 0	1 0
Thirty Scarlet-runner Beans	3 0	2 0	1 0
Six Parsnips	3 0	2 0	1 0

FRUIT.

	First.	Second.	Third.
One pound of black Currants	3 0	2 0	1 0
One pound of White ditto	3 0	2 0	1 0
One pound of Red ditto	3 0	2 0	1 0
Thirty Gooseberries (by weight)	3 0	2 0	1 0

FLOWERS.

	First.	Second.	Third.	Fourth.
For the best Collection of Flowers in pots, not fewer than four, of the exhibitor's own growth	5s.,	3s.,	2s.,	1s.

FLOWERS—continued.

	First.	Second.	Third.	Fourth.
For the best Bouquet of cut Flowers from exhibitor's own garden	4s.,	3s.,	2s.,	1s.

HONEY.

For the largest quantity of Honey taken by any Bee-keeper from his whole stock without destroying the Bees, *Prize* .... 5s. 0d.
For the largest quantity of Honey, taken from one stock, 1st Prize .... 3s. 6d.
For the second largest ditto, a Super, including 2s. 6d., given by Mr. W. Braddy.

ALLOTMENTS.

For the best cultivated Allotment in Kelvedon, a Steel Fork and .... 3s. 0d.
For the second-best ditto .... 6s. 0d.
For the third-best ditto .... 5s. 0d.
For the fourth-best ditto .... 4s. 0d.
For the fifth-best ditto .... 3s. 0d.
For the sixth-best ditto .... 2s. 0d.
For the best cultivated Allotment in Rivenhall, a Steel Fork and .... 5s. 0d.
For the second-best ditto .... 5s. 0d.
For the third-best ditto .... 4s. 0d.
For the fourth-best ditto .... 3s. 0d.
For the best cultivated Allotment in Feering, a Steel Fork and .... 3s. 0d.
For the second-best ditto .... 5s. 0d.
For the third-best ditto .... 4s. 0d.
For the fourth-best ditto .... 3s. 0d.

EXTRA PRIZES.

For Boys, under 18 or 20 Years of age, who have lived and worked with one Master the longest period, and who can bring a good character from his Master or Employer.
FIRST PRIZE .... 5s. 0d.
SECOND ditto .... 3s. 0d.
THIRD ditto .... 2s. 0d.

PRIZES

FOR AMATEURS AND GENTLEMEN'S GARDENERS,

IN THE PARISHES OF

KELVEDON, MESSING, Gt. BRAXTED, RIVENHALL, and INWORTH.

STRAWBERRIES.

FIRST PRIZE .... 4s. 0d.
SECOND ditto .... 3s. 0d.
THIRD ditto .... 2s. 0d.

CUCUMBERS.

FIRST PRIZE .... 4s. 0d.
SECOND ditto .... 3s. 0d.
THIRD ditto .... 2s. 0d.

12 FLOWERS IN POTS.

FIRST PRIZE .... 8s. 0d.
SECOND ditto .... 6s. 0d.
THIRD ditto .... 4s. 0d.

HOT-HOUSE GRAPES.

FIRST PRIZE .... 6s. 0d.
SECOND ditto .... 4s. 0d.
THIRD ditto .... 2s. 0d.

REGULATIONS FOR COTTAGE EXHIBITORS.

Agricultural Labourers residing in the Parishes of Kelvedon, Feering, Messing, Inworth, Braxted, and Rivenhall, and whose house-rent does not exceed £6 a year, are at liberty to compete for the above Prizes. The Prizes for Honey are open to general competition.

Competitors are allowed to exhibit in every class, but are only allowed to take one Prize in each class, and no competitor will be allowed to take more than one First Prize for which a Fork is offered. No Prize to be divided. Plates, dishes, baskets, &c., must be provided by the exhibitor. Any person who takes the First Prize for Allotment cultivation, will not be allowed to compete for the same the following year. The Allotment Gardeners are requested to Number their Allotments in figures.

The Booth will be open at 9 a.m., for the reception of Fruit, Vegetables, &c., and be closed at half-past 10 a.m.

Exhibitors on their arrival at the place of exhibition, must apply to the Secretary for numbers to be placed on the articles they bring.

A REWARD of FIVE SHILLINGS will be given for such information, as will lead to the detection of any one exhibiting for competition, Vegetables, Fruit or Flowers, not grown in his own Garden, or Allotment Ground. And any Person so detected will not be allowed a Prize, and will be excluded at any future Exhibition.

Every Article exhibited to remain the property of the exhibitor, but not to be removed from the table until 6 p.m.

Parties intending to compete, and resident in Kelvedon, Feering, Messing, and Inworth, are requested to enter their names with Mr. S. SEABROOK, or Mr. J. FULLER, Kelvedon; and those resident in Braxted and Rivenhall, are requested to enter their names with Mr. G. TABER, Rivenhall, on any day up to the 8th of August.

THE PRIZES WILL BE ANNOUNCED AT FIVE O'CLOCK.

W. GODFREY, PRINTER AND BINDER, KELVEDON.

464 Kelvedon Horticultural Society, notice of prizes, 1871.
Letterpress, printed by W. Godfrey, Kelvedon. 430 × 342 mm.
Essex County Record Office.

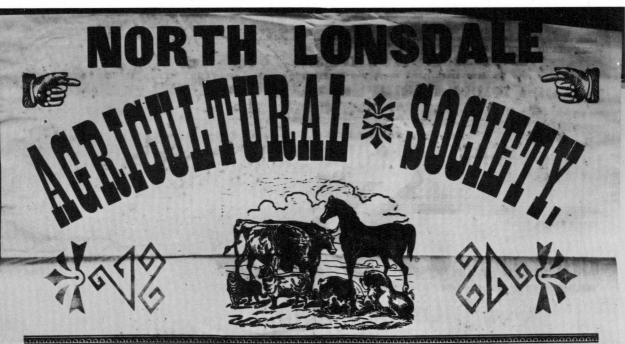

NORTH LONSDALE
AGRICULTURAL ❈ SOCIETY,

PATRON: HIS GRACE THE DUKE OF DEVONSHIRE, K.G.

THE ANNUAL

SHOW
OF
CATTLE, SHEEP, HORSES,
PIGS, COLLIE DOGS,
ROOTS, BUTTER & EGGS,

WILL BE HELD

On TUESDAY, September 18th, 1888,

In TOD BUSK PARK (near the Ry. Station), ULVERSTON,

WHEN PREMIUMS, &C., **£350** WILL BE OFFERED
TO THE VALUE OF FOR COMPETITION.

ENTRIES CLOSE, THURSDAY, the 6th day of SEPTEMBER, 1888.

Admission to the Show Ground, 1s.

CHILDREN UNDER TWELVE YEARS OF AGE HALF-PRICE.

THE FURNESS RAILWAY COMPANY will issue First, Second, and Third Class Return Tickets to Ulverston from all Stations on their line, and also from Ambleside and Bowness at about a Single FARE AND A QUARTER for the double journey.

LUNCHEON will be served on the Field at 1-30 p.m.

CERTIFICATES OF ENTRY, DETAILED LIST OF PRIZES, and other particulars may be obtained from

JNO. ATKINSON, Secretary,
NEW MARKET STREET, ULVERSTON.

13th August, 1888.

W. KITCHIN, PRINTER, BOOKBINDER & STATIONER, MARKET STREET, ULVERSTON.

465

Cattle Fair,
AT ULVERSTONE.

A FAIR FOR CATTLE WILL BE HOLDEN AT
ULVERSTONE,
On Tuesday the 24th of March, 1807;

WHERE a large quantity will be shewn, suitable for GENTLEMEN GRAZIERS, and BUTCHERS; this *Fair* has received the greatest encouragement from the FARMERS who purpose selling some of the Handsomest CATTLE bred in the *North* of *England*, and will be annually holden on *Tuesday* before *Easter*, which will suit *Preston*, *Bentham* and other Fairs in that week.

A SHEW of HORSES;
And *MALE* and *FEMALE SERVANTS* to be *HIRED*.

Ulverstone OCTOBER *Cattle Fair:*

The CATTLE FAIR will as usual be held on the 7th day of *October*, next.

J. SOULBY, *Printer*, Ulverstone.

466

CATTLE FAIR,
AT ULVERSTONE.

The SPRING FAIR for CATTLE, will be holden at
Ulverstone,
On TUESDAY *the* TWELFTH *Day of* APRIL, 1808,
WHERE A LARGE QUANTITY WILL BE SHEWN,
Suitable for
GENTLEMEN, GRAZIERS *AND* BUTCHERS:
The encouragement this FAIR has received promises a
FINE SHEW.

THE OCTOBER CATTLE FAIR,
Will be holden as usual, notice of which will be given.

N. B. *The* CATTLE *will be* SHEWN *in*
MARKET-PLACE, MARKET-STREET AND
KING-STREET.

ULVERSTONE:
Printed by J. SOULBY, in King-Street.

467

QUERIES,
PROPOSED BY THE
BOARD OF AGRICULTURE,
TO BE ANSWERED BY INTELLIGENT FARMERS.

QUERIES.	ANSWERS.
1. WHAT is the nature of the soil and climate in your neighbourhood?	
2. The manner in which the land is occupied, and whether the farms, are, in general, small or great?	
3. The manner in which the land is employed, whether in pasture, in husbandry, or a mixture of both.	
4. If in pasture, what grasses are cultivated? what species of stock is kept? Whether the breeds can be improved, or whether new breeds ought to be tried?	
5. Whether any of the land is watered, and whether any considerable extent of ground is capable of that improvement?	
6. If the land is employed in husbandry, what are the grains principally cultivated?	
7. What is the rotation of crops? and in particular whether green crops, as turnips, clover, &c. are cultivated, and how they are found to answer?	
8. Whether following is practised or otherwise?	
9. What	

468

465 North Lonsdale Agricultural Society, notice of annual show, Ulverston, 1888. Letterpress, with woodcut, printed in brown and blue on three sheets by W. Kitchin, Ulverston. 1390 × 890 mm. *Museum of English Rural Life, Reading University.*

466 Notice of cattle fair, Ulverston, 1807. Letterpress, printed by John Soulby (senior), Ulverston. 216 × 183 mm. *Barrow Public Library.*

467 Notice of cattle fair, Ulverston, 1808. Letterpress, printed by John Soulby (senior), Ulverston. 305 × 193 mm. *Barrow Public Library.*

468 Board of Agriculture questionnaire, late eighteenth or early nineteenth century. 4 pages, letterpress, anon. 270 × 215 mm. *Museum of English Rural Life, Reading University.*

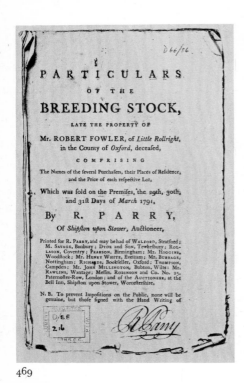

469

470

471

472

469, 470 Catalogue of sale of breeding stock, 1791. 32 pages, letterpress, anon. Page size 227 × 140 mm. *Museum of English Rural Life, Reading University.*

471, 472 Catalogue of sale of stock, 1795. 8 pages, letterpress, printed by J. Catnach, Alnwick. Page size 200 × 168 mm. *Museum of English Rural Life, Reading University.*

473 Auction bill, 1806. Letterpress, printed by H. Walmsley, Lancaster. 221 × 180 mm. *Barrow Public Library.*

474 Auction bill, 1818. Letterpress, printed by T. Jenkins, Swansea. 240 × 191 mm. *Museum of English Rural Life, Reading University.*

475 Auction bill, 1824. Letterpress, printed by John Soulby (junior), Ulverston. 180 × 215 mm. *Museum of English Rural Life, Reading University.*

476 Auction bill, 1826. Letterpress, printed by John Soulby (junior), Ulverston. 183 × 223 mm. *Museum of English Rural Life, Reading University.*

477 Auction bill, 1824. Letterpress, printed by John Soulby (junior), Ulverston. 275 × 224 mm. *Museum of English Rural Life, Reading University.*

TO BE SOLD,

BY AUCTION,

AT THE HOUSE OF MR. RICHARD GIBSON,

AT

BIRKLANDBARROW,

On WEDNESDAY the 22d of OCTOBER 1806,

The Sale to begin at one o'Clock;

ALL THE

STOCK OF CATTLE,

CONSISTING OF

8 Present and Spring Calvers, with other young goods to
the Number of sixteen Head.

2 good work Horses,

AND

20 *Sheep;*

Also, Carts, Wheels, Plows and Harrows, with various
other sorts of Husbandry Gear; and all sorts of HOUSE-
HOLD FURNITURE, viz. Bedsteads, Tables Chairs, &c.
with different sorts of Milking Vessels.

And also, will be let the WINTERAGE of the ESTATE.

Time for payment will be fixed at the place of Sale.

H. Walmsley, Printer, New-Street, Lancaster.

473

CAPITAL

FARMING STOCK,

Implements of Husbandry,

&c. &c.

TO BE SOLD BY AUCTION,

On MONDAY, the 23d of MARCH, 1818,

At Eglwysnunyd Farm,

NEAR MARGAM,

IN THE COUNTY OF GLAMORGAN,

Subject to such Conditions of Sale as will then be produced,

CONSISTING OF

TEN fat Oxen, Two fat Heifers, Eighteen Oxen, five and four years' old, Eight
three year-old Steers, Seven two year-old Ditto, Seven Yearling Ditto, Eleven
Cows and Six Heifers, Calved and in Calf, Seven two year-old Heifers, Seven
Yearling Ditto, a Bull; Six Cart Horses, Four Brood Mares, Four three year-old
Colts, Three two year-old Ditto, Three Yearling Ditto and Two Hacks; Fifty
Ewes, in Lamb, Sixty Yearling Sheep, Twenty-three fat Sheep, and Ten Pigs;
Waggons, Carts, Ploughs, Harrows, Horsehoes, Drags, &c. &c.; Three Hundred
Winchester Bushels of prime Seed Barley.

The above Stock are all of the improved Glamorgan Breed, selected by the late Mr.
Edward Thomas, of Eglwysnunyd, and have been long known and admired. Breeders,
Farmers, and others, will seldom have such have an opportunity of improving their Stock as
by a selection from the above.

The Stock may be viewed during the week preceding the sale.—The sale will commence
at ten o'clock precisely, the whole will be sold without reserve, and Six Months' Credit will
be given on approved Security.

T. JENKINS, PRINTER, SWANSEA.

474

To be Sold

BY AUCTION,

At the House of James Higginson,

AT OLD-PARK, NEAR HOLKER,

On Monday the 12th, Day of April,

1824,

AT 1 o'CLOCK IN THE AFTERNOON:

TWELVE HEAD OF YOUNG

CATTLE,

Of different ages, One Fat Cow,

NINETY SHEEP,

Of the improved Breed, and a quantity of Husbandry Gear, of different
sorts.

Time for Payment will be fixed at the Day of Sale.

Matthew Knowles Auctioneer.

J. Soulby, Printer, Market Place, Ulverston.

475

To be Sold

By Public Auction,

(BY VIRTUE OF A DISTRESS FOR RENT.)

FOR READY MONEY,

At UPPER STENNERLEY, in Lowick, in the Parish of Ulverston, in the
County of Lancaster.

On Saturday the 13th. of March

1824,

AT 1 o'CLOCK IN THE AFTERNOON.

7 MILCH COWS,

One Stirk,

3 Good Work

HORSES,

2 Stags, 2 Pigs, a quantity of

SHEEP,

Wheat, Barley, and Oats. ——A good Corn Machine, Carts, Wheels,
and Husbandry Gear; together with a variety of Household Goods
and Furniture.

J. Soulby, Printer, Market Place, Ulverston.

477

To be Sold

BY AUCTION,

On Tuesday the 28th Day of March

1826,

AT 1 o'Clock in the Afternoon,

At the House of Agnes Sill,

At Tottlebank, in Subberthwaite, in the Parish of Ulverston,

1 WORK HORSE,

5 COWS,

One Calf, two Carts and Wheels, Plough, Harrow, Cart Gear,

Household Furniture,

Corn in the Straw, Straw, Hay, Fire Wood, &c.

J. Soulby, Printer, Market Place, Ulverston.

476

478 Combined auction bill and catalogue for sale of farming stock at Hurley, 1827. Letterpress, printed by Hickman and Stapledon, Henley. 413 × 324 mm. *John Johnson Collection.*

479 Combined auction bill and catalogue for sale of farming stock at Saintbury, 1870. Letterpress, printed by H. A. Pearce, Evesham. 556 × 378 mm. *John Johnson Collection.*

SAINTBURY

GLOUCESTERSHIRE; 3 Miles from Campden, 2 from Broadway, and 7 from Evesham.

TO BE SOLD BY AUCTION, BY

H. W. SMITH

On THURSDAY, the 5th Day of MAY, 1870,

THE WHOLE OF THE LIVE & DEAD FARMING

STOCK,

Comprising **A FLOCK OF 120 CROSS-BRED SHEEP,**

Consisting of 52 Ewes and 69 Lambs, 67 Ewe and Wether Tegs, and a 2-shear Shropshire Ram;

30 HEAD OF WELL-BRED SHORT-HORN CATTLE

Including 10 Young Dairy Cows & Heifers, in or with Calf; 2 Barrens, 12 2-year-old Heifers & Oxen, 5 Fat Calves, & a 3-year-old Bull;

9 WAGGON HORSES & COLTS, COB, HALF-BRED BROWN MARE,

5-year-old, (a good Huntress,) **11 PIGS,** and the Modern

AGRICULTURAL IMPLEMENTS,

Which will include Waggons and Carts, Light Cart, Barley Roll, Wheat and Bean Drills, Ploughs, Harrows, Drags, Scuffles, Winnowing Machines, CHAMBER DAY'S Weighing Machine, GARDNER'S Turnip Cutters, Cake Breaker, Gearing, Rick Staddles, useful Gig, sets of Harness, Bridles and Saddles, and numerous other Farming Tools, also about

70 ACRES OF CAPITAL GRASS & SEED KEEPING

To be Grazed up to the 28th Day of September, 1870,

By order of the Executor of the late Mrs. MARY NIGHTINGALE, (Deceased,)

THE FARM BEING GIVEN UP.

Implements.

Lot
1 Waggon jack, grease pot and hammer
2 Ditto, dry tub and bench
3 Wheelbarrows and saddle horse
4 Two ditto
5 Iron furnace
6 Grindstone and bean mill
7 Seven wheels, two axle-trees, and 2 pair of shafts
8 Rick pegs
9 Three hen pens and coops
10 Pitch kettle and marks
11 Cross-cut saw
12 Farming tools, in lots
13 Two hay knives, lantern, scythe, and 7 cow ties
14 Two ditto and nine horse ties
15 Three ladders
16 Two iron pig troughs
17 Three stone troughs and three feeding ditto
18 Chaff box and knife
19 Ditto and three troughs
20 Eight sheep racks
21 Five sheep troughs
22 Six dozen wood hurdles, capped
23 Ten dozen ditto, and stakes
24 Set of long gears
25 Ditto
26 Ditto
27 Ditto
28 Ditto
29 Set of thiller's ditto
30 Ditto
31 Ditto
32 Miscellaneous harness
33 Five leather headstalls, 3 belly-bands and bend and traces
34 Two cow racks and calf ditto
35 Twenty sacks
36 Sack cart and large sheet
37 Bushel and strikeless
38 Two heel rakes and one cart rope
39 Ditto and two ditto
40 — flake hurdles
41 Long plough
42 Hutching's iron plough and traces
43 Ditto
44 Iron double plough
45 Ransome & Sims' ridging plough
46 Skim plough
47 Pair of seed harrows
48 Pair of two-horse ditto

49 Pair of two-horse harrows
50 Heavy drag
51 Bush harrow
52 Horse hoe
53 Iron skim and scuffle, combined
54 Scuffle, with shafts and wheels, complete
55 Barley roll
56 A 3-furrow wheat drill
57 Ditto
58 Bean drill
59 Two drills
60 Seed harrow
61 GARDNER'S turnip cutter
62 Ditto and box
63 Oil cake breaker
64 Ditto, by RANSOME & SIMS
65 CHAMBER DAY'S weighing machine and weights
66 Winnowing machine
67 Ditto
68 Five sieves
69 Two-knife chaff engine
70 Narrow-wheel cart with iron arms
71 Broad-wheel tip cart
72 Ditto
73 Ditto
74 Narrow-wheel waggon
75 Ditto
76 Ditto and slide
77 Ditto, with iron arms and slide
78 Dog cart, with lamps and cushions, complete
79 Set of gig harness
80 Saddle and bridle
81 Firewood
82 Hogshead cask
83 Ditto
84 Ditto
85 Ditto
86 Pipe
87 Ditto
88 Ditto
89 Ditto
90 Ditto
91 Ditto
92 Ditto
93 Ditto
94 Ditto

At the Hill Barn.

95 A six-stone staddle and timber
96 Ditto

At Lower Field Barn.

Lot
97 A six-stone staddle and timber
98 A nine-stone ditto
99 A seven-stone ditto
100 A nine-stone ditto
101 Ditto
102 Ditto
103 Staddle stones and caps

Flock of Cross-bred Sheep.

104 Five capital ewes and five lambs
105 Five ditto and five ditto
106 Five ditto and five ditto
107 Five ditto and five ditto
108 Five ditto and five ditto
109 Five ditto and five ditto
110 Five ditto and five ditto
111 Five ditto and ten ditto
112 Five ditto and ten ditto
113 Seven ditto and fourteen ditto
114 Five superior ewe tegs
115 Five ditto
116 Five ditto
117 Five ditto
118 Five ditto
119 Five ditto
120 Five ditto
121 Four ditto
122 Six strong wether tegs
123 Six ditto
124 Six ditto
125 Six ditto
126 Four ram tegs
127 A two-shear Shropshire ram

Dairy Stock.

128 A prime five-year-old cow
129 Her fat calf
130 A four-year-old cow
131 Her fat calf
132 A four-year-old cow, in or with calf
133 A choice three-year-old heifer
134 Her fat calf
135 A three-year-old heifer
136 Her fat calf
137 A three-year-old heifer
138 Her fat calf
139 A superior 3-year-old heifer, in or with calf

Lot
140 A superior 3-year-old heifer and calf
141 Ditto
142 Ditto 4-year-old ditto and calf
143 Very fresh barren cow
144 Ditto
145 Pair of two-year-old oxen
146 Ditto
147 Ditto
148 Pair of two-year-old heifers
149 Pair of yearling heifers
150 Ditto
151 A well-bred three-year-old short-horn bull

Horses.

152 Powerful black mare, *Poppet*
153 Ditto bay mare, *Diamond*
154 Ditto brown horse, 4-year-old, *Whitefoot*
155 Ditto roan mare, *Lively*, in foal to one of Mr. Wynn's horses
156 Powerful brown horse, *Tommy*
157 A promising 3-year-old brown cart colt, *Gilbert*
158 Ditto cart mare, *Smiler*
159 Ditto 3-year-old black cart filly
160 Yearling grey cart filly
161 Cream coloured pony, quiet to ride and drive
162 A half-bred brown mare, by "*Emperor*," 5-years-old, has been ridden and driven, and a capital huntress

Grass and Seed Keeping.

To be Grazed until the 28th day of September next.

		A.	R.	P.
163 Gibb's Meadow	- Grass	5	0	15
164 Ram Close	- "	2	2	14
165 Court Ground	- "	12	1	20
166 Lower Wood-Pile Ground	- "	12	0	0
167 Farmer's Ground	- "	4	0	0
168 Long Crofts	- "	4	0	0
169 Church Close	- "	9	1	35
170 The Conny Green	- "	3	0	0
171 Huntsill	- "	3	1	32
172 The Middle Three Ground, " Seeds	4	2	14
173 First Three Ground	- "	3	0	21
174 Dry Leys	- "	4	0	21

Parties are respectfully requested to view the above Keeping, also from Lot 95 to Lot 103, as the same will be sold at the Place of Sale.

Sale at 11 o'clock. Catalogues may be obtained at the Place of Sale, Inns in Broadway and Campden, and of the Auctioneer, Evesham.

H. A. Pearce, Printer, Bridge-street, Evesham.

WILFORD
Near NOTTINGHAM.

IMPORTANT SALE OF A VERY VALUABLE HERD OF
PURE-BRED
SHORT  HORNS

Horses, Sheep. Pigs, Greyhounds, Prize Geese, Poultry, Grass Keeping, &c.

WM. WRIGHT

Is favoured with instructions from JOHN BROWN, Esq., to SELL by AUCTION,

ON MONDAY, MARCH 6th, 1865,

The day preceding Nottingham MARCH FAIR, AT THE FARMSTEAD, WILFORD, his valuable

HERD OF 63
SHORT-HORNS

43 of which are pure-bred, comprising 32 COWS and HEIFERS, 12 BULLS and BULL CALVES, of various ages, descended from the celebrated Herds of Messrs. Towneley, Booth, Wilkinson, and others, and have the strongly-marked characteristics of their valuable breeds, without the extreme forcing so generally resorted to.

81   13
SHEEP  HORSES

60 Acres of GRASS KEEPING until April 6th, and also
18 GREYHOUNDS, of Mr. Brown's far-famed Breed.

REFRESHMENT BY TICKET.   SALE TO COMMENCE AT ELEVEN O'CLOCK.

The Place of Sale is within a short distance of the Great Northern and Midland Railway Stations, at Nottm.
Catalogues may be had at Place of Sale; "Guardian" Office, Nottingham; and of the Auctioneer, by post.
THRUMPTON, NEAR DERBY.

T. FORMAN, "GUARDIAN" OFFICE, NOTTINGHAM.

480

TO COVER THIS SEASON,

AT FURNESS ABBEY, 1804,

At one Guinea a Mare, and two Shillings and ſix Pence
the Groom;

YOUNG HEROD,

A full bred Horſe, fifteen Hands three Inches high,
and has proved himſelf a certain Foal-getter; he was
got by Norton Coniers, Norton Coniers was bred by the
late John Pratt, Eſq. of Aſkrigg, in Yorkſhire, Coniers'
Dam by Matcham, ſhe was the Dam alſo of Rockingham,
which was ſold by his Royal Highneſs the Prince of
Wales to Mr. Bulland for 2000 Guineas; the Sire of
young Herod was allowed to be as well bred a Horſe as
any in England.

Young Herod is a beautiful bright Bay, the Property
of Mr. Thomas Atkinson, of Furneſs Abbey, ſuppoſed
by Judges to be as good a Colt as any in the North of
England, and as full of Action,

Young Herod's Dam was a famous bred Mare, and
and was the Property of the late Mr. Batty Hodgson,
of Kendal, and an excellent Hunter, able to carry ſixteen
Stone either on the Road or Field.

YOUNG HEROD will be at Kendal, every Saturday.

Good Graſs for Mares, upon reaſonable Terms.

G. Ashburner, Printer, Ulverstone.

481

ASCHAM,

WILL COVER THIS SEASON,

At Twenty-five Shillings

A MARE.

Ascham is a beautiful Bay, with four black Legs, rising
five Years old, upwards of fifteen Hands high, strong made,
remarkable for Bone and Action, a swift Trotter, and has
proved himself a capital getter for the last three years.

He was got by Lord Lowther's Brown Ascham, Dam (a
well-bred Mare of Mr. Jefferson's, of Bulman Hill, by Royal
Prince, a Son of Grey Beard, out of Riot, Dam of Hercules,
by Match'em); Grandam, Old Ascham, (Sire of Bonny Brown,
&c.) by Regulus, out of Lord Lowther's Black Mare, by Mr.
Panton's Old Crab.----Brown Ascham's Dam was got by the
Gower Stallion, a Son of the Godolphin Arabian, (Sire of Cade,
Regulus, Blank, Babram, Bagazet, and Old England), and out
of Old Jason's Dam, by the Duke of Beauford's White Arabian.

ASCHAM WILL ATTEND AT

Ulverston, Cartmel, Dalton, Broughton, Bootle and Ravenglass,
during the Season;—and in the mean time may be seen,
at his own Stable in *Ulverston,* by applying to
Robert Crowdson, the Groom.

☞ The Money to be paid at Midsummer.

Ulverston:—*March,* 1809.

*Ulverston—*JOHN SOULBY, printer.

ZS V.22

482

SEASON 1918.

THE SHIRE STALLION
Leighton Conqueror II.
Brown (34103). Foaled 1915.
BRED BY THE EARL OF POWIS,
THE PROPERTY OF
Messrs. Cater Bros.,
Stonyhyll Farm, Great Warley,
BRENTWOOD, ESSEX.
This is a short-legged massive Horse of the waggon horse
stamp with grand feet and of the choicest breeding, as his
pedigree shows.
Holds Board of Agriculture Certificate 1918.

Sires.	PEDIGREE.	Dams
Sire—Guer Conqueror 25210, twice Champion London Shire Show. His dam 40998 Blaisden Jewel by Blaisden Conqueror 19989. His sire Hitchin Conqueror, also a London Champion.		Dam—57526 Leighton Primrose by Lord Wantage's Lockinge Albert 18695. His dam by the famous Royal Albert 1885. His sire Prince William 3956 twice London Champion.
G. Sire—Montford Jupitor 18940—let to the Crewe Society for 2 years, he was sire of Blaisden Jupiter 27051 (Lord Rothschild's) also London Champion.		G. Dam—42498 Leighton Beauty by Moore's Commander 18720 by Moore Zealot 15731. His dam by Harold 3703. also a London Champion.
G.G. Sire—Carbon 3523 (bred by Lord Ellesmere) a winner of many first and champion prizes. His dam by Matchless 1531.		G.G. Dam—42500 Leighton Beauty by Baron Chief 17141. His sire by Harold 3703, the London Champion.
☞ All the above sires referred to have been let from £500 to £1000 for the season.		

FEES.
Ten Guineas, and Five Guineas Tenant Farmers.
Grooms Fee, 5s.

J. JOBSON, *Groom.*

SEASON 1918.

THE SHIRE STALLION
Cockerton Kingmaker
Brown (33120). Foaled 1913.
(Has Board of Agriculture Certificate for 1918)
THE PROPERTY OF
Messrs. Cater Bros.
Here we have a short-legged well-proportioned Horse with
plenty of flat bone, good feet, and made as a cart horse
should be fore and aft. He is of the choicest breeding and
of the blood so much sought after to-day. His sire was let
for three years for 1000 guineas each season, his fillies at
Peterborough sale, March 1918, made from 200 to 525 gus.

Sires.	PEDIGREE.	Dams.
Sire—King of Tandridge 24351, sold for 1600 gus. A London and Royal winner. His dam by Vulcan, a London Champion.		Dam—50710 Cockerton Polly by Kedlinch Victor Chief 19056 by Bury Victor Chief 2105, a London Champion. His dam by Regent II. 6316. Here we have A 1 and Harold blood.
G. Sire—Lockinge Forest King 18867, the greatest sire of his day; his dam Lord Wantage's London winner 4470 The Forest Queen, by Royal Albert 1885, the sire of his day.		G. Dam—31417 Cockerton Smiler by Pearmone 4394 by Royal Albert 1885. G.G. Dam by Sir Garnet 4037
G.G. Sire—Lockinge Manners 16780 by Prince Harold 14228, a London Champion. His dam by Lord Arthur 9834. Here we have the Premier and What's Wanted (2332) blood.		G.G.G. Dam by Le Bon 1305 by Wosenam's Wonder 2357. the great foundation sire of all the best shires of to-day.
G.G.G. Sire—Harold 3703 Champion at London and many other shows.		☞ It will be seen that both Leighton Conqueror and Cockerton Kingmaker are of the choicest shire blood and those who wish to breed horses to pay cannot do better than patronise them.

FEES.
Three Guineas.

Groom's Fee 5/-

W. PAWLEY, *Groom.*

483

---

480 Auction bill for sale at Wilford, 1865. Letterpress, printed
by T. Forman, 'Guardian' Office, Nottingham. 760 × 504 mm.
Museum of English Rural Life, Reading University.

481 Stud bill, 1804. Letterpress, printed by G. Ashburner,
Ulverston. 251 × 187 mm. *Barrow Public Library.*

482 Stud bill, 1809. Letterpress, printed by John Soulby (senior),
Ulverston. 317 × 195 mm. *Barrow Public Library.*

483 Stud brochure, 1918. Letterpress, printed by W & W Ltd,
Romford. Page size 165 × 99 mm. *Museum of English Rural
Life, Reading University.*

484 Stud bill, 1835. Letterpress, printed by Bray, Stratton.
367 × 254 mm. *Andrew Jewell Esq.*

1835.

TO COVER THIS SEASON,

AT THE STABLE OF
Mr. CHARLES KINGDON, Solicitor, Bodmin Street,
Holsworthy, Devon,

At two SOVEREIGNS each MARE, and five
Shillings the Groom,

The GROOM'S Fee to be paid in hand, and the residue on or before the 9th. day of July next,

YOUNG
Luzborough,

(Out of a very fine Mare, more than half bred, by Bodkin,)
Got by Old Luzborough, which was got by Williamson's Ditto, his Dam by
Dick Andrews, out of Eleanor by Whiskey, (own sister to the Dams of Phantom
and Priam,) her dam Young Giantess, (the dam of Sorcerer,) by Diomed, out of
Giantess, by Matchem, &c.
**Luzborough's superior Blood, is a direct Cross
for most MARES.**
Williamson's ditto, was own brother to Walton, by Sir Peter, he won the
Derby so far that he absolutely trotted in. He also beat the speediest horses of his
time. Dick Andrews was an extraordinary four mile Horse, and Eleanor the
only Mare that ever won both Derby and Oaks. Lord Exeter's speedy Stallion
Sultan (Sire of Green Mantle, Varna, Augustus, Circassian &c. and now or
lately covering at **forty Sovereigns a Mare,**) is out of Williamson's
ditto Mare.

Old Luzborough was a beautiful brown bay, with black Legs, and
no white, about fifteen Hands and a half high, was an excellent runner, and
perhaps the gamest Horse in the Kingdom. He won twenty four times, beating
the famous Longwaist (who was afterwards sold for **3000 Guineas,**) Euphra-
tes, and many other celebrated runners. His extraordinary muscular power,
great bone, short legs, rare feet, fine temper, and excellent constitution, are
recommendations seldom to be met with. One thousand Guineas were refused
for him, for the sole purpose of a Stallion. He is of a large and well shaped
family, and his stock is very highly approved. Young Luzborough, resembles
him very much in beauty, size, colour, height &c.

Old Luzborough's Performances,
In 1824, then 4 Years old, he won a plate of £50 at Stockbridge, the
Hampshire Stakes at Winchester, the Gold Cup at Salisbury, the Southampton
stakes and £70 at Southampton, the Wellington Stakes at Basingstoke, the Gold
Cup and £50 Plate at Blandford. At 5 Years old he won the Gold Cup, the
Wellington Stakes and Handicap Stakes at Basingstoke. At 6 Years old he
won the great Somersetshire Stakes at Bath, the Gold Cup at Salisbury, the
Hampshire Stakes and Gold Cup at Winchester, the Oxfordshire Stakes at
Oxford, and the Gold Cup at Burcrop. At 7 Years old, he won the Gold Cup
again at Burderop, the King's Plate, at Weymouth, the Silver Tureen of 100
Sovereigns value, and the £100 Plate at Exeter. At 8 Years old, he won the
Gold Cup at Cheltenham, the Handicap stakes at Wells, the Gold Cup at Salis-
bury, and finished his racing career perfectly sound, and without blemish.

DATED, April, 6th 1835.

BRAY, Printer, & Bookbinder, STRATTON.

484

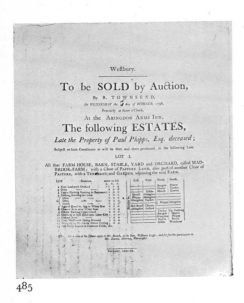

485

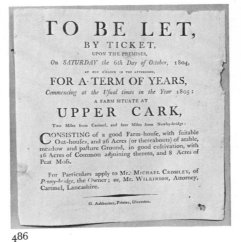

486

487

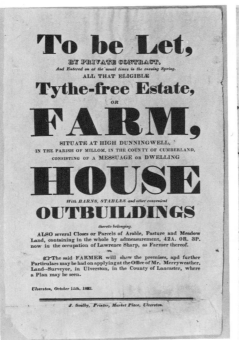

488

485 Auction bill, 1798. Letterpress, printed by Yockney. 412 × 336 mm. *Wiltshire County Record Office.*

486 Notice of farm to be let by ticket, 1804. Letterpress, printed by G. Ashburner, Ulverston. 195 × 178 mm. *Barrow Public Library.*

487 Notice of farms and grist mill to be let, 1824. Letterpress, printed by Baily, Calne. 334 × 215 mm. *Wiltshire County Record Office.*

488 Notice of farm to be let, 1822. Letterpress, printed by John Soulby (junior), Ulverston. 333 × 210 mm. *Museum of English Rural Life, Reading University.*

489 Auction bill, 1882. Letterpress, printed by R. & W. Wright, Stafford. 506 × 380 mm. *Museum of English Rural Life, Reading University.*

489

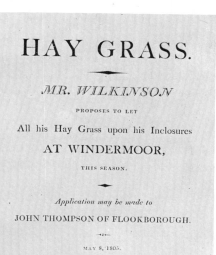

490

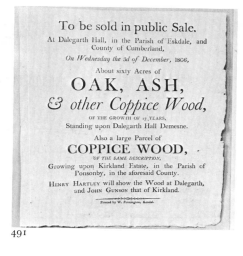

491

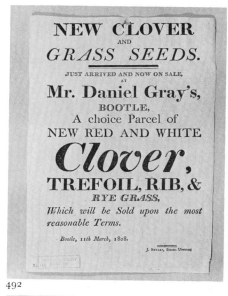

492

493

494

495

496

497

498

490 Notice of letting of hay grass near Ulverston, 1805. Letterpress, anon. 210 × 164 mm. *Barrow Public Library.*

491 Auction bill, 1806. Letterpress, printed by W. Pennington, Kendal. 212 × 186 mm. *Barrow Public Library.*

492 Notice of sale of clover, Bootle, 1808. Letterpress, printed by John Soulby (senior), Ulverston. 250 × 175 mm. *Barrow Public Library.*

493 Notice of letting of grass parks, 1801. Letterpress, printed by Lochhead & Gracie, Berwick. 145 × 192 mm. *Museum of English Rural Life, Reading University.*

494 Auction bill, 1824. Letterpress, printed by John Soulby (junior), Ulverston. 185 × 225 mm. *Museum of English Rural Life, Reading University.*

495 Auction bill, 1824. Letterpress, printed by John Soulby (junior), Ulverston. 187 × 222 mm. *Museum of English Rural Life, Reading University.*

496 Notice of grassings to be let, 1824. Letterpress, printed by John Soulby (junior), Ulverston. 235 × 235 mm. *Museum of English Rural Life, Reading University.*

497 Notice of sale of turnip seeds, 1827. Letterpress, printed by Soulby & Thornley, Ulverston. 236 × 268 mm. *Museum of English Rural Life, Reading University.*

498 Auction bill, 1826. Letterpress, printed by John Soulby (junior), Ulverston. 160 × 210 mm. *Museum of English Rural Life, Reading University.*

N

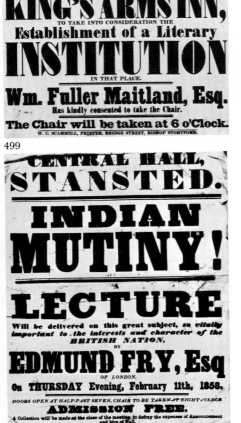

499 Notice of a meeting in Stansted to consider the establishment of a Literary Institution, 1849. Letterpress, printed by W. C. Scammell, Bishop's Stortford. 430 × 344 mm. *Essex County Record Office*.

500 Stansted Literary Institution, notice of a soirée, 1850. Letterpress, printed by W. C. Scammell, Bishop's Stortford. 428 × 342 mm. *Essex County Record Office*.

501 Stansted Literary Institution, notice of a lecture, 1852. Letterpress, printed by Mullinger, Bishop's Stortford. 319 × 252 mm. *Essex County Record Office*.

502 Notice of a lecture at Stansted Central Hall, 1858. Letterpress, printed by T. B. May, Bishop's Stortford. 430 × 340 mm. *Essex County Record Office*.

503 Stansted Literary Institution, notice of penny readings, 1862. Letterpress, anon. 573 × 450 mm. *Essex County Record Office*.

504 Stansted Literary Institution, notice of a musical entertainment, 1870. Letterpress, printed in black on orange paper by A. Boardman, Bishop's Stortford. 380 × 508 mm. *Essex County Record Office*.

505 Notice of a meeting in Stansted for the purpose of forming a society for the erection of an assembly room, 1854. Letterpress, printed by Mullinger, Bishop's Stortford. 430 × 342 mm. *Essex County Record Office*.

506 Notice concerning the opening of Stansted Central Hall, *c.* 1854. Letterpress, anon. 340 × 430 mm. *Essex County Record Office*.

Transport

Railway guides
Openings of railways
Railway timetables
Railway novelties
Coaching
Roads
Canals
Steam-boat notices
Disasters at sea
Steam-boat excursion guides
Tickets
Motor buses
The petrol engine
London's transport
Motor licences and certificates
The *Highway code*
Automobile Association
Imperial Airways

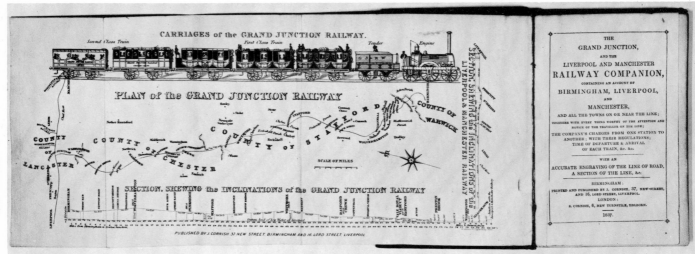

507

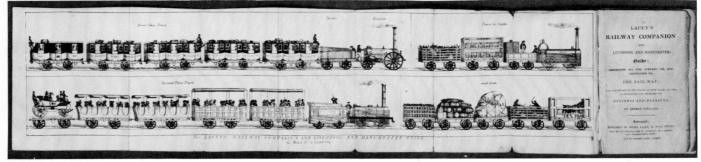

508

509

507 *The Grand Junction, and the Liverpool and Manchester Railway companion*, Birmingham and London, 1837. Letterpress, with engraved plate, printed and published by J. Cornish, the plate engraved by A. Johnson, Birmingham. Size of folding plate 142 × 315 mm. *John Johnson Collection.*

508 A. Freeling, *Lacey's railway companion and Liverpool and Manchester guide*, Liverpool, c. 1835. Letterpress, printed by Riddick & Kerr, Liverpool, with lithographed plate, anon. Size of folding plate 90 × 552 mm. *John Johnson Collection.*

509 Ticket for the opening of the London & Greenwich Railway, 1836. Steel-engraved by Rowe, Kentish & Co. 113 × 163 mm. *John Johnson Collection.*

510 Print commemorating the opening of the Shoreham branch of the London and Brighton Railway, 1840. Etching and aquatint, engraved by Charles Hunt, published by W. H. Mason, Brighton. 121 × 209 mm. *John Johnson Collection.*

510

511

512

513

514

511 Cover of *Railway Chronicle travelling charts: London Woking Guildford*, London, after 1845. Letterpress, with wood-engravings, printed on buff paper by James Holmes, London. 131 × 209 mm. *John Johnson Collection.*

512 Part of the folding chart from the item reproduced in Plate 511. Letterpress, with wood-engravings. Total size of folding chart 1130 × 209 mm.

513 Detail of Plate 512.

514 *The South Western, or London, Southampton, and Portsmouth Railway guide*, published by James Wyld, London, 1842. Letterpress, printed by William Clowes, London. Page size 143 × 88 mm. *John Johnson Collection.*

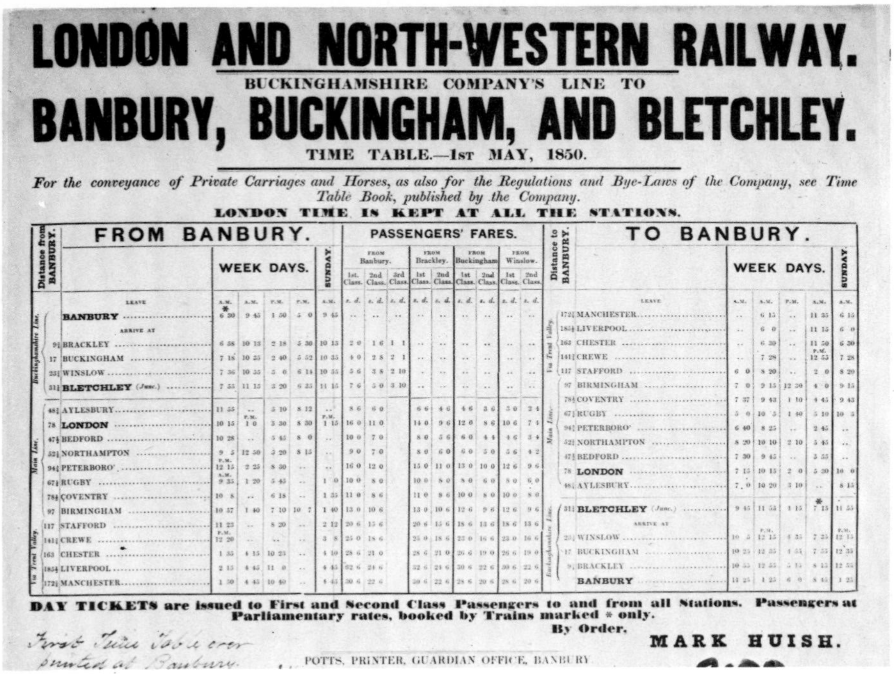

515

516

517

518

515 London and North-Western Railway timetable, 1850. Letterpress, printed by Potts, Banbury. 259 × 315 mm. *John Johnson Collection.*

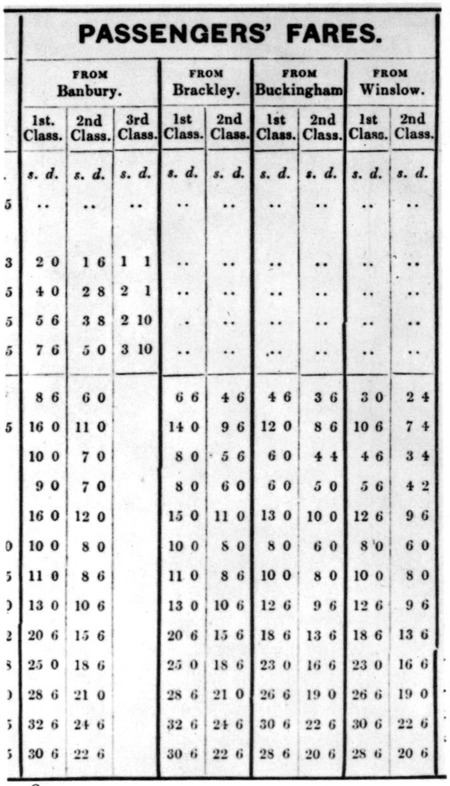

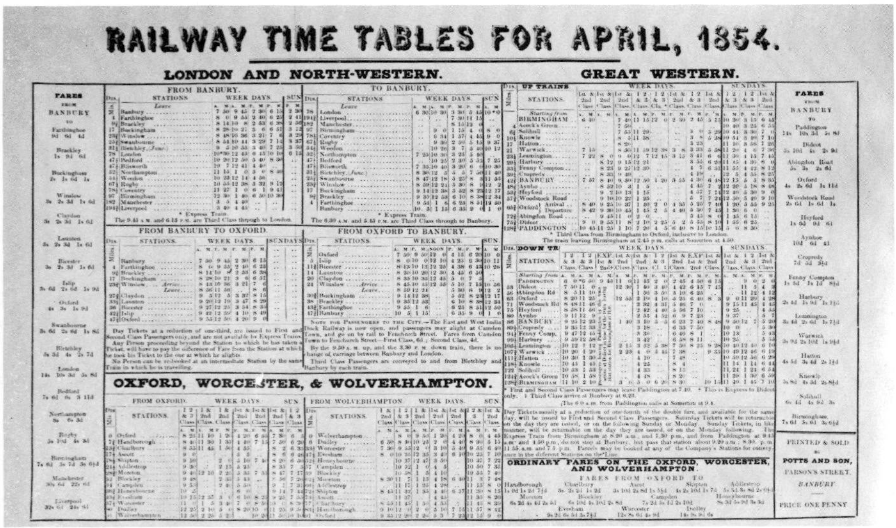

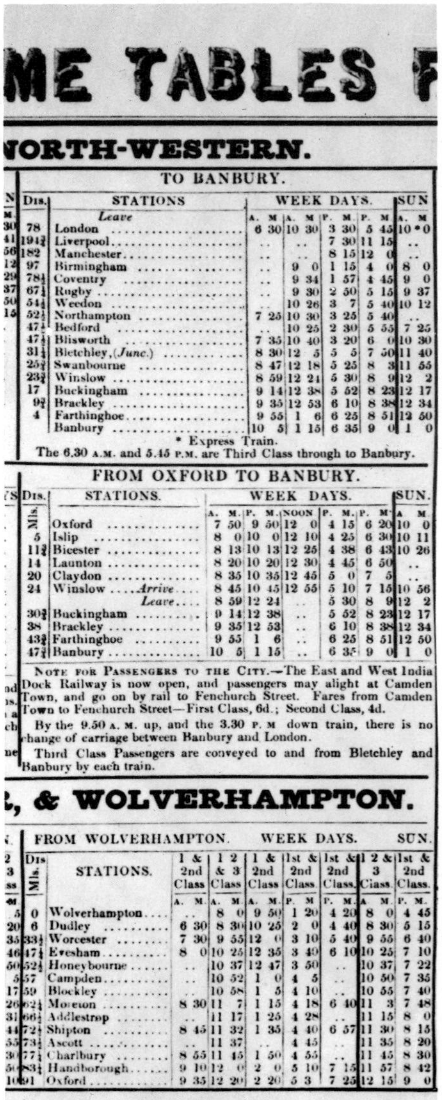

516 Detail of Plate 515.

517 Railway timetable relating to Banbury, 1854. Letterpress, printed and sold by Potts & Son, Banbury. 216 × 328 mm. *John Johnson Collection.*

518 Detail of Plate 517.

519

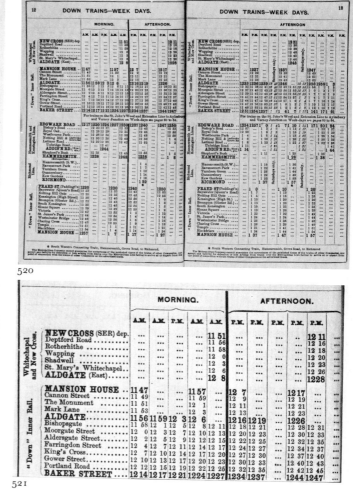

520

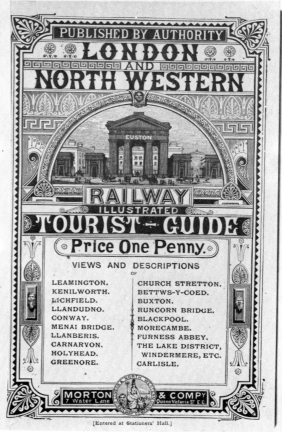

<table>
<thead>
<tr><th>12</th><th colspan="8">DOWN TRAINS—WEEK DAYS.</th></tr>
</thead>
</table>

521

522

523

524

519 Cover of Metropolitan Railway timetable, 1898. Letterpress, printed in green, blue, and black on cream paper by Waterlow & Sons Ltd, London. 220 × 139 mm. *John Johnson Collection.*

520 Facing pages from the item reproduced in Plate 519.

521 Detail of Plate 520.

522 Cover of *Great Eastern Railway illustrated tourist-guide*, 1879. Letterpress, printed in dark blue on yellow paper by the Camden Press, London. 243 × 150 mm. *John Johnson Collection.*

523 Cover of *Midland Railway illustrated tourist-guide*, 1882. Letterpress, printed in dark blue on buff paper. 235 × 150 mm. *John Johnson Collection.*

524 Cover of *London and North Western Railway illustrated tourist-guide*, 1882. Letterpress, printed in dark blue on pink paper. 235 × 150 mm. *John Johnson Collection.*

525

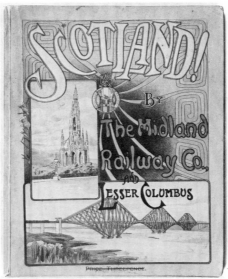

526

527

528

529

525 Cover of Great Northern Railway guide, *Tourist arrangements from London*, 1884. Letterpress, wood-engraved. 211 × 138 mm. *John Johnson Collection.*

526 Cover of Midland Railway Company and Lesser Columbus guide, *Scotland!*, 1898. Letterpress, printed in four colours. 245 × 185 mm. *John Johnson Collection.*

527 *To the English Lakes by LMS*, front of folded broadsheet. Gravure, printed in brown, green, and blue by Belcolor Ltd, Slough. 202 × 192 mm. *John Johnson Collection.*

528 Cover of LMS guide, *Cheap fares and other facilities*, 1938. Letterpress, printed in green and black by Bemrose & Sons Ltd, Derby and London. 176 × 120 mm. *John Johnson Collection.*

529 Cover of LMS guide, *Monthly return tickets*, 1935, designed by Ralph Mott. Gravure and lithography, printed in red and blue on primrose paper by McCorquodale & Co. Ltd, London. 242 × 150 mm. *John Johnson Collection.*

530 Cover of GWR guide, *Coronation tours from London*, 1937. Letterpress, printed in green and black by Joseph Wones Ltd, West Bromwich. 175 × 115 mm. *John Johnson Collection.*

531 Cover of booklet, *Facts about British Railways*, 1932, designed by Tom Purvis. Letterpress, printed in blue and black by Wellington Printers (1931) Ltd, London. 210 × 140 mm. *John Johnson Collection.*

530

531

532

533

532 A selection of mid-nineteenth century railway guides. *John Johnson Collection.*

533 Three of Wyld's railway guides: *The Great Western Railway guide, 1839; The South Western, London, and Southampton Railway guide, 1842; The London and Birmingham Railroad guide, 1838.* All in cloth-covered cases, gold-blocked. Size of each approximately 149 × 93 mm. *John Johnson Collection.*

534 Music cover. Lithographed in five colours by Concanen & Siebe, printed by Griffiths. 345 × 248 mm. *John Johnson Collection.*

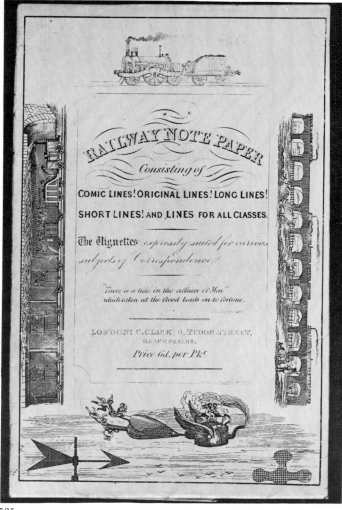

535

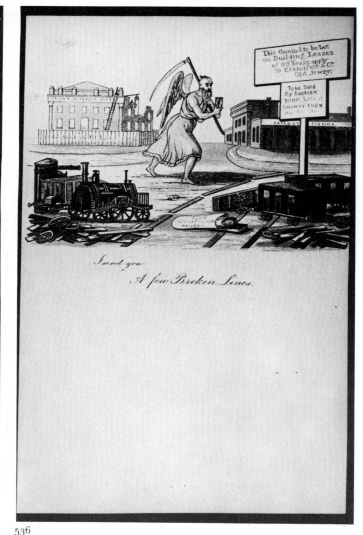

536

537

538

535 Packet for railway note-paper. Engraved. 190 × 120 mm. *John Johnson Collection.*

536 Sheet of railway note-paper. Aquatint. 180 × 111 mm. *John Johnson Collection.*

537 *Railway Times*, vol. 1, 1838. Letterpress, with wood-engraved heading, printed by J. T. Norris, London. Page size 273 × 206 mm. *Reading University Library.*

538 *Railway Magazine*, vol. 1, no. 1, July 1897. Letterpress cover, mostly wood-engraved, printed in turquoise on buff card by the Economic Printing and Publishing Co. Ltd, London. 245 × 172 mm. *John Johnson Collection.*

539 Railway novelty. Letterpress, with woodcut images, printed and published by M. Elliot, London. 335 × 218 mm. *John Johnson Collection.*

539

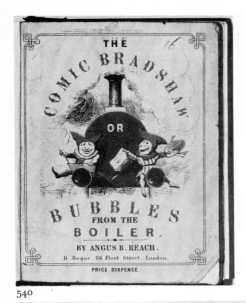

540

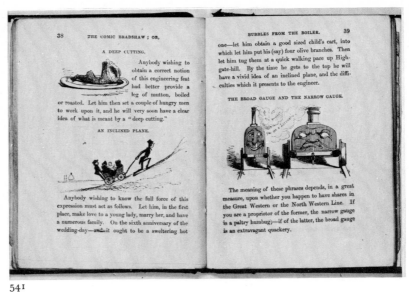

541

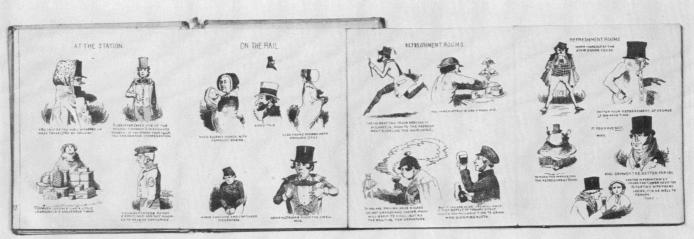

542

540 *The comic Bradshaw; or, bubbles from the boiler, by Angus B. Reach*, London, 1848, illustrated by H. G. Hine. Lithographed cover, printed in three colours. 139 × 105 mm. *John Johnson Collection.*

541 *The comic Bradshaw; or, bubbles from the boiler*, London, 1848. Letterpress, with wood-engravings, printed by T. C. Savill, London. Page size 139 × 105 mm.

542 George Sala, *Practical exposition of Mr J. M. W. Turner's picture 'Rain hail steam & speed': trifles for travellers*, London, n.d. Lithographed, folded in concertina. Size of each leaf 228 × 118 mm. *John Johnson Collection.*

543 Music cover, 'The express galop'. Lithograph, drawn by J. Brandard, printed in five colours by M. & N. Hanhart. 340 × 227 mm. *John Johnson Collection.*

544 Music cover, 'The locomotive galop'. Lithograph, drawn by T. Packer, printed in three workings, two of them in variegated colours, by Stannard & Dixon. 335 × 238 mm. *John Johnson Collection.*

543

544

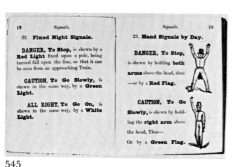

545

546

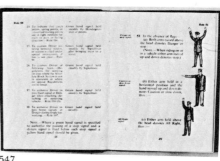

547

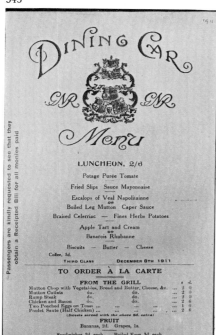

548

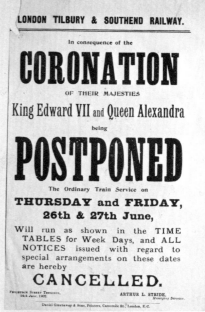

549

550

551

545, 546 Great Western Railway, *Code of signals and instructions*, 1852. Letterpress, with wood-engravings. Page size 130 × 100 mm. *John Johnson Collection.*

547 British Railways, *Rules for observance by employees*, 1950. Page size 139 × 107 mm.

548 Great Northern Railway luncheon menu, 1911. Letterpress, printed in red and black on green card, with gold die-stamping. 213 × 123 mm. *John Johnson Collection.*

549 Great Western Railway, excursion notice, 1860. Letterpress, printed by M'Corquodale & Co., London. 173 × 118 mm. *John Johnson Collection.*

550 London Tilbury & Southend Railway, notice of cancellation of arrangements in consequence of the postponement of the coronation of Edward VII, 24 June 1902. Letterpress, printed in red by Daniel Greenaway & Sons, London. 238 × 148 mm. *John Johnson Collection.*

551 Great Northern Railway, notice of football excursion, 1904. Printed by Waterlow & Sons Ltd, Dunstable and London, the text by letterpress in blue, the image of the football by lithography in brown. 235 × 235 mm. *John Johnson Collection.*

Three Cups Inn.
ALDERSGATE-STREET.

THE LEEDS
ROYAL UNION COACHES,
Every Morning at Seven, to

Welwyn	Buckden	Stamford	Retford
Baldock	Alconbury	Grantham	Bawtry
Biggleswade	Hill	Newark	Doncaster
Eaton	Stilton	Tuxford	Pontefract

And all Parts of the North, and arrive at the
WHITE HORSE INN, LEEDS,
Precisely at 8 o'Clock next Morning;
FROM WHENCE
The Huddersfield and Halifax Coaches set out at 10 o'Clock.

The Public are respectfully informed, that the Proprietors will endeavour to merit their Favours, by making this one of the most respectable Establishments in the Line.

552

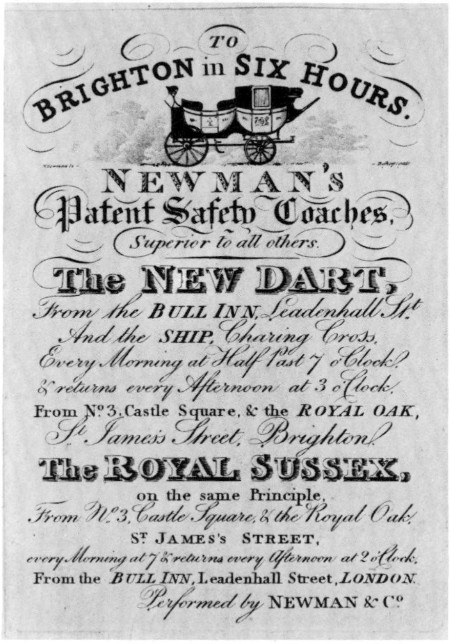

TO
BRIGHTON in SIX HOURS.

NEWMAN'S
Patent Safety Coaches,
Superior to all others.
The NEW DART,
From the BULL INN, *Leadenhall St.*
And the SHIP, *Charing Cross,*
Every Morning at Half past 7 o'Clock!
& returns every Afternoon at 3 o'Clock
From Nº 3, Castle Square, *& the* ROYAL OAK,
St. James's Street, Brighton,
The ROYAL SUSSEX,
on the same Principle,
From Nº 3, Castle Square, *& the Royal Oak,*
ST. JAMES'S STREET,
every Morning at 7 & returns every Afternoon at 2 o'Clock
From the BULL INN, *Leadenhall Street,* LONDON.
Performed by NEWMAN & Cº

553

CHEAP TRAVELLING. The Royal
Defiance Coach,
LEAVES THE KING AND QUEEN INN,
HIGHWORTH,
Every Monday, Wednesday, & Friday Morning, at 6 o'Clock;
The Bell Inn, Faringdon,
at a quarter before Seven;
ALFRED'S HEAD INN, WANTAGE,
a quarter before Nine;
through *Streatley,* at a quarter before Eleven; *Elephant and Castle Inn, Pangbourn,* at half-past Eleven; *White Hart Inn, Duke-street, Reading,* at a quarter past Twelve; and arrives at the GLOUCESTER COFFEE HOUSE, PICCADILLY, LONDON, at half-past Five.

Returns from the *Cross Keys, Wood-street, Cheapside, London,* every Tuesday, Thursday, and Saturday Morning, at a quarter before Seven; *Golden Cross,* at Seven; *Gloucester Coffee House,* a quarter past Seven.
Performed by Wm. Horne, J. Freeman & Co.
⁂ No Parcel above Five Pounds value accounted for if lost or damaged, unless entered and paid for accordingly.
N. B. No Breakfast on the Road.
[Cowslade & Co. Typ.

554

555

556

MATTHEWS'S
NEWLY INVENTED STAGE COACH,
which cannot be overturned, or broken down so as to hurt any one.

557

TO BE LETT,
By THOMAS LEWLING,
In Catherine Wheel-Yard, Great Windmill-Street,
the Top of the Hay-Market,
NEAT Four-wheel Post Chaises with good Horses and careful Drivers, at 9d a Mile, four Horses 15d to the George at Colnbrook, and from thence to Oxford, at the undermentioned Inns on the Road at 7d a Mile, four Horses 1s. short Journies at reasonable Rates, three People 9d a Mile,

From the George at Colnbrook,
To the Red Lyon at Maidenhead.
Bull and Heart, Nettlebed.
Dolphin, Oxford.
From thence to Enston, Chippingnorton on the Gloucester, Worcester and Birmingham Roads.
Cross Roads Nine Pence a Mile.
Please to enquire at the Bottom of Catherine Wheel Yard.

558

ISAAC SALTER,
At Mr. Jeffery's Flour Store, High Street, and near the Baths, George Street, Ryde,
LICENSED TO LET NEAT FOUR WHEEL CARS.

DAY JOURNEYS.	MILES.	THREE DAY'S TOUR.	MILES.	FOUR DAY'S TOUR.	MILES.
1		1		1	
Ryde to St. Helens	5	Ryde to Brading	4	Ryde to St. Helens	4
Brading	2	Sandown	2	Brading	2
Bembridge	3	Lake	1	Yaverland	1
Sandown	4	Shanklin	1½	Bembridge	3
Lake	1	Luccombe	2	Sandown	4
Shanklin	2	Bonchurch	1	Lake	1
Return to Brading	5	Ventnor	1	Shanklin	2
Ryde	4 27	St. Lawrence	1	Bonchurch	3
		Niton	3 18	Ventnor	1 21
Ryde to Ashey Down	4				
Newchurch	2	2		2	
Appuldurcombe	4	Niton to Chale	2¼	Ventnor to Steephill	1
Godshill	1	Kingston	2	St. Lawrence	1
Rookley	2	Shorwell	1½	Niton	3
Shide	3	Brixton	2	Chale	2¼
Newport	1	Mottistone	2	Kingston	2
Carisbrooke	1	Brooke	2	Shorwell	1½
Return to Newport	1	Freshwater Gate	4½	Brixton	2
Ryde	7 26	Alum Bay	2 18½	Mottistone	2
				Brooke	2
Ryde to Brading	4	3		Freshwater Gate	4½ 21½
Sandown	2	Alum Bay to Fresh-			
Lake	1	water	2	3	
Shanklin	1	Yarmouth	3	Freshwater Gate to	
Bonchurch	4	Shalfleet	4	Alum Bay	2
Ventnor	1	Newtown	1	Freshwater	2
Wroxall	2	Carisbrooke	5	Yarmouth	3
Appuldurcombe	1	Newport	1½	Shalfleet	4
Newchurch	2	Wootton Common	2½	Newtown	1
Ashey Down	2	Wootton Bridge	1½	Carisbrooke	5
Ryde	4 26	Ryde	4 23	Newport	5
				Ashey Down	2
Ryde to Wootton Br.	3			Ryde	4 23
Sandown	2				
Carisbrooke	1	**Common Carrier**		**4**	
Newport	1	**to Newport and**		Ferry to East Cowes	
West Cowes	5	**Cowes, daily.**		Whippingham	2½
Return through				Newport	2½
Newport to Ryde	12	**LUGGAGE con-**		Shide	3
Or Ferry to East Cowes.		**veyed to any part**		Arreton	2
Whippingham	2½	**of the Island.**		Godshill	4
Wootton Bridge	2½			Appuldurcombe	4
Ryde	3 23			Newchurch	2
				Ashey Down	2
				Ryde	4 23

Residence, High Street, near the Swan Inn.

559

552 Coach notice. Letterpress, with wood-engraving. 90 × 61 mm. *John Johnson Collection.*

553 Coach notice. Copper-engraved by W. Newman, London. 111 × 78 mm. *John Johnson Collection.*

554 Coach notice. Letterpress, with wood-engraving, printed by Cowslade & Co., Reading. 112 × 75 mm. *John Johnson Collection.*

555 'Posting in Scotland', 1805. Hand-coloured etching by C. Loraine Smith, published by H. Humphrey, London. 310 × 387 mm. *John Johnson Collection.*

556 'Travelling in England', 1819. Etching by George Cruikshank, published by G. Humphrey, London. 126 × 167 mm. *John Johnson Collection.*

557 Advertisement for Matthews's newly invented stage coach. Letterpress, with wood-engraving by Byn. 124 × 191 mm. *John Johnson Collection.*

558 Coach notice. Letterpress. 82 × 116 mm. *John Johnson Collection.*

559 Coach notice, *c.* 1835. Letterpress, with copper-engraved map on the reverse. 126 × 90 mm. *John Johnson Collection.*

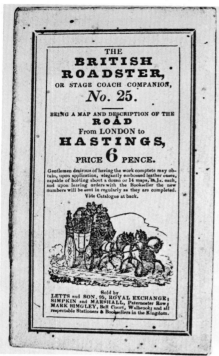

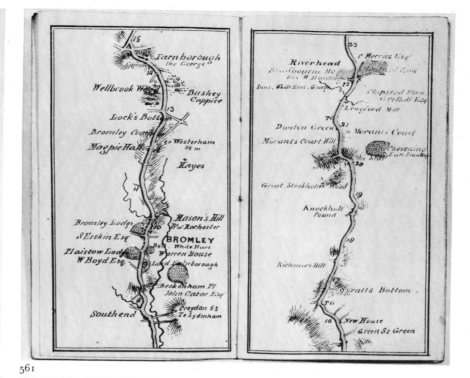

560 Cover of the *British Roadster*, no. 25, 1839. Letterpress, with wood-engraving, printed on buff paper. 104 × 60 mm. *John Johnson Collection.*

561 Route maps from the *British Roadster*, no. 25, 1839. Lithographed and coloured by hand. Page size 104 × 60 mm.

562 Notice of cab fares, Penzance, 1859. Letterpress, printed by Rowe, Penzance. 413 × 324 mm. *John Johnson Collection.*

563 Notice of Shillibeer's omnibus, 1829. Letterpress, printed by Howlett & Brimmer, London. 148 × 215 mm. *John Johnson Collection.*

564 Coach notice, 1822. Letterpress, printed in blue by Terry, London. 187 × 222 mm. *John Johnson Collection.*

565

TO

Surveyors

OF

ROADS.

THE

SITUATION OF SURVEYOR

OF THE

Crewkerne

TURNPIKE ROADS,

Will become vacant on the First of MAY next.

Persons wishing to fill the Office, may present Testimonials of
Character and Qualification to the TRUSTEES, at their next
MEETING, to be held at the GEORGE INN, CREWKERNE, on
SATURDAY the 28th. of APRIL, at Twelve o'Clock.

SALARY, £60 a Year.

The Person appointed will be expected to keep Accounts, and
to devote the Whole of his Time to the Duties of his Situation.

DATED 22nd. March, 1838.

JOLLIFFE, PRINTER, CREWKERNE.

566

CREWKERNE TURNPIKE.

To Road-Makers, Excavators,

AND

Earth-Removers.

Any Person or Persons willing to Contract with the TRUSTEES of

THE

CREWKERNE

TURNPIKE ROADS,

For widening, lowering, and improving the

ROAD,

LEADING FROM

Crewkerne to Clapton,

From a given Point near Maiden Beech Tree, to opposite the Lane
leading to Marsh Common, in Length about 440 Yards, and also from the
Hewish Toll Gate to the County Boundstone, near Clapton Bridge, in
Length about 1672 Yards, may deliver TENDERS in Writing, on or before
the 20th. Day of JANUARY next, to Mr. SPARKS and Mr. MURLY,
Crewkerne, Clerks to the said Trustees, with whom a Plan, Section, and
Specification of the intended Alterations and Improvements are left for Inspection, and who will direct the Surveyor of the Roads to point out the
several Works to the Persons applying.

As it is expected that the Work will be done in a complete and workmanlike Manner, within a given Period, none but Persons who can give
ample Security for the due Performance of the Contract will be treated with.

DATED 26th. January, 1836.

JOLLIFFE, Printer, Sheep-Market Street, CREWKERNE.

567

TO

Road-Makers,

Excavators,

AND

Earth-Removers.

ANY Person or Persons willing to contract with the
Trustees of the **CREWKERNE TURNPIKE ROADS,** for
forming, cutting, and making an entirely new Line of Road,
on the North Side of the present Turnpike Road, at the West
End of the Town of **CREWKERNE,** commencing at or near
a Stake Gate in **GOULD's ORCHARD,** and extending West-
ward through, and over, divers enclosed Lands, to, or near the
Gate of a Close at **HOAR STONE,** belonging to Mr. **PHELPS,**
where it is intended it shall unite with the old Road, may deliver Tenders in Writing, on or before the 7th of December next,
to **Mr. SPARKS,** or **Mr. MURLY, CREWKERNE,** Clerks
to the Trustees, with whom a Plan, Section, and Specification
of the intended new Road, are left for Inspection, and who will
direct the Surveyor of the Roads to point out the Line to the
Persons applying.

As it is expected that the Work will be done in a complete and workmanlike Manner, within a given Period, none
but Persons who can give ample Security for Performance of
the Contract, (the Form of which may be seen at the Offices
of Mr. SPARKS and Mr. MURLY,) will be treated with.

S. JOLLIFFE & SON, SHEEP-MARKET STREET, CREWKERNE.

568

Caution

TO

DRIVERS

OF

WAGGONS and CARTS.

NOTICE is hereby given, That the DRIVERS
of WAGGONS, or CARTS, of any Kind, who shall be
found riding upon any such Carriages in any TURNPIKE
ROAD, not having some other Person on Foot, or on
Horseback, to guide the same, (such light Carts as are usually driven with Reins, and are conducted by some Person
holding the Reins of the Horse, or Horses, not being more
than two, drawing the same, excepted,) or who shall be guilty of any of the Offences specified in the 132d. Section
of an Act passed in the Third Year of the Reign of His
late Majesty King GEORGE the Fourth, intituled " An Act to
" amend the general Laws now in being for regulating Turn-
" pike Roads, in that Part of Great Britain, called Eng-
" land," will be prosecuted as the Law in that behalf directs, and the Commissioners of the Crewkerne Turnpike
Roads have directed their Surveyor to inform against every
Person offending in the Premises.

Dated CREWKERNE, January 17, 1839.

JOLLIFFE, PRINTER, CREWKERNE.

---

565 Notice of vacancy for the office
of surveyor of roads, 1838. Letterpress,
printed by Jolliffe, Crewkerne. 282 ×
222 mm. *John Johnson Collection.*

566 Notice of letting of contract for road
work, 1836. Letterpress, printed by
Jolliffe, Crewkerne. 390 × 258 mm. *John
Johnson Collection.*

567 Notice of letting of contract for road
work. Letterpress, printed by S. Jolliffe
& Son, Crewkerne. 378 × 254 mm.
John Johnson Collection.

568 Turnpike road notice, 1839. Letterpress, printed by Jolliffe, Crewkerne.
259 × 194 mm. *John Johnson Collection.*

569 Notice of new road, 1791. Letterpress,
printed by Cruttwell. 545 × 450 mm.
Reading University.

569

THE ⬥ ROYAL

Foreſt Road,

To BATH, BRISTOL, &c.

Through Windſor.

To the *Nobility, Gentry,* and *Others,* travelling the
Great Weſtern Road to *Bath, Briſtol, &c.*

THE KING's moſt Excellent MAJESTY has
been graciouſly pleaſed to make a ROAD from WINDSOR, over
CRANBOURN-CHACE, thro' WINDSOR-FOREST, leading to the rural Villages of
WINKFIELD, WARFIELD, and BINFIELD, to READING; which is allowed to
be the moſt delightful Ride of any in this Kingdom, from the many Beautiful
and Pictureſque Views of Noblemen and Gentlemen's Seats, and Parks, the
whole Way.

The great Annoyance gen~rally complained of by Perſons Travelling the
other Road, on Account of the frequent Obſtructions from the paſſing of
large Droves of Oxen, Sheep, and other Cattle, Stage-Coaches, Road-Wag-
gons, and other Carriages, is ſuch, as to render it very diſagreeable, particularly at this Seaſon of the Year.

The ſaving of a *very heavy Turnpike,* and *Bridge Toll,* and the diſtance from
Hyde-Park Corner to *Reading* being equally the ſame, it is hoped, will recom-
mend to the Nobility, Gentry, and Others, a Preference to the ROAD
leading through WINDSOR.

New Road to READING *through* WINDSOR.

	Miles.
From HYDE-PARK CORNER to HOUNSLOW - - -	10
From HOUNSLOW to WINDSOR - - - - - -	12
From WINDSOR to READING - - - - - - -	18
MAY 1ſt, 1791.	40

N. B. *Beware of Miſinformation from intereſted Perſons.*

CRUTTWELL, PRINTER.

570

571

Pleasure

And PACKET BOATS are daily starting from BATH and BRADFORD, on the Kennet and Avon Canal, in which Parties may enjoy a most delightful Ride, and beautiful Picturesque Scenery,

Without

The Inconvenience of Horse Exercise or Walking.
No Expence has been spared to render them Commodious, and remove every Idea of

Fatigue.

Terms and Hours of Starting may be known at the Boat Office, N.E. Side of Sydney Garden, or of Mr. Andras, Milsom-St.
GYE, Printer, *MARKET-PLACE*, Bath.

572

The Regents Canal & Dock Company.

CAUTION.

The following offences are punishable under the Company's Acts of Parliament:—

TRESPASSING.
BATHING.
DAMAGING FENCES.
THROWING REFUSE,
LIVE OR DEAD
ANIMALS INTO
CANAL OR ON TO THE
COMPANY'S LAND.

Notice is Hereby Given that Action will be taken against Offenders.

E. CLARKSON, Secretary.

573

570 'The famous packet from Paddington to Uxbridge on the Grand Junction Canal', 1801. Hand-coloured etching, published by S. W. Fores, London. 229 × 387 mm. *John Johnson Collection*.

571 'A view from the left of the first bridge at Paddington with the company and barges', 1801. Etching and aquatint, drawn by H. Milbourne, engraved by J. Jeakes, published by G. Riebau, London. 276 × 340 mm. *John Johnson Collection*.

572 Packet-boat notice. Letterpress, printed by Gye, Bath. 450 × 640 mm. *John Johnson Collection*.

573 Canal notice. Letterpress, printed by Palmer, Sutton & Co., London. 641 × 508 mm. *British Waterways Museum*.

574 Canal notice, 1887. Letterpress, printed by Duncan Campbell & Son, Glasgow. 762 × 509 mm. *British Waterways Museum*.

CRINAN CANAL
NOTICE.

CHILDREN and Others are hereby Prohibited from Running along the Canal Banks after the Passenger Steamer; and Passengers are requested not to encourage them by throwing Money on to the bank.

Children are further warned not to throw Flowers into the Boat.

SALE OF MILK.

THE SALE OF MILK on the Property of the Canal Commissioners is only permitted on the understanding that no annoyance is caused to Passengers.

Any person who, by urging to purchase, or otherwise, inconveniences or annoys any Passenger will be prohibited from selling, and, if necessary, dealt with according to law.

Passengers are requested to report any such case to the Purser, and also to point out the delinquent to the nearest Lockkeeper or Canal Official.

Crinan Canal Office,
Ardrishaig. 30th June. 1887.

L. JOHN GROVES,
SUPERINTENDENT.

574

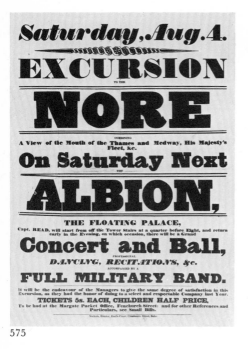

576

577

575

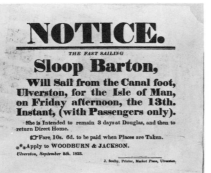

578

575 Packet-boat excursion notice, *c.* 1833.
Letterpress, printed in black on green
stained paper by Nichols, London.
793 × 535 mm. *St Bride Printing Library.*

576 Notice of sailing, 1826. Letterpress,
printed by Jackson, Lancaster. 208 ×
166 mm. *Museum of English Rural Life,
Reading University.*

577 Steamer excursion notice, Fleetwood,
1844. Letterpress, printed by W. T. Aston,
Fleetwood. 278 × 225 mm. *Museum of
English Rural Life, Reading University.*

578 Notice of sailing, Ulverston, 1823.
Letterpress, printed by John Soulby
(junior), Ulverston. 168 × 210 mm.
*Museum of English Rural Life, Reading
University.*

579 Packet-boat notice. Letterpress,
printed by Teape, London. 378 ×
254 mm. *John Johnson Collection.*

579

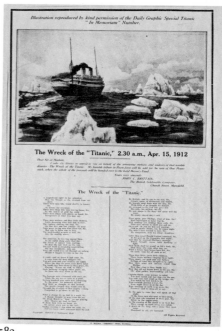

580

581

582

584

580 Account of the loss of the *Comet* steam-boat. Letterpress, with wood-engraving, printed by J. Catnach, London. 500 × 380 mm. *John Johnson Collection.*

581 Account of the wreck of the *Princess Alice*, 1878. Letterpress, with wood-engraving, anon. 508 × 365 mm. *John Johnson Collection.*

582 Appeal on behalf of the orphans and widows of the *Titanic*, 1912. Letterpress, with half-tone image, printed by F. Willman, 'Chronicle' Office, Mansfield. 438 × 273 mm. *John Johnson Collection.*

583 Steam-boat excursion guide, after 1843. Letterpress, with wood-engravings. 425 × 340 mm. *John Johnson Collection.*

584 Steam-boat excursion guide, 1841. Letterpress, with wood-engravings. 508 × 381 mm. *John Johnson Collection.*

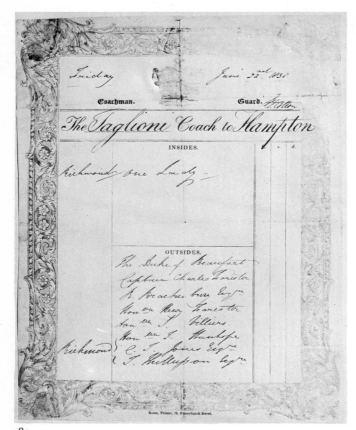

585

586

587

588

LYONSHALL GATE

Frees Hergest, Floodgates, Sunset, Headbrook, Kingswood, Moseley, Crossway, Eardisley, Titley, Avenue, Next-end, Noke, Milton, and Pembridge Gates & Bars.

Horse	-
Waggon	-
Cart	-
Gig	-
Chaise	-
Cattle	-
Pigs	-
Sheep	-
Asses	-

187

589

585 Coach passenger list, 1838. Letterpress, printed in blue and gold by Balne, London. 252 × 195 mm. *John Johnson Collection.*

586 Coach ticket, 1811. Etched and engraved on copper. 118 × 97 mm. *John Johnson Collection.*

587 Toll ticket. Letterpress. 40 × 48 mm. *John Johnson Collection.*

588 Toll ticket. Letterpress. 37 × 43 mm. *John Johnson Collection.*

589 Toll ticket, 1871. Letterpress. 73 × 49 mm. *John Johnson Collection.*

590 Passenger-boat ticket. Letterpress, printed on green card. 38 × 77 mm. *British Waterways Museum.*

Forth and Clyde Canal Swift Passenger Boats.
KIRKINTILLOCH TO SHIRVA AND TWECHAR.
STEERAGE.
No. 51 3d.
This Ticket to be kept clean, and delivered to the Master before leaving the Boat.

590

591

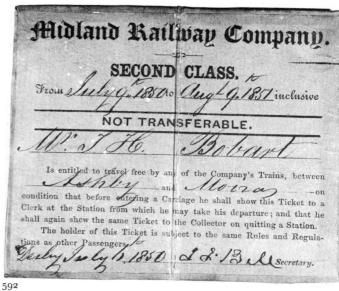

592

593

594

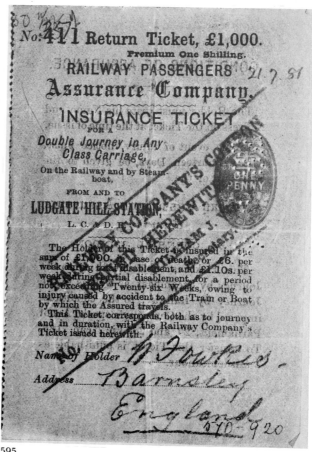

595

591 Railway season ticket, 1864. Intaglio, printed in green. 80 × 120 mm. *John Johnson Collection.*

592 Railway season ticket, 1850. Letterpress, printed in black on cerise paper and mounted in a folder. Size of folder 85 × 100 mm. *John Johnson Collection.*

593 Railway tickets, 1896-7. Letterpress, printed on buff card. Each ticket 30 × 57 mm. *John Johnson Collection.*

594 Railway excursion ticket, 1862. Letterpress, printed in black on blue paper. 60 × 91 mm. *John Johnson Collection.*

595 Railway passenger's insurance ticket, 1881. Letterpress, printed in black on grey paper, overprinted in brown. 115 × 77 mm. *John Johnson Collection.*

596

597

598

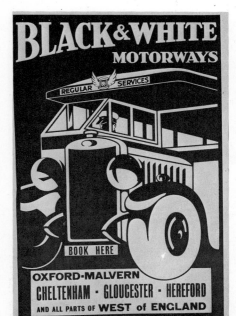

599

596 Cover of *Daves' guide to London's motor omnibus service*, 1906. Letterpress, printed in black on pink paper. 134 × 109 mm. *John Johnson Collection.*

597 Cover of London General Omnibus Company guide to coach tours. Letterpress, three-colour process, printed at the Baynard Press by Sanders Phillips & Co. Ltd, London. 165 × 107 mm. *John Johnson Collection.*

598 Cover of East Kent bus timetable, 1940. Letterpress, printed in red. 190 × 122 mm. *John Johnson Collection.*

599 Poster for Black & White Motorways. Lithographed. 733 × 508 mm. *John Johnson Collection.*

600 Poster for Percival's char-à-bancs. Hand-drawn lithography, printed in colours by Thurnams, Carlisle. 890 × 535 mm. *John Johnson Collection.*

600

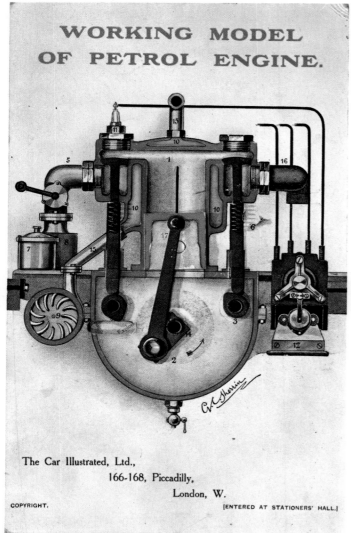

601

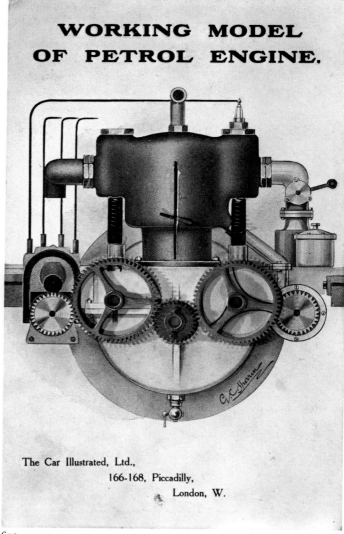

602

601 Working model of a petrol engine, signed G. C. Sherrin, published by The Car Illustrated Ltd. Letterpress, printed in four colours on card, the working parts made of metal. 215 × 133 mm. *John Johnson Collection.*

602 The reverse of the item reproduced in Plate 601. Letterpress, printed in two colours, the working parts made of metal.

603 A selection of London Transport folding maps, 1924-38. *John Johnson Collection.* The details given below refer to the covers and not to the actual maps.
Top row:
Map of the London general bus routes, no. 12, 1924; lithography, printed in two colours by Waterlow & Sons Ltd, 149 × 75 mm.
Map of the electric railways of London, 1928; lithography, printed in two colours by Waterlow & Sons Ltd, 150 × 74 mm.
Map of the general omnibus routes, no. 5, 1928; lithography, printed in two colours by Waterlow & Sons Ltd, 144 × 75 mm.
Map of routes, no. 1, 1930; lithography, printed in two colours by Waterlow & Sons Ltd, 144 × 74 mm.
Tram map, no. 1, 1935; lithography, printed in two colours by the Baynard Press, 151 × 76 mm.
continued on page 206

603

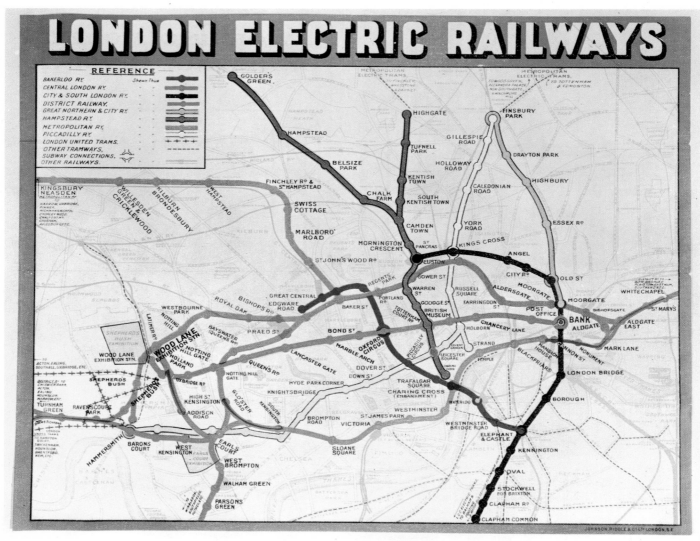

604

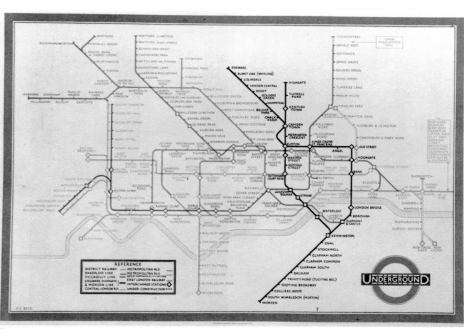

605

continued from page 205
Bottom row :
Green Line coach map, no. 1, 1936;
lithography, printed in two colours by the
Dangerfield Printing Co. Ltd, 142 ×
75 mm.
Railway map, no. 1, 1937; lithography,
printed in two colours by Johnson,
Riddle & Co. Ltd, 153 × 76 mm.
Bus map central area, no. 1, 1937;
lithography, printed in two colours by
Waterlow & Sons Ltd, 142 × 74 mm.
Underground Railway map, no. 1, 1937;
lithography, printed in four colours by
Geographia Ltd, 150 × 76 mm.
Trolleybus and tram map, no. 1, 1938;
lithography, printed in two colours by the
Baynard Press, 151 × 76 mm.

604 Map of London Electric Railways.
Lithography, printed in eight colours by
Johnson, Riddle & Co. Ltd. 285 ×
360 mm. *John Johnson Collection.*

605 London Underground map, 1933,
designed by H. C. Beck. Lithography,
printed in six colours by Waterlow &
Sons Ltd, London, Dunstable, and Watford.
157 × 226 mm. *John Johnson Collection.*

606

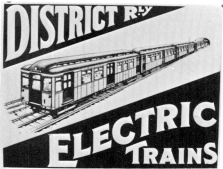

607

608

609

606 Great Northern, Piccadilly & Brompton Railway notice, 1906. Letterpress. Uncovered in a subway at King's Cross Station during renovations. Photograph. *London Transport Board.*

607 District Railway poster, 1908. 1016 × 1270 mm. *London Transport Board.*

608 Metropolitan Railway poster, 1886. Letterpress. 1016 × 1270 mm. *London Transport Board.*

609 Joseph Pennell, Charing Cross Underground Station, 1913. Lithograph, proof state of a poster, without letters. 780 × 525 mm. *Victoria & Albert Museum.*

610 London Underground poster, 1908. Lithograph, printed by Johnson, Riddle & Co. Ltd, London. 1016 × 635 mm. *London Transport Board.*

610

207

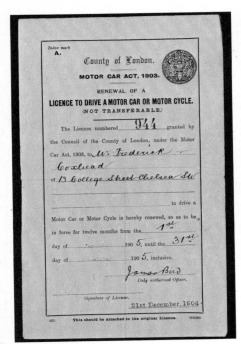

611

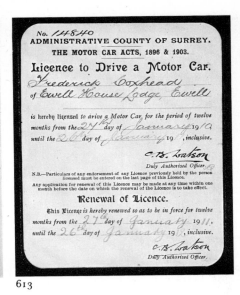

612

613

614

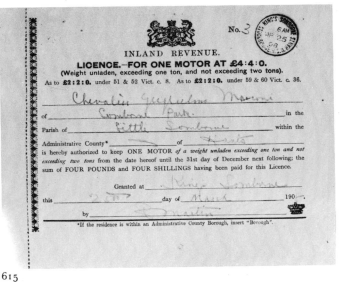

615

611 Licence to drive a motor car or motor cycle, 1904. Letterpress. 217 × 137 mm. *Automobile Association.*

612 Licence to drive a motor car or motor cycle, 1905. Letterpress, mounted in a folder. 171 × 133 mm. *John Johnson Collection.*

613 Licence to drive a motor car, 1910. Letterpress, mounted in a folder. 126 × 98 mm. *Automobile Association.*

614 Road fund licence, 1922. Probably letterpress. 75 × 75 mm. *John Johnson Collection.*

615 Road fund licence, 1908. Letterpress. 148 × 155 mm. *John Johnson Collection.*

616 Royal Automobile Club driving certificate, 1912. Letterpress, mounted in a folder. 98 × 124 mm. *Automobile Association.*

617 Ministry of Transport, diagram of distinguishing mark to be displayed on a motor vehicle whilst being driven by a person holding a provisional licence, 1935. Letterpress, printed in red. 284 × 221 mm. *John Johnson Collection.*

616

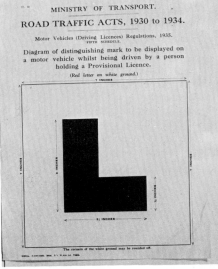

617

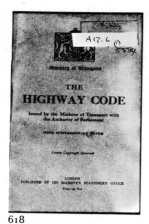

618

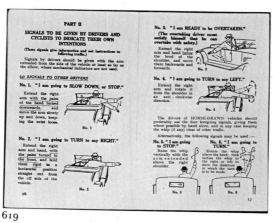

619

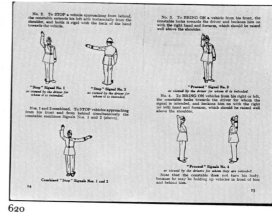

620

621

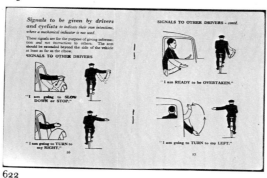

622

623

624

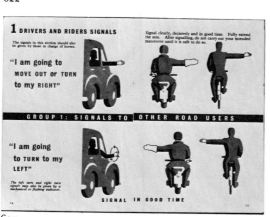

625

626

627

628

629

618-20 The *Highway code*, c. 1935 (24 pp). Letterpress, the cover printed black on blue paper, the text pages monochrome throughout. Page size 161 × 101 mm. *Road Research Laboratory*.

621-3 The *Highway code*, c. 1946 (32 pp). Lithographed cover, printed in black on brown paper; letterpress text, printed monochrome throughout. Page size 136 × 106 mm. *Road Research Laboratory*.

624-6 The *Highway code*, 1957 (32 pp). Lithographed cover in four colours, printed on yellow paper; the text pages lithographed in up to four colours. Printed by Sir Joseph Causton & Sons Ltd, Eastleigh. Page size 165 × 105 mm. *Road Research Laboratory*.

627-9 The *Highway code*, 1969 (52 pp). Lithographed cover, printed in two colours; the text pages lithographed in up to four colours. Printed by Sir Joseph Causton & Sons Ltd, Eastleigh. 184 × 115 mm.

630

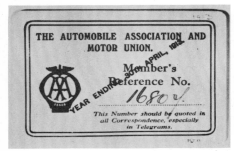

631

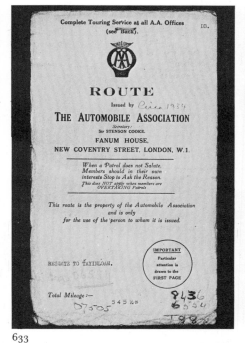

633

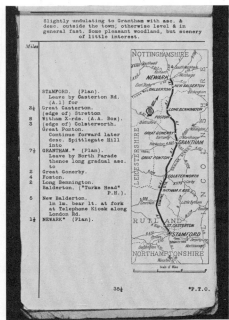

634

632

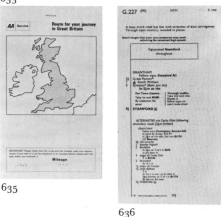

635

636

630 Automobile Association handbooks, 1908-68. *From left to right:* 1908, stone cloth-covered case, 140 × 85 mm.; 1920, grey paper-covered boards, 140 × 87 mm.; 1930, green cloth-covered case, 187 × 112 mm.; 1954, yellow paper-covered boards, 209 × 127 mm.; 1966/67, yellow Linson-covered boards, 216 × 134 mm.; 1968/69, Linson-covered boards, printed in colour, 210 × 128 mm. All from the *Automobile Association.*

631 Membership card of the Automobile Association and Motor Union, 1913. Letterpress, printed in red and green, overprinted in black. 54 × 80 mm. *John Johnson Collection.*

632 Membership certificate of the Automobile Association, 1969. Letterpress. 110 × 117 mm.

633 Cover of route issued by the Automobile Association, *c.* 1934. Letterpress, printed in black on buff. 220 × 128 mm. *Automobile Association.*

634 Sheet of route issued by the Automobile Association, *c.* 1934. Letterpress. 195 × 126 mm. *Automobile Association.*

635 Cover of route issued by the Automobile Association, 1969. Lithographed, black on yellow. 222 × 128 mm.

636 Sheet of route issued by the Automobile Association, 1969. Letterpress. 212 × 109 mm.

637, 638 *The Automobile Association and Motor Union handbook,* 1914. Letterpress, printed by Charles Knight. Facing pages and detail. Page size 135 × 81 mm. *Automobile Association.*

639, 640 *The Automobile Association handbook,* 1927. Letterpress, printed by Whitehead Morris Ltd, London. Facing pages and detail. Page size 181 × 103 mm. *Automobile Association.*

641, 642 *The Automobile Association handbook,* 1949. Letterpress, printed by Hazell, Watson & Viney and Sun Printers Ltd, Aylesbury and Watford. Facing pages and detail. Page size 210 × 122 mm. *Automobile Association.*

643, 644 *The Automobile Association members handbook,* 1961. Letterpress, printed by Hazell, Watson & Viney, Aylesbury and Slough. Facing pages and detail. Page size 210 × 125 mm. *Automobile Association.*

645, 646 *AA members handbook,* 1968. Lithography, printed in red and black by Petty & Sons Ltd, Leeds. Facing pages and detail. Page size 210 × 125 mm. *Automobile Association.*

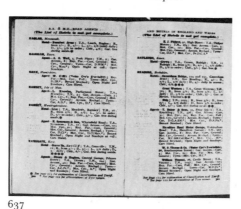

637

A.A. & M.U. ROAD AGENTS
AND HOTELS IN ENGLAND AND WALES

RAYLEIGH, Essex.
Hotel—Crown ; T.A., Crown, Raleigh ; T.N., 11
Raleigh ; R., from 3/6 ; B., 2/- ; L., 2/6 daily ;
D., 3/6 to order ; Chfr., 5/- ; Gar. free. ★

READING, Berkshire.
Hotel:—Caversham Bridge, 229 and 231, *Caversham
Road* ; T.N., 800 Reading ; R., 4/- ; B.,
2/6 ; L., 2/6 daily ; D., 4/- daily in season ;
Chfr., 6/6.★★★

Great Western ; T.A., Great Western ; T.N.,
785 ; R., from 3/6 ; B., from 1/6 ; L., 2/-
daily ; D., 3/6 to order ; Chfr., 5/- ; Gar. at
Messrs. Vincent's.★★

Ship ; T.N. 1029 ; R., from 3/6 ; B., from
2/- ; L., 2/6 daily ; D., from 3/6 to order ;
Chfr., 5/- ; Gar. free during meals. ★★

638

639

RAYLEIGH (3,125), Essex. [*Map* 7.C.5.] London 31½ miles.
E. Closing—Wed. Post—8.0 p.m.

GARAGE.
★ Colvin & Hinksman, Rayleigh Garage, High Street ; T.N., 33 ; G.A.—C. 30 ; M/C. 100 ; O.N. at call ; O.S.

READING (92,600), Berks. [*Map* 5.B.7.] London 39 miles.
L.H. 10-2, 6-10 w.d. ; 12-2, 7-10 S. M. Day—Sat. E. Closing—Wed. Post—7.15 p.m.
Parking Facilities available (except Sat.).

HOTELS.
★★★ Caversham Bridge, Caversham Road ; T.N., 800 ; 30 brms. ; S.R. 5/6 to 6/6 ; D.R. 10/- to 13/- ; B. 2/- to 3/6 ; L.c. 3/- to 3/6 ; L.h. 3/6 to 4/- ; T. 1/6 ; D. daily 5/6 ; Ch. 12/6 ; R.W.T. ; G.A.—C. 9, f.d.m. ; 1/- N. ; C.H.L.
★★★ Great Western ; T.N., 785 ; 25 brms. ; S.R. 6/6 to 8/6 ; D.R. 16/- to 25/- ; B. 3/6 ; L. 4/- ; T. 1/6 ; D. 5/6 ; Ch. 10/- ; Pub. G. adj.
★★★ Mansfield House (Unlic.), Kendrick Road ; T.A., Mansfield House ; T.N., 597 ; 30 brms. ; S.R. 5/6 ; D.R. 11/- ; B. 3/- ; L. daily 3/- ; T. 1/6 ; D. 4/- ; Ch. 10/6 ; Pub. G. 50 yards.
★★★ Ship, Duke Street ; T.N., 1029 ; 32 brms. ; S.R. 5/- to 7/- ; D.R. 10/- to 14/- ; B. 3/6 ; L.c. 3/- ; L.h. 3/6 ; T. 1/6 ; D. 5/- ; Ch. 8/6 ; G.A.—C. 14 f.d.m. ; 1/- to 1/6 N.

640

641

REA] A.A. HOTELS AND GARAGES, ENGLAND AND WALES **212**

READING—(continued)
★★★ George. T.N. 3445 : 40 Rms: H & C: N.P.: Ga-22: Lu-1: SAC. B & B 18/6: W.T. 7 Gns.
★★★ Great Western. T.N. 3255 : 41 Rms: H & C: N.P.
★★★ Ship. T.N. 302911: 43 Rms: H & C: N.P.: Ga-20: SAC. B & B 13/6: W.T. 7 Gns.
★★ Gate House, Bath Rd. (Cond.) T.N. 2019 : 12 Rms: H & C: Ga-4: Lu-4 B & B 15/-: W.T. 6 Gns.
★★ Upcross, Berkeley Ave. (Unlic.). T.N. 319211: 14 Rms: H & C: Ga-7: Lu-7. B & B 12/6 to 17/6: W.T. 4½ to 7 Gns.
Coley Avenue. (Cond.) T.N. 60039: 9 Rms: h & c: SAC. B & B 14/6: W.T. 5½ Gns.
Queens, Queens Rd. T.N. 219411: 12 Rms: H & C: Ga-12. B & B 13/6: W.T. 5 to 5½ Gns.
T. Baker & Sons, 35 Friar St. T.N.

REDDITCH (Worcs.). 27,300. MAP 14 42/0 6. E.C.Wed. M.D.Sat. LONDON 106, Birmingham 14, Bromsgrove 6, Evesham 16, Kidderminster 16, Stratford-on-Avon 16, Warwick 17, Wolverhampton 26.
Bordesley Garage, Birmingham Rd. T.N. 437: O.S.
Pitts (Redditch) Ltd., Motor House. T.N. 91: Ford: Lanchester: M.G.: Morris: Riley: Wolseley.
Wyatt's Garage, Rectory Rd. T.N. 229: O.S.

REDHILL (Notts.). map 21 43/5 4. LONDON 125, Nottingham 4.
Lea Pool Garage. T.N. Arnold, Nottingham 68112: O.S.

REDHILL (Surrey). 40,660 (with Reigate). MAP 8 51/2 5.

642

643

★Lion High St T 3175 6rm ch G CA Dgbc NCP BB 21/- L 5/6:7/6 & alc D 7/6:10/6 & alc (m#) WT 9r 9n
7pm Richardson's Bury Rd T 3145 M/c G Sc vts
6pm Sycamore's Whytefield Rd T 3237 G MG/Mor/Ril/Wol
RAMSEY IOM See Isle of Man
RAMSGATE Kent 36,100 MB Map 9D
LH 1030-230 6-1030 S 12-2 7-10 LP845 S530 Accom
Bur T Thanet 51096 EC Thu London 74 Canterbury 18 Dover 20 Herne Bay 15 Margate 5 Sandwich 8
★★Court Stairs Pegwell Rd (C) T Thanet 51850 12rm (A)6 dad CH G CA TV Dg bcd NCP BB 22/6: 35/- L fr 8/6 D fr 10/6 LM WT 12:17gn Se%, 10
★★Sanclu East Cliff Prom T Thanet 52345 60rm pb2 ch L NP G OnPl/- CA TV Dg b NCP BB 17/6:30/- L fr 8/- D fr 8/- WT 10½:14gn Se%, 10
★★Foy Boat Sion Hill T Thanet 52662 7rm CH TV Dg ad BB 18/6:21/6 L 5/6:8/6 & alc (m/6) D 8/6: 12/6 & alc (m8/6) (mt) LM WT 11:12gn Se%, 10 (on request)
Ap. Dawson's Chatham St (CI) T Thanet 51964 22rm G CA TV Dg d NCP closed Oct 1:Oct 16 BB fr 16/- L 3/6 & alc 4/6:6/6 LM WT 6:7gn
GH. Milton Mount 11 Nelson Cres (U) T Thanet 53717 11rm CA TV Dg d April:Sept30 BB 14/6
GH. Shoals 16 Carlton Ave (U) T Thanet 52084 6rm CH CA TV Dg bd BB 15/- WT 7gn
RC. L'Ambassadeur 3 Turner St T Thanet 52838 closed Sun Oct:Apr L 4/6:8/6 & alc (m5/6) D 6/6: 5/6 & alc (m3/6) D 8/6:12/6 & alc (m6/6) open weekdays Oct:Apr 9am:3pm Sat 9am:m/n
24hr A & B Garages Ltd Grange Rd T Thanet 51456 M/c G Sc Hil/Mor/Kov/Wol vts

RAYLEIGH Essex 17,700 UD Map 18F
EC Wed MD Wed London 34 Southend 7
7pm Hinksman's High St T 33 G Aus/Mor vts
7pm Rayleigh Garage Ltd High Rd T 270 NS Hil vts
READING Berks 118,200 CB Map 7B
Address
Fanum House 75 London Road
T 54481
24-hour emergency service:
Telephone Reading 54481 by day or night
LH 1030-230 6-10 S 12-2 7-10 LP615 S615 EC Wed MD Sat London 39 Aldershot 20 Alton 24 Andover 33 Aylesbury 32 Basingstoke 17 Cirencester 53 Guildford 28 Henley 8 Maidenhead 12 Marlborough 35 Marlow 14 Newbury 17 Oxford 27 Salisbury 50 Slough 18 Staines 23 Swindon 42 Wantage 25 Winchester 34 Windsor 18
★★★Caversham Bridge Caversham T 53793 30rm (A)13 ch G CA TV Dg d BB 25/-:27/6 L fr 7/6 & alc (m7/6) D fr 9/6 & alc (m9/6) WT fr 13gn
★★George King St T 53445 45rm pb1 CH NP G CA Dg d BB fr 25/- L fr 7/6 & alc (m7/6) D fr 9/6 & alc (m9/-) WT fr 14gn
★★Great Western Station Rd T 53255 45rm pb3 ch NP CA Dg d BB 27/6:37/6 L 9/- & alc D 10/- & alc Se% 10 (on request) WT
★★Ship Duke St T 302911 38rm CH NP G CA WT fr 13gn Se% 10
★★Upcross Berkeley Ave (C) T 50796 20rm ch Lu7 TV Dg cd BB 23/6:25/6 L 7/6:12/6 D 8/6:12/- WT 10½:12gn
Ap. Calcot Bath Rd Calcot (C) T 67346 11rm (A)4

644

645

Hawker's, Lea Pool Nottingham 268112 R9 G cdh
Willoughby's Nottingham 268111 N 263683 Sin G
Redhill 550 *Somerset* Map 7ST46
*London*125 Bristol 9
LH10-230 6-1030 12-2 7-1030 Lp430 2 EcSat MM Paradise Wrington 277 rm17 pb17 (A4 pb21) TV Btr37/6 M9/6:15/6 & alc Ld11 Robert's Wrington 272 RS8 Aus Ril G sdh
Redhill 20,238 *Surrey* Map12TQ25
*London*21 Brighton 33 Crawley 10 Croydon 11 East Grinstead 14 Guildford 20 Haywards Heath 18 Horsham 17 Kingston upon Thames 17 Maidstone 34 Reigate 2 Westerham 12 Lh 11-2 630-1030 12-2 630-1030 Lp11 8 EcWed MdSet
Lane's 41043 rm16 TV Btr42/6 M13/-:17/6 & alc Ld 1030
★ Mill House (2½m S A23) 63796 rm14 TV B37/6 M12/6:35/- & alc Ld10
Baker's, Redstone Hill 63262 No Merstham 2501
Kennings, London Rd 64354 Aus Ril sdh
Redland see Bristol
Redruth 36,700 *Cornwall* Map4SW64

646

647 648 649 650 651

652

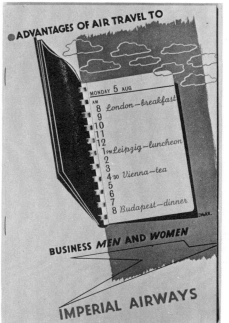

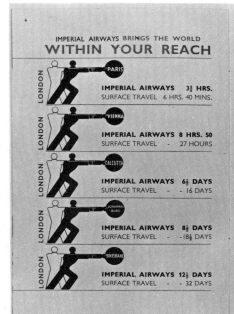

653

654

647-50 Covers of Imperial Airways time-tables, 1933-4. Letterpress, all printed in black and one colour by the Curwen Press, London. Each brochure approximately 221 × 93 mm. *John Johnson Collection.*

651, 652 Covers of Imperial Airways time-tables, 1937, designed by E. McKnight Kauffer. Letterpress, printed in two colours by Spottiswoode, Ballantyne & Co. Ltd, London, Colchester, and Eton. 225 × 98 mm. *John Johnson Collection.*

653, 654 Imperial Airways travel brochure, the cover design by E. McKnight Kauffer. Letterpress, printed in black and blue throughout by Spottiswoode, Ballantyne & Co. Ltd. Page size 205 × 132 mm. *John Johnson Collection.*

655 Imperial Airways poster, designed by E. McKnight Kauffer. Lithographed in black and blue. 1015 × 622 mm. *John Johnson Collection.*

656 Cover of *A book about Imperial Airways*, 1935, designed by Barbara Hepworth. Letterpress half-tone, printed in blue by the Curwen Press, London. 254 × 203 mm. *John Johnson Collection.*

655

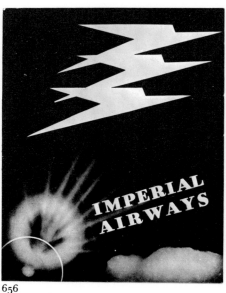

656

Wars

Propaganda
Anti-war bills
Recruiting
Militia notices
Anti-militia bills
Conscription and anti-conscription
Representations of battles
Service certificates, record books, and forms
Notice of casualties
News of war and peace
Glorification of war
The home effort
Second World War information leaflets
Air raids
Celebration of peace

TO ARMS! TO ARMS!
Britons
Strike Home!

AT a time when our *Freedom*, our *Wealth*, and our *Lives* are threatened by *Frenchmen*, it becomes every *True Briton* to stand forward in defence of his *Country*. In former Wars we fought for *Glory*, in this War we must fight for *Life*.—Let all who have health and strength TAKE ARMS.

Do not think our *Fleets* can always protect us. In *One Night* the French Army may land.—Last War they landed *twice* at *Killala* and once at *Bantry* in *Ireland*; and once at *Fisgard* in *Wales*. BONAPARTE swears he will lose *One Hundred Thousand Men*, but he will conquer England.—His Generals and Soldiers are eager to Rob and Plunder. MASSENA declares, if he cannot conquer England, or hold it, he will *make it unfit even for Englishmen to live in*. The French have Maps of all your Roads, and Lists of all the Shops they can *pillage*. They will *burn* your Corn and your Houses—They will *kill* your Old Men—They will force your *Young Men* to fight against the *Savage Blacks* (in St. Domingo)—They will *ravish* your Wives and Daughters—They will toss your *Young Children* on their *Pikes* and *Bayonets*.

There is no Safety but in Arms.

Remember GRANBY! Remember ABERCROMBIE!

Fight like *Men*, for you fight for every thing that is *dear to Man*!

You fight for a GOOD KING, and GOOD OLD ENGLAND, against *French Slaves* and *Robbers*, led on by an ITALIAN POISONER!

To ARMS! To ARMS!
Britons Strike Home!

[F. Hodson, Printer, Cambridge.

657

Plain Answers to Plain Questions,
IN A
DIALOGUE
BETWEEN
JOHN BULL
AND
Bonaparte,
Met *Half-Seas over* between DOVER and CALAIS.

John Bull. HOW do you do?

Bonaparte.—Pretty well; but hope to be better when I am in *London*.

John Bull.—When do you expect to get there?

Bonaparte.—About the end of September; or October at latest.

John Bull.—Why would not you remain at PEACE with us; which you know we were anxious to preserve?

Bonaparte.—Because I had set my heart on the recovery of EGYPT, which I had disgracefully quitted; and in recovering EGYPT, to pave the way for driving you out of INDIA, to the productions of which you owe so much of the Wealth, the Strength, and the Prosperity, which you enjoy.

John Bull.—But what did *Malta* signify?

Bonaparte.—I could not cleverly get to EGYPT without it.

John Bull.—Why are you such an enemy to our LIBERTY OF THE PRESS?

Bonaparte.—That's a foolish Question, John. Why?—Because it exposes all my deep designs. Because it makes me odious amongst my own subjects, and in all Europe, by pointing out all the bloodshed, desolation and rapine by which I have obtained power, and by which I must preserve it. Because it recommends love, loyalty, and support to a King whom I mean to dethrone; and unanimity to a country, which I mean to conquer, to ravage, and to annihilate.

John Bull.—What RELIGION are you of?

Bonaparte.—None.—I was first a Deist; then a Papist in *Italy*; afterwards a Mahometan in *Egypt*; and am now an Atheist.

John Bull.—Why then did you restore the Catholic Religion in France?

Bonaparte.—Because it answered my purpose best.

John Bull.—Why have you suffered your Soldiers to burn so many Towns, shed so much innocent blood, destroy Cottages as well as Palaces so indiscriminately, murder in cold blood Thousands of poor Men, and ravish Thousands of poor Women, in ITALY, in EGYPT, in SYRIA, and lately in HANOVER?

Bonaparte.—Foolish again, John.—I did not merely suffer it—I encouraged it.—My object has always been to strike terror. I don't mince matters. Witness the deliberate massacre of four thousand Turks at *Jaffa*, who were my prisoners; and my poisoning several hundred of my own soldiers, who were of no use to me.

John Bull.—What do you mean to do if you come here?

Bonaparte.—I won't tell you. It would make your hair stand an end.

John Bull.—Arn't you a bit afraid of us?

Bonaparte.—To tell you the truth, I am. But I am not afraid to sacrifice 100,000 men in an attempt to invade you.

John Bull.—As an honest man, what do you most depend upon for success?

Bonaparte.—On foggy weather—long nights—a want of discipline in your troops—a want of spirit and of union in your people.

John Bull.—You had better let it alone, *Bony*;—if these are your only grounds for hope, you're a damn'd Fool if you attempt it.

Bonaparte.—To tell you the truth, *John*, I don't much like some of your late proceedings in Parliament. But I am determined on the attempt; so, look to it.

F. HODSON, PRINTER, CAMBRIDGE.

658

---

657 Propaganda bill, early nineteenth century. Letterpress, printed by F. Hodson, Cambridge. 383 × 252 mm. *Cambridge Folk Museum.*

658 Propaganda bill, early nineteenth century. Letterpress, printed by F. Hodson, Cambridge. 385 × 250 mm. *Cambridge Folk Museum.*

659 First World War propaganda bill, 1918. Hand-drawn lithograph, printed in five colours by J. W. Ltd, signed David Wilson & W.F.D. 375 × 252 mm. *John Johnson Collection.*

660 First World War propaganda bill, Hand-drawn lithograph, printed in five colours by H. & C. Graham Ltd, London, signed David Wilson & W.F.B. 375 × 256 mm. *John Johnson Collection.*

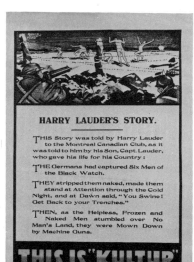

659

660

661 Peace bill, Stockport, 1808. Letterpress, printed by W. Cowdroy, Manchester. 242 × 190 mm. *John Johnson Collection.*

662 Anti-war bill, *c.* 1900. Letterpress, anon. 464 × 333 mm. *John Johnson Collection.*

663 Campaign for Nuclear Disarmament leaflet, 1969. Lithographed. 210 × 133 mm.

664 British Campaign for Peace in Vietnam leaflet, 1969. Lithographed. 210 × 132 mm.

TEN GUINEAS  BOUNTY!

VOLUNTEERS

FOR

His Majesty's Royal Regiment

OF

DRAGOONS,

Late the EARL of PEMBROKE's

COMMANDED BY

Major GENERAL GOLDSWORTHY.

ALL YOUNG MEN, willing to serve in the above-named Regiment, shall immediately enter into present Pay & good Quarters, by applying to the COMMANDING OFFICER, at the *Head Quarters* in DORCHESTER, BLANDFORD and WINBORNE or with the RECRUITING PARTIES stationed at WARMINSTER, TROWBRIDGE, DEVIZES and YEOVIL, where each Volunteer will receive

The King's full Bounty of Ten Guineas

WITH AN

INCREASE of PAY;

ALSO, A GOOD

HORSE, ARMS, CLOATHS, ACCOUTREMENTS,

And every Thing necessary to complete a Gentleman Dragoon.

Young Men wishing to be entertained as ROYAL DRAGOONS, must be well made, and well looking, perfectly found and healthy, having no bodily Infirmity whatever, from the Age of Sixteen to Twenty-Six Years, and from Five Feet Seven Inches, to Six Feet high. Growing handsome Lads, of Sixteen, if full Five Feet Six Inches and Three Quarters high, will not be rejected.

No SEAFARING MEN need apply, nor any MILITIA MEN not having served their Time, or any APPRENTICES whose Indentures are not given up; as it is the Intention of the Regiment to inlist none but HONEST FELLOWS, that wish to serve their KING and COUNTRY with Honesty and Fidelity.

Bringers of *good Recruits* shall receive *Two Guineas* for each Man approved of.

GOD SAVE THE KING.

DORCHESTER: Printed by LOCKETT, 1794.

665

G R

Not to go Abroad.

For the Defence solely of the CHURCH & KING

Against the FRENCH and all other Enemies.

Young Men of true Spirit are wanted for his Majesty's

Perth Highland Fencible Regiment,

COMMANDED BY

Col. ROBERTSON,

And by CAPT. FRAZIER.

Of the Establishment of his Royal Highness the

PRINCE of WALES.

None will be taken, but those who are desirous of serving his Majesty. No Apprentices. The Men are sure of being kindly treated by the Officers, who are all Men of well known Character and Consequence.

The Soldiers are not to GO ABROAD, or to be Draughted into any other Regiment. They who serve in this Corps will be entitled to their Freedom in any Corporation in *GREAT BRITAIN & IRELAND*: and when reduced on the Establishment of Peace, they are to be Disembodied as near as possible to the place they were raised.

666

17th NOVEMBER, 1914.

100,000 MEN
ARE NEEDED AT ONCE

To add to the ranks of the New Armies.

JOIN FOR THE WAR.

Extension of Age Limit and Reduction of Height to the Normal Standard.

Age on Enlistment—19 to 38 years
Height for Infantry—5ft. 3ins. and upwards
Chest—34½ ins. at least

PAY AT ARMY RATES.

SEPARATION ALLOWANCE under Army conditions is issuable AT ONCE to the wife of a married man who signs the necessary form at the time of enlistment, and in certain circumstances to the dependants of other soldiers. Pamphlets with full details from any Post Office.

Enquire at any Post Office, Police Station or Labour Exchange for address of nearest Recruiting Office.

GOD SAVE THE KING.

W 2552—5057 500m 11/14
8257—1127 80,000 11/14
Printed for His Majesty's Stationery Office by Hazell, Watson & Viney, Ld., 52, Long Acre, London, W.C.

667

HAVE YOU A
REASON=
OR ONLY AN
EXCUSE~
FOR NOT ENLISTING

668

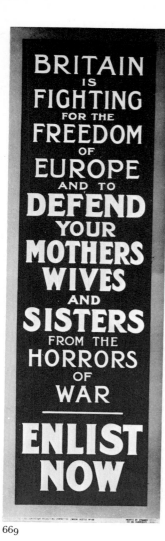

669

670

671

665 Recruiting bill for the Royal Regiment of Dragoons, 1794. Letterpress, printed by Lockett, Dorchester. 562 × 447 mm. *John Johnson Collection.*

666 Recruiting bill for the Perth Highland Fencible Regiment. Letterpress, anon. 508 × 375 mm. *John Johnson Collection.*

667 First World War recruiting bill, 1914. Letterpress, printed in black on blue paper by Hazell, Watson & Viney Ltd, London. 438 × 346 mm. *John Johnson Collection.*

668 First World War recruiting poster, published by the Parliamentary Recruiting Committee. Lithograph, printed in four colours by the Abbey Press, London. 755 × 495 mm. *John Johnson Collection.*

669 First World War recruiting poster, published by the Parliamentary Recruiting Committee. Lithograph, printed in red and blue by Straker Brothers Ltd, London. 755 × 255 mm. *John Johnson Collection.*

670 First World War recruiting poster, published by the Parliamentary Recruiting Committee. Lithograph, printed in red and blue by Straker Brothers Ltd, London. 755 × 255 mm. *John Johnson Collection.*

671 The *Recruiting Times*, no. 1, March 1915, published by the Voluntary Recruiting League, London. Letterpress, printed by Punnett, Cooper & Co., London. Page size 263 × 205 mm. *Imperial War Museum Library.*

672 The *Times*, Recruiting Supplement, 3 November 1915. Letterpress, printed and published for the Times Publishing Co. Ltd by John Parkinson Bland, London. Page size 470 × 315 mm. *Imperial War Museum Library.*

672

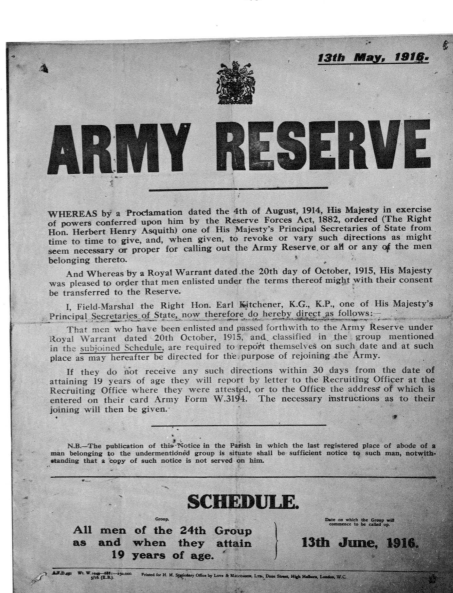

673 Militia return form, 1820. Letterpress, printed by Stephen Tyson, Ulverston. 372 × 225 mm. *Museum of English Rural Life, Reading University.*

674 Militia notice, 1809. Letterpress, printed by G. Ashburner, Ulverston. 250 × 200 mm. *Barrow Public Library.*

675 Militia notice, 1809. Letterpress, printed by J. Brown, Wigan. 320 × 210 mm. *Barrow Public Library.*

676 Recruiting reply form, 1914. Letterpress. 173 × 208 mm. *Imperial War Museum Library.*

677 Army reserve call-up notice, 1916. Letterpress, printed in brown by Love & Malcomson Ltd, London. 572 × 455 mm. *John Johnson Collection.*

673

674

675

676

677

678 Anti-militia bill, late eighteenth or early nineteenth century. Letterpress, anon. 413 × 260 mm. *John Johnson Collection.*

679 Anti-militia bill, published by the Peace Society, 1844 or after. Letterpress, with wood-engraving, printed by R. Barrett, London. 500 × 315 mm. *John Johnson Collection.*

680 Anti-militia bill, published by the Peace Society, mid-nineteenth century. Letterpress, printed by R. Barrett (junior), London. 447 × 280 mm. *John Johnson Collection.*

681 Will Dyson, *'Conscript 'em!'*. Cover of a collection of anti-conscription cartoons. Letterpress, printed by the Victoria House Printing Co. Ltd, London, published by the *Herald*. 357 × 261 mm. *John Johnson Collection.*

682

683

682 Popular broadsheet description of the battle of Talavera (1809). Letterpress, with woodcut, published in Glasgow. 535 × 403 mm. *John Johnson Collection.*

683 Popular broadsheet commemorating the battle of Waterloo (1815). Letterpress, with woodcuts, printed by Pitts, London. 498 × 368 mm. *John Johnson Collection.*

684 Victory of Vittoria (1813). Aquatint, etched by H. Moses and aquatinted by F. C. Lewis after a painting by L. M. Wright, published by Thomas Rickards, London, 1814. *Victoria & Albert Museum.*

684

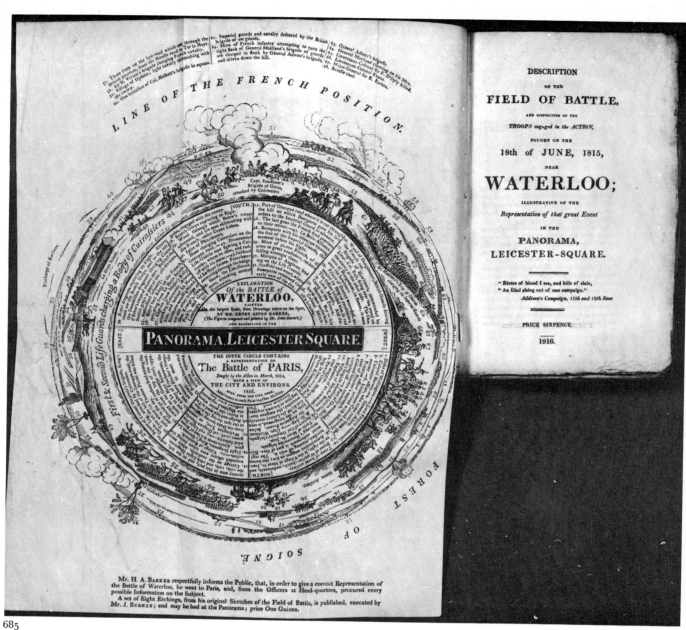

685

DESCRIPTION

OF THE

FIELD OF BATTLE,

AND DISPOSITION OF THE

TROOPS engaged in the ACTION,

FOUGHT ON THE

18th of JUNE, 1815,

NEAR

WATERLOO;

ILLUSTRATIVE OF THE

Representation of that great Event

IN THE

PANORAMA,
LEICESTER-SQUARE.

" Rivers of blood I see, and hills of slain,
" An Iliad rising out of one campaign."
Addison's Campaign, 11th and 12th lines

PRICE SIXPENCE.

1816.

685 Guide to Barker's panorama of the battle of Waterloo exhibiting at Leicester Square, 1816. Letterpress, printed by J. Adlard, London, with a representation of the battle engraved on wood by Lane. Page size 220 × 135 mm., size of the image and text on the folding plate 373 × 270 mm. *John Johnson Collection.*

686 Plate from the guide to Barker's panorama of the battle of Vittoria, 1814. Letterpress, printed by J. Adlard, London, the representation of the battle engraved on wood by Lane. Sheet size 400 × 320 mm. *John Johnson Collection.*

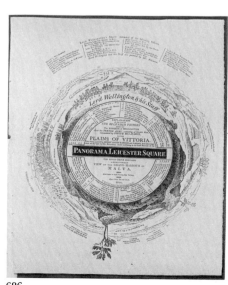

686

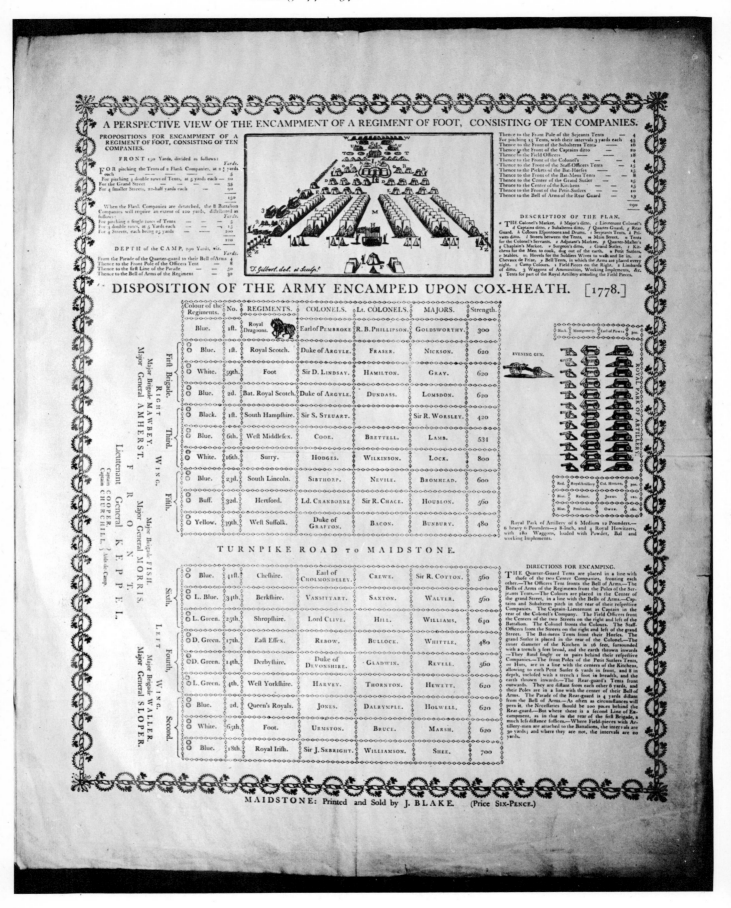

687 Representation of the disposition of the army encamped on
Cox-heath, 1778. Letterpress, printed by J. Blake, Maidstone,
with a woodcut drawn and engraved by J. Gilbert. 600 ×
483 mm. *John Johnson Collection.*

THE EXPLOSION OF THE RIGHT SIEGE-TRAIN, NEAR INKERMAN MILL.—SKETCHED BY E. A. GOODALL.—(SEE PAGE 608.)

688

688 E. A. Goodall, 'The explosion of the
right siege-train, near Inkerman Mill',
from the *Illustrated London News*, 15 December 1855. Wood-engraving. 230 ×
340 mm.

689 The *Daily Mirror*, 1 October 1914.
Letterpress, with process half-tones.
389 × 303 mm. *St Bride Printing Library*.

690 The *Daily Call*, 5 October 1914.
Letterpress, with process half-tones.
496 × 337 mm. *St Bride Printing Library*.

689

690

691

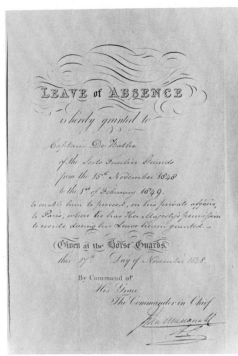

692

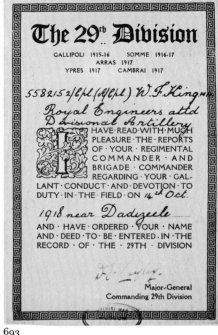

693

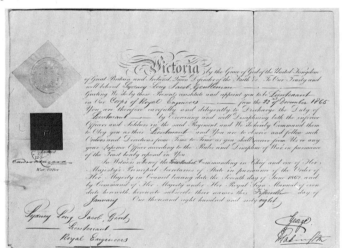

694

691 Certificate of admission to the
Order of Merit, 1846. Lithography, anon.
330 × 235 mm. *John Johnson Collection.*

692 Certificate of leave of absence, 1848.
Engraved, anon. 327 × 201 mm. *John
Johnson Collection.*

693 Certificate of gallant conduct and
devotion to duty, 1918. Letterpress,
printed on parchment. 175 × 112 mm.
Imperial War Museum Library.

694 Certificate of appointment to
Lieutenant, 1868. Copper-engraved by
Warrington, London. 305 × 403 mm.
John Johnson Collection.

695 Army form, 1917. Letterpress, printed
by Hazell, Watson & Viney Ltd.
152 × 114 mm. *Imperial War Museum
Library.*

696 Army form, 1917. Letterpress, printed
by Hazell, Watson & Viney Ltd. 234 ×
130 mm. *Imperial War Museum Library.*

695

696

731

732

733

731 First World War poster, issued by the National Organising Committee. Lithography, printed in red and blue by David Allen & Sons Ltd, Harrow. 762 × 508 mm. *John Johnson Collection.*

732 A. S. Hartrick, 'Bus conductor', from his *War work 1914-18*. Lithograph, printed in black and red. 425 × 251 mm. *John Johnson Collection.*

733 A. S. Hartrick, 'Ticket collector', from his *War work 1914-18*. Lithograph, printed in black and beige. 421 × 254 mm. *John Johnson Collection.*

734 First World War poster, issued by the National War Savings Committee, 1917. Hand-drawn lithography, printed in colours by Eyre & Spottiswoode Ltd. 990 × 635 mm. *John Johnson Collection.*

734

735

736

737

738

735 Second World War leaflet, issued by the Ministry of Information. 212 × 137 mm.

736 Second World War leaflet, issued by the Ministry of Information, 1941. Letterpress. 279 × 213 mm.

737 Second World War air raid precautions training pamphlet, issued by the Ministry of Home Security, 1941. Letterpress. 215 × 139 mm.

738 Second World War leaflet, issued by the Ministry of Information in co-operation with the War Office and the Ministry of Home Security, 1941. Letterpress, 275 × 210 mm.

739

740

741

739 Cover of Ministry of Home Security booklet, *Air raids*, published by His Majesty's Stationery Office, 1940. Photogravure, printed in red and brown. 183 × 118 mm.

740, 741 Facing pages of Ministry of Home Security booklet, *Air raids*, published by His Majesty's Stationery Office, 1940. Letterpress, with line and tone illustrations. Page size 183 × 118 mm.

742 Air raid warden's appointment card, 1941. Letterpress, printed by Shaw & Sons Ltd, London. 131 × 91 mm.

743 Air raid warden's report form, *c.* 1941. Letterpress. 191 × 128 mm.

LOCAL AUTHORITY :—
Oxfordshire County Council
AIR RAID PRECAUTIONS ORGANISATION
OF THE LOCAL AUTHORITY.

ENROLMENT No.....................

APPOINTMENT OF AIR RAID WARDEN.

(SECTOR..............................)

Mr *Walter R. Barlow*

of *1 Grove Villas, Grove Road*

Sonning Common

IS HEREBY APPOINTED ONE OF THE LOCAL AUTHORITY'S AIR RAID WARDENS.

THE DUTIES ASSIGNED TO AN AIR RAID WARDEN IN TIME OF PEACE ARE AS FOLLOWS :—

(1) TO VISIT EACH HOUSE IN HIS OR HER SECTOR AND TO ASCERTAIN THE NUMBER OF PERSONS RESIDING IN SUCH HOUSE AND THE SIZE OF GAS RESPIRATOR REQUIRED BY EACH PERSON.

(2) TO DISSEMINATE INFORMATION AS TO THE PRECAUTIONARY MEASURES RECOMMENDED TO BE TAKEN TO REDUCE RISK TO THE POPULATION IN THE EVENT OF AN EMERGENCY ARISING.

THE LOCAL AUTHORITY WILL BE GRATEFUL IF FULL FACILITIES ARE ACCORDED TO THEIR AIR RAID WARDENS TO ENABLE THEM TO CARRY OUT THESE IMPORTANT DUTIES.

LT. COLONEL,
SUB CONTROLLER
HENLEY BORO. A.R.D.

WARDEN'S SIGNATURE } *W R Barlow*

DATE...............

NOTE.—AIR RAID WARDENS WEAR A SILVER A.R.P. BADGE OR BROOCH.

COPYRIGHT. A.R.27. SHAW & SONS LTD., FETTER LANE, E.C.4. S 2506 (X)

742

WARDEN'S REPORT FORM. A.R.P./M.I.
Form of Report to Report Centres.

(Commence with the words) "AIR RAID DAMAGE"

Designation of REPORTING AGENT
(e.g., Warden's Sector Number)

POSITION of occurrence

TYPE of bombs :—H.E. Incendiary Poison Gas

Approx. No. of CASUALTIES :—
(If any trapped under wreckage, say so)

IF FIRE say so :—

Damage to MAINS :—Water Coal Gas Overhead electric cables Sewers

Names of ROADS BLOCKED

Position of any UNEXPLODED BOMBS

Time of occurrence (approx.)

Services already ON THE SPOT or COMING :—

Remarks :—

(Finish with the words) "MESSAGE ENDS"

ORIGINAL } These words are for use with a report sent by messenger.
DUPLICATE } Delete whichever does not apply.

743

744

745

746

744 Peace festival notice, Soham, 1814.
Letterpress, printed by Playford,
Mildenhall. 208 × 162 mm. *Cambridge
Folk Museum.*

745 Peace festival notice, Saffron Walden,
1856. Letterpress, printed in black on
blue paper by Hart, Saffron Walden.
565 × 444 mm. *Essex County Record Office.*

746 Peace festival notice, Saffron Walden,
1856. Letterpress, printed by Hart,
Saffron Walden. 430 × 339 mm. *Essex
County Record Office.*

747 News bill to celebrate peace, 1918 (?).
Hand-drawn lithography, printed in
red and blue on orange paper by Vincent
Brooks, Day & Son Ltd, London.
743 × 507 mm. *John Johnson Collection.*

747

Exhibitions

Dioramas and panoramas
Models and curiosities
Waxworks
Madame Tussaud's exhibition
Great Exhibition, official printing
Views of the Great Exhibition
Great Exhibition novelties
Trade advertising at the Great Exhibition
International Exhibition, 1862
Empire exhibitions
Festival of Britain, 1951
Trade exhibitions
Art exhibition notices and posters
Art exhibition tickets and private view cards
Art exhibition catalogues

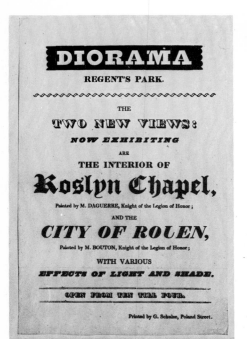

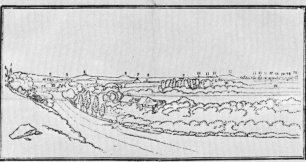

748 Diorama notice, 1826. Letterpress, printed by G. Schulze, London. 222 × 142 mm. *John Johnson Collection.*

749 Panorama notice, 1824. Letterpress, printed by Whiting, London. 220 × 128 mm. *John Johnson Collection.*

750 Panorama notice. Letterpress, printed by J. & G. Nichols, London. 107 × 138 mm. *John Johnson Collection.*

751 Diorama notice, 1827. Letterpress, with woodcut, printed by G. Schulze, London. 316 × 205 mm. *John Johnson Collection.*

752 Guide to Barker and Burford's panoramic view of Rome, 1817. Letterpress, with wood-engraved plate by Lane, printed by J. Adlard, London. Page size 223 × 133 mm, size of folding plate 343 × 305 mm. *John Johnson Collection.*

753 Guide to Barker and Burford's panoramic view of Venice, 1819. Letterpress, with wood-engraved plate by James Lee, printed by J. and C. Adlard, London. Page size 223 × 130 mm, size of folding plate 313 × 455 mm. *John Johnson Collection.*

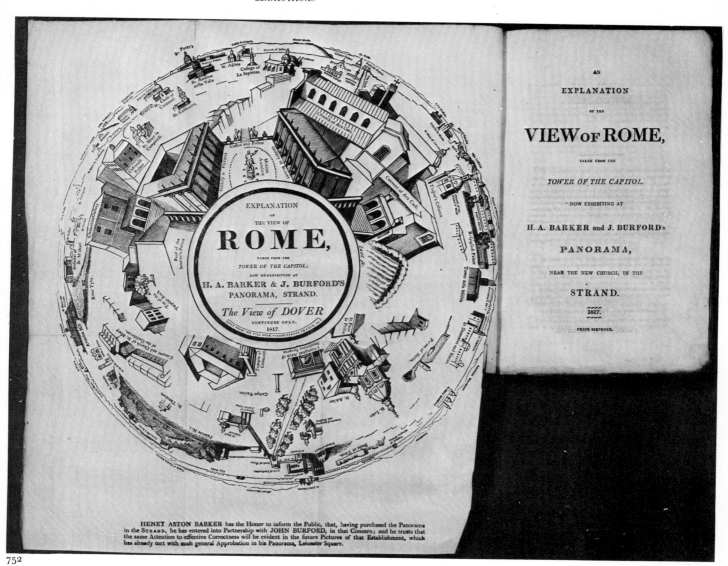

HENRY ASTON BARKER has the Honor to inform the Public, that, having purchased the Panorama in the STRAND, he has entered into Partnership with JOHN BURFORD, in that Concern; and he trusts that the same Attention to effective Correctness will be evident in the future Pictures of that Establishment, which has already met with such general Approbation in his Panorama, Leicester Square.

752

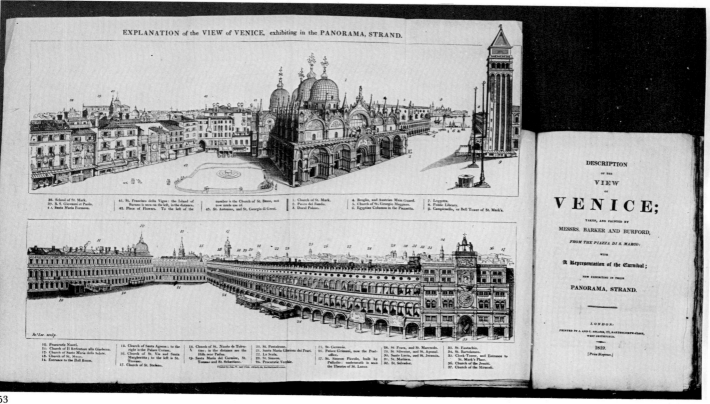

753

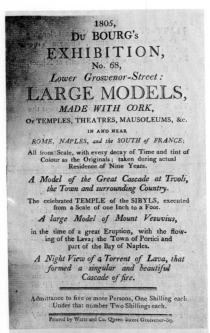

754

755

757

754 Catalogue of exhibition of cork models, 1805. Letterpress, printed by Watts & Co., London. 196 × 123 mm. *John Johnson Collection.*

755 Notice of James Wyld's large model of the earth, bears MS. date 1853. Letterpress, printed by Crozier & Mullin, London. 187 × 124 mm. *John Johnson Collection.*

756 Notice of exhibition of Lequoy's model of Paris, bears MS. date 1777. Letterpress, anon. 228 × 166 mm. *John Johnson Collection.*

757 Notice of exhibition of 'The miraculous giantess' and other phenomena, early 1840s. Letterpress, printed by J. W. Peel, London. 735 × 495 mm. *John Johnson Collection.*

756

Now under Exhibition at the
COSMORAMA ROOMS
No. 209, REGENT-STREET,
THE ANATOMICAL
PARISIAN
VENUS

As a Work of Art, this exquisite Dissected Wax Model of the Human Body is perfectly unique, and most assuredly surpasses in beauty and accuracy any Figure of a similar kind ever introduced into Britain ; neither time nor effort has been spared to render it worthy the attention of the Philosopher and the general Public.   Its perfect accordance with Nature, in the form, proportion, and relative position of the various parts, has been certified by some of

The Highest Living Authorities in this Country and in France.

This full size Figure, while it displays with truth the beautiful and complicated series of Organs which enter into our Constitution, cannot give offence even to the most refined delicacy ; and no one who has witnessed the demonstration of its various parts, can ever forget its extraordinary appearance of reality, inconveying true and forcible ideas of that wonderful and transcendant Organism to which, whether individually or as a species, we are indebted for our existence.

arious parts will be shewn and described by the Medical Proprietor ; first, in their natural and relative position, and afterwards, removed and drided into sections, to reveal their internal structure, while constant reference will be made to the functions which they perform, to their morbid appearances, pincipal diseases, and to the remedial means instituted by Nature and Art for the re-establis   ent of Health.

On removing the Integuments of the Face, the various Blood Vessels and Nerves are brought into view, together with the Muscles which they supply. N Work of Art can exceed the perfection and beauty of the parts thus exposed : the Muscles which give expression to the various passions and emotions of the mind—to joy and sorrow—to rage, anguish, and despair—are here pointed out, and their actions explained ; and cannot fail to gratify all who may view them, but especially the Artist and Philosopher, to whom a knowledge of these parts is essential.   For the sake of convenience part of the Cranium is removed, and the Membranes which cover and protect the Brain brought under observation ; these in their turn are seen drawn aside, and the Brain itself,

" The dome of thought, the image of the soul,"

with all its external convolutions, strikingly and correctly displayed.

On removing the Breastbone and part of the Ribs, a beautiful and correct view is obtained of the great Organs of Circulation and Respiration, *in situ*. This view is highly interesting on account of the numerous serious and fatal diseases to which the Heart and Lungs are liable.   After displacing the Lungs, the Heart is separated into sections, and the wonderful and admirable mechanism of its interior fully demonstrated : here are seen the beautiful series of Valves, and the accessory parts, accompanied by a description of their uses and mode of action.   If in one part of the Body there are evidences of design more than in another, it is here ; for so palpable is the adaptation of the various means to their respective ends, that no one who has seen and reflects on this portion of our Organization can fail to pay a tribute to the Great First Cause.

On removing the Abdominal Parieties, a view exceedingly accurate and interesting is presented.   The parts are seen in the situation which they occupy during life, and their connexion one with another is immediately discovered.   The Stomach is here seen, and a simple and a concise account given of the changes which the food undergoes during digestion. The Liver, with its uses in the animal economy, is next pointed out. A general outline will thus be afforded of the Anatomy of the Organs of Assimilation, together with their physiological action, and frequent reference will be made to their morbid states, and to the effect produced on them by remedial and other agents.   When it is borne in mind how many of the diseases which afflict humanity are traceable to a vitiation of the Digestive Organs, the views and explanations here given cannot fail to ensure the liveliest interest.   Other Organs which are situated in the region of the Abdomen, and to which special reference is not here required, will, in like manner, be described.

When the Skin is lifted off, a very correct view is obtained of the Muscles, Blood Vessels, and Nerves, of the upper and lower extremities.   To the general enquirer these parts are unfolded in a manner so truly beautiful, that their very simplicity, yet their efficiency, cannot fail to excite admiration. The Arteries which convey the Blood for the nutrition of the Limbs, the Veins which return the Blood to the Heart, and the Nerves which transmit sensation and motor power, are all so faithfully displayed, that an impression of reality is instantly conveyed to the mind of the beholder.

However useful and meritorious Drawings and Paintings of Anatomical Subjects may be ; however beautiful and accurate may be their execution ; still no representation on any flat surface can convey such definite and correct ideas of our Corporeal Organization as the

PARISIAN VENUS.

Neither to the non-professional portion of the community can even recent preparations be compared with this attractive Work of Art ; for it is an important fact, that no sooner is vitality extinct, than many parts completely change their appearance ; while to every part of this Model is imparted the natral colour, at the same time making no infringement on correct taste and feeling.

ADMISSION ONE SHILLING.
Open Daily from Ten in the Morning till Six in the Evening.
LADIES in Parties admitted by themselves Daily.

COSMORAMA ROOMS, 209, REGENT. STREET.   Star Press, 20, Cross Street, Hatton Garden—J. TURNER.

758 Exhibition notice, 'The anatomical Parisian Venus'. Letterpress, printed by J. Turner, London. 293 × 211 mm. *John Johnson Collection.*

ROYAL EXHIBITION.

The Duke and Dutchefs of *YORK*,

With an exact REPRESENTATION of
Their MARRIAGE CEREMONY,

Are now to be feen at Mrs. SALMON's WAX-WORK, No. 189, *Fleet-Street*.

Admittance One Shilling.

759

1785.

EXHIBITION.

The SPEAKING FIGURE,

At the GLASS-WAREHOUSE,

COVENTRY-STREET, near the HAY-MARKET,

Where it is to be feen every Day, (Sundays excepted) from
Twelve till *Nine* at Night.

A MECHANIC has compofed a Figure about the Size of a New
Born Infant, the moft Surprifing and Curious that ever was feen.

Thofe Ladies and Gentlemen who go to fee this Figure, may queftion
it promifcuoufly in any Language they think proper, and the Figure
will anfwer to every Queftion with that Precifion, as though it had been
prepared for thofe Queftions. If agreeable to the Company, the Figure
will put the Queftion.

Any Perfon may fpeak either with a loud Voice, or whifper that no
Perfon in the Room can hear, and the Figure will anfwer to every Queftion
afked; and to prevent any Communication, the Figure will be fufpended
in the Air by a Ribband, which may be examined or exchanged.

The Author has had the Honour of fhowing it to the King and Queen
of France, and all the Royal Family; and to that of Portugal, where fhe
was the Wonder and Admiration of them all.

And at Madrid, fhe caufed fo much Surprife, that the whole Spanifh
Inquifition affembled, and fat together to interrogate her; to all which
Queftions fhe anfwered very well.

The MECHANICAL BIRD,

Who flies in all Senfes, and is very ufeful for the Direction of an Air Balloon;
It is the firft piece of Mechanifm that was ever known to fly.

The DANCING AUTOMATON,

Which performs Surprifing Feats of Activity, and follows exactly the
Notes of Mufic.

ALSO SEVERAL OTHER

Very curious Mechanical and Phyfical Pieces.

At the fame Place may be had, (Price 1s) a Book defcribing the
Powers, &c. of the Magic Tub, or the Way to Magnetife, now in great
Vogue at *Paris*.

Admittance One Shilling each Perfon.

760

Sep.t 1833

209, Regent Street.

JUST OPENED,

A NEW AND EXTRAORDINARY

EXHIBITION

OF

NAPOLEON

BREATHING,

SIMILAR TO WHEN HE WAS ALIVE.

NAPOLEON, whose extraordinary genius has
excited the admiration of the civilized World, (but
more particularly the English Nation, who are generally
acknowledged as the most correct appreciators of great
merit,) is represented Breathing on a couch, clad in the
Dress which he generally wore.

The Body is constructed of materials of a new
invention, and the effect produced is so extraordinary that
you may see and hear the phenomenon of Respiration,—
feel the softness of the Skin, and the elasticity of the Flesh,
—the existence of the Bones, and the entire structure of
the Human Body.

The Likeness, Dress, and Motion are so striking,
as to cause such an uncommon illusion, that many who
have lived in intimacy with that great man, have thought
they beheld him alive again. From such a happy combination we may say for the future,

NAPOLEON IS NOT DEAD!

Admittance 1s. *To Examine the Body 1s. extra.*

Open from Ten 'till Dusk.

Printed by A. A. Paris, 49, Holywell Street, Strand, London.

761

EXHIBITION OF

WaxWorks,

At the Rotunda,

NEAR BLACKFRIARS BRIDGE.

MRS. HOJOS, the Proprietor, respectfully informs the
Ladies and Gentlemen of London, and its Vicinity, that the
Exhibition is just arrived from the Continent, consisting of
a Splendid Cabinet of ANCIENT & MODERN

WAX FIGURES;

THE FIRST & PRINCIPAL GROUP REPRESENTING THE HISTORY OF

SAMSON

AND

DELILAH,

SAMSON

Is a fine anatomical figure, for which great sums of money
have been offered. It was seen by Napoleon Bonaparte in
1813, and so much admired, that he presented the celebrated
artist, CABALE, with a medal.

One of the Attendants on DELILAH is the figure of an

Old Woman

And a subject worthy of the notice of every artist.
The figures are of the life size, and perfect resemblances of
human nature.

In the Collection, there is also a beautiful figure of the

GRECIAN

DAUGHTER!

Being an exact representation of the noble father in prison,
doomed to starvation, with the daughter sustaining his life
from her breast.

WITH A VARIETY OF OTHER FIGURES
TOO NUMEROUS TO MENTION.

Admittance to Ladies and Gentlemen, One Shilling—Servants and Children, Sixpence.

Open from Ten in the Morning till Ten at Night.

N. B.—It is requested that no Person will touch the Figures. *July 1830.*

Fruit and Refreshments may be had at the Bar,
and in the Coffee Room of the Rotunda.

762

---

759 Notice of Mrs Salmon's waxwork exhibition, *c.* 1793.
Letterpress, anon. 65 × 180 mm. *John Johnson Collection.*

760 Notice of exhibition of speaking figure, bears MS. date
1785. Letterpress, anon. 197 × 154 mm. *John Johnson Collection.*

761 Notice of exhibition of model of Napoleon breathing, bears
MS. date 1833. Letterpress, printed by A. A. Paris, London.
189 × 132 mm. *John Johnson Collection.*

762 Notice of Mrs Hojos's waxwork exhibition, bears MS.
date 1830. Letterpress, anon. 413 × 193 mm. *John Johnson
Collection.*

Just Arrived, from Edinburgh,
THE GRAND EUROPEAN

Cabinet of Figures,

MODELLED FROM LIFE,

Exhibiting in the GREAT ROOM, at the WHITE
HART INN, Old Flesh-Market,

Where the Curious may be gratified with a View of all the Characters at once.

Madame TUSSAUD, Artist,

Respectfully informs the Nobility, Gentry, and Public of Newcastle and the Vicinity, that her Unrivalled Collection will positively remain here but a short Time.

The full-length Portrait-Models of their Most Gracious Majesties

George III. & Queen Charlotte,

THEIR ROYAL HIGHNESSES, THE
PRINCE and PRINCESS CHARLOTTE of WALES, DUKE of YORK,

Prince Charles Stuart,

Lieutenant-General Sir JOHN MOORE,
ADMIRAL LORD NELSON,
General WASHINGTON,
Right Hon. CHARLES JAMES FOX—Right Hon. WILLIAM PITT,
Sir FRANCIS BURDETT,
Right Hon. H. GRATTAN—Right Hon. J. P. CURRAN,
The Philanthropic Mr. ROSEBERRY of Dublin,
Mons. TALLEYRAND—L'ABBE SIEYES,
The famous BARON TRENCK—The ARTIST and her DAUGHTER,
MADAME CATALANI, the celebrated Singer—A sleeping Child,
The EMPRESS of FRANCE—The celebrated Mrs. CLARKE,
JOHN KNOX and JOHN WESLEY.

An EXACT LIKENESS of the beautiful

MARY QUEEN of SCOTS.

A COACH AND A CANNON,

Formed in Gold, Ivory, and Tortoise-Shell—to the Astonishment of the Spectator is, with great facility,

DRAWN BY A FLEA.

763

MADAME TUSSAUD'S
Exhibition and Promenade,

Consisting of Full Length Figures of Public Characters, Instructive to Youth, and Interesting to all,

IS NOW OPEN,

In the LOWTHER ROOMS, King William St.,
WEST STRAND.

SELECTIONS FROM THE PUBLIC PRINTS.

This Exhibition is deserving of encouragement, being by far the most splendid thing of the kind ever seen in this Metropolis.—*Times.*

This is one of the most remarkable Exhibitions that has been seen in London for a considerable time, being Portraits in Wax, presenting much of the exterior semblance of the originals. It is highly interesting.—*Morning Herald.*

Admittance One Shilling.

CHILDREN under EIGHT Years of Age Sixpence.—Second Room Sixpence.
Open every Day from 11 till 6, in the Evening from 7 till 10.

PHAIR, Printer, 67, Great Peter Street, Westminster.

764

Exhibition de Mᵐᵉ TUSSAUD & FILS,
58, Baker Street, Portman Square,

Ouverte depuis 11 heures du Matin jusqu' à 4, et depuis 7 heures du Soir jusqu' à 10.

MADAME TUSSAUD ET FILS ont l'honneur d'informer les Etrangers et le Public, qu'ils ont ajouté à leur MAGNIFIQUE EXHIBITION DE FIGURES DE CIRE, la plus curieuse Collection qui existe d'objets ayant appartenu à Napoléon, comme Général, Consul, et Empereur, et qui sont exposés dans deux nouvelles Salles décorées avec la plus grande richesse et ornées de tous les emblèmes de l'Empire. On pourra se faire une idée de leur magnificence par la somme énorme de 6,000 livres sterling qu'elles ont coûté. MADAME TUSSAUD ET FILS ne voulant point que le public conçoive le moindre doute sur l'authenticité des objets qu'ils ont l'honneur de répresenter, et dont la plus grande partie provient du Prince Lucien et du Docteur O'Meara, ont cru devoir mettre tous ses yeux, dans l'une des Salles, tous les titres, pièces et certificats qui attestent leur origine.

PARMI CES PRECIEUSE RELIQUES ON REMARQUE PRINCIPALEMENT.

LE LIT DE CAMP avec la Courtepointe, le Traversin et les Deux Matelas sur lesquels Napoléon est mort à Ste. Hélène. Les Matelas et la Courtepointe sont tachés de son sang par suite de l'autopsie faite par le Docteur Antomarchi. LE MANTEAU qu'il portait à la Bataille de Marengo, et qu'il a légué à son Fils. UN COSTUME complet porté par lui à Ste. Hélène ainsi que plusieurs Mouchoirs, et paires de Bas. LA CHEMISE, le Gilet de Flanelle et le Madras, qu'il avait sur lui quand il est mort. UNE DENT, et l'Instrument dont s'est servi le Docteur O'Meara pour la lui extraire. LA ROBE de son couronnement et celle de Joséphine. LE SABRE qu'il portait à la Bataille des Pyramides. LE SABRE d'honneur qui lui a été offert par le Directoire à son retour de sa première campagne d'Italie. LE SERVICE EN PORCELAINE, le couvert en vermeil et la tasse à café dont il se servait à Ste. Hélène. LA CROIX D'HONNEUR qu'il a constamment portée à l'Île d'Elbe, SA TABATIERE en or avec son chiffre, et UN CAMEE à son image monté en bague; Ces trois objets ont été offerts par lui à son frère Lucien lors de leur réconciliation en 1815. LE COFFRE de son nécessaire pris dans sa voiture à Waterloo, et dont la serrure a été brisée par les soldats. LE SUPERBE BERCEAU du Roi de Rome fait par Jacob. LA VOITURE MILITAIRE de Napoléon prise à Waterloo, et achetée par Mr. Bullock à S. M. George IV. pour la somme de 2,500 livres sterling. LE PORTRAIT EN PIED de l'Empereur peint par Robert Lefèvre. Ceux idem de Joséphine, Marie Louise, Lucien, Caroline sa Sœur, Reine de Naples, Madame Mère, et le Duc de Reischtadt, peint par David, Gérard, Lethière et Sales, (ce dernier, peintre de S. M. l'Empereur d'Autriche). Enfin, la magnifique TABLE DES MARECHAUX, chef-d'œuvre de la manufacture de Sèvres, peinte par Isabey et donnée par Napoléon à la ville de Paris. Après avoir été exposée cinq ans dans la grande galerie du Louvre, ce précieux monument national fut vendu sous la restauration en 1815.

MADAME TUSSAUD prévient également le Public qu'elle a en sa possession, depuis plus de 50 ans, la Chemise qu' Henry IV. avait sur le corps quand il fut assassiné par Ravaillac, elle est ensanglantee, et parcée des deux coups de poignard dont il a été frappé. (Cette relique inappréciable fait partie de l'exhibition.)

A l'extrémité de la grande Salle des figures, est située la Salle du trône où est représenté la figure de S. M. George IV revêtue de la veritable robe de son couronnement. Ce magnifique costume a coûté dans l'origine 18,000 livres sterling.

Au nombre des Anciennes Figures, dont le nombre dépasse 130, on remarque toujours le Groupe intéressant de Louis XVI. et Marie Antoinette, avec Madame la Duchesse d'Angoulême dans son enfance, et le Dauphin, et parmi les nouvelles, on distingue particulièrement celles du Marquis de Wellesley, frère du Duc de Wellington, d'Espartero, et du Père Mathew.

Prix d'Entrée :—1 Shilling pour la Grande Salle, et 6 Pence de Supplément pour des Deux Salles des Reliques de Napoléon et la Chambre des Criminels.

☞ La musique commence à 8 heures du Soir, heure à laquelle toutes les Salles sont brillamment illuminées.

G. COLE, Carteret Street, Westminster.

765

---

763 Notice of exhibition of Madame Tussaud's waxworks in Newcastle, early nineteenth century. Letterpress, printed on grey paper, anon. 323 × 178 mm. *John Johnson Collection.*

764 Notice of Madame Tussaud's waxwork exhibition, *c.* 1835. Letterpress, printed by Phair, London. 124 × 248 mm. *John Johnson Collection.*

765 Notice of Madame Tussaud's waxwork exhibition, *c.* 1825. Letterpress, with wood-engraving, printed by G. Cole, London. 340 × 214 mm. *John Johnson Collection.*

766

767

768

769

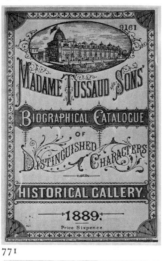

770

771

772

773

774

775

776

777

A selection of covers of Madame Tussaud's exhibition catalogues. All from the *John Johnson Collection*.

766 1822. Letterpress title-page, printed by J. Clarke, Manchester. 202 × 127 mm.

767 [1835]. Letterpress, printed by J. Phair, London. 208 × 130 mm.

768 1856. Letterpress on peach coloured paper, printed by G. Cole, London. 206 × 138 mm.

769 1869. Letterpress on pink paper, printed by W. S. Johnson, 'Nassau Steam Press', London. 215 × 135 mm.

770 1879. Lithography, printed in three colours by Ben George, London. 240 × 148 mm.

771 1889. Letterpress, printed on blue paper by F. W. Potter & Co. Ltd, London. 211 × 131 mm.

772 [c. 1896]. Chromolithography, printed in seven colours, anon. 213 × 139 mm.

773 1897. Chromolithography, printed in eight colours, anon. 213 × 139 mm.

774 [c. 1920]. Letterpress, printed in brown by Bruton & Co., London. 214 × 139 mm.

775 1925. Letterpress, printed in grey and brown on cream paper by Bruton & Co., London. 212 × 135 mm.

776 1930. Lithography, printed in blue on buff paper by the Reader Printing Co. Ltd, Leicester and London. 198 × 124 mm.

777 [c. 1941]. Letterpress, printed in red and blue by the Broadway Press Ltd, London. 200 × 125 mm.

14   BIOGRAPHICAL SKETCHES.

which his grandfather had lost by weakness and bigotry; but the attempt was unsuccessful, for, on the 16th of April, 1746, the rebels were totally defeated at Culloden, by the Duke of Cumberland. Charles, after many hair-breadth escapes and hardships, got out of the kingdom in safety; but many of his followers, noblemen as well as persons of inferior rank, fell sacrifices to the House of Stewart. The Pretender died abroad, in 1788.

21.—LORD VISCOUNT NELSON.

Taken from a Bust, executed a short time before his Death.

Horatio Viscount Nelson was the fourth son of the Reverend Mr Nelson, Rector of Burnham Thorpe, in Norfolk, at which place Horatio was born, September 29th, 1758. His actions, like those of Wellington, have been attended with important consequences to this country. The fame they have procured him is so great, that it is almost superfluous to name them.—He went to sea at the early age of twelve years, under his uncle, Captain Suckling, of the Reasonable man of war. He passed for Lieutenant in 1777, and was made Post-Captain in 1779; in 1796 he was appointed Commodore on board the La Minerve. Having shifted his flag on board the Culloden, 74, he in the battle of St. Vincent, under Admiral Jervis, attacked the Santisima Trinidada, of 136 guns, and boarded and took the San Nicholas, of 80 guns, and the San Joseph, of 112 guns: for this glorious action he was made Rear Admiral of the Blue. The battle of Aboukir, on the 1st of August, 1798, was another glorious triumph of the Naval hero. On the 21st of October, 1805, he conquered in the battle of Trafalgar, and died in the arms of Victory. What noble mind does not envy the fate of Nelson? He died as he

BIOGRAPHICAL SKETCHES.   15

much classical knowledge, his father taking him early from the grammar-school at Stratford, to follow his business as a dealer in wool. But our Poet's genius soared above every disadvantage—the muses had marked him for their own; and his works will live as long as taste and knowledge irradiate the country which had the honour of giving him birth. He died in 1616, and was buried in the church at Stratford.

23.—J. P. KEMBLE, ESQ.

Taken from Life, in 1800.

This celebrated gentleman is the eldest son of Mr Roger Kemble, who was many years manager of a company of comedians. His first appearance in the metropolis was in Hamlet; and but few first appearances in London have given greater satisfaction. He is here represented in the character of Coriolanus, to which his solemn demeanour and style of acting have admirably suited him. Whether we view him as an actor or as an author, we must observe, in justice to his character, that he possesses wonderful talents.

24.—MRS SIDDONS.

Taken from a Bust, executed in 1804.

This much admired actress is the daughter of Mr Roger Kemble.

778

16   MADAME TUSSAUD AND SONS' CATALOGUE.

HALL OF KINGS.

HOUSE OF BRUNSWICK FROM THE TIME OF GEORGE I

The following characters are placed in the new room, called the "Hall of Kings," so named from containing several portraits, in oil, by eminent artists. It is probably the most splendid room ever seen as an exhibition, and on the walls are placed the full length portrait of her Majesty Queen Victoria, in her sacerdotal robes, painted with her Majesty's most gracious permission by Sir George Hayter; his Royal Highness Prince Albert, from life, by Patten; his Majesty William IV., from life, by Simpson; George III. and Queen Charlotte, from the collection of her late Majesty the Queen Dowager; his Majesty George IV., painted by Sir Thomas Lawrence and presented by his Majesty to General Nicolay; George II., by Hudson; the Duchess of Nassau, by De Vos; Queen Anne, by Sir Peter Lely; the original picture of Charles X. of France, by Lefevre; Equestrian Picture of Louis XIV., by Parosel. The beautiful ceiling was painted by Sir James Thornhill, and is a masterpiece of art; it was restored in its present high state by Mr. Holder, of Great Queen Street, Holborn.

This Group is intended to convey an idea of characters dear to every Englishman and lover of his country; and, at the same time, presents the most complete view of the four National Orders, the Garter, Bath, Thistle, and St. Patrick—costumes with which every one must desire to be acquainted, and which are now for the first time brought before the public. The throne is the original from Carlton Palace, under which his Majesty George the Fourth received the Allied Monarchs.

Also, a full-length Model of the Great Duke, taken from life during his frequent visits to the Napoleon Relics, of which it was said, that "If this figure alone constituted the whole of the Exhibition, it would well repay the trouble of a visit."—*Evening Sun.*

[117.] HIS MAJESTY GEORGE THE FOURTH. (The figure of his Majesty, wearing the orders of the Garter, Bath, and Guelph, was modelled from life; the attitude copied from a picture by Sir Thomas Lawrence. The robe, complete in every respect, measuring seven yards long, was worn by his Majesty in the procession to Westminster Abbey, and borne by nine eldest sons of peers. The robe on the extreme right was used at the opening of Parliament; that on the left, similarly

779

MADAME TUSSAUD AND SONS' CATALOGUE.   17

[118.] HIS MAJESTY WILLIAM IV., in the magnificent coat worn by him as Lord High Admiral of England, embroidered by Messrs. Holbecks, of Bond-street, the only one ever made. His Majesty was born Aug. 21, 1765; married, July 11, 1818, Adelaide, eldest daughter of the late Duke of Saxe Meiningen; ascended the throne June 26, 1830; was crowned Sept. 8, 1831; and died June 20, 1837, leaving no issue, to the great grief of the whole nation, having, during seven years of peace, conferred on his subjects many reforms, which before his reign were regarded as hopeless.

[119.] THE LATE QUEEN DOWAGER, in the actual train, &c., worn by her at her coronation. Amelia Adelaide Louisa Theresa, sister to the reigning Duke of Saxe Meiningen, was born Aug. 13, 1791; married July 11, 1818; crowned September 8, 1831. Her Majesty, to a highly cultivated mind, united elegance of manner and an amiable disposition.

[120.] HER MOST GRACIOUS MAJESTY VICTORIA. (Taken in 1838.) Her Majesty was born at Kensington Palace May 24, 1819; succeeded William IV. June 20, 1837; and was crowned June 28, 1838. Her Majesty, to a prepossessing exterior, unites those qualities calculated to endear her to her country, and to place her in that exalted situation, in the hearts of a free people, which must render her the envy as well as the admiration of the world.

[121.] QUEEN CAROLINE, in a court dress of the period. (From life in 1808.) Her Majesty Caroline Amelia Elizabeth, second daughter of the late Duke of Brunswick, was born May 17, 1768. She was married to his Majesty George IV., then Prince of Wales, April 8, 1795. She died August 7, 1821.

[122.] PRINCESS CHARLOTTE OF WALES, attired in a full court costume of the period. (Taken from the beautiful model for which her Royal Highness graciously sat on the day of her marriage, from which circumstance it received the appellation of the Nuptial bust.) Charlotte Caroline Augusta, daughter of George IV., was born January 7, 1796. May 2, 1816, she was married to the Prince of Saxe Coburg (now King of the Belgians), from which union every Englishman anticipated the happiest results; her Royal Highness

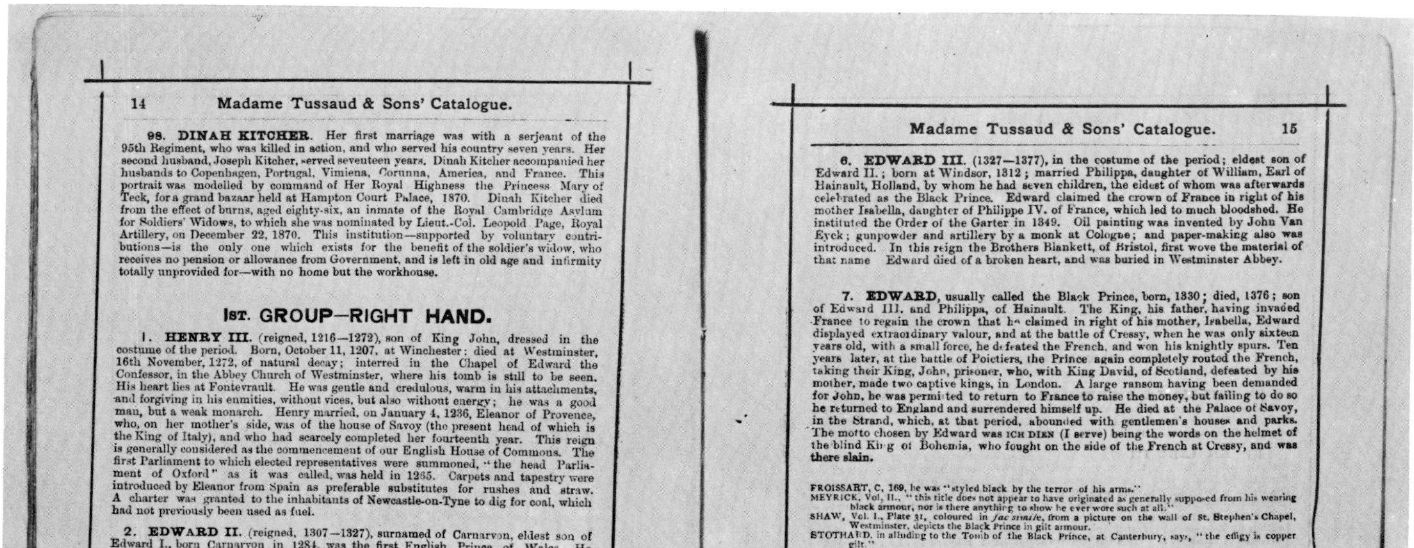

14   Madame Tussaud & Sons' Catalogue.

98. DINAH KITCHER. Her first marriage was with a serjeant of the 95th Regiment, who was killed in action, and who served his country seven years. Her second husband, Joseph Kitcher, served seventeen years. Dinah Kitcher accompanied her husbands to Copenhagen, Portugal, Vimiera, Corunna, America, and France. This portrait was modelled by command of Her Royal Highness the Princess Mary of Teck, for a grand bazaar held at Hampton Court Palace, 1870. Dinah Kitcher died from the effect of burns, aged eighty-six, an inmate of the Royal Cambridge Asylum for Soldiers' Widows, to which she was nominated by Lieut.-Col. Leopold Page, Royal Artillery, on December 22, 1870. This institution—supported by voluntary contributions—is the only one which exists for the benefit of the soldier's widow, who receives no pension or allowance from Government, and is left in old age and infirmity totally unprovided for—with no home but the workhouse.

1st. GROUP—RIGHT HAND.

1. HENRY III. (reigned, 1216—1272), son of King John, dressed in the costume of the period. Born, October 11, 1207, at Winchester; died at Westminster, 16th November, 1272, of natural decay; interred in the Chapel of Edward the Confessor, in the Abbey Church of Westminster, where his tomb is still to be seen. His heart lies at Fontevrault. He was gentle and credulous, warm in his attachments, and forgiving in his enmities, without vices, but also without energy; he was a good man, but a weak monarch. Henry married, on January 4, 1236, Eleanor of Provence, who, on her mother's side, was of the house of Savoy (the present head of which is the King of Italy), and who had scarcely completed her fourteenth year. This reign is generally considered as the commencement of our English House of Commons. The first Parliament to which elected representatives were summoned, "the head Parliament of Oxford" as it was called, was held in 1265. Carpets and tapestry were introduced by Eleanor from Spain as preferable substitutes for rushes and straw. A charter was granted to the inhabitants of Newcastle-on-Tyne to dig for coal, which had not previously been used as fuel.

2. EDWARD II. (reigned, 1307—1327), surnamed of Carnarvon, eldest son of Edward I., born Carnarvon in 1284, was the first English Prince of Wales. He married the daughter of the King of France, Philippe IV., and had issue two sons and one daughter. Regardless of the dying requests of his father in disinheriting

MADAME TUSSAUD & SONS' CATALOGUE.   15

6. EDWARD III. (1327—1377), in the costume of the period; eldest son of Edward II.; born at Windsor, 1312; married Philippa, daughter of William, Earl of Hainault, Holland, by whom he had seven children, the eldest of whom was afterwards celebrated as the Black Prince. Edward claimed the crown of France in right of his mother Isabella, daughter of Philippe IV. of France, which led to much bloodshed. He instituted the Order of the Garter in 1349. Oil painting was invented by John Van Eyck; gunpowder and artillery by a monk at Cologne; and paper-making also was introduced. In this reign the Brothers Blankett, of Bristol, first wove the material of that name. Edward died of a broken heart, and was buried in Westminster Abbey.

7. EDWARD, usually called the Black Prince, born, 1330; died, 1376; son of Edward III. and Philippa, of Hainault. The King, his father, having invaded France to regain the crown that he claimed in right of his mother, Isabella, Edward displayed extraordinary valour, and at the battle of Cressy, when he was only sixteen years old, with a small force, he defeated the French, and won his knightly spurs. Ten years later, at the battle of Poictiers, the Prince again completely routed the French, taking their King, John, prisoner, who, with King David, of Scotland, defeated by his mother, made two captive kings in London. A large ransom having been demanded for John, he was permitted to return to France to raise the money, but failing to do so he returned to England and surrendered himself up. He died at the Palace of Savoy, in the Strand, which, at that period, abounded with gentlemen's houses and parks. The motto chosen by Edward was ICH DIEN (I serve) being the words on the helmet of the blind King of Bohemia, who fought on the side of the French at Cressy, and was there slain.

FROISSART, C. 169, he was "styled black by the terror of his arms."
MEYRICK, Vol. II., "this title does not appear to have originated as generally supposed from his wearing black armour, nor is there anything to show he ever wore such at all."
SHAW, Vol. I., Plate 31, coloured in *fac simile*, from a picture on the wall of St. Stephen's Chapel, Westminster, depicts the Black Prince in gilt armour.
STOTHARD, in alluding to the Tomb of the Black Prince, at Canterbury, says, "the effigy is copper gilt."
PLANCHE, in his "British Costume," says, "the query of Edward being called the Black Prince from the colour of his armour has already been exploded by Sir Samuel Meyrick." "The *first* mention of Edward the Black Prince in England occurs in a Parliamentary Roll of the second year of

780

778-80 Top half of facing pages from Madame Tussaud's exhibition catalogues: 1822, 1856, 1879. *See opposite page for details.*

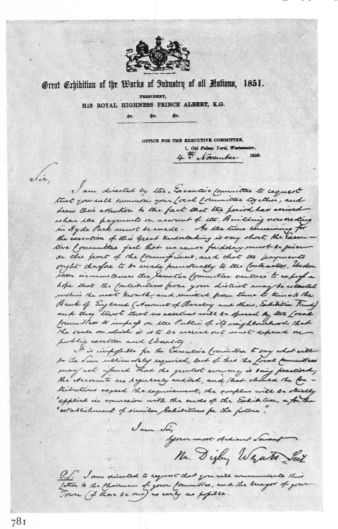

781

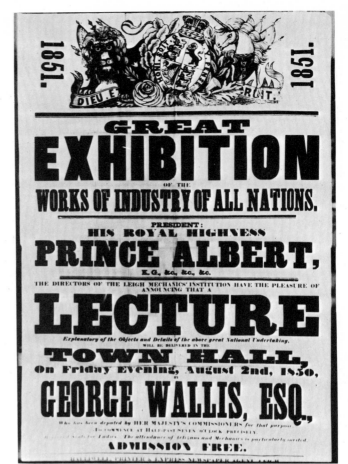

782

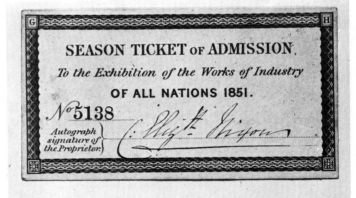

783

781 Circular from Digby Wyatt to local committees appealing for financial support for the Great Exhibition of 1851, 1850. Lithographed by Waterlow & Sons. 323 × 200 mm. *Reading University Library.*

782 Notice of a lecture about the Great Exhibition of 1851, Leigh, 1850. Letterpress, printed by Halliwell, Leigh. From an old photograph. *Reading University Library.*

783 Season tickets for the Great Exhibition of 1851 showing front and back. Engraved, printed in black on pink card. 46 × 83 mm. *John Johnson Collection.*

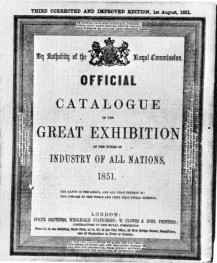

784

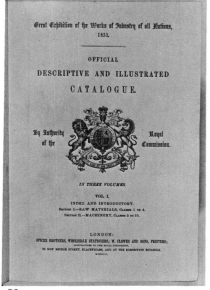

786

785

Class 17. PAPER, PRINTING, AND BOOKBINDING.

Areas F. 27 to 29; G. H. I. J. 26, 27.

1 ACKERMAN & Co. 96 Strand.— Envelope case. Sea weeds. Pole screens. Ornamental colour box. Scrap book.

4 HUGHES, E. Greenwich Hospital Schools, Des.—An improved map of the British islands, physical, political, and industrial. Map of Palestine and adjacent countries.

5 REMNANT, EDMONDS, & REMNANT, 9 Lovell's Ct. Paternoster Row.— Specimens of binding in morocco, vellum, Russia, and calf, elegant, plain, and antique. Sheep and cloth, plain and elegant.

7 HAWTHORNE, J. 77 Charrington St. Manu.— Various descriptions of writing inks, and the materials from which they are made. Specimens of hair dyeing with ink. Nutgalls, fruit of the Terminalia Chebula, from Bengal. Inks.

8 EVANS, J. S. 64 Berwick St. Soho, Manu.— Bookbinding; and leather stained in imitation of woods.

9 FAIRBAIRN, R. 37 Gt. Cambridge St. Hackney Rd. Manu.— Specimens of wood type for printing, &c.

10 FISHER, J. H. New North Rd. Hoxton, Inv.— Specimen of bank note printed in chemical water-colour, in two colours at one operation.

11 GALLARD, W. 30 Lisson Grove, Des.— Portable frame for cases at the imposing stone, or for extra cases.

12 GILL, T. D. 27 Charlotte St. Fitzroy Sq. Inv.— Post-

note paper. Stamping in relief. Smith's improved stamping press. Medal, button, and other dies.

34 ROYSTON & BROWN, 40 & 41 Old Broad St. Manu.— Specimens of bank notes and bills of exchange, engraved by a patent process to prevent forgery. Various account books.

35 SAPSFORD, N. 17 Kirby St. Hatton Garden, Manu.— Specimen of bookbinding.

36 SAUNDERS, T. H. Queenhithe, and Dartford, Kent, Manu.— Parchment paper. Bank-note papers. Glass transparency to show the water mark. Safety paper for cheques, &c.

37 SAUNDERSON, C. Kilburn Lodge. Kilburn, Prop.— Map of Ireland, by J. Dower.

38 SCHLESINGER & Co. 8 Old Jewry — Registered metallic memorandum books. Pocket-books. Letter-clips. Parallel rulers.

40 SILVERLOCK, H. 3 Wardrobe Ter. Doctors' Commons, Des.— Letterpress printing from stereotype plates of medallion and machine engraving.

41 SMITH, J. 42 Rathbone Pl. Inv. and Manu.— Adhesive envelopes. &c. Dowse's tracing and writing cloth.

42 SPICER BROTHERS, New Bridge St. London, Wholesale and Export Stationers, Prop.— Writing papers, Joynson's extra superfine quality. Large bank post. Imperial, royal, and demy. Foolscap, for account books. Superfine plate

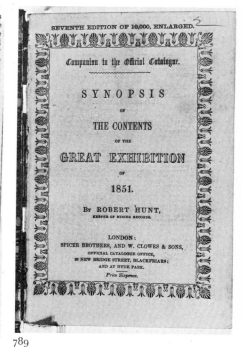

787

The improvement in these treble beat hydraulic valves consists in making the outer beats as near as possible of one size, and allowing the water to act against the middle plate to lift the valve, which will give a third beat, and a third discharge of water, and consequently reduce the lift, prevent concussion, and increase the durability not only of the valve, but other parts of the machinery.—Registered 1851.

202 ASHBY, JONATHAN, *Croydon Common*—Inventor. Screw friction clutch, for engaging and disengaging machinery, while the moving power is in motion.

204 LEES, T., *Stockport*—Inventor. Water-gauge, alarm valve, &c.

205 NEWCOMB, THOMAS, *12 Norfolk Place, East Lane, Walworth*—Inventor and Maker. Brass model of machine, for rolling tanned hides. Its objects are, increased speed in drying hides, less power in working, and a finer finish in the leather. The pressure on the hides may be varied from 1 cwt. to 2 tons. Brass model of patent furnace for marine or stationary steam engines; it supplies itself with fuel, consumes its own smoke, and burns small coal.

206 HASKETH, —, *Redruth*—Inventor. A lubricator for machinery.

208 GADD & BIRD, *Manchester*—Inventors. An expansive piston.

300 LLOYD, GEORGE, *70 Gt. Guildford Street, Southwark* —Inventor and Manufacturer. Patent centrifugal disc blowing machine. The centrifugal exhauster differs from the ordinary

788

789

784 Cover of the *Official catalogue of the Great Exhibition, 1851*. Letterpress, printed on grey paper by William Clowes & Sons, London. 206 × 167 mm. *Reading University Library*.

785 Upper part of a page from the *Official catalogue of the Great Exhibition, 1851*. Letterpress, printed by William Clowes & Sons, London.

786, 787 Title-page and facing pages from the first volume of the *Official descriptive and illustrated catalogue* of the Great Exhibition, 1851. Letterpress, with wood-engravings, printed by William Clowes & Sons, London. Page size 256 × 175 mm. *Reading University Library*.

788 Detail of Plate 787.

789 Cover of the *Synopsis of the contents of the Great Exhibition of 1851*. Letterpress, printed on grey paper by William Clowes & Sons, London. 157 × 102 mm. *Reading University Library*.

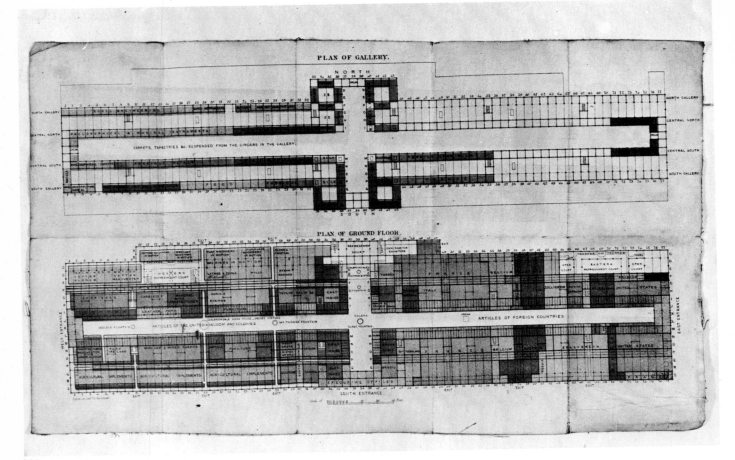

790

791

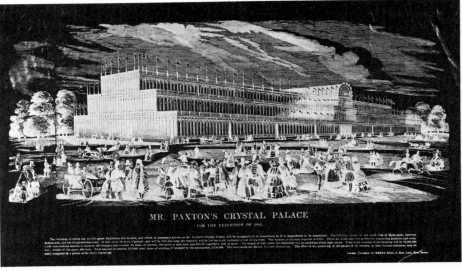

792

790 Plan of the building, Great Exhibition,
1851. Lithography, printed in three
colours by Day & Son, mounted on linen.
255 × 418 mm. *Reading University Library.*

791 'Building for the Great Exhibition
of 1851.' Steel-engraving on coated card,
engraved and published by Layton's,
London. 40 × 62 mm. *Reading University
Library.*

792 'Mr. Paxton's Crystal Palace', 1851.
Letterpress, printed in gold on black
paper, published by Henry Beal, London.
187 × 333 mm. *Reading University Library.*

793 'View of the interior of the building
in Hyde Park for the exhibition of 1851.'
Etching and aquatint, published by
G. Berger, London. 185 × 453 mm.
Reading University Library.

793

248

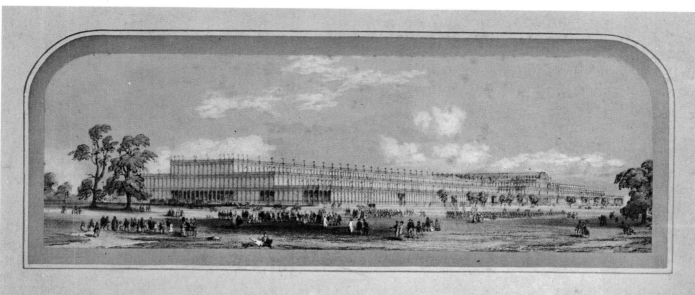

794

795

794 'The building for the Great Exhibition, 1851', published by Ackermann & Co., 1851. Lithograph, printed in six colours by Day & Son, mounted on card within a gold border with letterpress text beneath. Image, including letterpress, 142×253 mm. *Reading University Library.*

795 'Interior of the Great Exhibition', designed, printed, and published by George Baxter, 1851. Printed from one aquatint key plate and eleven relief blocks, mounted on card within a gold border. 155 × 334 mm. *Reading University Library.*

796 Detail of Plate 795. 80 ×, 100 mm.

796

797

798

797 Joseph Nash, 'The Great Industrial
Exhibition of 1851', published by
Dickinson Brothers, Plate 1, 'The
Inauguration'. Lithograph, printed in
colours and coloured by hand. 605 ×
755 mm. *Reading University Library*.

798 Detail of Plate 797. 105 × 135 mm.

THE GREAT INDUSTRIAL EXHIBITION OF 1851.

Plate 4 The Transept.

799

799 Joseph Nash, 'The Great Industrial Exhibition of 1851', published by Dickinson Brothers, Plate 4, 'The Transept'. Lithograph, printed in colours and coloured by hand. 612 × 754 mm. *Reading University Library*.

800 William Simpson, 'The Transept from the Grand Entrance', published by Ackermann & Co., 1851. Lithograph, printed in colours by Day & Son, with some hand-colouring. 357 × 464 mm. *Reading University Library*.

800

801

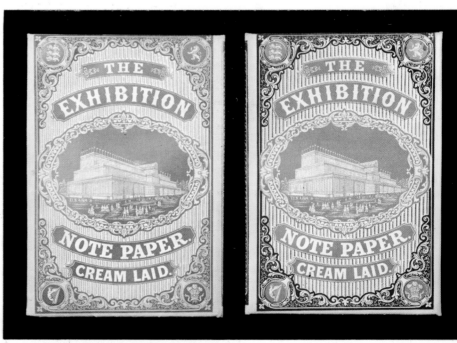

802

801 Stationery box with a view of the
Crystal Palace on its lid. Printed in
colours by lithography, with some hand-
colouring. 160 × 217 mm. *John Johnson
Collection.*

802 Great Exhibition note-paper packets.
Each lithographed in two colours. 182 ×
122 mm. *John Johnson Collection.*

803

804

805

806

807

803 Great Exhibition note-paper bearing steel-engraved view of the building, published by Harris Brothers, London. 176 × 115 mm. *John Johnson Collection.*

804 Cover of 'The Great Exhibition Songster', 1851. Letterpress, with wood-engraving, black on yellow paper, printed and published by W. S. Johnson, London. *John Johnson Collection.*

805 Music cover, 'Fantasia on airs of all nations, composed in honour of the Royal Exhibition for 1851'. Lithographed in colours by Stannard & Dixon, London. 360 × 265 mm. *Reading University Library.*

806, 807 Animated Christmas card with views of the Great Exhibition, shown closed and open. Chromolithographed. Size when open 105 × 92 mm. *Victoria & Albert Museum.*

808 Street ballad, 'How's your poor feet', c. 1851. Letterpress with wood-engraving, printed by W. S. Fortey at the Catnach Press, London. From a photograph in *Reading University Library.*

809 George Cruikshank, 'The first Shilling-day—going in. The first Shilling-day—coming out'. Etching. 264 × 194 mm. *Reading University Library.*

808

809

253

810

811

812

814

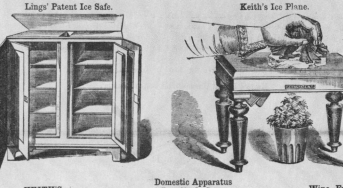

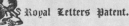

813

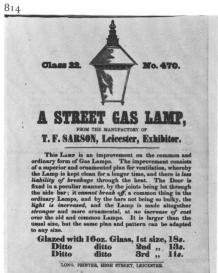

815

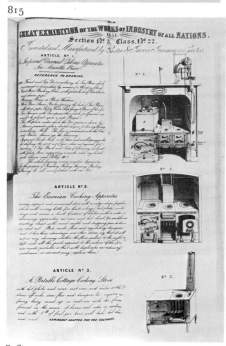

810-12 Trade catalogues issued at the Great Exhibition, 1851: *left*, letterpress, printed by Anthony Pickard, Leeds, 183 × 108 mm.; *centre*, letterpress and intaglio on green card, printed by John Wright, Bristol, 214 × 135 mm.; *right*, letterpress, printed on cream coated paper at the Thames Press, 206 × 130 mm. All from *Reading University Library*.

813 Trade advertisement issued at the Great Exhibition, 1851. Letterpress, with wood-engravings. 230 × 192 mm. *Reading University Library*.

814 Trade advertisement issued at the Great Exhibition, 1851. Letterpress, with wood-engravings, printed by C. Clark, Bath. 248 × 188 mm. *Reading University Library*.

815 Trade advertisement issued at the Great Exhibition, 1851. Letterpress, with wood-engraving, printed by Long, Leicester. 245 × 186 mm. *Reading University Library*.

816 Trade advertisement issued at the Great Exhibition, 1851. Lithographed by W. Spreat, Exeter. 440 × 280 mm. *Reading University Library*.

816

817

818

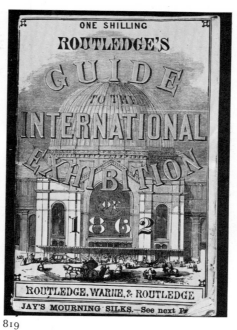

819

820

NOTICE TO EXHIBITORS.

No. 328.

Unless Exhibitors remove their straw and other inflammable materials, daily, at 4 o'clock, the Building will be closed at 3 o'clock, in order to give time to the Officers of Her Majesty's Commissioners to clear away the rubbish, the accumulation of which endangers the safety of the Building.

By order,

F. R. SANDFORD, General Manager.

821

INTERNATIONAL EXHIBITION. 1862.

Demand for Space.

822

823

817, 818 Season tickets for the International Exhibition, 1862. Printed in two colours by J. Biden, London. 47 × 87 mm. *John Johnson Collection.*

819 Cover of *Routledge's guide to the International Exhibition of 1862.* Wood-engraved, printed in red and black. 183 × 121 mm. *John Johnson Collection.*

820 John Leighton, advertisement produced for the International Exhibition, 1862, in the form of a certificate. Printed in colours by Bradbury, Wilkinson & Co., London. 463 × 387 mm. *John Johnson Collection.*

821 Notice to exhibitors at the International Exhibition of 1862. Letterpress. 325 × 490 mm. *Reading University Library.*

822 Form of demand for space at the International Exhibition of 1862, 1861. Letterpress, printed on blue paper by Eyre & Spottiswoode, London. 338 × 205 mm. *Reading University Library.*

823 Perforated form with receipt relating to season tickets for the International Exhibition of 1862. Letterpress, printed on pink paper. 122 × 300 mm. *Reading University Library.*

S

824

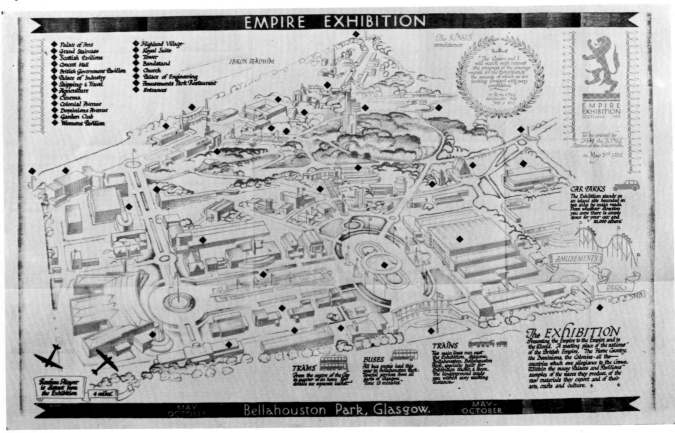

825

824 Plan of the British Empire Exhibition, Wembley, 1924, designed by Kennedy North, 1923. Lithography, printed in six colours by Dobson, Molle & Co. Ltd, Edinburgh, Liverpool, and London. 505 × 750 mm. *Reading University Library.*

825 Plan of the Empire Exhibition, Glasgow, 1938, signed HWW. Lithography, printed in three colours (letterpress on the reverse printed by McCorquodale, Glasgow). 508 × 758 mm. *Reading University Library.*

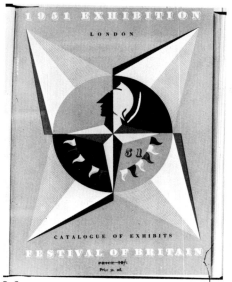

826

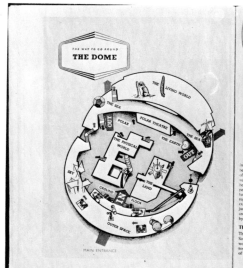

827

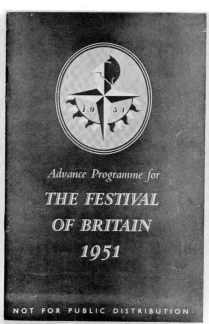

828

829

830

831

826, 827 Festival of Britain, South Bank Exhibition, *Catalogue of exhibits*, 1951. Cover design by Abram Games, printed by lithography in four colours by Fosh & Cross Ltd. Text pages designed by Will Carter and printed letterpress by McCorquodale & Co. Ltd. Page size 241 × 178 mm. *Reading University Library.*

828 Festival of Britain, South Bank Exhibition, *A guide to the story it tells*, by Ian Cox, 1951. Text pages designed by Will Carter, printed letterpress in two colours by Purnell & Sons Ltd. 235 × 175 mm. *Reading University Library.*

829 Cover of *Advance programme for the Festival of Britain 1951*. Letterpress, printed in orange by Sanders Phillips & Co. Ltd, London. 210 × 133 mm. *Reading University Library.*

830 Publicity brochure for the Festival of Britain, 1951, designed by London Press Exchange. Lithography, printed in three colours by Waterlow & Sons Ltd. 215 × 100 mm. *Reading University Library.*

831 Publicity brochure for the Festival of Britain, 1951, designed by London Press Exchange, with cover motif by Eric Fraser. Photogravure, printed in two colours by L. T. A. Robinson Ltd. 227 × 102 mm. *Reading University Library.*

832

833

834

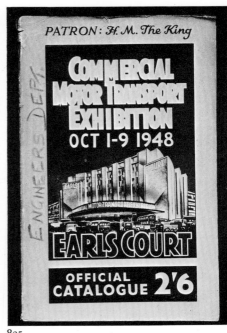

835

832 Complimentary season ticket for the Motor Exhibition, 1907. Letterpress, printed in black and green. 76 × 117 mm. *John Johnson Collection.*

833 Complimentary season ticket for the Commercial Motor Vehicle Exhibition, 1910. Letterpress, printed in green. 115 × 77 mm. *John Johnson Collection.*

834 Cover of catalogue of the International Motor Exhibition, 1938. Four-colour photolithography, printed at the Stanhope Press, Rochester. 235 × 143 mm. *Automobile Association.*

835 Cover of catalogue of the International Commercial Motor Transport Exhibition, 1948. Four-colour photolithography, printed at the Stanhope Press, Rochester. 235 × 150 mm. *Automobile Association.*

836 Invitation to Printers, Stationers & Paper Makers' Exhibition, 1881. Letterpress, printed in two colours by Field & Tuer, London. 141 × 173 mm. *John Johnson Collection.*

837 Invitation to the International Food Exhibition, 1881. Lithography, printed in green and red by Frederick Dangerfield, London. 110 × 158 mm. *John Johnson Collection.*

838 Season ticket for the Ideal Home Exhibition, 1925. Letterpress, printed in black and red. 67 × 90 mm. *John Johnson Collection.*

839 Exhibitor's season ticket for the British Industries Fair, 1930. Letterpress, printed in black and red on brown card. 122 × 77 mm. *John Johnson Collection.*

840 Invitation to exhibition of American packages of 1934. Letterpress, printed in red and blue, the carton produced by Wm W. Cleland Ltd, Belfast and London. 237 × 200 mm. *John Johnson Collection.*

836

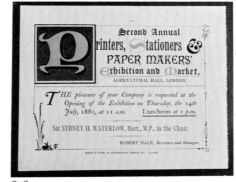

837

838

839

840

841

842

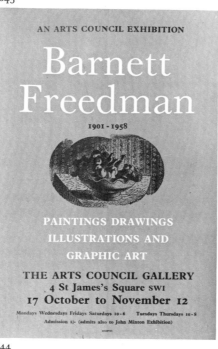

843

844

845

841 Exhibition notice, bears MS. date 1809. Letterpress, printed by Jones, London. 185 × 147 mm. *John Johnson Collection.*

842 Exhibition notice, bears MS. date 1839. Letterpress, printed by G. Stevens, London. 125 × 187 mm. *John Johnson Collection.*

843 Exhibition notice, 1862. Letterpress, printed in black on yellow paper. 745 × 500 mm. *John Johnson Collection.*

844 Exhibition poster, 1958. Silkscreen, printed in black and tan by the Shenval Press. 760 × 505 mm.

845 Exhibition poster, 1965. Designed by Ken Briggs and printed by silkscreen in orange and grey by J. & P. Atchison. 760 × 508 mm.

846

850

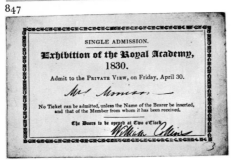

847

851

848

852

849

853

846 Exhibition ticket, 1761. Letterpress, printed two up. 55 × 140 mm. *John Johnson Collection.*

847 Exhibition ticket, 1763. Etching. 60 × 88 mm. *John Johnson Collection.*

848 Private view card, 1830. Letterpress, printed in blue. 86 × 126 mm. *John Johnson Collection.*

849 Private view card, *c.* 1850. Lithography. 106 × 153 mm. *John Johnson Collection.*

850 Private view card, *c.* 1840. Lithography, printed in four colours. 114 × 173 mm. *John Johnson Collection.*

851 Private view card, *c.* 1860. Lithography, printed in five colours. 120 × 182 mm. *John Johnson Collection.*

852 Private view card, 1860. Lithography. 88 × 125 mm. *John Johnson Collection.*

853 Invitation to exhibition. Letterpress, printed in red and black on antique card. 113 × 146 mm. *John Johnson Collection.*

854 Private view card, 1913. Letterpress, printed in grey and black. 122 × 156 mm. *John Johnson Collection.*

855 Private view card, 1914. Letterpress. 123 × 154 mm. *John Johnson Collection.*

856 Private view card, 1928. Letterpress, printed in grey and black. 116 × 139 mm. *John Johnson Collection.*

857 Private view card, *c.* 1933. Letterpress, printed in ochre and black. 113 × 150 mm. *John Johnson Collection.*

858 Private view card, 1936. Letterpress, printed in blue and black by Lund Humphries. 128 × 158 mm. *John Johnson Collection.*

859 Private view card, 1936. Letterpress, printed on antique lilac paper. 100 × 125 mm. *John Johnson Collection.*

860 Notice of exhibition, 1934. Designed by E. McKnight Kauffer, printed letterpress in black and blue by Lund Humphries. 165 × 300 mm. *John Johnson Collection.*

861 Private view card, 1934. Letterpress, printed in pale blue and black. 177 × 308 mm. *John Johnson Collection.*

862 Private view card, 1960. Letterpress, printed in black and tan on light blue card. 127 × 102 mm.

863 Private view card, 1966, front and back. Letterpress, printed in blue and orange and black and orange respectively. Diameter 185 mm.

854

855

856

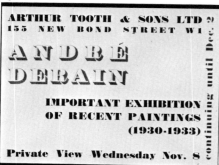

857

858

LONDON GROUP

We request the pleasure of your company at the Private View on Wednesday, November 11, at the New Burlington Galleries, Burlington Gardens, W.1, between 10 and 5. Exhibition closes November 28

34th Exhibition

859

AN EXHIBITION OF PHOTOGRAPHY BY MAN RAY AT LUND HUMPHRIES & CO LTD 12 BEDFORD SQUARE WC1
NOV 22–DEC 8 1934 ADMISSION FREE FROM 10-6

860

861

862

863

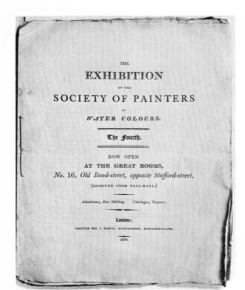

864

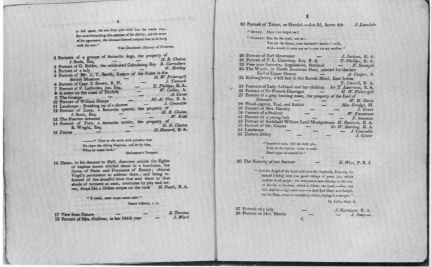

865

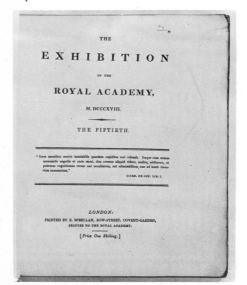

866

867

864, 865 Catalogue of the exhibition of the Society of Painters in Water Colours, London, 1808. Letterpress, printed by J. Barfield, London. Page size 255 × 202 mm. *John Johnson Collection.*

866, 867 Catalogue of the exhibition of the Royal Academy, London, 1818. Letterpress, printed by B. McMillan, London. Page size 248 × 204 mm. *John Johnson Collection.*

868 'Portraits of their Majesty's and the Royal Family viewing the exhibition of the Royal Academy, 1788.' Copperengraving by P. Martini. 357 × 497 mm. *Victoria & Albert Museum.*

868

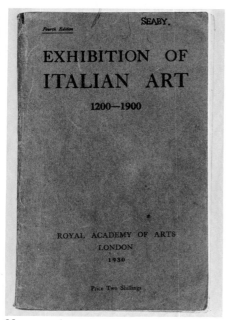

869

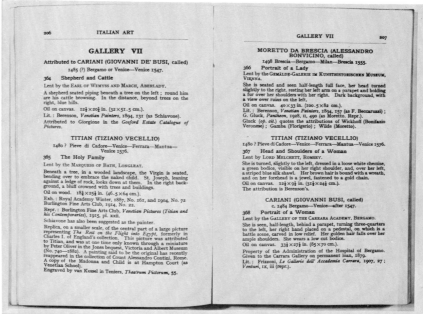

870

871

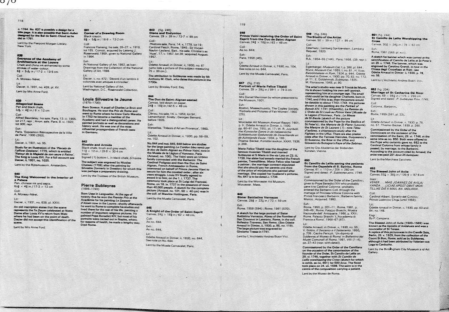

872

869, 870 Royal Academy of Arts catalogue,
Exhibition of Italian Art 1200-1900, London,
1930. Letterpress, the cover on green paper,
printed by William Clowes & Sons Ltd,
London. Page size 215 × 140 mm.

871, 872 Royal Academy of Arts Catalogue,
France in the eighteenth century, London, 1968.
Designed by Gordon House. Letterpress,
the cover in five colours, printed by the
Hillingdon Press, Uxbridge. Page size
300 × 209 mm.

873 Official guide to the National Art
Treasures Exhibition, Folkestone, 1886.
Printed in green by R. Turner, Dover.
212 × 137 mm. *John Johnson Collection.*

874 Catalogue of the tenth exhibition of
the London Group, 1919. Letterpress, the
motif designed by E. McKnight Kauffer.
204 × 129 mm. *John Johnson Collection.*

875 Catalogue of Arts Council exhibition
of work by Edward Lear, 1958. Letterpress, printed in purple and black by the
Curwen Press, London. 216 × 140 mm.

873

874

875

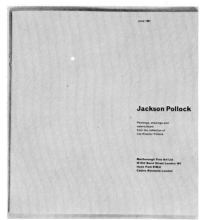

876

877

Landscape with figures

Oil on canvas on hardboard
7½ × 8 (sight measurements)

Possibly an industrial scene, though the thickness of the paint obscures specific detail. The simplified forms of the foreground figures may be connected with the undulating forms in No.5.

Untitled Painting c.1936

Oil on board 10½ × 16½
Exhibited:
Sidney Janis Gallery 1958
Reproduced:
Janis 1958 4
O'Hara 3
BR 106

At the time this painting was done (Lee Krasner estimates c.1936) it may not have seemed too far from Pollock's contemporary work. It could have been interpreted as a subjective marine (like *Seascape, BR* 104) or as a pseudo-Dantesque scene (*The Flame, BR* 103). With hindsight, however, the facture of this painting seems prophetic. Although there is a lingering pyramidal composition, Pollock shows himself able to establish forms wholly by means of paint. It is applied with a fat medium, so that the paint finds its own level, and, here and there, slight paint trails have been dropped. The paint, which is generally sluggish in the earlier paintings, takes on a mobility and sensuality that Pollock was to extend for the rest of his painting life. The painted area is irregularly filled; presumably cut from a larger board.

Drawing c.1935

Ink and gouache on paper.
10½ × 19½ (sight measurements)

Three drawings, contained by bounding lines, with sketches in the margins. The subject at left may be *Christ Carrying the Cross.* The central scene is not readable as a specific subject, but neither is it non-figurative. The implication of a dramatic figure or figures anticipates later black paintings, such as No.21, 1951 (repro *Parsons* 1951). The scene on the right is a cubist-type interior. The knotted rattlesnakes in the margins, as well as the profile with a feathered bonnet, recall Pollock's interest in American Indian art. The mixture of motives on this single sheet is characteristic of Pollock's wide ranging and feverish imagination.

'Panel' G c.1936
Oil on hardboard 4½ × 7½

Of the same piece or make of hardboard as Nos.8, 9, and 10, though not originally mounted with 8 and 9.
The central figure is in the traditional pose of a rider breaking in a horse, one arm stretched behind him holding his hat. The movement of the scene is expressed by staccato curves. Though more highly abstracted than Thomas Hart Benton, the basic idea of celebrating mid-Western subjects probably comes from Benton who 'translated the flame-like distortions of Tintoretto and el Greco into a simplified modern idiom which served admirably to express the romantic dynamism with which he viewed American life' (John I. H. Baur, *Revolution and Tradition in American Art,* Harvard University Press, 1951, p40).

'Panel' A c.1936
Oil on hardboard 7½ × 4½ (sight measurements)
Exhibited:
Sidney Janis Gallery 1958
Reproduced:
Janis 1958 3 (as first on left of a group of four paintings described as a panel, though, in fact, on hardboard).
Arts. William Rubin. *Notes on Masson and Pollock.* 34. 2. 1959 (as one of a group).
BR 108 (as one of a group).

One of a series of paintings originally done on a single piece of hardboard. On several occasions Pollock painted runs of pictures on one board or canvas (see Nos. 53 and 57). Subject problematic. Lee Krasner Pollock considers it might be a 'male and female' subject. My reading tends towards a simplified figure bent over a desk or apparatus. Given Pollock's romantic interests an alchemist (?) may be intended or an image of research (?) influenced by the themes of Mexican murals. At any rate, the painting seems provocative of meanings, rather than purely non-figurative.

'Panel' B c.1936
Oil on hardboard 7½ × 5½
Exhibited:
Sidney Janis Gallery 1958
Reproduced:
Janis 1958 3 (as second from left of a group of four paintings).
Arts. 34. 2. 1959 (as one of a group).
BR 108 (as one of a group).

878

880

876-8 Marlborough Fine Art Ltd, catalogue of exhibition of work by Jackson Pollock, 1961. Designed by Herbert Spencer. Letterpress, the cover on buff card, printed by Tillotsons (Bolton) Ltd, London and Bolton. Page size 229 × 210 mm.

879, 880 Exhibition catalogue, *Painting & sculpture of a decade,* 1964. Designed by Edward Wright and Robin Fior. Lithography, printed by the Shenval Press Ltd, London, Hertford, and Harlow, the cover in four-colour half-tone. 254 × 190 mm.

879

Select bibliography

Index of illustrations

General index

Select bibliography

The sections of this bibliography follow fairly closely the chapter divisions of the book. Works are listed once only; at the end of each section references are given to the most relevant items in other sections

In general, articles in *Penrose Annual* are not included since a checklist of them has recently been published (*See* **Bibliographies,** Taylor)

Bibliographies

Bigmore, E. C., and Wyman, C. W. H., *A bibliography of printing*, 3 vols, London, 1880-6

Bland, D., *A bibliography of book illustration (The book, number 4)*, London, 1955

Gaskell, P., Barber, G., and Warrilow, G., 'An annotated list of printers' manuals to 1850', *Journal of the Printing Historical Society*, no. 4, 1968, pp. 11-32

Handover, P. M., 'A handlist of the writings of Stanley Morison, 1950-1959', *Motif*, no. 3, 1959, pp. 51-7

Hassall, J., *Wood engraving: a reader's guide*, London, 1949

Howe, E., 'Bibliotheca typographica', *Signature*, new series, no. 10, 1950, pp. 49-64

Kampmann, C., *Die Literatur der Lithographie von 1798-1898*, Vienna, 1899

Levis, H. C., *A descriptive bibliography of the most important books in the English language relating to the art & history of engraving and the collecting of prints*, London, 1912

Newberry Library, *Dictionary catalogue of the history of printing from the John M. Wing Foundation in the Newberry Library*, 6 vols, Boston, 1961

Overton, J., *A bibliography of paper and paper-making (The book, number 3)*, London, 1955

St Bride Foundation, *Catalogue of the periodicals relating to printing and allied subjects in the technical library of St Bride Institute*, London, 1950

—, *Catalogue of the technical reference library of works on printing and the allied arts*, London, 1919

Singer, H. W., and Strang, W., *Etching, engraving and the other methods of printing pictures*, London, 1897 (Bibliography, pp. 188-219)

Spencer, H., *The visible word*, London, 1968 (Bibliography of works relating to legibility, pp. 77-99)

Taylor, J., 'A checklist of Penrose articles 1895-1968', *Penrose Annual*, vol. 62, 1969, pp. 253-92

Ulrich, C. F., and Küp, K., *Books and printing: a selected list of periodicals, 1800-1942*, New York, 1943

Watson, G. (ed.), *The new Cambridge bibliography of English literature*, vol. 3, 1800-1900, Cambridge, 1969 (Book production and distribution, cols 25-90)

Williamson, H., *Book typography: a handlist for book designers (The book, number 1)*, London, 1955

General

An adept of 35 years' experience, *Publicity. An essay on advertising*, London, 1878

Alford, B. W. E., 'Business enterprise and the growth of the commercial letterpress printing industry, 1850-1914', *Business History*, vol. vii, no. 1, January 1965, pp. 1-14

—, 'Government expenditure and the growth of the printing industry in the nineteenth century', *Economic History Review*, 2nd series, vol. xvii, no. 1, 1964, pp. 96-112

Altick, R. D., *The English common reader: a social history of the mass reading public 1800-1900*, Chicago, 1957

Ashton, T. S., *The industrial revolution, 1760-1830*, London, 1948

Aspinall, A., *Politics and the press c.1780-1850*, London, 1949

Bain, I., 'James Moyes and his Temple Printing Office of 1825', *Journal of the Printing Historical Society*, no. 4, 1968, pp. 1-10

Barnes, J. J., *Free trade in books: a study of the London book trade since 1800*, Oxford, 1964

Bensusan, G., *The benevolent years: some notes on the Printers' Pension Corporation and its background in the trade*, London, 1955

Berry, W. T., and Poole, H. E., *Annals of printing: a chronological encyclopaedia from the earliest times to 1950*, London, 1966

British Federation of Master Printers, *Economic study of the printing industry*, London, 1965

Clair, C., *A chronology of printing*, London, 1969

—, *A history of printing in Britain*, London, 1965

Collet, C. D., *History of the taxes on knowledge*, 2 vols, London, 1899

Curtis, S. J., *History of education in Great Britain*, London, 1948 (4th ed. 1957)

Delafons, A., *The structure of the printing industry*, London, 1965

Glaister, G. A., *Glossary of the book*, London, 1960

Handover, P. M., *Printing in London from 1476 to modern times*, London, 1960

Hartwell, R. M., 'The causes of the industrial revolution. An essay in methodology', *Economic History Review*, 2nd series, vol. xviii, no. 1, 1965, pp. 164-82

Howe, E., 'The Hansard family', *Signature*, new series, no. 6, 1948, pp. 19-35

—, *The London compositor; documents relating to wages, working conditions and customs of the London printing trade 1785-1900*, London, 1947

—, '*The trade*'; passages from the literature of the printing craft 1550-1935, London, 1943

Isaac, P. C. G., and Watson, W. M., 'The history of the book trade in the North: a review of a research project', *Journal of the Printing Historical Society*, no. 4, 1968, pp. 87-98

Johnson, J., *The printer, his customers and his men*, London, 1933

Kendall, M. G. (ed.), *The sources and nature of the statistics of the United Kingdom*, 2 vols, London, 1952-7: Deane, M., 'Publishing', vol. 1, pp. 331-52

Klingender, F. D., *Art and the industrial revolution*, London, 1947

Lang, P. H., 'Charles Knight and "The art of printing"', *Printing Review*, vol. 8, no. 4, 1939, pp. 926-30

Luckhurst, K. W., *The story of exhibitions*, London and New York, 1951

McMurtrie, D. C., *The book: the story of printing & bookmaking*, 3rd ed., Oxford University Press, 1943

Marrot, H. V., 'William Bulmer', *The Fleuron*, no. 5, 1926, pp. 63-91

Meynell, F., *English printed books*, London, 1946

Minto, J., *A history of the public library movement in Great Britain and Ireland*, London, 1932

Moran, J., *Natsopa seventy-five years: The National Society of Operative Printers and Assistants (1889-1964)*, London, 1964

Morison, S., *The English newspaper; some account of the physical development of journals printed in London between 1622 & the present-day*, Cambridge, 1932

—, *Four centuries of fine printing*, London, 1924 (Revised octavo ed. 1949)

—, *John Bell, 1745-1831*, Cambridge, 1930

Munford, W. A., *Penny rate: aspects of British public library history 1850-1950*, London, 1951

Musson, A. E., *The Typographical Association*, London, 1954

Plant, M., *The English book trade. An economic history of the making and sale of books*, London, 1939 (2nd ed. 1965)

Plomer, H. R., *A short history of English printing 1476-1898*, London, 1900 (2nd ed. 1915)

Printing and the mind of man, catalogue of the exhibitions at the British Museum and at Earls Court, London, 1963

Sampson, H., *A history of advertising from the earliest times*, London, 1874

Smith, C. M., *The working man's way in the world*, reprinted from the third issue of 1857, with a preface and notes by Ellic Howe, London, Printing Historical Society, 1967

Smith, W., *Advertise. How? When? Where?* London, 1863

Smith, W. O. L., *Education in Great Britain*, London, 1949 (2nd ed. 1956)

Steinberg, S. H., *Five hundred years of printing*, Penguin Books, 1955 (2nd ed. 1961)

Stutterheim, K. von, *The press in England*, translated by W. H. Johnston, London, 1934

Swan Electric Engraving Co., *Progress of British newspapers in the nineteenth century, illustrated*, London, n.d. [c. 1901]

The Times, Printing in the twentieth century, reprinted from the special number of *The Times*, 29 October 1929, London, 1930

The Times Literary Supplement, Printing Number, 13 October 1927

The Times printing number, reprinted from the 40,000th issue of *The Times*, 10 September 1912, London, 1912

Trevelyan, G. M., *British history in the nineteenth century and after*, London, 1922 and 1937 (Penguin Books, 1965)

—, *Illustrated English social history. Volume four: the nineteenth century*, London, 1949-52 (Penguin Books, 1964)

Turner, E. J., *The shocking history of advertising*, London, 1952

Webb, R. K., *The British working class reader, 1780-1848*, London, 1955

Williamson, H., *Methods of book design*, London, 1956 (2nd ed. 1966)

Young, G. M., *Victorian England, portrait of an age*, London, 1936

Jobbing and other ephemeral printing

Alderson, F., *The comic postcard in English life*, Newton Abbot, 1970.

Allsop, J. C., 'Tram ticket typography', *Typography*, no. 2, 1937, pp. 23-5

Ballinger, J., *Gleanings from a printer's file*, Aberystwyth, 1928

Barman, C., 'Timetable typography', *Typography*, no. 5, 1938, pp. 9-17

Beaujon, P., 'Job printing', *Curwen Press Newsletter*, no. 12, 1936

Buday, G., *The history of the Christmas card*, London, 1954

—, *The story of the Christmas card*, London, [1951]

Carline, R., *Pictures in the post, the story of the picture postcard*, Bedford, 1959

Daish, A. N., *Printers' pride; the house of Yelf at Newport, Isle of Wight, 1816-1966*, Newport, 1967

Davis, A., *Package and print: the development of container and label design*, London, 1968

—, 'Printers on their metal', *British Printer*, vol. 83, no. 1, 1970, pp. 80-3

Ettlinger, L. D., and Holloway, R. G., *Compliments of the Season*, London, 1947

Gould, A., 'Protest by design', *Typographica*, new series, no. 14, 1966, pp. 41-56

Heal, A., '17th-century booksellers' and stationers' trade cards', *Alphabet and Image*, no. 8, 1948, pp. 51-62

Hussey, C., 'Pictorial note-paper', *Country Life*, 30 March 1945, pp. 550-1

Imeson, W. E., *Illustrated music-titles and their delineators*, London, 1912

Isaac, P. C. G., *William Davison of Alnwick: pharmacist and printer, 1781-1858*, Oxford, 1968

—, 'William Davison of Alnwick, pharmacist and printer', *The Library*, 5th series, vol. xxiv, no. 1, March 1969, pp. 1-32

Jackson, H., 'A sanctuary of printing: the record room at the University Press, Oxford', *Signature*, no. 1, 1935, pp. 1-23

Johnson, J., 'The development of printing, other than book-printing', *The Library*, 4th series, vol. xvii, no. 1, June 1936, pp. 22-35

Katin, L., 'One hundred years of Bradshaw', *Printing Review*, vol. 8, no. 2, 1939, pp. 863-5
King, A. Hyatt, 'English pictorial music title-pages 1820-1885. Their style, evolution, and importance', *The Library*, 5th series, vol. iv, no. 4, March 1950, pp. 262-72
—, 'Some Victorian illustrated music titles', *Penrose Annual*, vol. 46, 1952, pp. 43-5
Knaster, R., 'Paper-valentines', *Typography*, no. 4, 1937, pp. 13-17
—, 'Watchpapers: a neglected conceit', *Alphabet and Image*, no. 7, 1948, pp. 26-32
Lang, P. H., 'An aspect of nineteenth-century French jobbing, with special reference to a collection of pieces in the possession of Mr Ellic Howe', *Signature*, no. 11, 1939, pp. 44-54
Lee, R.W., *A history of valentines*, Batsford, 1953
Lewis, J., 'In pursuit of ephemera', *Motif*, no. 7, 1961, pp. 84, 89
—, *Printed ephemera*, Ipswich, 1962 (2nd ed., London, 1969)
Museum Street Galleries, exhibition catalogue, *The art of Alfred Concanen*, London, 1962
Nuttall, D., *A history of printing in Chester from 1688 to 1965*, Chester, 1969
Orwell, G., 'The art of Donald McGill', *Horizon*, vol. iv, no. 21, September 1941, pp. 153-63
Pickard, P., 'The history of the letterhead', *Printing Review*, vol. 75, Autumn 1957, pp. 5-20
Rickards, M., *Posters at the turn of the century*, London, 1968
—, *Posters of the First World War*, London, 1968
—, *Posters of the nineteen-twenties*, London, 1968
Ridler, V., 'Desiderata for the sanctuary of printing, The University Press, Oxford', *Signature*, no. 5, 1937, pp. 39-47
Righyni, S. L., 'News bills: a retrospectus', *Alphabet and Image*, no. 2, 1946, pp. 34-49
Schuwer, P., *Histoire de la publicité*, Geneva, 1965
Scott, W. J., *All about postcards*, Leeds, 1903
Speaight, G., *Juvenile drama; the history of the English toy theatre*, London, 1946
Staff, F., *The penny post, 1680-1918*, London, 1966
—, *The picture postcard & its origins*, London, 1966
—, *The valentine & its origins*, London, 1969
Tracy, W., 'Telephone directories', *Typographica*, no. 15, pp. 4-15
Twyman, M., *John Soulby, printer, Ulverston*, Reading, 1966
White, G., *Christmas cards and their chief designers* (*Studio* special number, 1894)
See also
General: Handover, Sampson, Smith, W., Turner
Design: survivals and new approaches: Kauffer, Spencer (1952)

New processes

Bain, I., 'Thomas Ross & Son, copper- and steel-plate printers since 1833', *Journal of the Printing Historical Society*, no. 2, 1966, pp. 3-22
Bankes, H., *Lithography; or, the art of making drawings on stone, for the purpose of being multiplied by printing*, Bath, 1813 (2nd ed., London, 1816)
Bathe, G. and D., *Jacob Perkins, his inventions, his times and his contemporaries*, Philadelphia, 1943
Berthiaud and Boitard, *Nouveau manuel complet de l'imprimeur en taille douce*, Paris, 1837
Biggs, J. R., *Illustration and reproduction*, London, 1951
Blaney, H. R., *Photogravure*, New York, 1895
Bliss, D. P., *A history of wood-engraving*, London, 1928 (reprinted 1964)
Bradbury, H., *Nature printing: its origins and objects*, London, 1856
Brunner, F., *A handbook of graphic reproduction processes*, London, 1962
Burton, W. K., *Practical guide to photographic and photo-mechanical printing*, London, 1892
Chatto, W. A., and Jackson, J., *A treatise on wood engraving, historical and practical*, London, 1839 (2nd ed. 1861)
Chelsum, J., *A history of the art of engraving in mezzotinto*, Winchester, 1786
Curwen, H., *Processes of graphic reproduction in printing*, 3rd ed. revised by Charles Mayo, London, 1963
De la Motte, P., *On the various applications of anastatic printing and papyrography*, London, 1849
Deleschamps, P., *Traité complet de la gravure*, Paris, 1836
Denison, H., *A treatise on photogravure in intaglio*, London, [1895]
Donlevy, J., *The rise and progress of the graphic arts*, New York, 1854
Duchochois, P. C., *Photographic reproduction processes*, London, 1892
Farquhar, H. D., *The grammar of photo-engraving*, New York, 1893
Federation of Master Process Engravers, *The process engraver's compendium*, London, [*c.* 1932]
Fielding, T. H., *The art of engraving, with the various modes of operation*, London, 1841 (2nd ed. 1844)
Gamble, C. W., *Modern illustration processes: an introductory textbook for all students of printing methods*, 3rd ed., London, 1950
Goodman, J., *Practical modern metalithography*, Letchworth, 1914
Griffits, T. E., *The rudiments of lithography*, London, 1956
Halbmeier, C., *The history of lithography*, New York, 1926
Hamerton, P. G., *The graphic arts, a treatise on the varieties of drawing, painting, and engraving, in comparison with each other and with nature*, London, 1882
Harper, C. G., *A practical handbook of drawing for modern methods of reproduction*, London, 1894 (2nd ed. 1901)
Harris, E. M., *Experimental graphic processes in England 1800-1859*, Ph.D. thesis, Reading University, 1965
—, 'Experimental graphic processes in England 1800-1859', *Journal of the Printing Historical Society*, no. 4, 1968, pp. 33-86, no. 5, 1969, pp. 41-80 (to be continued in no. 6)
Hayter, S. W., *New ways of gravure*, 2nd ed., London, 1966
Hind, A. M., *An introduction to a history of woodcut*, London, 1935 (reprinted New York, 1963)
—, *A short history of engraving and etching*, London, 1908 (3rd ed. 1923, reprinted New York, 1963)
—, *The processes and schools of engraving*, 4th ed., London, 1952
Hodgson, T., *An essay on the origin and progress of stereotype printing*, Newcastle-upon-Tyne, 1820
Hullmandel, C., *The art of drawing on stone*, London, 1824 (2nd ed. 1833, 3rd ed. 1835)
Kainen, J., *The development of the halftone screen*, Washington, 1952 (from the Smithsonian Report for 1951, pp. 409-25)
—, *Why Bewick succeeded: a note in the history of wood engraving*, United States National Museum, Bulletin 218, Washington, 1959
Landseer, J., *Lectures on the art of engraving, delivered at the Royal Institution of Great Britain*, London, 1807
Library of the Fine Arts, 'History and processes of lithography', vol. i, no. 1, February, 1831, pp. 44-58; 'A view of the present state of lithography in England', vol. i, no. 3, April 1831, pp. 201-16
Linton, W. J., *Wood-engraving, a manual of instruction*, London, 1884
Mackenzie, A. D., *The Bank of England note, a history of its printing*, Cambridge, 1953
Palmer, E., *Glyphography or engraved drawing, for printing at the type press after the manner of wood-cuts*, London, 1843 (2nd ed. 1843, 3rd ed. 1844)
Partington, C. F., *The engravers' complete guide*, London, 1825
Pennell, J. and E. R., *Lithography and lithographers, some chapters in the history of the art*, London, 1898 (2nd ed. 1915)
Perrot, A. M., *Nouveau manuel de gravure*, Paris, 1844
Pring, J. A., *An account of a method of etching or engraving by means of voltaic electricity*, London, 1843
Richmond, W. D., *The grammar of lithography*, London, 1878 (numerous later editions)
Sampson, T., *Electrotint*, London, 1842
Schnauss, J., *Collotype and photo-lithography*, translated by E. C. Middleton, London, 1889
Schoenberg, L., *Metallic engravings in relief for letterpress printing being a greatly improved substitute for wood engraving called acrography*, London, 1842
Senefelder, A., *A complete course of lithography*, London, 1819
Short, F., *The making of etchings*, London, 1888
Singer, H. W., and Strang, W., *Etching, engraving and the other methods of printing pictures*, London, 1897
Smee, A., *Elements of electro-metallurgy*, London, 1841 (2nd ed. 1843, 3rd ed. 1851)
Smith, W. J., Turner, E. L., and Hallam, C. D., *Photo-engraving in relief*, London, 1932
Stannard, W. J., *The art exemplar*, London, [*c.* 1859]
Trivick, H. H., *Autolithography, the technique*, London, 1960
Twyman, M., *Lithography 1800-1850: the techniques of drawing on stone in England and France and their application in works of topography*, London, 1970
Verfasser, J., *The half-tone process*, Bradford, 1894 (5th ed., London, 1912)
Verry, H. R., *Document copying and reproduction processes*, London, 1958
Watt, P. B., 'Early English lithography', *The Artist*, May 1896, pp. 224-6
Weber, W., *A history of lithography*, London, 1966
Wilkinson, W. T., *Photo-engraving, photo-litho, collotype and photogravure*, 5th ed., 1894
Williams, W. S., 'On lithography', *Transactions of the Society for the Encouragement of Arts, Manufactures, and Commerce*, London, 1847-8, pp. 226-50
Woods, H. T., *Modern methods of illustrating books*, London, 1887
See also
From craft to technology: Legros and Grant, *Printing patents*
Pictures into print: Abbey, Blackburn, Dalziel, Gernsheim (1955), Hayter, Lewis and Smith, Linton, Man (1963), Prideaux, Spielmann, Weekley

Colour printing

Bloy, C. H., *A history of printing ink, balls and rollers 1440-1850*, London, 1967
Burch, R. M., *Colour printing and colour printers*, 2nd ed., London, 1910
Chevreul, M. E., *The principles of harmony and contrast of colours, and their applications to the arts*, translated from the French by Charles Martel, 2nd ed., London, 1855
Docker, A., *The colour prints of William Dickes*, London, 1924
Frankau, J., *Eighteenth century colour prints*, London, 1900 (2nd ed. 1906)
Gower, L. G., 'How a chromo-lithograph is printed', *Strand Magazine*, vol. 27, January 1904, pp. 33-9
Gray, N., 'The nineteenth-century chromo-lithograph', *Architectural Review*, vol. 84, 1938, pp. 177-8, 187
Griffits, T. E., *Colour printing*, London, 1948
—, 'The Lyons lithographs', *Printing Review*, vol. 16, no. 57, 1951-2, pp. 32-4
—, *The technique of colour printing by lithography*, 2nd ed., London, 1944
Hardie, M., *English coloured books*, London, 1906
Harris, E. M., *Sir William Congreve and his compound-plate printing*, United States National Museum, Bulletin 252, Washington, 1967
Kainen, J., *John Baptist Jackson: 18th-century master of the color woodcut*, United States National Museum, Bulletin 222, Washington, 1962
Lang, L., 'Godefroy Engelmann de Mulhouse, imprimeur lithographe', *Trois siècles d'art alsacien*, Strasbourg and Paris, 1948, pp. 159-87
Lewis, C. T. C., *George Baxter, the picture printer*, London, [1924]
—, *The story of picture printing in England during the nineteenth century*, London, n.d.
McLean, R., *The reminiscences of Edmund Evans*, Oxford, 1967
—, *Victorian book design & colour printing*, London, 1963
Mellerio, A., *La lithographie en couleurs*, Paris, 1898
Savage, W., *On the preparation of printing ink: both black and coloured*, London, 1832
—, *Practical hints on decorative printing*, London, 1822
Tooley, R. V., *English books, with coloured plates, 1790-1860*, 2nd ed., London, 1954
Twyman, M., 'The tinted lithograph', *Journal of the Printing Historical Society*, no. 1, 1965, pp. 39-56
See also
New processes: Hayter, Weber
Pictures into print: Gray, Hayter, Lewis and Smith

From craft to technology

Babbage, C., *On the economy of machinery and manufactures*, London, 1832
Birkbeck, J. A., 'How machine-cast type became accepted by British printers', *British Printer*, vol. 83, no. 1, 1970, pp. 61-3
Bluhm, A., *Photosetting*, Oxford, 1968
Bowden, B. V. (ed.), *Faster than thought: a symposium on digital computing machines*, London, 1953
Clapperton, R. H., *Modern paper-making*, 3rd ed., Oxford, 1952
—, *Paper. An historical account of its making by hand from the earliest times down to the present day*, Oxford, 1934
—, *The paper-making machine, its invention, evolution and development*, Oxford, 1967
Coleman, D. C., *The British paper industry 1495-1860*, Oxford, 1958
Duncan, C. J., 'Look! No hands!', *Penrose Annual*, vol. 57, 1964, pp. 121-67
Elliott, R. C., 'The "Monotype" from infancy to maturity', *Monotype Recorder*, vol. 31, no. 243, 1932
Evans, J., *The endless web: John Dickinson & Co. Ltd 1804-1954*, London, 1955
Exhibition of the works of industry of all nations, 1851, *Reports by the juries*, London, 1852, pp. 396-455
Faulmann, K., *Illustrirte Geschichte der Buchdruckerkunst*, Vienna, 1882
Green, R., *History of the platen jobber*, Chicago (Ill.), 1953
Hansard, T. C., *Typographia*, London, 1825

Hart, H., *Charles Earl Stanhope and the Oxford University Press* (reprinted from *Collectanea*, 111, 1896, of the Oxford Historical Society, with notes by James Mosley), London, Printing Historical Society, 1966

[Hoe & Co.], *A short history of the printing press* (issued by the firm of Hoe), New York, 1902

Howe, E., 'Newspaper printing in the nineteenth century', *Alphabet and Image*, no. 4, 1947, pp. 5-31

—, 'The typecasters', *Monotype Recorder*, vol. 41, no. 1, 1957

—, 'Typefounding and mechanical typesetting in the nineteenth century', *Typography*, no. 2, 1937, pp. 5-12

Hunter, D., *Papermaking: the history and technique of an ancient craft*, 2nd ed., London, 1947

Huss, R. E., 'A chronological list of type-setting machines and ancillary equipment, 1822-1925', *Journal of Typographic Research*, vol. 1, no. 3, 1967, pp. 245-74

Isaacs, G., *The story of the newspaper printing press*, London, 1931

Johnson, J., *Typographia*, London, 1824

Kainen, J., *George Clymer and the Columbian press*, New York, 1950

Legros, L. A., and Grant, J. C., *Typographical printing surfaces: the technology and mechanism of their production*, London, 1916

McIntosh, A., *Typewriter composition and standardization in information printing*, together with the technical supplement, *Typewriter composition*, Old Woking, 1965

Maddox, H. A., 'The offset method of printing', *The Imprint*, vol. 2, 1913, pp. 30-6

Mengel, W., *Ottmar Mergenthaler and the printing revolution*, Brooklyn, New York, 1954

Monotype Newsletter, special film-setting number, no. 62, August 1961

Moran, J., 'An assessment of Mackie's steam type-composing machine', *Journal of the Printing Historical Society*, no. 1, 1965, pp. 57-67

—, 'The Columbian press', *Journal of the Printing Historical Society*, no. 5, 1969, pp. 1-23

—, *The composition of reading matter*, London, 1965

Mosley, J., 'The press in the parlour: some notes on the amateur printer and his equipment', *Black Art*, vol. 2, no. 1, Spring 1963, pp. 2-16

Munson, J. H., 'Computer recognition of hand-printed text', *Journal of Typographic Research*, vol. 3, no. 1, 1969, pp. 31-61

Musson, A. E., 'Newspaper printing in the industrial revolution', *Economic History Review*, 2nd series, vol. x, no. 3, 1958, pp. 411-26

Penny Magazine, vol. 2, 1833, 'The commercial history of a Penny Magazine': I, Papermaking, pp. 377-84; II, Wood-cutting and type-founding, pp. 417-24; III, Compositors' work and stereotyping, pp. 465-72; IV, Printing presses and machinery—Bookbinding, pp.505-11

Phillips, A. H., *Computer peripherals and typesetting*, London, 1968

Pollard, G., 'Notes on the size of the sheet', *The Library*, 4th series, vol. xxii, no. 2, 3, September-December 1941, pp. 105-37

Powell, D. T., 'Offset and offset machinery', *The Imprint*, vol. 1, 1913, pp. 212-22

Printing patents: abridgements of patent specifications relating to printing, 1617-1857, reprinted with a prefatory note by James Harrison, London, Printing Historical Society, 1969

Richards, G. T., *The history and development of typewriters*, London, HMSO, 1964

Ringwalt, J. L., *American encyclopaedia of printing*, Philadelphia, 1871

Rosner, C., *Printer's progress: a comparative survey of the craft of printing 1851-1951*, London, 1951

Savage, W., *A dictionary of the art of printing*, London, 1841

Singer, C. (ed., with others), *A history of technology*, Oxford, 1954-8, vol. v, 'Printing and related trades', pp. 683-715, by W. Turner Berry

Southward, J., *Progress in printing and the graphic arts during the Victorian era*, London, 1897

Stone, R., 'The Albion press', *Journal of the Printing Historical Society*, no. 2, 1966, pp. 58-73

Stower, C., *The printer's grammar*, London, 1808

Tarr, J. C., *Printing to-day*, London, 1945 (2nd ed. 1949)

Thompson, J. S., *History of composing machines*, Chicago, 1904

[*The Times*], *The history of 'The Times'*, 3 vols, London, 1935-47

—, *A newspaper history 1785-1935* (reprinted from the 150th anniversary number of *The Times*, 1 January 1935), London, 1935

—, *Printing 'The Times' since 1785. Some account of the means of production and changes of dress of the newspaper*, London, 1953

Tomlinson, C. (ed.), *Cyclopaedia of useful arts*, London, 1854, vol. ii, 'Printing', pp. 471-508

Twyman, M., 'The lithographic hand press 1796-1850', *Journal of the Printing Historical Society*, no. 3, 1967, pp. 3-50

Wallis, L. W., 'Filmsetting in focus', *Monotype Recorder*, vol. 43, no. 2, 1965

Wilson, F. J. F., and Grey, D., *A practical treatise upon modern printing machinery and letterpress printing*, London, 1888

See also

General: Howe (1943), *Printing and the mind of man*

New processes: Goodman

Colour printing: Bloy

Design: survivals and new approaches: Society of Industrial Artists and Designers

Types and other letterforms

Bartram, A., 'Reading by machine', *Typographica*, new series, no. 5, 1962, pp. 3-11

—, 'Typewriter type faces', *Typographica*, new series, no. 6, 1962, pp. 42-60

Beaujon, P., 'Eric Gill: sculptor of letters', *The Fleuron*, no. 7, 1930, pp. 27-59

Berry, W. T., and Johnson, A. F., *Catalogue of specimens of printing types by English and Scottish foundries, 1665-1830*, London, 1935

—, 'A note on the literature of British type specimens with a supplement to the *Catalogue of specimens of printing types by English and Scottish printers and founders 1665-1830*', *Signature*, new series, no. 16, 1952, pp. 29-40

—, and Jaspert, W. P., *The encyclopaedia of type faces*, 3rd ed., revised and enlarged, London, 1962

Biggs, J. R., *An approach to type*, London, 1949

British Computer Society, *Character recognition*, London, 1967

Burgess, F., 'Tombstone lettering on slates', *Typographica*, new series, no. 13, 1966, pp. 3-19

Burt, C., *A psychological study of typography*, London, 1959

Callingham, J., *Sign-writing and glass embossing*, London, 1871

Carter, J., 'The woodcut calligraphy of Reynolds Stone', *Signature*, no. 2, 1936, pp. 21-8

Cheetham, D., and Grimbly, B., 'Design analysis: typeface', *Design*, 186, 1964, pp. 61-71

—, and Poulton, E. C., 'The case for research', *Design*, 195, pp. 48-51

Day, L. F., *Alphabets old & new*, London, 1898

Dowding, G., *Factors in the choice of type faces*, London, 1957

Dowding, G., *An introduction to the history of printing types*, London, 1961

Dreyfus, J., *The work of Jan van Krimpen*, London, 1952

Fairbank, A., *A book of scripts*, Penguin Books, 1949

Frutiger, A., 'OCR-B: a standardized character for optical recognition', *Typographische Monatsblätter*, January 1967, pp. 29-36

—, 'Typography with the IBM Selectric Composer', *Journal of Typographic Research*, vol. 1, no. 3, 1967, pp. 285-92

—, with Delamarre, N., and Gürtler, A., 'OCR-B: a standardized character for optical recognition', *Journal of Typographic Research*, vol. 1, no 2, 1967, pp. 137-46

Gill, E., *Autobiography*, London, 1944

Gray, N., 'Berthold Wolpe', *Signature*, no. 15, 1940, pp. 20-7

—, 'David Jones and the art of lettering', *Motif*, no. 7, 1961, pp. 69-80

—, *Lettering on buildings*, London, 1960

—, *19th century ornamented types and title pages*, London, 1938 (2nd impression 1951)

Handover, P. M., 'Black serif. The career of the nineteenth-century's versatile invention: the slab-seriffed letter design', *Motif*, no. 12, 1964, pp. 79-89

—, 'Grotesque letters: a history of unseriffed type faces from 1816 to the present day', *Monotype Newsletter*, no. 69, March 1963

—, 'Letters without serifs', *Motif*, no. 6, 1961, pp. 66-81

Harling, R., 'An account of the LNER type standardisation', *Monotype Recorder*, vol. 32, no. 4, 1933

—, 'The story of Gill Sans', *Monotype Recorder*, vol. 34, no. 4, 1935

—, 'The type designs of Eric Gill', *Alphabet and Image*, no. 6, 1948, pp. 55-69

Johnson, A. F., 'The evolution of the modern-face roman', *The Library*, 4th series, vol. xi, no. 3, December 1930, pp. 353-77

—, 'Fat-faces: their history, forms and use', *Alphabet and Image*, no. 5, 1947, pp. 43-55

—, 'A guide to present-day types', *Paper & Print*, nos. 1-9, March 1932 to Spring 1934

—, *Type designs: their history and development*, London, 1934 (3rd ed. 1966)

Johnston, E., *Writing & illuminating & lettering*, London, 1906 (numerous later editions)

Johnston, P., *Edward Johnston*, London, 1959

Lang, P., 'Times Roman: a revaluation', *Alphabet and Image*, no. 2, 1946, pp. 5-17

McLean, R., 'Printers' type-specimen books in England, 1920-40', *Signature*, new series, no. 5, 1948, pp. 33-49

Megaw, D., '20th century sans serif types', *Typography*, no. 7, 1938, pp. 27-35

Mergler, H. W., and Vargo, P. M., 'One approach to computer assisted letter design', *Journal of Typographic Research*, vol. 2, no. 4, 1968, pp. 299-322

Monotype Corporation, 'The L.N.E.R. reforms its typography', *Monotype Recorder*, vol. 32, no. 4, 1933, pp. 7-11

Monotype Recorder, commemorating an exhibition of lettering and type designs by Eric Gill, vol. 41, no. 3, 1958

—, special issue describing the Times New Roman type, vol 21, no. 246, 1932

Morison, S., 'Decorated types', *The Fleuron*, no. 6, 1928, pp. 95-130

—, *A tally of types cut for machine composition and introduced at the University Press, Cambridge, 1922-1932*, Cambridge, 1953

Morison, S., *Type designs of the past and present*, London, 1926

Mosley, J., 'English vernacular: a study in traditional letter forms', *Motif*, no. 11, 1963-4, pp. 3-55

—, 'The nymph and the grot: the revival of the sanserif letter', *Typographica*, no. 12, pp. 2-19

—, 'Trajan revived', *Alphabet*, 1964, pp. 17-36

—, 'The type foundry of Vincent Figgins 1792-1831', *Motif*, no. 1, 1958, pp. 29-36

Muir, P. H., 'The engraved letter-forms of Reynolds Stone', *Alphabet and Image*, no. 7, 1948, pp. 3-13

Ovink, G. W., *Legibility, atmosphere-value, and forms of printing types*, Leiden, 1938

Reed, T. B., *A history of the old English letter foundries*, first published 1887, new edition revised and enlarged by A. F. Johnson, London, 1952

Rogers, B., *Report on the typography of the Cambridge University Press*, London, Wynkyn de Worde Society, 1968

Roman lettering, Victoria & Albert Museum, 1958

Shewring, W., *The letters of Eric Gill*, London, 1947

Speaight, R., *The life of Eric Gill*, London, 1966

Sutton, J., and Bartram, A., *An atlas of typeforms*, London, 1968

Thorp, J., 'Towards a nomenclature for letter forms', *Monotype Recorder*, April-May, 1931

—, 'Experimental application of a nomenclature for letter forms', *Monotype Recorder*, July-August 1932 and Spring 1933

Updike, D. B., *Printing types, their history, forms, and use*, 2 vols, 3rd ed., Cambridge (Mass.), 1962

Western typebook, The, London, 1960

Wolpe, B., 'Caslon architectural', *Alphabet*, 1964, pp. 57-72

—, *Vincent Figgins type specimens 1801 and 1815*, London, Printing Historical Society, 1967

Zachrisson, B., *Studies in the legibility of printed text*, Stockholm, 1965

Zapf, H., 'The changes in letterforms due to technical developments', *Journal of Typographic Research*, vol. 2, no. 4, pp. 351-68

See also

General: Morison (1930), Morison (1932), Williamson

Jobbing and other ephemeral printing: Lewis (1962), Twyman

Design: survivals and new approaches: Spencer (1968)

Pictures into print

Abbey, J. R., *Life in England in aquatint and lithography 1770-1860*, London, 1953

—, *Scenery of Great Britain and Ireland in aquatint and lithography 1770-1860*, London, 1952

—, *Travel in aquatint and lithography 1770-1860*, 2 vols, London, 1956, 1957

Alexander, W. B., 'Ornithological illustration', *Endeavour*, vol. xii, no. 47, July 1953, pp. 144-53

Balston, T., 'English wood-engraving 1900-1950', *Image*, no. 5, 1950, pp. 3-84

Bingley, B., 'Bewickiana', *Signature*, new series, no. 9, 1949, pp. 35-46

Blackburn, H., *The art of illustration*, London, 1894 (2nd ed. 1896)

Blunt, W., *The art of botanical illustration*, London, 1950

Carter, H., *Orlando Jewitt*, London, 1962

Curle, R., *The Ray Society: a bibliographical history*, London, 1954

Dalziel, G. and E., *The brothers Dalziel; a record of fifty years' work*, London, 1901

George, M. D., *Hogarth to Cruikshank: social change in graphic satire*, London, 1967

Gernsheim, H., 'Photography: documentation and reportage', *Motif*, no. 3, 1959, pp. 70-85

Gernsheim, H. and A., *The history of photography*, London, 1955

—, *Roger Fenton*, London, 1954

Gray, B., *The English print*, London, 1937

Handover, P. M., 'Rudolph Ackermann', *Motif*, no. 13, 1967, pp. 81-9

Hasler, C., 'Britain's Royal Arms', *Typographica*, new series, no. 1, 1960, pp. 2-17

—, 'The emergence of the printer's stock block', *Typographica*, new series, no. 10, 1964, pp. 30-48

Hayter, S. W., *About prints*, London, 1962

Hemsley, W. B., 'Walter Hood Fitch, botanical artist, 1817-92', *Royal Botanic Gardens, Kew, Bulletin of Miscellaneous information*, 1915, pp. 277-84

Hindley, C., *The history of the Catnach Press*, London, 1886

Howe, O. and E., 'Vignettes in type-founders' specimen books 1780-1900', *Signature*, no. 11, 1939, pp. 15-35

Ivins, W. M., *Prints and visual communication*, London, 1953 (reprinted Cambridge, Mass., 1969)

Jackson, M., *The pictorial press: its origin and progress*, London, 1885

Kitton, F. G., *Dickens and his illustrators*, London, 1899

Lapage, G., *Art and the scientist*, Bristol, 1962

Laver, J., *English book illustration 1800-1900*, London, 1947

—, Hutchison, H. F., and Griffits, T. E., *Art for all: London Transport Posters 1908-1949*, London, 1949

Lewis, J., *The twentieth century book*, London, 1967

—, and Smith, E., *The graphic reproduction and photography of works of art*, Ipswich, 1969

Linton, W. J., *The masters of wood-engraving*, London, 1889

Man, F. H., *150 years of artists' lithographs 1803-1953*, London, 1953

—, 'Lithography in England (1801-1810)', in C. Zigrosser (ed.), *Prints*, London, 1963, pp. 97-130

Morison, S., *Richard Austin, engraver to the printing trade*, Cambridge, 1937

Mosley, J., 'Printers' ships', *Motif*, no. 7, 1961, pp. 85-8

Pennell, J., 'The coming illustration', *The Imprint*, vol. 1, 1913, pp. 24-32

—, *Pen drawing and pen draughtsmen*, London, 1889 (2nd ed. 1894)

Prideaux, S. T., *Aquatint engraving*, London, 1909

Reade, B., 'The birds of Edward Lear', *Signature*, new series, no. 4, 1947, pp. 3-15

Reid, F., *Illustrators of the sixties*, London, 1928

Shepard, L., *John Pitts, ballad printer of Seven Dials, London 1765-1844*, Pinner, 1969

Simpson, W., *The autobiography of William Simpson*, edited by G. E. Todd, London, 1903

Sitwell, S., *Morning, noon and night in London*, London, 1948

Spielmann, M. H., *The history of 'Punch'*, London, 1895

Sullivan, E. J., *The art of illustration*, London, 1921

Thorpe, J., *English illustration: the nineties*, London, 1935

—, 'The posters of the Beggarstaff Brothers,' *Alphabet and Image*, no. 4, 1947, pp. 33-47

—, 'Some draughtsmen of the early "Daily Graphic"', *Alphabet and Image*, no. 2, 1946, pp. 59-71

Weekley, M., *Thomas Bewick*, London, 1953

White, G., *English illustrators: 'The Sixties', 1855-1870*, London, 1897

Whitman, A., *The masters of mezzotint*, London, 1898

Vizetelly, H., *Glances back through seventy years*, 2 vols, London, 1893

Vries, Leonard de, *Victorian advertisements*, London, 1968

See also

Jobbing and other ephemeral printing: Alderson, Buday, Carline, Ettlinger and Holloway, Hussey, Imeson, King, Orwell, Rickards, Staff, White

New processes: Bliss, Chatto and Jackson, Hamerton, Harper, Hayter, Hind (1935), Hind (1908), Hullmandel, Pennell, Singer and Strang, Twyman

Colour printing: Burch, Lewis

Design: survivals and new approaches: Kauffer, McLean (1969), Neurath

Design: survivals and new approaches

Bayer, H., *Herbert Bayer: painter, designer, architect*, New York, 1967

Betjeman, J., 'Ecclesiastical typography', *Typography*, no. 6, 1938, pp. 23-30

Blackwell, B., 'Bernard Newdigate: typographer', *Signature*, new series, no. 1, 1946, pp. 19-36

Bradshaw, C., *Design*, London, 1964

Carter, H., 'The typographical design of Government printing', *Alphabet and Image*, no. 5, 1947, pp. 3-15

Dreyfus, J., 'Mr Morison as "Typographer"', *Signature*, new series, no. 3, 1947, pp. 3-26

Evers, C. H., 'Adjustment to unjustified composition on the *Rotterdamsch Nieuwsblad*', *Journal of Typographic Research*, vol. 2, no. 1, 1968, pp. 59-74

Gane, C. P., Horabin, I. S., and Lewis, B. N., *Flow charts, logical trees and algorithms for rules and regulations*, CAS occasional paper no. 2, London, 1967

—, 'The simplification and avoidance of instruction', *Industrial Training International*, July 1966, pp. 160-5

Garland, K., 'Typophoto', *Typographica*, new series, no. 3, 1961, pp. 2-20

Gerstner, K., *Designing programmes*, London, 1964

Gill, E., *An essay on typography*, 2nd ed., London, 1936

Gloag, J. E., *Victorian taste: some social aspects of architecture and industrial design, from 1820-1900*, London, 1962

Gray, C., 'Alexander Rodchenko: a Constructivist designer',

Typographica, new series, no. 11, 1965, pp. 2-20

Jackson, H., 'A cross-section of English printing: the Curwen Press 1918-1934', *The Curwen Press Newsletter*, no. 9, 1935, pp. 1-14

—, 'The nonage of nineteenth-century printing in England', *The Fleuron*, no. 2, 1924, pp. 87-97

Jones, S., 'Why can't leaflets be logical?', *New Society*, 16 September 1964, pp. 16-17

Kauffer, E. McKnight, *The art of the poster*, London, 1924

Lewis, J., *Typography: basic principles*, London, 1963

—, and Brinkley, J., *Graphic design*, London, 1954

Lockwood, A., *Diagrams, a visual survey of graphs, maps, charts and diagrams for the graphic designer*, London, 1969

McLean, R., *Magazine design*, London, 1969

—, *Modern book design*, London, 1958

—, 'Who designs print?', *Printing Review*, vol. 8, no. 4, 1939, pp. 930-1

Meynell, F., *The typography of newspaper advertisements*, London, 1929

Miles, H., 'The printed work of Edward Bawden', *Signature*, no. 3, 1936, pp. 23-39

Monotype Recorder, modern typography number, vol. 32, no. 4, 1933

Moorsel, L. Leering-van, 'The typography of El Lissitzky', *Journal of Typographic Research*, vol. 2, no. 4, 1968, pp. 323-40

Morison, S., 'First principles of typography', *The Fleuron*, no. 7, 1930, pp. 61-72 (reprinted Cambridge University Press, 1936)

—, *Modern fine printing*, London, 1925

—, 'On advertisement settings', *Signature*, no. 3, 1936, pp. 1-6

—, *The typographic arts*, London, 1949

Morris, W., and Walker, E., 'Printing', in *Arts and crafts essays* by Members of the Arts and Crafts Exhibition Society, with a preface by William Morris, London, 1893

Neumann, E., 'Henryk Berlewi and Mechano-faktura', *Typographica*, new series, no. 9, 1964, pp. 21-8

—, 'Herbert Bayer's photographic experiments', *Typographica*, new series, no. 11, 1965, pp. 34-44

Neurath, O., *International picture language*, London, 1936

Pevsner, N., *Pioneers of modern design*, Penguin Books, 1960

Raffé, W. G., *Graphic design*, London, 1927

Read, H., 'Ashley Havinden and the art of printing', *Typography*, no. 3, 1937, pp. 8-10

Ridler, V., 'Artistic printing: a search for principles', *Alphabet and Image*, no. 6, 1948, pp. 4-17

Royal Academy of Arts, catalogue of an exhibition of the work of the Bauhaus, London, 1968

Simon, O., 'English typography and the industrial age', *Signature*, new series, no. 7, 1948, pp. 17-41

—, *Introduction to typography*, 3rd ed., edited by David Bland, London, 1963

Simon, O., 'To *The Fleuron*', *Signature*, new series, no. 13, 1951, pp. 3-29

—, and Rodenberg, J. (eds.), *Printing of to-day: an anthology of modern typography*, London, 1928

Smallwood, A., 'The ratios of margins', *Printing Review*, vol. 8, no. 2, 1939, pp. 835-8

Society of Industrial Artists and Designers, *Computers in visual communication*, proceedings of an SIAD/STD Typographers' Computer Working Group symposium, London, 1968

Spencer, H., *Design in business printing*, London, 1952

—, 'H. N. Werkman, printer-painter', *Typographica*, no. 11, [c. 1955], pp. 18-26

—, 'Piet Zwart', *Typographica*, new series, no. 7, 1963, pp. 25-32

—, *Pioneers of modern typography*, London, 1969

—, 'The responsibilities of the design profession', *Penrose Annual*, vol. 57, 1964, pp. 18-23

—, *The visible word*, London, 1968

Steer, V., *Printing design and layout*, 4th ed., London, n.d.

Swann, C., *Techniques of typography*, London, 1969

Symons, A. J. A., 'An unacknowledged movement in fine printing: the typography of the eighteen-nineties', *The Fleuron*, no. 7, 1930, pp. 83-119

Themerson, S., 'Idéogrammes lyriques', *Typographica*, new series, no. 14, 1966, pp. 2-24

Thorp, J., 'The work of Bernard H. Newdigate', *Printing Review*, vol. 8, no. 1, 1938-9, pp. 1-9

Tolmer, A., *Mise en page: the theory and practice of lay-out*, London, 1931

Tomkins, J., 'DIN—a new, old cause', *Typographica*, new series, no. 5, 1962, pp. 45-56

Tschichold, J., *Asymmetric typography*, London and Toronto, 1967 (translation by Ruari McLean of *Typographische Gestaltung*, Basle, 1935)

—, *Designing books*, New York, 1951

—, *Die neue Typographie*, Berlin, 1928

—, 'Type mixtures', *Typography*, no. 3, 1937, pp. 2-7

Typoclastes, 'A plea for reform of printing', *The Imprint*, vol. 1, 1913, pp. 391-402

'Typography in Britain', *Typographica*, new series, no. 7, 1963, pp. 2-24

Updike, D. B., 'On the planning of printing', *The Fleuron*, no. 2, 1924, pp. 13-27

Warde, B., *The crystal goblet*, sixteen essays on typography selected and edited by Henry Jacob, London, 1955

Wissing, B., 'Paul Schuitema', *Typographica*, new series, no. 8, 1963, pp. 35-46

Working Party on Typographic Teaching, *Interim report*, London, 1968

See also

General: Morison (1924), Williamson

Jobbing and other ephemeral printing: Katin, Lewis (1962), Twyman

Colour printing: Harris, Kainen, McLean (1963), Twyman

From craft to technology: Duncan, McIntosh

Index of illustrations

General index